Critical Acclaim
for Disappearing Cryptography

Disappearing Cryptography is a witty and entertaining look at the world of information hiding. Peter Wayner provides an intuitive perspective of the many techniques, applications, and research directions in the area of steganography. The sheer breadth of topics is outstanding and makes this book truly unique. A must-read for those who would like to begin learning about information hiding.

Deepa Kundur, Ph.D., University of Toronto

Peter Wayner's *Disappearing Cryptography* is thorough, accurate, and entertaining. It's especially relevant given the restrictions on speech, code, and research that groups like SDMI and RIAA have won via the Digital Millennium Copyright Act. Wayner provides an easy-to-follow introduction to all of the major techniques in information hiding as well as the attacks against them. This book could easily become the standard stego reference text in the same way that Schneier's *Applied Cryptography* has for crypto.

Mike Stay, staym@datawest.net

Wayner's second edition offers a much updated and very accessible introduction to the hidden world of steganography, the science of hiding the very existence of information. The book covers the technical aspects of the parallel arms races surrounding steganography and watermarking—the battle of wits between the statistician and the steganographer, and between the watermarker and free-wheeling digital copying. It's accessible and informative, with worked examples, source code, and reviews of software packages and references to the literature.

Dr. Adam Back, founder of Cypherspace Internet Security

Disappearing Cryptography

Information Hiding:
Steganography & Watermarking

Second Edition

Disappearing Cryptography

Information Hiding:
Steganography & Watermarking

Second Edition

Peter Wayner

MORGAN KAUFMANN PUBLISHERS

An Imprint of Elsevier

AMSTERDAM   BOSTON   LONDON   NEW YORK
OXFORD   PARIS   SAN DIEGO   SAN FRANCISCO
SINGAPORE   SYDNEY   TOKYO

Acquisitions Editor   Tim Cox
Assistant Publishing Services Manager   Edward Wade
Production Editor   Howard Severson
Editorial Coordinator   Stacie Pierce
Cover Design   Frances Baca
Cover Image   Peter H. Sprosty/Photonica
Text Design   Detta Penna
Composition and Illustration   Interactive Composition Corporation
Copyeditor   Carol Leyba
Proofreader   Erin Milnes
Indexer   Steve Rath
Printer   Courier Corporation

Designations used by companies to distinguish their products are often claimed as trademarks or registered trademarks. In all instances in which Morgan Kaufmann Publishers is aware of a claim, the product names appear in initial capital or all capital letters. Readers, however, should contact the appropriate companies for more complete information regarding trademarks and registration.

Morgan Kaufmann Publishers
An Imprint of Elsevier
340 Pine Street, Sixth Floor
San Francisco, CA 94104-3205, USA
www.mkp.com

06   5 4 3 2

Library of Congress Control Number: 2001099790
ISBN-13: 978-1-55860-769-9
ISBN-10: 1-55860-769-2
This book is printed on acid-free paper.

Contents

Preface

Notes on the Second Edition

The world of steganography and hidden information changed dramatically during the five years since the first edition of this book appeared. The interest from the scientific community grew, and separate conferences devoted to the topic flourished. A number of new ideas, approaches, and techniques appeared, many of which are included in this book.

The burgeoning interest was not confined to science labs. The business community embraced the field in the hope that using hidden information would give creators of music and images a chance to control their progeny. This hidden information is usually called a *watermark*. The hidden payload might include information about the creator, the copyright holder, the purchaser, or even special instructions about who is allowed to consume the information and how often they will be allowed to push the button.

While private companies have helped the art of information hiding, sometimes the drive for scientific advancement has clashed with the desires of some in the business community. The scientists want the news of the strengths and weaknesses of steganographic algorithms to flow freely. Some businesspeople fear that this information will be used to attack their systems, and so they push to keep the knowledge hidden.

This struggle erupted into an open battle when the recording industry began focusing on the work of Scott A. Craver, John P. McGregor, Min Wu, Bede Liu, Adam Stubblefield, Ben Swartzlander, Dan S. Wallach, Drew Dean, and Edward W. Felten. This group of programmers attacked a number of techniques distributed by the Secure Digital Music Initiative (SDMI), an organization devoted to creating a watermark system and sponsored by members of the music industry. The attacks were invited by SDMI in a public contest intended to test the strengths of the algorithms. Unfortunately, the leaders of SDMI also tried to hamstring the people who entered the contest by forcing them to sign a pledge of secrecy to collect their prize. In essence, SDMI was trying to gain all of the political advantages of public scrutiny while trying to silence anyone who attempted to spread the results of their scrutiny to the public. When the group tried to present their work at the Information Hiding Workshop in April in Pittsburgh, the Recording Industry Association of America (RIAA) sent them a letter suggesting that public discussion would be punished by a lawsuit. The group withdrew the paper and filed their own suit claiming that the RIAA and the music industry were attempting to stifle their First Amendment rights. The group later presented their work at the USENIX conference in August 2001 in Washington, D.C., but it is clear that the battle lines still exist. On one side are people who believe in open sharing of information, even if it produces an unpleasant effect, and on the other are those who believe that censorship and control will keep the world right.

This conflict seems to come from the perception that the algorithms for hiding information are fragile. If someone knows the mechanism in play, they can destroy the message by writing over it or scrambling the noise. The recording industry is worried that someone might use the knowledge of how to break the SDMI algorithms to destroy the watermarking information—something that is not difficult to do. The only solution, in some eyes, is to add security by prohibiting knowledge.

This attitude is quite different from the approach taken with cryptography. Most of the industry agrees that public scrutiny is the best way to create secure algorithms. Security through obscurity is not as successful as a well-designed algorithm. As a result, public scrutiny has identified many weaknesses in cryptographic algorithms and has helped researchers develop sophisticated solutions.

Some companies trying to create watermarking tools may feel that they have no choice but to push for secrecy. The watermarking tools aren't secure enough to withstand assault, so the companies hope that some additional secrecy will make them more secure.

Unfortunately, the additional secrecy buys little extra. Hidden information is easy to remove by compressing, reformatting, and re-recording the camouflaging information. Most common tools used in recording studios, video shops, and print shops are also good enough to remove watermarks. There's nothing you can do about it. Bits are bits and information is information. There is not a solid link between the two.

At this writing the battle between the copyright holders and the scientists is just beginning. Secret algorithms have never worked for long before, and there's no reason why they will work now. In the meantime, enjoy the information in the book while you can. There's no way to tell how long it will be legal to read this book.

Using the Book

The early chapters of this book are devoted to material that forms the basic bag of tricks such as private-key encryption, secret sharing, and error-correcting codes. The later chapters describe how to apply these techniques in various ways to hide information. Each chapter is designed to give you an introduction and enough information to use the data if you want.

The information in each chapter is roughly arranged in order of importance and difficulty. Each begins with a high-level summary for those who want to understand the concepts without wading through technical details, and an introductory set of details for those who want to create their own programs from the information. People who are not interested in the deepest, most mathematical details can skip the last part of each chapter without missing any of the highlights. Programmers who are inspired to implement some algorithms will want to dig into the last pages.

All of the chapters (except Chapter 1) also come with allegorical narratives that attempt to illustrate some of the ideas in the chapters. You may find them funny, you may find them stupid, but I hope you'll find some better insight into the game afoot. Also, at the end of each chapter, you will find a chapter summary, along with a list of all the chapter's major points.

For the most part, this book is about having fun with information. But knowledge is power and people in power want to increase their control. So the final chapter is an essay devoted to some of the political questions that lie just below the surface of all of these morphing bits.

Book Notes

The copy for this book was typeset using LaTeX typesetting software. Several important breaks were made with standard conventions in order to remove some ambiguities. The period mark is normally included inside the quotation marks like this: "That's my answer. No. Period." This can cause ambiguities when computer terms are included in quotation marks because computers often use periods to convey some meaning. For this reason, my electronic mail address is "p3@wayner.org". The periods and commas are left outside of quotes whenever leaving them inside might cause confusion.

Hyphens also cause problems when they're used for different tasks. LISP programmers often use hyphens to join words together into a single name like this: `Do-Not-Call-This-Procedure`. Unfortunately, this causes grief when these longer words occur at the end of a line. In these cases, there will be an extra hyphen included to specify that there was an original hyphen in the word. This isn't *hyper-compatible* with the standard rules that don't include the extra hyphen. But these rules are for readers who know that *self-help* is a word that should be hyphenated. No one knows what to think about `A-Much-Too-Long-Procedure-That-Should-Be-Shortened--For-Every-one`.

Acknowledgments

This book is a second edition and so that means more thanks for everyone. There is no doubt that I owe a debt of gratitude to the participants in the cypherpunks and coderpunks mailing lists. Their original contributions inspired me to write the first book, and their continual curiosity makes the list one of the best sources of information around.

Some newer mailing lists are more focused on the topic. The watermarking list and the stegano list both offer high-quality discussions with a high signal-to-noise ratio. Other lists like the RISKS digest and Dave Farber's Interest People list helped contribute in unexpected ways. Of course, modern list-like Web sites like Slashdot,

Kuro5hin, and InfoAnarchy contributed by offering solid, moderated discussions that help the signal jump out of the noise. It is impossible to thank by name all of the members of the community who submit plenty of solid information and deep thought in their high-quality postings.

The organizers of the Information Hiding Workshops brought some academic rigor to the area by sponsoring excellent workshops on the topic. The discipline of creating, editing, reviewing, presenting, and publishing a manuscript advanced the state of the art in numerous ways. The collected papers published by Springer-Verlag are a great resource for anyone interested in the development of the field.

Some others have helped in other ways. Peter Neumann scanned the first manuscript and offered many good suggestions for improving it. Bruce Schneier was kind enough to give me an electronic version of the bibliography from his first book [Sch94]. I converted it into Bibtex format and used it for some of the references here. Ross Anderson's annotated bibliography on information hiding was also a great help.

Scott Craver, Frank Hartung, Deepa Kundur, Mike Stay, and three anonymous reviewers checked the second edition. Their comments helped fix numerous errors and also provided many suggestions for improving the book. David Molnar and Greg Ruse also helped identify errors in the first edition.

The original book was published by AP PROFESSIONAL, a division of Harcourt-Brace. The team responsible for producing the first edition included Chuck Glaser, Jeff Pepper, Mike Williams, Barbara Northcott, Don DeLand, Tom Ryan, Josh Mills, Gael Tannenbaum, and Dave Hannon.

Of course, this new edition would not exist without the vision and support of Tim Cox at Morgan Kaufmann. I would like to thank Tim, Stacie Pierce, and Howard Severson for all their help and encouragement.

chapter one

Framing Information

1.1

Introduction

On its face, information in computers seems perfectly defined and certain. A bank account either has $1,432,442 or it has $8.32. The weather is either going to be 73 degrees or 74 degrees. The meeting is either going to be at 4 pm or 4:30 pm. Computers deal only with numbers and numbers are very definite.

Life isn't so simple. Advertisers and electronic gadget manufacturers like to pretend that digital data is perfect and immutable, freezing life in a crystalline mathematical amber, but the natural world is filled with noise, and numbers can only begin to approximate what is happening. Digital information comes with much more precision than the world may provide.

Numbers themselves are strange beasts. All of their certainty can be scrambled by arithmetic, equations, and numerical parlor tricks designed to mislead and misdirect. Statisticians brag about lying with numbers. Car dealers and accountants can hide a lifetime of sins in a balance sheet. Encryption can make one batch of numbers look like another with a push of a button.

Language itself is often beyond the grasp of rational thought. Writers dance around topics and thoughts relying on nuance, inflection, allusion, metaphor, and dozens of other rhetorical techniques to deliver a message. None of these tools are perfect and people seem to find a way to argue about the definition of the word "is".

This book describes how to hide information by exploiting this uncertainty and imperfection. This book is about how to take words, sounds, and images and hide them in digital data so they look like other words, sounds, or images. It is about converting secrets into innocuous noise so that the secrets disappear in the ocean of bits flowing through the Net. It describes how to make data mimic other data to disguise its origins and obscure its destination. It is about submerging a conversation in a flow of noise so that no one can know if a conversation exists at all. It is about taking your being, dissolving it into nothingness, and then pulling it out of the nothingness so it can live again.

Traditional cryptography succeeds by locking up a message in a mathematical safe. Hiding the information so it can't be found is a similar but often distinct process that is often called *steganography*. There are many historical examples of it, including hidden compartments, mechanical systems such as microdots, or burst transmissions, that make the message hard to find. Other techniques such as encoding the message in the first letters of words disguise the content and make it look like something else. All of these have been used again and again.

David Kahn's *Codebreakers* provides a good history of the techniques [Kah67].

Digital information offers wonderful opportunities not only to hide information, but also to develop a general theoretical framework for hiding the data. It is possible to describe general algorithms and make some statements about how hard it will be for someone who doesn't know the key to find the data. Some algorithms offer a good model of their strength. Others offer none.

Some of the algorithms for hiding information use keys that control how they behave. Some of the algorithms in this book hide information in such a way that it is impossible to recover the information without knowing the key. That sounds like cryptography, even though it is accomplished at the same time as cloaking the information in a masquerade.

Is it better to think of these algorithms as "cryptography" or "steganography"? Drawing a line between the two is both arbitrary and dangerously confusing. Most good cryptographic tools also produce data that looks almost perfectly random. You might say that they are trying to hide the information by disguising it as random noise. On the other hand, many steganographic algorithms are not trivial to break even after learning that there is hidden data to find. Placing an algorithm in one camp often means forgetting why it could exist in the other. The best solution is to think of this book as a collection of tools for massaging data. Each tool offers some amount of misdirection and some amount of security. Users can combine a number of different tools to achieve their end.

This book is published under the title "Disappearing Cryptography" for the simple reason that few people knew about the word "steganography" when the book first appeared. We've kept the title for this, and other, practical reasons, but this doesn't mean that the title is just a convenient mechanism for giving the buyer a cover text to use for judging the book. Thinking of these algorithms as tools for simply disguising information is a mistake. Some offer cryptographic security at the same time as an effective disguise. Some are deeply intertwined with cryptographic algorithms, while others act independently. Some are difficult to break without the key, while others offer only basic protection. Trying to classify the algorithms as purely steganography or cryptography imposes only limitations. While all may be digital information, there are an infinite number of forms, shapes, and appearances the information may assume.

1.2

Reasons for Secrecy

There are many different reasons for using the techniques of this book, and some are scurrilous. There is little doubt that the Four Horsemen of the Infocalypse—drug dealers, terrorists, child pornographers, and money launderers—will find a way to use the tools in this to their benefit in the same way that they've employed telephones, cars, airplanes, prescription drugs, box cutters, knives, libraries, video cameras, and many other common, everyday items. There's no need to explain how people can hide behind the veils of anonymity and secrecy to commit heinous crimes.

But these tools and technologies can also protect the weak. In the interest of defending this book, here's a list of some possible good uses:

1. So you can seek counseling about deeply personal problems such as suicidal thoughts.

2. So you can inform colleagues and friends about a problem with odor or personal hygiene.

3. So you can meet potential romantic partners without danger.

4. So you can play roles and act out different identities for fun.

5. So you can explore job possibilities without revealing where you currently work and potentially losing your job.

6. So you can turn a person in to the authorities anonymously because you fear recriminations.

7. So you can leak information to the press about gross injustice or unlawful behavior.

8. So you can take part in a contentious political debate about, say, abortion, without losing the friendship of those who happen to be on the other side of the debate.

9. So you can protect your personal information from being exploited by terrorists, drug dealers, child pornographers, and money launderers.

10. So the police can communicate with undercover agents infiltrating the gangs of bad people.

The Afterword examines the promises and perils of this technology in more detail.

There are many other reasons, but I'm surprised that government officials don't recognize how necessary these freedoms are to the world. Much of government functions through back-corridor bargaining and power games. Anonymous communication is a standard part of this level of politics. I often believe that all governments would grind to a halt if information was as strictly controlled as some would like it to be. No one would get any work done. They would just spend hours arguing about who should and should not have access to information.

The Central Intelligence Agency, for instance, has been criticized for missing the signs of the pending collapse of the former Soviet Union. They continued to issue pessimistic assessments of a burgeoning Soviet military while the country imploded. Some blame greed, power, and politics. I blame the sheer inefficiency of keeping information secret. Spymaster Bob can't share the secret data he got from Spymaster Fred because everything is compartmentalized. When people can't get new or solid information, they fall back on their basic prejudices—which in this case was that the Soviet Union is a burgeoning empire. There will always be a need for covert analysis for some problems, but it will usually be much more inefficient than overt analysis.

Anonymous dissemination of information is a grease for the squeaky wheel of society. As long as people question its validity and recognize that its source is not willing to stand behind the text, then everyone should be able to function with the information. When it comes right down to it, anonymous information is just information. It's merely a torrent of bits, not a bullet, a bomb, or a broadside. Sharing information generally helps society pursue the interests of justice.

Secret communication is essential for security. The police and the defense department are not the only people who need the ability to protect their schedules, plans, and business affairs. The algorithms in this book are like locks on doors and cars. Giving this power to everyone gives everyone the power to protect themselves against crime and abuse. The police do not need to be everywhere because people can protect themselves.

For all these reasons and many more, these algorithms are powerful tools for the protection of people and their personal data.

1.3

How It Is Done

There are a number of different ways to hide information. All of them offer some stealth, but not all of them are equally strong. Some provide startling mimicry with some help from the user. Others are largely automatic. Some can be combined with others to provide multiple layers of security. All of them exploit some bit of randomness, some bit of uncertainty, or some bit of unspecified state in a file. Here is an abstract list of the techniques used in this book:

- *Use the Noise.* The simplest technique is to replace the noise in an image or sound file with your message. A digital file consists of numbers that represent the intensity of light or sound at a particular point in time or space. Often, these numbers are computed with extra precision that can't be detected effectively by humans. For instance, one spot in a picture might have 220 units of blue on a scale that runs between 0 and 255 total units. An average eye would not notice if that one spot was converted to having 219 units of blue. If this process is done systematically, it is possible to hide large volumes of information just below the threshold of perception. A digital photo-CD image has 2048 by 3072 pixels that each contain 24 bits of information about the colors of the image. As much as 756K of data can be hidden in the three least significant bits for each color of each pixel. That's probably more than the text of this book. The human eye would not be able to detect the subtle variations, but a computer could reconstruct all of it.

- *Spread the Information Out.* Some of the more sophisticated mechanisms spread the information out over a number of pixels or moments in a sound file. This diffusion protects the information and also makes it less susceptible to detection, either by humans looking at the information or by computers looking for statistical profiles. Many of the techniques that fall into this category came from the radio communication arena where engineers first created them to cut down on interference, reduce jamming, and add some secrecy. Adapting them to digital communications is not difficult.

  Spreading the information out often increases the resilience to destruction by either random or malicious forces. The spreading algorithms often distribute the information in such a way that not all of the bits are required to reassemble the original data. If some parts get destroyed, the message still gets through.

Many of the techniques are closely related to the process of generating cryptographically secure random numbers—that is, a stream of random numbers that can't be predicted. Some algorithms use this number stream to choose locations, others blend the random values with the hidden information, and others replace some of the random values with the message.

  Many of these spreading techniques hide information in the noise of an image or sound file, but there is no reason why they can't be used with other forms of data as well.

- *Adopt a Statistical Profile.* Data often falls into a pattern and computers often try to make decisions about data by looking at the pattern. English text, for instance, uses the letter "p" far more often than the letter "q". If data can be reformulated so it adopts the statistical profile of the English language, then a computer program minding p's and q's will be fooled.

- *Adopt a Structural Profile.* Mimicking the statistics of a type of file is just the beginning. More sophisticated solutions rely upon sophisticated models of the underlying data to better mimic it. For instance, information can be hidden by making it look like the transcript of a baseball game. The bits are hidden by using them to choose between the nouns, verbs, and other parts of the text. The data are recovered by sorting through the text and matching up the words with the bits that selected them. This technique can produce startling results, although the content of the messages often seems a bit loopy or directionless. This is often good enough to fool humans or computers that are programmed to algorithmically scan for particular words or patterns.

- *Replace Randomness.* Many software programs use random number generators to add realism to scenes, sounds, and games. Monsters look better if a random number generator adds blotches, warts, moles, scars, and gouges to a smooth skin defined by mathematical spheres. Information can be hidden in the place of the random number. The location of the splotches and scars carries the message.

- *Change the Order.* A grocery list may be just a list, but the order of the items can carry a surprisingly large amount of information.

- *Split Information.* There is no reason why the data needs to travel in one package. Data can be split into any number of packets that take different routes to their destination. Sophisticated algorithms can also split the information so that any subset of k of the n parts are enough to reconstruct the entire message.

- *Hide the Source.* Some algorithms allow people to broadcast information without revealing their identity. This is not the same as hiding the information itself, but it is still a valuable tool in some situations.

These different techniques can be combined in many different ways. First information can be hidden by hiding it in a list, then the list can be hidden in the noise of some file, which is then broadcast in a way to hide the source of the data.

1.4

How Steganography Is Used

Hidden information has a variety of uses in products and protocols. Hiding slightly different information or combining the various algorithms creates different tools with different uses. Here are some of the most interesting applications:

- *Enhanced Data Structures*. Most programmers know that standard data structures get old over time. Eventually there comes a time when new, unplanned information must be added to the format without breaking old software. Steganography is one solution. For example, you can hide extra information about photos in the photos themselves. This information travels with the photos but will not disturb old software that doesn't know of its existence.

  Some researchers suggest another use: you could embed comments from a radiologist in the background of a digitized X ray. The file would still work with standard tools, saving hospitals the cost of replacing all their equipment.

Digital Watermarking by Ingemar J. Cox, Matthew L. Miller, and Jeffrey A. Bloom is a good introduction to watermarks and the challenges particular to the subfield [CMB01].

- *Strong Watermarks*. The creators of digital content such as books, movies, and audio files may want to add hidden information into the file to describe the restrictions they place on the file. This message might be as simple as "This file copyright 2002 by Big Fun" or as complex as "This file can only be played twice before 12/31/2002 unless you purchase three cases of soda and submit their bottle tops for rebate, in which case you get four song plays for every bottle top."

  Some watermarks are meant to be found even after the file undergoes a great deal of distortion. Ideally, the watermark will still be detectable even after someone crops, rotates, scales, and compresses a document. The only way to truly destroy the watermark is to alter the document so much it is no longer recognizable.

  Other watermarks are deliberately made as fragile as possible. If someone tries to tamper with the file, the watermark will disappear. Combining strong and weak watermarks is a good option when tampering is possible.

- *Document Tracking Tools*. Hidden information can identify the legitimate owner of a document. If the document is leaked or distributed to unauthorized people, it can be tracked back to the rightful owner. Adding individual tags to each document is an idea attractive to both content-generating industries and government agencies with classified information.

- *Document Authentication.* The hidden information bundled with a document can also contain a digital signature certifying its authenticity. A regular software program would simply display (or play) the document. If someone wanted some assurance, the digital signature embedded in the document could verify that the right person signed it.

- *Private Communications.* Software for hiding information or preserving anonymity is also useful in political situations when communication is dangerous. There will always be moments when two people can't exchange messages because their enemies are listening. Many governments continue to see the Internet, corporations, and electronic conversations as an opportunity for surveillance. In these situations, hidden channels offer the politically weak a chance to elude the powerful who control the networks [Sha01].

Many uses for hidden information don't come classified as steganography or cryptography. Anyone who needs to deal with old data formats and old software knows that programmers don't always provide ideal data structures with full documentation. Many basic hacks aren't much different from the steganographic tools in this book. Clever programmers find ways to stretch a data format by packing extra information where it wasn't needed before. This kind of hacking is bound to yield more applications than people imagined for steganography. Somewhere out there, a child's life may be saved thanks to clever data handling and steganography!

1.5

Attacks on Steganography

Steganography algorithms provide stealth and security to information. The degree of stealth and security, though, is hard to measure. As data blends into the background, when does it effectively disappear? One way to judge the strength of a steganographic algorithm is to imagine different attacks and then assess whether the algorithm can successfully withstand them. This approach is far from perfect, but it is the best available. There's no way to anticipate all possible attacks, although you can try.

Attacking steganographic algorithms is very similar to attacking cryptographic algorithms, and many of the same techniques apply.

Of course, steganographic algorithms promise some stealth as well as security so they are also vulnerable to additional attacks.

Here's a list of some of the possible attacks:

- *File Only.* The attacker has access to the file and must determine if there is a message hidden inside it. This is the weakest form of attack, but it is also the minimum threshold for successful steganography.

  Many of the basic attacks of this form rely upon a statistical analysis of digital images or sound files to reveal the presence of a message in the file. This type of attack is often more of an art than a science because the person hiding the message can try to counter the attack by adjusting the statistics.

- *File and Original Copy.* In some cases, the attacker may have a copy of the file with the encoded message and a copy of the original, pre-encoded file. Clearly, detecting the presence of some hidden message is a trivial operation. If the two files are different, there must be some information hidden inside it.

  The real question is what the attacker may try to do with the data. The attacker may try to destroy the hidden information, something that can be accomplished by replacing it with the original. The attacker may try to extract the information or even replace it with his or her own.

- *Multiple Encoded Files.* The attacker gets *n* different copies of the files with *n* different messages. One of them may or may not be the original unchanged file. This situation may occur if a company is inserting different tracking information into each file and the attacker is able to gather a number of different versions. If music companies sell digital sound files with personalized watermarks, then several fans with legitimate copies can get together and compare their files.

  Some attackers may try to simply destroy the tracking information, while some may try to replace it with their own version of the information. One of the simplest attacks in this case is to blend the files together, either by averaging the individual elements of the file or by creating a hybrid by taking different parts from each file.

- *Access to the File and Algorithm.* An ideal steganographic algorithm can withstand scrutiny even if the attacker knows the algorithm itself. Clearly, simple algorithms that hide and unveil information can't resist this attack. Anyone who knows the algorithm can use it to extract the information.

  But this can work if you keep some part of the algorithm secret and use it as the "key" to unlock the information. Many algorithms in this book use a cryptographically secure random number generator to control how the information is blended into a file. The seed value to this random number stream acts like a key. If you don't know it, you can't generate the random number stream and you can't unblend the information.

- *Destroy Everything Attack.* Some people argue that steganography is not particularily useful because an attacker could simply destroy the message. This is certainly true, but cryptography and many other protocols are also vulnerable to this charge.

- *Random Tweaking Attacks.* Some attackers may not try to determine the existence of a message with any certainty. An attacker could simply add small, random tweaks to all files in the hope of destroying whatever message may be there. During World War II, the government censors would add small changes to numbers in telegrams in the hopes of destroying covert communications. This approach is not very useful because it sacrifices overall accuracy for the hope of squelching a message. Many of the algorithms in this book can resist such an attack by using error-correcting codes to recover from a limited number of seemingly random changes.

- *Add New Information.* One simple attack is to use the same software to encode a new message in the file. Some algorithms are vulnerable to these attacks because they overwrite the channel used to hide the information. The attack can be resisted with good error-correcting codes and by using only a small fraction of the channel chosen at random.

- *Reformat Attack.* One possible attack is to change the format of the file. This can work because different file formats don't store data in exactly the same way. There are a number of different image formats, for instance, that use a variety of bits to store the individual pixels. Many basic tools help the graphic artist deal with the different formats by converting one file format into another. Because these conversions cannot always be perfect, the hidden information is often destroyed in the process.

Watermark algorithms for images are often designed to resist this type of attack because reformatting is so common in the world of graphic arts. An ideal audio watermark, for instance, would still be readable after someone played the music on a stereo and recorded it after it traveled through the air.

Of course, there are limits to this. Reformatting can be quite damaging, and it is difficult to anticipate all the cropping, rotating, scaling, and shearing that a file might undergo. Some of the best algorithms do come close.

- *Compression Attack.* One of the simplest attacks is to compress the file. Compression algorithms try to remove the extraneous information from a file, and "hidden" is often equivalent to "extraneous". The dangerous compression algorithms are the so-called *lossy* ones that do not reconstruct a file exactly during decompression. The JPEG image format, for instance, does a good job of approximating, rather than accurately reconstructing, the original.

  Some of the watermarking algorithms can resist compression by the most popular algorithms, but there are none that can resist all of them. The only algorithms that can resist all compression attacks hide the information in plain sight by changing the "perceptually salient" features of an image or sound file.

Unfortunately, steganography is not a very solid science, in part because there's no simple way to measure how well it is doing. How hidden must the information be before no one can see it? Just how invisible is invisible? The models of human perception are often too simple to measure what is happening.

The lack of a solid model means it is difficult to establish just how well the algorithms resist attack. Many algorithms can survive cursory scrutiny but will fail if a highly trained or talented set of ears and eyes analyzes the results. Some people with so-called 'golden ears' can supposedly hear changes in an audio file that are inaudible to the average person. A watermark may be completely inaudible to most of the buying public, but if the musicians can hear it, the record company may not use it.

Our lack of a solid model does not mean that the algorithms don't have practical value. A watermark heard by 1 percent of the population is of no concern to the other 99 percent. An image with hidden information may be detectable, but this only matters if someone is trying to detect it.

There is also little doubt that a watermark or a steganographic tool does not need to resist all attackers to have substantial value. A watermark that lives on after cropping and basic compression still carries its message to many people. A hacker may learn how to destroy it, but most people have better things to do with their time.

Our lack of understanding also does not mean that the algorithms do not offer some security. Some of the algorithms insert their information with mechanisms that offer cryptographic strength. Borrowing these ideas and incorporating them provides both stealth and security.

1.6

Adding Context

One reviewer of the book who was asked for a back cover blurb joked that the book should be "essential bedside reading for every terrorist." After a pause he added, "and every freedom fighter, Hollywood executive, police officer, abused spouse, chief information officer, and anyone needing privacy anywhere."

You may be a terrorist or you may be a freedom fighter. Who knows? This book is just about technology, and technology is neutral. It teaches you how to cast shape-shifting spells that make data look like something completely different. You may have good plans for these ideas. Perhaps you want to expose a local chemical company dumping toxic waste into the ground. Or you might be filled with the proverbial malice aforethought, and you can't wait to hatch a maniacal plan. You might be part of that cabal of executives using these secret algorithms to plan where and when to dump the toxic waste. Technology is neutral.

There is some human impulse that would like to believe that all information is ordered, correct, structured, organized, and above, all true. We dream that computers and their vast collection of trivia about the world will keep us safe, secure, and moving toward some glorious goal, even if we don't know what that goal is. We hope that the databases held by the government, the banks, the insurance companies, the retail stores, the doctors, and practically everyone else will deliver unto us a perfectly ordered world.

Alas, nothing could be further from the truth. Even the bits can hide multiple meanings. They're supposed to be either on or off, true or false, 0 or 1, but even the bits can conspire to carry secret messages and hidden truths. Information is not as certain or as precise as it may seem to be. Sometimes a cigar carries a freight train load of meaning, and sometimes it is just a cigar. Sometimes it is close and no cigar at all.

Through it all, only a human can make sense of it. Only a human can determine the difference between an obscene allusion to a cigar and reference to an object for delivering nicotine. We keep hoping that artificial intelligence and database engines will be able to parse all of the data, all of the facts, and all of the bits, and identify the terrorists that need punishing, the good people that need help, and the split ends that need another dose of special conditioner. You, the reader, are the human who must decide how to use the information in this book. You can solve crimes, coordinate a wedding, plan a love that will last forever, or concoct dastardly schemes. The technology is neutral. The book is just equations on a page. You will determine what the equations mean for the world.

chapter two

Encryption

Pure White

In the final years of the 20th century, Pinnacle Paint was purchased by the MegaGoth marketing corporation in a desperate attempt to squeeze the last bit of synergy from the world. The executives of MegaGoth, who were frantic with the need to buy something they didn't already own so they could justify their existence, found themselves arguing that the small, privately owned paint company fit nicely into their marketing strategy for dominating the entertainment world.

Although some might argue that people choose colors with their eyes, the executives quickly began operating under the assumption that people purchased paint that would identify them with something. People wanted to be part of a larger movement. They weren't choosing a color for a room, they were buying into a lifestyle—how dare they choose any lifestyle without licensing one from a conglomerate? The executives didn't really believe this, but they were embarrassed to discover that their two previous acquisition targets were already owned by MegaGoth. Luckily, their boss didn't know this either when he gave the green light to those projects. Only the quick thinking of a paralegal saved them from the disaster of buying something they already owned and paying all of that tax.

One of the first plans for MegaGoth/Pinnacle Paints is to take the standard white paint and rebottle it in new and different product lines to target different demographic groups. Here are some of the plans:

- *Moron and Moosehead's Creative Juice.* What would the two lovable animated characters paint if they were forced to expand their creativity in art class? Moron might choose a white cow giving milk in the Arctic for his subject. Moosehead would probably try to paint a little lost snowflake in a cloud buffeted by the wind and unable to find its way to its final destination: Earth.

- *Empathic White.* White is every color. The crew of *Star Trek: They Keep Breeding More Generations* will welcome Bob, the "empath," to the crew next season. His job is to let other people project their feelings onto him. Empathic White will serve the same function for the homeowner as the mixing base for many colors. Are you *blue*? Bob, the empath, could accept that feeling and validate it. Do you want your living room to be blue? That calls for Empathic White. Are you *green* with jealousy? Empathic White at your service.

- *Fright White.* MegaGoth took three British subjects and let them watch two blood-draining horror movies from the upcoming MegaGoth season. At the end they copied the color of their skin and produced the purest white known to the world.

- *Snow White.* A cross-licensing product with the MegaGoth/Disney division ensures that kids in their nursery won't feel alone for a minute. Those white walls will be just another way to experience the magic of a movie produced long ago when Disney was a distinct corporation.

- *White Dwarf White.* The crew of "Star Trek" discovers a white dwarf star and spends an entire episode orbiting it. But surprise! The show isn't really about white dwarf stars qua white dwarfs, it's really about using their super-strong gravitational fields as a metaphor for human attraction. Now, everyone can wrap themselves in the same metaphor by painting their walls with White Dwarf White.

2.1

Encryption and White Noise

Hiding information is a tricky business. Although the rest of this book will revolve around camouflaging information by actually making the bits look like something else, it is a good idea to begin with examining basic encryption. The standard encryption functions such as AES (Advanced Encryption Standard) or RSA (the algorithm developed by Ron Rivest, Adi Shamir, and Len Adleman at MIT) hide data by making it incomprehensible. They take information and convert it into total randomness or white noise. This effect may not be a good way to divert attention from a file, but it is still an important tool. Many of the algorithms and approaches described later in this book perform best when they have a perfectly random source of data. Encrypting a file before applying any of the other approaches is a good beginning.

The world of cryptography began attempting to produce perfect white noise during World War II. This is because Claude Shannon, a mathematician then working for Bell Labs, developed the foundations of information theory that offered an ideal framework for actually measuring information.

Most people who use computers have a rough idea about just how much information is contained in a particular file. A word processing document, for instance, has some overhead and about one byte for each character. But most people are also aware that there is something slippery about measuring information. If the number of bytes in a computer file were an accurate measurement of the information in it, then there would be no way that a compression program could squeeze files to be a fraction of the original size. Real estate can't be squeezed and diamonds can't be smooshed, but potato chips always seem to come in a bag filled with air. That's why they're sold by weight, not volume. The success of compression programs such as PKZIP or StuffIt indicates that measuring a file by the number of bytes is like selling potato chips by volume.

Compression is discussed in Chapter 5.

Shannon's method of measuring information "by weight" rests upon probability. His idea is that a message has plenty of information if you can't anticipate the contents, but it has little information if the contents are easy to predict. A weather forecast in Los Angeles doesn't contain much information because it is often sunny and 72 degrees Fahrenheit. A weather forecast in the Caribbean during hurricane season, though, has plenty of potential information about coming storms that might be steaming in.

Shannon measured information by totaling up the probabilities. A byte has 8 bits and 256 different possible values between 00000000 and 11111111 in base two. If all of these possible values occur with the same probability, then there are said to be 8 bits of information in this byte. On the other hand, if only two values such as 00101110 and 10010111 happen to appear in a message, then there is only one bit of information in each byte. The two values could be replaced with just a 0 and a 1, and the entire file would be reduced to one-eighth the size. The number of bits of information in a file is called, in this context, its *entropy*.

Shannon also provided a precise formula for measuring the size of information (a topic found later in Section 2.2). This measurement of information offered some important insights to cryptographers. Mathematicians who break codes rely upon deep statistical analysis to ferret out patterns in files. In English, the letter "q" is often followed by the letter "u", and this pattern is a weak point that might be exploited by attackers trying to get at the underlying message. A good encryption program would leave no such patterns in the final file. Every one of the 256 possible values of a byte would occur with equal probability. It would seem to be chock full of information.

The *one-time pad* is an encryption system that is a good example of the basic structure behind information theory. The one-time pad received its name because spies often carried pads of random numbers that served as the encryption key. They would use each sheet once and then dispose of it.

A simple one-time pad system can be built by using a simple method of encryption. Assume for the moment that a key is simply a number such as 5, and a message consists of all uppercase letters. To encrypt the letter "C" with a key number 5, count over five letters to get "H". If the counting goes past "Z" at the end of the alphabet, simply go back to "A" and keep going. The letter "Y" encrypted with the key number 6 would produce "E". To decrypt work backward.

Here is a sample encryption:

H	E	L	L	O
9	0	2	1	0
Q	E	N	M	O

The key, in this case, is the five numbers 9, 0, 2, 1, and 0. They would constitute the one-time pad that encrypted this message. In practice, the values should be as random as possible. A human might reveal some hidden short circuits in his or her brain.[1]

Shannon proved that a one-time pad is an unbreakable cipher because the information content of the final file is equal to the information content of the key. An easy way to see why this is true is to break the message "QENMO" described above. Any five-letter word could be the underlying message because any key is possible. The name "BRUNO", for instance, would have generated "QENMO"

A secret can be split into parts using an extension of one-time pads described in Section 4.1.1.

---

[1]Or the limitations of creativity brought on by too much television.

if the key numbers were 15, 13, 19, 25, and 0. If all possibilities are available, then the attacker can't use any of the information about English or the message itself to rule out solutions. The entropy of the message itself should be greater than or equal to the entropy in the key. This is certainly the case here because each byte of the message could be any value between 0 and 255 and so could the key. In practice, the entropy of the key would be even greater because the distribution of the values in the message would depend upon the vagaries of language, whereas the key could be chosen at random.

A real one-time pad would not be restricted to uppercase characters. You could use a slightly different encryption process that used all 256 possible values of a byte. One popular method is to use the operation known as *exclusive-or* (XOR), which is simply addition in the world of bits ($0 + 0 = 0$, $0 + 1 = 1$, and $1 + 1 = 0$ because it wraps around). If the one-time pad consists of bytes with values between 0 and 255 and these values are evenly distributed in all possible ways, then the result will be secure. It is important that the pad not be used again because statistical analysis of the underlying message can reveal the key. The United States was able to read some crucial correspondence between the Soviet Union and its spies working in the United States during the early Cold War because the same one-time pad was reused [Age95]. The number of bits in the key was now less than the number of bits of information in the message, and Shannon's proof that the one-time pad is a perfect encryption no longer holds.

The one-time pad is an excellent encryption system, but very impractical. Two people who want to communicate in secret must arrange to exchange one-time pads securely long before they need to start sending messages. It would not be possible, for instance, for someone to use a Web browser to encrypt the credit card numbers being sent to a merchant without exchanging a one-time pad in person. Often, the sheer bulk of the pad is too large to be practical.

Many people have tried to make this process more efficient by using the same part of the pad over and over again. If they were encrypting a long message, they might use the key 90210 over and over again. This makes the key small enough to be remembered easily, but it introduces dangerous repetition. If the attackers are able to guess the length of the key, they can exploit this pattern. They would know in this case that every fifth letter would be shifted by the same amount. Finding the right amount is often trivial, and it can be as easy as solving a crossword puzzle or playing Hangman.

2.1.1   DES and Modern Ciphers

There are many different encryption functions that do a good job of scrambling information into white noise. One of the more practical and secure encryption algorithms available today is the Data Encryption Standard (DES) developed by IBM in the 1970s. The system uses only 56 bits of key information to encrypt 64-bit blocks of data. Today the number of the bits in the key is considered too small because some computer scientists have assembled computers that can try all 2^{55} possible keys in about 48 hours [Fou98].

One of the newest and most efficient replacements for DES is the Advanced Encryption Standard (AES), an algorithm chosen by the U.S. government after a long, open contest. The algorithm, Rijndael, came from Joan Daemen and Vincent Rijmen and narrowly defeated four other highly qualified finalists [DR00, DR01].[2]

The basic design of most modern ciphers such as DES and Rijndael was inspired, in part, by some other work of Claude Shannon in which he proposed that encryption consists of two different and complementary actions: confusion and diffusion. *Confusion* consists of scrambling up a message or modifying it in some nonlinear way. The simple one-time pad system confuses each letter. *Diffusion* involves taking one part of the message and modifying another part so that each part of the final message depends on many other parts of the message. There is no diffusion in the one-time pad example because the total randomness of the key made it unnecessary.

DES consists of 16 alternating rounds of confusion and diffusion. There are 64 bits that are encrypted in each block of data. These are split into two 32-bit halves. First, one half is confused by passing it through what is called an *S-box*. This is really just a random function that is preset to scramble the data in an optimal way. Then these results are combined with the key bits and used to scramble the other half. This is the diffusion, because one half of the data is affecting the other half. This pattern of alternating rounds is often called a *Feistel network*.

The alternating rounds would not be necessary if a different S-box were used for each 64-bit block of the message. Then it would be the equivalent of a one-time pad. But that would be inefficient because a large file would need a correspondingly large set of S-boxes. The

---

[2]Daemen and Rijmen suggest pronouncing the name: "Reign Dahl," "Rain Doll," or "Rhine Dahl."

alternating rounds are a compromise designed to securely scramble the message with only 64 bits.

The confusion and diffusion functions were designed differently. Confusion was deliberately constructed to be as nonlinear as possible. Linear functions, straight lines, are notoriously easy to predict. For this reason, the S-boxes that provide the confusion for DES were chosen to be as nonlinear as possible.

Creating a nonlinear S-box is not an easy process. The original technique was classified, leading many to suspect that the U.S. government had installed a trapdoor or secret weakness in the design. The recent work of two Israeli cryptographers, Eli Biham and Adi Shamir, however, showed how almost-linear tendencies in S-boxes could be exploited to break a cipher like DES. Although their technique was very powerful and successful against DES-like systems, the authors discovered that DES itself was optimally designed to resist this attack.

The diffusion function, on the other hand, was limited by technology. Ideally, every bit of the 64-bit block will affect the encryption of any other bit. If one bit at the beginning of the block is changed, then every other bit in the block may turn out differently. This instability ensures that those attacking the cipher won't be able to localize their effort. Each bit affects the others.

The process of using one half of the function to scramble the other is shown in Figure 2.1. Alternating which half scrambles the

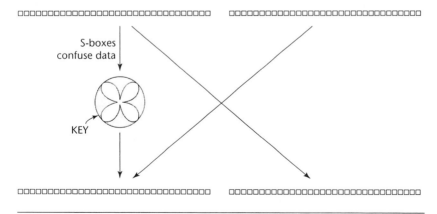

Figure 2.1   A schematic view of one round of DES. 64 bits enter and are split into two 32-bit halves. The left half is scrambled up with the key using the S-boxes. This result is then mixed in with the right half, and the result of adding these two together becomes the new left half. The new right half is just a copy of the old left half.

000000 → 1110	000001 → 0100	000010 → 1101	000011 → 0001
000100 → 0010	000101 → 1110	000110 → 1011	000111 → 1000
001000 → 0011	001001 → 1010	001010 → 0110	001011 → 1100
001100 → 0101	001101 → 1001	001110 → 0000	001111 → 0111
010000 → 0000	010001 → 1111	010010 → 0111	010011 → 0100
010100 → 1110	010101 → 0010	010110 → 1101	010111 → 0001
011000 → 1010	011001 → 0110	011010 → 1100	011011 → 1011
011100 → 1001	011101 → 0101	011110 → 0011	011111 → 1000
100000 → 0100	100001 → 0001	100010 → 1110	100011 → 1000
100100 → 1101	100101 → 0110	100110 → 0010	100111 → 1011
101000 → 1111	101001 → 1100	101010 → 1001	101011 → 0111
101100 → 0011	101101 → 1010	101110 → 0101	101111 → 0000
110000 → 1111	110001 → 1100	110010 → 1000	110011 → 0010
110100 → 0100	110101 → 1001	110110 → 0001	110111 → 0111
111000 → 0101	111001 → 1011	111010 → 0011	111011 → 1110
111100 → 1010	111101 → 0000	111110 → 0110	111111 → 1101

Figure 2.2   This table shows how the first DES S-box converts 6-bit values into 4-bit ones. Note that a change in one input bit will generally change two output bits. The function is also nonlinear and difficult to approximate with linear functions.

other is a good way to ensure that the contents of one half affect the other. The diffusion in DES is even more subtle. Although the information in one half would affect the other after only one round, the bits inside the halves wouldn't affect each other quite as quickly. This part of the book does not go into the design of the S-boxes in detail, but suffice it to say at this point that the amount of scrambling was limited by the technology available in the mid-1970s when the cipher was designed. It takes several rounds of this process to diffuse the information thoroughly.

Figure 2.2 shows one of the eight S-boxes from DES. It is simply a table. If the input to the S-box is 000000, then the output is 1110. This is the simplest form of scrambling and it is fairly easy to reverse. The S-box takes 6 bits as input to implement diffusion. The 32 bits of one half are split into eight 4-bit blocks. Each of the 4-bit blocks then grabs one bit from the block to the left and one bit from the block to the right. That means that each 4-bit block influences the processing of the adjacent 4-bit block. This is how the bits inside each of the halves affect each other.

This is already too much detail for this part of the book. The rest of DES is really of more interest to programmers who actually need to implement the cipher. The important lesson here is how the designers of DES chose to interleave some confusion functions with some diffusion functions to produce incomprehensible results.

The best way to judge the strength of an encryption system such as DES is to try to break it. Talking about highly technical subjects like code-breaking at a high level can be futile because the important details can often be so subtle that the hand-waving metaphors end up flying right over the salient fact. Still, a quick sketch of an attack on the alternating layers of confusion and diffusion in DES can give at least an intuitive feel for why the system is effective.

Imagine that you're going to break one round of DES. You have the 64 bits produced by one step of confusion and one step of diffusion. You want to reconstruct the 64 bits from the beginning and determine the 56 key bits that were entered. Since only one round has finished, you can immediately discover one half of the bits. The main advantage that you have is that not much diffusion has taken place. 32 bits are always unchanged by each round. This makes it easier to determine if the other half could come from the same file. Plus, these 32 bits were also the ones that fed into the confusion function. If the confusion process is not too complicated, then it may be possible to run it in reverse. The DES confusion process is pretty simple, and it is fairly straightforward to go backward. It's just a table lookup. If you can guess the key or the structure of the input, then it is simple.

Now imagine doing the same thing after 16 rounds of confusion and diffusion. Although you can work backward, you'll quickly discover that the confusion is harder to run in reverse. After only one round, you could recover the 32 bits of the left half that entered the function. But you can't get 32 bits of the original message after 16 rounds. If you try to work backward, you'll quickly discover that everything is dependent upon everything else. The diffusion has forced everything to affect everything else. You can't localize your search to one 4-bit block or another because all of the input bits have affected all of the other bits in the process of the 16 rounds. The changes have percolated throughout the process.

Rijndael is similar in theme to DES, but much more efficient for modern CPUs. The S-boxes from DES are relatively simple to implement on custom chips, but they are complicated to simulate with the general-purpose CPUs used in most computers. The confusion in AES is accomplished by multiplying by a polynomial, and the diffusion occurs when the subblocks of the message block are scrambled. This math is much simpler than the complex S-boxes because the general-purpose CPUs are designed to handle basic arithmetic.

The other four AES finalists can also be shoehorned into this simple model of alternating rounds of confusion and diffusion. All of them are considered to be quite secure, which means they all provide more "whitening".

2.1.2   Public-Key Encryption

Public-key encryption systems are quite different from the popular private-key encryption systems such as DES. They rely on a substantially different branch of mathematics that still generates nice, random white noise. Even though these foundations are different, the results are still the same.

The most popular public-key encryption system is the RSA algorithm that was developed by Ron Rivest, Adi Shamir, and Len Adleman when they were at MIT during the late 1970s. The system uses two keys. If one key encrypts the data, then only the other key can decrypt it. The first key is worthless. This is not a bug, but a feature. Each person can create a pair of keys and publicize one of the pair, perhaps by listing it in some electronic phone book. The other key is kept secret. If someone wants to send a message to you, they look up your public key and use it to encrypt the message to you. Only the other key can decrypt this message now, and only you have a copy of that key.

In a very abstract sense, the RSA algorithm works by arranging the set of all possible messages in a long, long loop in an abstract mathematical space. The circumference of this loop, call it n, is kept a secret. You might think of this as a long necklace of pearls or beads. Each bead represents a possible message. There are billions of billions of billions of them in the loop. You send a message by giving someone a pointer to a bead.

The public key is just a relatively large number, call it k. A message is encrypted by finding its position in the loop and stepping around the loop k steps. The encrypted message is the number at this position. The secret key is the circumference of the loop minus k. A message is decrypted by starting at the number marking the encrypted message and marching along the $n - k$ steps. Because the numbers are arranged in a loop, this will bring you back to where everything began, the original message.

There are two properties about this string of pearls or beads that make it possible to use it for encryption. The first is that given a bead, it is really hard to know its exact position on the string. If there is some special first bead that serves as the reference location as on a rosary, then you would need to count through all of the beads to determine the exact location of one of the beads. This same effect happens in the mathematics. You would need to multiply numbers again and again to determine if a particular number is the one you want.

The second property of the string of beads in this metaphor does not make as much sense, but it can still be explained easily. If you want to move along the string k beads or pearls, then you can jump there almost instantaneously. This allows you to encrypt and decrypt messages using the public-key system.

The two special features are similar but they do not contradict each other. The second says that it is easy to jump an arbitrary number of beads. The first says it's hard to count the number of beads between the first bead and any particular bead. If you knew the count, then you could use the second feature. But you don't so you have to count by hand.

The combination of these two features makes it possible to encrypt and decrypt messages by jumping over large numbers of beads. But it also makes it impossible for someone to break the system because they can't determine the number of steps in the jump without counting.

This metaphor is not exactly correct, but it captures the spirit of the system. Figure 2.3 illustrates it. Mathematically, the loop is constructed by computing the powers of a number modulo some other number. That is, the first element in the loop is the number.

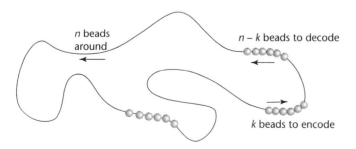

Figure 2.3 RSA encryption works by arranging the possible messages in a loop with a secret circumference. Encryption is accomplished by moving a random amount, k, down the loop. Only the owners know the circumference, n, so they can move $n - k$ steps down the loop and recover the original message.

The second is the square of the number, the third is the cube of the number, and so on. In reality, the loop is more than one-dimensional, but the theme is consistent.

2.1.3   How Random Is the Noise?

How random is the output of an encryption function like DES or RSA? Unfortunately, the best answer to that question is the philosophical response, "What do you mean by random?" Mathematics is very good at producing consistent results from well-defined questions, but it has trouble accommodating capricious behavior.

At the highest level, the best approach is indirect. If there were a black box that could look at the first n bits of a file and predict the next set of bits with any luck, then it would be clear that the file is not completely random. Is there such a black box that can attack a file encrypted with DES? The best answer is that no one knows of any black box that will do the job in any reasonable amount of time. A brute-force attack is possible, but this requires a large machine and some insight into the structure of the encrypted file. So, we could argue that the results of DES or AES should appear random because we can't predict them successfully [Way92, Fou98].

The same arguments also hold for RSA. If there were some black box that could take a number and tell you where it stood in the loop, then you would be able to break RSA. If the input didn't fall in a pattern, then the output would be very random. If there were some way of predicting it, then that could be used to break RSA. Of course, the bits coming out of a stream of RSA-encrypted values are not perfectly random, at least at the level of bits. The values in the output are all computed modulo n so they are all less than n. Since n is not a power of 2, some bits are somewhat less likely.

Even if the values can't be predicted, they still might not be as random looking as we might want. For instance, an encrypted routine might produce a result that is uncrackable but filled with only two numbers such as 7 and 11. The pattern might be incomprehensible and unpredictable, but you still wouldn't want to use the source as the random number generator for your digital craps game. One immediate clue is that if the 7 and the 11 occur with equal probability, then the entropy of such a file is clearly 1 bit per number.

It is easy to construct a high-level argument that this problem will not occur with DES. All possible output values should be produced with equal probability. Why? Because DES can be decoded successfully. 64 bits go into DES and 64 bits go out. Each possible output can only have one matching input and vice versa. Therefore each possible output can be produced.

The same argument also holds for RSA. The loop contains a number for each of all possible messages, and these numbers are distributed around the loop in a way that defies cognition. Therefore, each output value has practically the same probability of emerging from the function.

Although these two arguments don't prove that the output from an encryption function is random, they do suggest that DES and RSA will pass any test that can be thrown at them. If a test is good enough to detect a pattern, then it would be a good lever for breaking the code. In practice, the simple tests support these results. The output of DES is quite random.[3] Many tests show that it is a good way to "whiten" a random number source to make it more intractable. For instance, some people experiment with using a random physical process such as counting cosmic rays to create random numbers. However, there might be a pattern caused by the physics of the detector. A good way to remove this possibility is to use DES to encrypt the random data and produce the whitest noise possible.

2.2

Measuring Information and Encrypting It

Information is a slippery notion. Just how big is a fact? How much data must be accumulated before you have a full-fledged concept? None of these questions are easy to answer, but there are approximations that help with digital data. Shannon's measure of information is closely tied to probability and randomness. In a sense, information is defined by how much randomness it can remove. Our goal is to harness randomness and replace it with a hidden message. Knowing the size, length, depth, or breadth of our target is a good beginning.

---

[3]The level of randomness depends upon the input file if there is no key feedback mechanism being used. In some versions of DES, the results of one block are XORed with the inputs for the next block so that there will be diffusion across the blocks. If this is not used, someone could input a file with a pattern and get out a file with a pattern as long as the pattern repeats in an even multiple of 8 bytes.

2.2.1 Entropy

Let an information stream be composed of n characters between x_0 and x_{n-1} that occur in the stream with probability $\rho(x_i)$. Shannon's measure of the *entropy* in the information stream, that is, the number of bits per character, can be written as

$$\sum_{i=0}^{n-1} \rho(x_i) \log\left(\frac{1}{\rho(x_i)}\right).$$

The log is taken base two.

If a stream is made up of bytes with values between 0 and 255 and every byte value occurs with equal probability of $\frac{1}{256}$, then the entropy of the stream is 8 bits per byte. If only two bytes, say 43 and 95, each occur half of the time and the other 254 bytes don't occur at all, the entropy of this stream is only 1 bit per byte. In this simple example, it should be obvious how the bit stream can be compressed by a factor of 8 bits to 1 per character. In more complex examples, the entropy is still a good rough measure of how well a simple compression algorithm will do.

The limitations of Shannon's measure of information are pretty obvious. An information stream that repeats the bytes $0, 1, 2, \ldots, 254, 255, 0, 1 \ldots$ ad infinitum would appear to contain 8 bits of information per byte. But, there really isn't that much information being conveyed. You could write a short two-line program in most computer languages that would duplicate the result. This computer program could stand in for this stream of information, and it would be substantially cheaper to ship this program across the network than pay for the cost of sending an endless repeat stream of bytes.

In a sense, this repeating record computer program is a very good compressed form of the information. If the data were the potato chips discussed earlier, you would hope that it were measured by the number of lines in a computer program that could generate the data were the data, *not* the Shannon entropy. There is another measure of information known as the *Kolmogorov* complexity that attempts to measure the information by determining the size of the smallest program that could generate the data. This is a great theoretical tool for analyzing algorithms, but it is entirely impractical. Finding the smallest program is both theoretically and practically impossible because no one can test all possible programs. It might be a short program in C, but what about in Pascal, Smalltalk, or a language that no one has written yet.

The Shannon measure of information can be made more complicated by including the relationship between adjacent characters:

$$\sum_{i,j} \rho(x_i \mid x_j) \log \left(\frac{1}{\rho(x_i \mid x_j)} \right).$$

$\rho(x_i \mid x_j)$ means the probability that x_i follows x_j in the information stream. The sum is computed over all possible combinations. This measure does a good job of picking up some of the characteristics of the English language. The occurrence of a letter varies significantly. The letter "h" is common after a "t" but not after a "q". This measure would also pick up the pattern in the example of 0, 1, 2, ..., 255, 0, 1, ... But there are many slightly more complicated patterns that could be generated by a simple computer program yet still confound this second-order entropy calculation. Shannon defined the entropy of a stream to include all orders up to infinity. Counting this high may not be possible, but the higher-order terms can usually be safely ignored. While it may be practical to compute the first- or second-order entropy of an information stream, the amount of space devoted to the project obviously becomes overwhelming. The number of terms in the summation grows exponentially with the order of the calculation. Shannon created several experimental ways for estimating the entropy, but the limits of the model are still clear.

2.2.2 RSA Encryption

Section 2.1, "Encryption and White Noise", described RSA encryption with the metaphor of a long circle of beads. Here's the true mathematics. The system begins with two prime numbers p and q. Multiplying p and q together is easy, but no one knows of an efficient way to factor pq into its components p and q if the numbers are large (i.e., about 1024 to 2048 bits).

This is the basis of the security of the system. If you take a number x and compute the successive powers of x, then there is some number ϕ such that $x^\phi \bmod pq = x$. ($x \bmod y$ means the remainder after x is divided by y. So, 9 mod 7 is 2; 9 mod 3 is 0.) That is, if you keep multiplying a number by x modulo pq, then it returns to x after $\phi+1$ steps.

A message is encrypted by treating it as the number x. The sender encrypts the number x by multiplying it by itself e times; that is, computing $x^e \bmod pq$. The receiver decrypts the message by multiplying it by itself d times; that is, computing $(x^e)^d \bmod pq = x^{ed} \bmod pq$. If $d \times e = \phi$, then the result will be x.

How do we compute ϕ? The value depends upon the modulus, p or pq, used in the computation. There is a function for $\phi(n)$ called the *Euler Totient* function, and it is the number of integers less than n that are relatively prime to n. If x is a prime number, then $\phi(n)$ is $n - 1$ because all of the integers less than n are relatively prime to it. Luckily, $\phi(n) = \phi(n)\phi(n)$, so that $\phi(pq) = pq - p - q + 1$; for example, $\phi(15) = 8$. The numbers 1, 2, 4, 7, 8, 11, 13, and 14 are relatively prime. The values 3, 5, 6, 9, 10, and 12 are not.

Calculating the value of $\phi(pq)$ is easy if you know both p and q, but no one knows an efficient way to do it if you don't. This is the basis for the RSA algorithm. The circumference of this string of pearls or beads is $\phi(pq)$. Moving one bead along the string is the equivalent of multiplying by x.

Neal Koblitz's book [Kob87] gives a good introduction to finding this inverse.

The two keys for the RSA are chosen so they both multiply together to give 1 modulo $\phi(pq)$. One is chosen at random, and the other is calculated by finding the inverse of it. Call these e and d where $de = 1 \bmod \phi(pq)$. This means that

$$x^{ed} \bmod pq = x.$$

This can be converted into an encryption system very easily. To encrypt with this public key, calculate $x^e \bmod pq$. To decrypt, raise this answer to the d power. That is, compute

$$(x^e \bmod pq)^d \bmod pq = x^{de} \bmod pq = x.$$

This fulfills all of the promises of the public-key encryption system. There is one key, e, that can be made public. Anyone can encrypt a message using this value. No one can decrypt it, however, unless they know d. This value is kept private.

The most direct attack on RSA is to find the value of $\phi(pq)$. This can be done if you can factor pq into p and q. There is no better computational approach that anyone knows.

Actually implementing RSA for encryption requires attention to a number of details. Here are some of the most important ones, in no particular order:

- *Converting Messages into Numbers.* Data is normally stored as bytes. RSA can encrypt any integer that is less than pq. So there needs to be a solid method of converting a collection of bytes into and out of integers less than pq. The simplest solution is to glue together bytes until the string of bytes is a number that is greater than pq. Then remove one byte and replace it with random bits so that the value is just less than pq. To convert back to bytes, simply remove this padding.

- *Fast Modulo Computation.* Computing $x^e \bmod pq$ does not require multiplying x together e times. This would be prohibitive because e could be quite large. An easier solution is to compute $x, x^2 \bmod pq, x^4 \bmod pq, x^8 \bmod pq, \ldots$. That is, keep squaring x. Then choose the right subset of them to multiply together to get $x^e \bmod pq$. This subset is easy to determine. If the ith bit of the binary expansion of e is 1, then multiply in $x^{2^i} \bmod pq$ into the final answer.

  [BFHMV84], [Bri82], [Mon85], and [QC82] discuss efficient multiplication algorithms.

- *Finding Large Prime Numbers.* The security of the RSA system depends upon how easy it is to factor pq. If both p and q are large prime numbers, then this is difficult. Identifying large prime numbers is, as luck would have it, pretty easy to do. There are a number of tests for primality that work quite well. The solution is just to choose a really large, odd number at random and then test it to see if it is prime. If it isn't, then choose another. The length of time it takes to find a prime number close to an integer x is roughly proportional to the number of bits in x.

  The Lehman test [Leh82] is a simple way to determine if n is prime. To do so, choose a random number a and compute $a^{(n-1)/2} \bmod n$. If this value is not 1 or -1, then n is not prime. Each value of a has at least a 50 percent chance of showing up a nonprime number. If we repeat this test m times, then we're sure that we have a 1 in 2^m chance that n is not prime, but we haven't found an a that would prove it yet. Making $m = 100$ is a good starting point. It is not absolute proof, but it is good enough.

  RSA encryption is a very popular algorithm used for public-key encryption. Many other algorithms are also available. The discussion of these variants is beyond the scope of this book. Both Bruce Schneier's book [Sch94] and Gus Simmons's book [Sim93] offer good surveys.

2.3

Summary

Pure encryption algorithms are the best way to convert data into white noise. This alone is a good way to hide information in data. Some scientists, for instance, encrypt random data to make it even

more random. Encryption is also the basis for all of the other algorithms used in steganography. The algorithms that take a block of
data and hide it in the noise of an image or sound file need data that
is as close to random as possible. This lowers the chance that it can
be detected.

Of course, nothing is perfect. Sometimes data that is too random
can stick out too. Chapter 17 describes how to find hidden information by looking for values that are more random than they should be.

- *The Disguise.* Good encryption turns data into white noise that
  appears random. This is a good beginning for many algorithms
  that use the data as a random source to imitate the world.

- *How Secure Is It?* The best new encryption algorithms such as
  Rijndael and the other four AES finalists have no practical attack
  known to the public. These algorithms are designed and
  evaluated solely on their ability to resist attack. DES is still
  relatively secure, although brute-force attacks on the relatively
  small 56-bit key are very feasible.

- *How To Use It?* Encryption code can be downloaded from a
  number of places on the Net. See Appendix D.

chapter three

Error Correction

Close but No Cigar

1. Speedwalking

2. America Online, CompuServe, and Prodigy

3. Veggie burgers

4. Using a StairMaster

5. Winning the Wild Card pennant

6. Driving 55 mph

7. Living in suburbia

8. New Year's resolutions

9. Lists as poetry

10. Lists as a simple way to give structure to humor

11. Cigarettes

3.1

Correcting Errors

The theory of computers rests on an immutable foundation: a bit is either on ("1") or off ("0"). Underneath this foundation, however, is the normal, slightly random, slightly chaotic world in which humans spend their time. Just as the sun is sometimes a bit brighter than usual and sometimes it rains for a week straight, the physics that govern computer hardware is a bit random. Sometimes that spot on the hard disk that is responsible for remembering something doesn't behave exactly perfectly. Sometimes an alpha particle from outer space screams through a chip and changes the answer.

Computer designers manage to corral all this randomness through a mixture of precision and good mathematics. Clean machines eliminate the dirt that screws up things, and the mathematics of error-correcting codes is responsible for fixing up the rest of the problems that slip through. This mathematics is really one of the ideas that is most responsible for the digital explosion. The math makes it possible to build a digital circuit with a bit of sloppiness that can never be present in an analog world. Designers know that the sloppiness can be fixed by a bit of clever mathematics.

Error-correcting codes can be used effectively to hide information in a number of important ways. The most obvious approach is to simply introduce small errors into a file in an organized fashion. If someone tries to read the file with ordinary tools, the error correction would patch up these changes and no one would be the wiser. More sophisticated tools could find these changes by comparing the original file with the cleaned-up version or simply using the error-correcting principles to point to the location. The message could be encoded in the position of the errors.

Some music CD manufacturers are taking advantage of the differences between the error-correcting mechanisms in computers and CD players. Strategically placed errors will be corrected by a CD player but labeled as disk failure by the mechanisms in computers. Voilà, copy protection that prevents a CD from being used in a computer.

A high number of errors might indicate the existence of a message. Chapter 17 describes how to build statistical models to detect abnormal patterns such as a high error rate.

Error-correcting codes can also be used to help two people share a channel. Many semipublic data streams make ideal locations for hiding information. It might be possible to insert bits in a photograph or a music file on the Internet by grabbing the file and replacing it with a copy that includes your message. This works well until someone else has the same idea. Suddenly one message could overwrite another. An ideal solution would be to arrange it so no one took up more than a small fraction of a channel like this one. Then, they would write their information with an error-correcting code. If two messages interacted, they would still only damage a fraction of each other's bits, and the error-correcting code would be used to fix it. This is the same way that the codes are used in many radio systems.

Of course, error-correcting codes can also help deal with errors introduced by attackers, a noisy channel, or a format conversion. Some

Web sites reduce the size of images or apply subtle color corrections. In some cases, these modifications introduce only a few changes to the file, and the error-correcting codes can recover them. This additional strength is hard to measure because there is no easy way to predict the damage waiting for the file.

On occasion, it makes sense to split a message into a number of different parts to be shipped through different channels. Ideally, the message could be reconstructed if a few of the parts were compromised along the way. The part could either be lost or scrambled by a malicious courier. In either case, error-correcting codes can defend against this problem.

Systems of error-correcting codes come in any number of flavors. Many of the most commonly used codes have the ability to carry k bits in a packet of n bits and find the right answer if no more than m errors have been made. There are many different possible codes that come with different values of k, n, and m, but you never get anything for free. If you have 7 bits and you want each block to carry at least 4 bits of information, then one standard code can only correct up to one error per block. If you want to carry 6 bits of information in a 7-bit block, then you can't successfully correct errors and you can only detect them half of the time.

The best metaphor for understanding error-correcting codes is to think about spheres. Imagine that each letter in a message is represented as the center of a sphere. There are 26 spheres, one for each letter, and none of them overlap. You send a message by sending the coordinates to this point at the center. Occasionally, a transmission glitch might nudge the coordinates a bit. When the recipient decodes the message, he or she can still get the correct text if the nudges are small enough so the points remain inside the sphere. The search for the best error-correcting codes involves finding the best way to pack these spheres so that you can fit the most spheres in a space and transmit the most characters.

Although the mathematicians talk about sphere packing on an abstract level, it is not immediately obvious how this applies to the digital world where everything is made up of binary numbers that are on or off. How do you nudge a zero a little bit? If you nudge it enough, when does it becomes a one? How do you nudge a number like 252, which is 11111100 in binary? Obviously, a small nudge could convert this into 111111101, which is 253. But what if the error came along when the first bit was going through the channel? If the first bit was changed, the number would become 011111100. That is 114, a change of 128, which certainly doesn't seem small. This

Section 9.2.6 shows how to construct a system using random walks. Ross Anderson, Roger Needham, and Adi Shamir used a similar approach to hide information in their steganographic file system [ANS98].

Better secret splitting solutions are found in Chapter 4.

would imply that the spheres really couldn't be packed too closely together.

The solution is to think about the bits independently and to measure the distance between two numbers as the number of bits that are different. So 11111100 and 11111101 are one unit apart because they differ in only one bit. So are 11111100 and 01111100. But 01111100 and 11111101 are two units apart. This distance is often called the *Hamming distance*.

This measure has the same feel as finding the distance between two corners in a city that is laid out on a Manhattan-like grid. The distance between the corner at 5th Avenue and 42nd Street and the corner at 6th Avenue and 45th Street is 4 blocks, although in Manhattan they are blocks of different lengths. You just sum up the differences along each of the different dimensions. In the street example, there are two dimensions: the avenues that run north and south, and the streets that run east and west. In the numerical example, each bit position is a different dimension, and the 8-bit examples above have eight dimensions.

Error-correcting codes spread the information out over a number of bits in the same fashion as the spread-spectrum algorithms do in Chapter 14.

The simplest example of an error-correcting code uses 3 bits to encode each bit of data. The code can correct one error in a bit but not two. There are eight possible combinations of three bits: 000, 001, 010, 011, 100, 101, 110, and 111. You can think of these as the eight corners of a cube as shown in Figure 3.1. A message 0 can be encoded as "000" and a 1 can be encoded as "111". Imagine there is an error in which the "000" was converted into a "001". The closest possible choice, "000", is easy to identify.

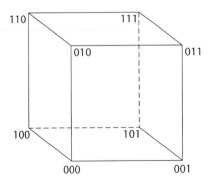

Figure 3.1   The eight corners of the cube. The two corners 000 and 111 are used to send the message of either 0 or 1. If there is an error in one bit, then it can be recovered by finding the closest corner.

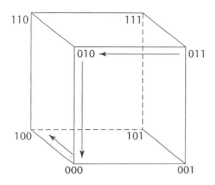

Figure 3.2   The Hamming distance shows that the corner "011" is three steps or units away from "100". That's the longest distance in this cube.

The sphere of "000" includes all points that are at most one Hamming unit away: 001, 010, and 100. Two errors, however, would nudge a point into the adjacent sphere. Figure 3.2 illustrates the calculating of the Hamming distance in three dimensions.

Obviously, the technique can be extended into higher-dimensional spaces. The trick is to find an optimal number of points that can be packed into a space. For instance, imagine a five-dimensional space made up of the points 00000, 00001, 00010, ..., 11111. Every point has an opposite point that is five units away from it. Point 00000 is five steps away from 11111, and 10111 is five units away from 01000. It is easy to construct a sphere with a radius of two units around each point. That means 0 could be encoded as 00000, and 1 would be encoded as 11111. Up to two errors could occur and the correct answer would be found. Point 10110 is two units away from 11111, so it would fall in its sphere of influence and be decoded as a 1.

Generally, odd-dimensional spaces are much better than even-dimensional spaces for this simple scheme. Imagine the six-dimensional space created from the points 000000, 000001, 000010, ..., 111111. Both 000000 and 111111 are six units apart. But if you draw a sphere of radius 3 around each point, then the spheres overlap. The point 010101, for instance, is both three units away from 000000 and three units away from 111111. It's in both spheres. If you were to try to construct an error-correcting code using this arrangement, then you would only be able to fit two spheres of radius 2 in the space and the code would only be able to resist up to two errors per block. Obviously, the 5-bit code in the five-dimensional space is just as error-resistant while being more efficient.

There is no reason why you need to pack only two spheres into each space. You might want to fit in many smaller spheres. In seven-dimensional space, you can fit in two spheres of radius 3 centered around any two points that are seven units apart. But you can also fit in a large number of spheres that have a radius of only 1. For instance, you can place spheres with a single unit radius around 0000000, 0000111, 1110000, 0011001, 1001100, 1010001, and 1000101. None of these spheres overlap and the space is not full. You could also add a sphere centered around 1111110. There are eight code words here, so eight different messages or 3 bits of information could be stored in each 7-bit code word. Up to one bit error could be found and resolved.

In general, packing these higher-dimensional spaces is quite difficult to do optimally (see Figures 3.3 and 3.4). It should be clear that there are many other points that are not in any of eight different spheres. This reflects a gross inefficiency.

Section 3.2, "Constructing Error-Correcting Codes", describes how to build general Hamming codes. It is possible to use the algorithm given there to construct an error-correcting code that packs 4 bits of information, or 16 different messages, into one 7-bit code word. That's one extra bit of data. The code can also resist up to 1 bit

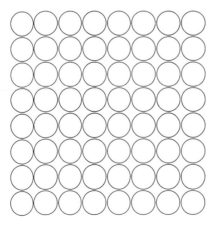

Figure 3.3   A poor way to pack circles. If the system error can't shift the signal more than the radius of the sphere, then the space between the circles is wasted. Figure 3.4 shows a better approach.

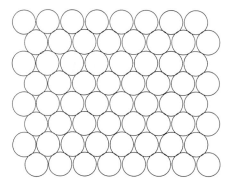

Figure 3.4 A better approach to packing the circles from Figure 3.3. This is about 86.6 percent of the original height. It is wider by one half of the radius of a circle.

of error. The 16 centers generated by this method are as follows:

0000000	0001111	0010011	0011100
0100101	0101010	0110110	0111001
1000110	1001001	1010101	1011010
1100011	1101100	1110000	1111111

There are many other types of error-correcting codes. The metaphor of sphere packing is a good way to understand the basic idea, but it offers little guidance on how it can be done effectively. It is easy to imagine stacking pool balls in a rack, but it is impossible to visualize how to do this in multiple dimensions—especially if the Hamming distance is used.

In practice, error-correcting codes rest upon algorithms that take the data and add extra *parity bits* that can be used to recover the data. The parity bits "puff up" the data into more dimensions and move the points away from each other. For instance, in four dimensions the points 1110 and 1111 are right next to each other. But if three parity bits are added to the end of each one, the result, 1110000 and 1111111, are four units apart.

If you look carefully at the table above, the first four bits represent all of the possible points in a four-dimensional space. The last three bits are parity bits that were added to puff it out into seven dimensions.

The location of the parity bits varies significantly between different codes. Some codes can correct a certain number of errors that occur anywhere in a block of data. Other codes can correct errors that happen in bursts. They might be able to correct only one burst of errors, but the burst can contain anywhere between one flipped bit and an upper limit of k. If the errors don't occur next to each other, however, then the code can't fix the error. Each of these different codes places the parity bits in different arrangements to grab different types of errors.

The rest of this book will rely upon error-correcting codes to add robustness to protocols, perhaps add randomness, and provide another way to split information into a number of different parts. Using error-correcting codes is essential if information might bump into other information in channels.

3.1.1 Error Correction and White Noise

Error-correcting codes may be intended to correct errors, but they can also be used to make a bit stream conform to some pattern. Once a collection of bits is encoded in an error-correcting code, then changes can be introduced without destroying the underlying information. These changes might add randomness or, with some difficulty, make the data conform to a pattern.

In practice, the best choice for this approach is error-correcting codes that can sustain a high number of errors. A simple choice might be the 3-bit error-correcting code that conveys 1 bit. You write 000, 001, 010, or 100 for the 0 bit and 111, 110, 101, or 011 for the 1 bit. Any of the three are acceptable choices. This will triple the size of the file, but it will allow plenty of flexibility in rearranging the structure of the data.

Adding randomness is easy, but there are limitations to making the data fit some other pattern. Obviously, the underlying data must come close enough to the pattern so that errors can be introduced successfully. In an abstract sense, the pattern must fall into the spheres. The bigger the sphere, the more patterns that can work successfully. For instance, you could easily use the 3-bit code described above to produce a bit stream that never had more than three 1s or three 0s occurring in a row. Each bit could be encoded with a pattern that started with a 1 or a 0. On the other hand, you could not produce a pattern that required that there were always five 1s or 0s in a row.

This technique can be taken one step further that takes it outside the realm of error-correcting codes entirely. If you're planning to use the error-correcting codes to give you enough room to add some randomness to the data, then you're going to lose many of the error-correcting properties. For instance, one flipped bit can convert 110, a value representing 1, into 010, a value representing 0. In essence, you might want to forget about the error-correcting ability altogether and just construct a list of codes for representing each bit: 1 might be encoded as 001, 100, 011, and 111, while 0 would be encoded as 110, 101, 010, and 000. The main advantage of this approach is that the distribution of 0s and 1s can be even more balanced. In the 3-bit code used as an example in this section, there are an average of 2.25 bits used to encode a 1 and .75 used to encode a 0. This means a file with a high percentage of 1s, for instance, will still have a high percentage after the encoding. Using random codes assigned to each bit can remove this bias. But this is drifting away from the focus of the chapter.

3.1.2 Error Correction and Secret Sharing

Error-correcting codes have a functional cousin known as *secret sharing*—that is, a class of algorithms that allow a file to be split into m parts so that only $m - k$ parts are necessary to reconstruct it. Obviously, an error-correcting code that could handle up to k errors in m bits would work very similarly. Simply encode the file using this method and then break up the m bits into m different files.

Chapter 4 describes secret sharing.

There is one problem with this approach. Some bits are more privileged than others in some error-correcting schemes. For instance, the next section on Hamming codes describes a code that takes 11 bits and adds 4 parity bits that will correct any single error. Ideally, a file encoded with this code could be broken into 15 parts, and any 14 parts would suffice to recover the data. But there are only 11 bits of data in every block of 15 bits. The other 4 parity bits are just used to correct the errors. If the ith bit of each block always went in the ith part, then the right 11 parts would suffice. The key is to distribute the bits so this never happens. Here are the steps:

1. Choose an error-correcting code that offers the right recovery properties. It is easy to find Hamming codes that recover single errors.

2. Encode the file using this technique.

3. If there are n bits in each block and n files, then place one bit from each block in each file. That is, place bit i in file $i + j \bmod n$. The choice of j should vary with each block. It can either increase sequentially or be chosen by a random number

generator. If a random number generator is used, it should be a pseudo–random number generator that can be reseeded to recover the information later.

For most practical purposes, error-correcting codes are not ideal ways to share secrets. While it is easy to construct a Hamming code that can sustain one error, it is pretty inefficient to generate an error-correcting code that contains n bits per block and still survive, say, $n - 2$ errors. The theory is just not optimized around this solution.

A better secret-sharing technique emerges directly from geometry. Imagine that you encode a message as a point in a plane. One solution is to draw three lines through the point and distribute the lines to different people. Two lines are enough to reconstruct the point. The process can be turned into an error-correcting code by simply choosing the one point that represents the largest intersection of lines. If you want to encode larger amounts of data, you can use higher-dimensional spaces and use planes or higher dimensions. This is close to what the Hamming codes are doing, but it is difficult to think in these terms when only bits are being used.

3.2

Constructing Error-Correcting Codes

[Ara88] and [LJ83] were the sources for this material. More information can be found there.

Hamming codes are easy and elegant error-correcting codes. Constructing them and using them is relatively easy. The problem can be thought of as taking your incoming message bits and then adding parity bits that will allow you to correct the errors. The net effect is to create an overdetermined collection of linear equations that can be solved in only one way.

The easiest way to introduce the algorithm is by constructing an example code that takes 11 bits and adds 4 new parity bits to the mix so that an error of at most 1 bit can be corrected if it occurs. The input bits will be $a_1, \ldots, a_{11}$. The output bits are $b_1, \ldots, b_{15}$. For the purpose of illustrating the algorithm, it is easier to use binary subscripts: b_{0001} through b_{1111} (see Table 3.1).

The best way to illustrate the process is with a table of the output bits. The input bits are simply copied over into an output slot with a different number. This is easy to do in hardware if you happen to be implementing such an algorithm in silicon. The extra parity bits are computed by adding up different sets of the input bits modulo 2. They are found in output bits b_{0001}, b_{0010}, b_{0100}, and b_{1000}.

Table 3.1 An 11-bit correcting code.

Output Bit	Where It Comes From
b_{0001}	$a_1 + a_2 + a_4 + a_5 + a_7 + a_9 + a_{11} \bmod 2$
b_{0010}	$a_1 + a_3 + a_4 + a_6 + a_7 + a_{10} + a_{11} \bmod 2$
b_{0011}	a_1
b_{0100}	$a_2 + a_3 + a_4 + a_8 + a_9 + a_{10} + a_{11} \bmod 2$
b_{0101}	a_2
b_{0110}	a_3
b_{0111}	a_4
b_{1000}	$a_5 + a_6 + a_7 + a_8 + a_9 + a_{10} + a_{11} \bmod 2$
b_{1001}	a_5
b_{1010}	a_6
b_{1011}	a_7
b_{1100}	a_8
b_{1101}	a_9
b_{1110}	a_{10}
b_{1111}	a_{11}

Errors are detected by calculating four formulas that will give the location of the error:

$$c_0 = b_{0001} + b_{0011} + b_{0101} + b_{0111} + b_{1001} + b_{1011} + b_{1101} + b_{1111} \bmod 2$$
$$c_1 = b_{0010} + b_{0011} + b_{0110} + b_{0111} + b_{1010} + b_{1011} + b_{1110} + b_{1111} \bmod 2$$
$$c_2 = b_{0100} + b_{0101} + b_{0110} + b_{0111} + b_{1100} + b_{1101} + b_{1110} + b_{1111} \bmod 2$$
$$c_3 = b_{1000} + b_{1001} + b_{1010} + b_{1011} + b_{1100} + b_{1101} + b_{1110} + b_{1111} \bmod 2$$

These four equations yield 4 bits. If they're combined into a single number, then they'll reveal the location of an error. For instance, imagine that bit b_{1011} was flipped by an error. This is the incoming bit a_7, and this bit is part of the equation that produces parity bits b_{1000}, b_{0010}, and b_{0001}. The pattern should be obvious. The parity bits are stuck at slots that have only a single 1 in the binary value of their subscript. A normal bit is added into the equation by examining the binary value of its subscript. If there is a 1 at position i, then it is added into the parity bit that has a 1 at position i. Bit b_{1011} has three 1s, so it ends up in four equations.

The effect of an error in b_{1011} is easy to follow. Bit b_{0001} will not match the sum $b_{0011} + b_{0101} + b_{0111} + b_{1001} + b_{1011} + b_{1101}$. This will mean that c_0 will evaluate to 1. The same effect will set $c_1 = 1$ and $c_3 = 1$. Formula c_2 will stay 0. If these are combined in the proper order, 1011, then they point directly at bit b_{1011}.

These equations will also correct errors that occur in the parity bits. If one of these should be flipped, then only one of the equations will produce a 1. The rest will yield 0s because the parity bits are not part of their equations.

The general steps for constructing such an error-correcting code for n bits can be summarized:

1. Find the smallest k such that $2^k - k - 1 \leq n$. This set of equations will encode $2^k - k - 1$ bits and produce $2^k - 1$ bits.

2. Enumerate the output bits with binary subscripts: $b_{00...01}, \ldots, b_{11...11}$.

3. The parity bits will be the output bits with a single 1 in their subscript.

4. Assign the input bits to the nonparity output bits. Any order will suffice, but there is no reason not to be neat and do it in order.

5. Compute the parity bit with a 1 at position i by adding up all of the output bits with a 1 at the same position i *except* the parity bit itself. Do the addition modulo 2.

6. To decode, compute c_i, which is the sum of all output bits that have a 1 in position i *including* the parity bit. This will yield a 0 if the parity bit matches and a 1 if it doesn't. Aggregating the c_i values will reveal the position of the error. This code will only detect one error.

What is the most efficient choice of k for this algorithm? Given that the number of parity bits is proportional to the log of the number of input bits, it is tempting to lump the entire file into one big block and use only a small number of parity bits. This requires a large number of additions. There are about $\frac{n \log n}{2}$ additions in a block of n bits. Large blocks require fewer parity bits but need more computation. They also only correct one error in the entire block, and this substantially limits their usefulness. The best trade-off must be based upon the noisiness of the channel carrying the information.

Implementations of Hamming codes like this one are often fastest when they are done a word at a time. Most CPUs, including all of the major ones, have instructions that will do a bitwise XOR of an instruction word, which is usually either 32 or 64 bits long. XOR is addition modulo 2. These fast XORs provide a good way of doing up to 32 or 64 encodings in parallel. This is done by using all of the above equations, but doing the calculations with words instead of bits and XOR instead of basic arithmetic.

This approach is a very fast way to encode the error-correcting bits, and it is a quick way to detect errors, but correcting the error can be slow. Testing for errors can be done just by seeing if all of the c_i values are 0. If one of the c_i is not 0, then the code must step through each of the bits individually and compute the location of the errors. This is much slower, but not any slower than computing the code in a bitwise fashion.

The Hamming codes described in this section are particularly elegant, in my opinion, because of the way that the results of the c_i are aggregated to find the location of the error. This is simply a result of the arrangements of the parity bits. The same basic algorithm could be used no matter what order the bits were found in. Any permutation of the bits b_{0001} through b_{1111} would work. The recovery process wouldn't be as elegant.

This elegant arrangement is not really necessary for hardware-based implementations because the correction of the error does not need to be done by converting the c_i values into an index that points to the error. It is quite possible to simply create a set of AND gates for each bit that looks for a perfect match. This means the parity bits could be placed at the beginning or the end of each block. This might simplify stripping them out.

3.2.1   Periodic Codes

The codes described in the previous section correct only one bit error per block. This may suffice, but it can be pretty inefficient if the block sizes are small. The Hamming codes need three parity bits to correct one error in four bits. That's almost a 50 percent loss just to correct one bit out of four.

The Hamming codes are also less than optimal because of the nature of noise that can corrupt digital data. The errors may not be randomly distributed. They are often grouped in one big burst that might occur after an electrical jolt or some other physical event disrupts the stream. A scratch on a CD-ROM may blur several bits that are right next to each other. These errors would mangle any Hamming solution that is limited to correcting one bit in each block.

Periodic codes are a better solution for these occasions that demand detecting and recovering errors that occur in bursts. In this case, the parity bits will be distributed at regular intervals throughout the stream of bits. For instance, every fourth bit in a stream might be a parity bit that is computed from some of the previous bits. As before, the location of the parity bits can be varied if the number of parity bits per set of bits is kept constant, but it is often cleaner to arrange for them to occur periodically.

The Hamming codes are designed to work with predefined blocks of bits. The convolutional codes described here will work with rolling blocks of bits that overlap. The same convolutional technique will also work with fixed blocks, but it is left out here for the sake of simplicity. To avoid confusion, this section will use the word *subblock* to refer to the smaller sets of bits that are used to create the rolling block.

The periodic code will consist of a subblock of bits followed by a set of parity bits that are computed from the bits present in any number of the preceding subblocks. The parity might also depend on some of the bits in the following subblocks, but this configuration is left out in the interest of simplicity.

A simple set of bits from a convolutional code might look like this:

$$b_{(i,1)}, \ b_{(i,2)}, \ b_{(i,3)}, \ b_{(i,4)}, \ b_{(i,5)}, \ p_{(i,1)}.$$

Here, $b_{(i,1)}$ stands for the first data bit in subblock i. $p_{(i,1)}$ is the first parity bit. There are five data bits and one parity bit in this example.

The parity bit could be any function of the bits in the previous subblocks. For simplicity, let

$$p_{(i,1)} = b_{(i,1)} + b_{(i-1,2)} + b_{(i-2,3)} + b_{(i-3,4)} + b_{(i-4,5)} \bmod 2.$$

That is, each parity bit is affected by one of the bits in the previous five subblocks.

These parity bits can detect one burst of up to five bits that occurs in each rolling set of five subblocks. That means the error will be detected if every two error bursts have at least five subblocks between them. The error, once detected, can be fixed by asking for a retransmission of the data. It can also be recovered in some cases that will be described later.

The error can be detected by watching the trail it leaves in the parity bits that follow it. A burst of errors in this case might affect any of the five parity bits that come after it. When the parity bits don't match, the previous set of five subblocks can be retransmitted to fix the problem. It should be simple to see how spreading out the parity bits makes it possible for the code system to detect bursts of errors. None of the equations used to calculate the parity bits depends upon neighboring bits. In this example, there are at least five bits in the bit stream between each of the bits used to calculate each parity bit. In the Hamming example, each of the parity equations depended on some adjacent bits. If both of those bits were flipped because of a burst of error noise, then the errors would cancel out and the error would be recoverable.

Recovering a parity error is normally not possible with a simple code like this example. If one of the parity bits doesn't agree in this example, then the error could have been introduced by an error in six different bits. Finding which one is impossible. To some extent, a larger burst of errors will make the job easier. For instance, if three bits in a row are flipped, then three consecutive parity bits will also be flipped. If the parity bits are examined individually, then each one could have been caused by up to six different errors. But periodic codes like this are designed to handle bursts of errors. So it is acceptable to assume that the three errors would be adjacent to each other. This limits the location to two different spots.

For instance, here is a data stream with correct parity bits:

... 01010 0 01010 1 1001 1 01111 1 00011 1 ...

If the first three bits are flipped, then the first three parity bits are also flipped:

... 10110 1 01010 0 11001 0 01111 1 00011 1 ...

Each individual error could occur in any of the previous five blocks, but the overlapping nature of the code limits the error to the first block shown here or to either of the two blocks that preceded it. If five bits were flipped in a row, then the exact location would be known and it would be possible to correct the errors. This pushes the code to an extreme, and it would be better not to hope for bursts to come at the extreme limit of the ability of the codes to detect the errors.

The periodic code described in this section is a good way to detect bursts of errors, but it cannot help correct them unless the burst is at the extreme. There is some information available, but it is clearly not enough to recover the data.

Both [LJ83] and [Ara88] are good sources of more information about error-correcting codes.

3.3

Summary

Error-correcting codes are one of the most important tools for building digital systems. They allow electronic designers to correct the random errors that emerge from nature and provide the user with some digital precision. If the electronics were really required to offer perfect accuracy, then they would be prohibitively expensive.

These codes are useful for correcting problems that emerge from the transmission systems. It might be desirable, for instance, for several people to use the same channel. If several people use a small part of the channel chosen at random, then the codes will correct any occasional collisions.

The field is also blessed with a deep body of literature exploring many different variations that lie outside the scope of this introduction. Unfortunately, this book does not have the space to consider them all nor outline the different ways that they can be more or less useful for steganography.

Chapter 14 describes spread-spectrum-like applications to hiding information. These techniques also rely upon distributing the message over a relatively large number of elements in the file. If several of the elements are disturbed or mangled, the spread-spectrum solutions can still recover the message.

- *The Disguise.* If you want to use these codes to hide information, the best solution is to disturb a small subset of bits. If each block has 8 bits, for instance, you can send 3 bits per block. If you want to send 000, then flip bit 0. If you want to send 011, then flip bit 3, and so on. When the bits are finally read at the other end, the error-correcting codes will remove the errors and the casual reader won't even know that they were there. You can use the error-correcting codes to recover them.

  Of course, this solution trades accuracy for steganography. Accidental or intentional errors will destroy the message. The error-correcting powers of the equation will be spent on carrying the information.

- *How Secure Is It?* Error-correcting codes are not secure at all against people who want to read them. The patterns between the bits are easy to detect. They are, however, quite resistant, to errors.

- *How to Use Them?* Error-correcting codes are rarely sold to consumers directly, but consumers use them all the time. Many electronic devices, however, such as CD players and cell phones, rely upon them. Programmers who need to use error-correcting codes should search out complete books on this large and engaging topic.

chapter four

Secret Sharing

Two out of Three Musketeers

In Bob's Manhattan living room, three high school chums are confronting a middle-age crisis over scotch and soda. They're all lawyers and disenchanted by the way that money and corruption have ruined the justice system. So, inspired by movies like *Batman*, they decide to recreate *The Three Musketeers* and prowl about the night looking for people in need of help.

Bob: Okay. It's settled. We'll file for our license to carry concealed weapons tomorrow. On Friday, we pick out our Glocks.

Harry: Yes. 9 mm.

Together: All for one and one for all!

Harry: You know, I just thought of something. My wife promised we would go to dinner at her cousin's house on Friday. She planned it last month. Could we get the Glocks another day?

Bob: Sunday's out for me. We're going to my mother's house after church.

Mark: Well, doesn't fighting evil count for something in the eyes of God?

Bob: Yes. But I still think we need a contingency. We're not going to always be available. There will be business trips, family visits, emergencies.

Mark: This is a good point. We might be stuck in traffic or held up in court. We need a plan.

Harry: Well, what if we said, "All available for one and one for who's there that evening?"

Mark: Not bad. It's more flexible. But what if just one of us is there?

Harry: What's the difference?

Mark: That one person really wouldn't be a group. He would be acting as a vigilante. He could do anything he wanted that evening. Maybe even something that was less than just.

Harry: So you want a quorum?

Mark: Yes. I say two out of three of us should be there before someone can start invoking the name of the Three Musketeers.

Bob: What about costumes? What do we wear if we're alone?

Mark: Doesn't matter. The most important thing is what we shout as we vanquish the foes. Are we together on this?

Together: Two out of Three for One and One for Two out of Three!

4.1

Splitting Up Secrets

There are many occasions when you need to split a key or a secret into numerous puzzle parts so that the secret can only be recovered if all the parts are available. This is a good way to force people to work together. Many nuclear weapons systems, for instance, require two people to turn two different keys simultaneously. Bank safe deposit boxes have two locks, and one key is held by the owner, the other by the bank.[1]

Splitting information into a number of parts is a good way to make information disappear. Each part may look like noise, but together they create the message. These different parts can take different paths, adding further confusion to the entire process.

There are many neat ways to mathematically split a secret into a number of parts. This secret might be the key to an encrypted file, or it might be the important factoid itself. The goal is to create n

---

[1]It is not clear to me why the bank needs to have its own key to the box. The combination to the vault serves the same purpose.

different files or numbers that must all be present to reconstruct the original number. There are also threshold schemes that let you recover the secret if you have some smaller subset of the original parts. If a corporation has five directors, for instance, you might require that three be present to unlock the corporation's secret key used to sign documents.

The mathematics of these schemes is really quite simple and intuitive. Chapter 3 showed how error-correcting codes can be used to serve as primitive secret-sharing devices. That is, you can split up a secret by encoding it with an error-correcting code that can correct wrong bits. (The 11-bit code from page 42 shows how you can split up a secret into seven parts so that it can be recovered if any ten parts are available.)

There are numerous problems with this approach. First, some bits can be more privileged than others. In the 11-bit scheme from page Table 3.1, 7 of the 11 bits hold the original message. The other 4 are parity bits. If the right 7 are put together, then the original secret is unveiled. If one of these bits is missing, however, then the parity bits are needed to get the secret.

Second, there can be some redundancy that allows people to unveil the secret even if they don't hold all of the parts. For instance, the 3-bit error-correcting code described in Section 3.1 can recover the correct answer even if one of the three bits is changed. This is because each bit is essentially turned into three copies of itself. If these three copies were split into three parts, then they wouldn't prevent each person from knowing the secret. They would have it in their hands. Their part was an exact copy of the whole. This example is extreme, but the same redundancies can exist in other versions.

> Deliberately adding errors is one way to prevent this redundancy.

A better solution is to use algorithms designed to split up secrets so they can't be recovered unless the correct number of parts are available. There are many different algorithms available to do this, most of which are geometric in nature. Such algorithms are often easiest to understand with figures and diagrams.

4.1.1   Requiring All Parts

Many of the algorithms described later in this section can recover a secret split into n parts only if k parts are available. There are many times when you might want to require that all parts be present. There are good algorithms that work quite well when $n = k$ but are not flexible when k is less than n. These simple algorithms are described here before explaining the other solutions.

The most straightforward approach is to imitate the safe deposit boxes and use n layers of encryption. If $f(k_i, X)$ encrypts a message X with key k_i, then you can simply take the secret and encrypt it repeatedly with each of n different keys. That is, compute

$$f(k_1, f(k_2, f(k_3, \ldots, f(k_n, X) \ldots))).$$

Each person gets one of the n keys, and it should be obvious that the secret can't be recovered unless all of them are present. If one is missing, then the chain is broken and the layers of encryption can't be stripped off.

A simpler approach is to think of the secret as a number, X, and then split it into n parts that all add up to that number, $X_1 + X_2 + X_3 + \cdots + X_n = X$. If one number is missing, it is impossible to determine what X might be. This solution is an extension of the one-time pad, and it is just as secure. There is no way that the people who hold the $n-1$ parts can guess what the value of the missing part might be.

In practice, this solution is often computed for each bit in the secret. That is, the secret is split into n parts. If the first bits of the parts are added together, they will reveal the first bit of the secret. If the second bits of the different parts are added together, the result is the second bit of the secret. This addition is done modulo 2, so you're really just determining whether there is an odd or even number of ones in the bits. Here's an example:

$$X_1 = 101010100$$
$$X_2 = 101011010$$
$$X_3 = 110010010$$
$$X_4 = 010101100$$
$$X_1 + X_2 + X_3 + X_4 = 100110000$$

If you wanted to split up a secret, then you would generate the first $n - 1$ parts at random. Then you would compute X_n so that $X_1 + \cdots + X_n = X$. This is actually easy.

$$X_n = X + X_1 + \cdots + X_{n-1}.$$

Are both of these solutions equally secure? The addition method, which is just an extension of the one-time pad, is perfectly secure. There is no way that the system can be broken if you don't have access to all of the parts. There is no additional pattern. The layers of encryption are not necessarily as secure. There are so many different variables in the choice of encryption function and the size of the keys, that some choices might be breakable.

Another way of understanding this is to examine the entropy of the equation, $X_1 + X_2 + X_3 + \cdots + X_n = X$. If each value of X_i has m bits, then there are mn bits of entropy required to determine the equation. If $n - 1$ values of X_i are recovered, there are still m bits of entropy or 2^m possible solutions to explore.

Intuitively, the encryption equation, $f(k_1, f(k_2, f(k_3, \ldots, f(k_n, X) \ldots)))$, has the same properties. If each key, k_i, has m bits, then there are still mn bits of entropy in the equation. Unfortunately, the complexity of the function f makes it difficult to provide more mathematical guarantees. If the basic function f, however, is secure enough to use for basic encryption, then it should be secure in this case. But there are many interesting and unanswered questions about what happens if the same system is used to encrypt data over and over again with different keys. (Some beginning papers include [CW93].) The simplest approach is the best in this case.

4.1.2 Letting Parts Slide

There are many reasons why you might want to recover some secret if you don't have all of the parts. The simplest algorithms are based on geometry. Imagine that your secret is a number, x. Now choose an arbitrary value for y and join the two values together so they represent a point on a plane. To split up this secret into two parts, just pick two lines at random that go through the point (see Figure 4.1).

Gus Simmons's chapter on shared secrets in [Sim93] is a great introduction to the topic.

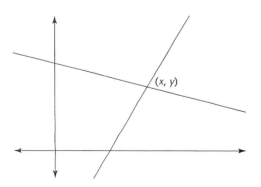

Figure 4.1 A secret, x, is split into two parts by finding two random lines that intersect at (x, y). (y is chosen at random.)

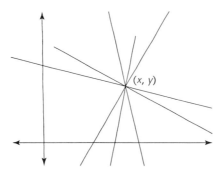

Figure 4.2   A secret, x, is split into n parts by finding n random lines that intersect at (x, y). (y is chosen at random.) Any pair is enough to recover the secret.

The secret can be recovered if the intersection of the two lines is found. If only one line is available, then no knows what the secret might be.

If there are two lines, then both parts need to be available to find the solution. This technique can be extended so there are n parts, but any two parts are enough to recover the secret.

Simply choose n lines that go through (x, y) at random. Any pair will intersect at (x, y) and allow someone to recover the secret, as shown in Figure 4.2.

When the secret must be split into n parts and any k must be available to recover the secret, then the same approach can be used if the geometry is extended into k dimensions. If $k = 3$, then planes are used instead of lines. Three planes will only intersect at the point. Two planes will form a line when they intersect. The point (x, y, z) will be somewhere along the line, but it is impossible to determine where it is.

It is also possible to flip this process on its head. Instead of hiding the secret as the intersection point of several lines, you can make the line the secret and distribute points along it. The place where the line meets the y axis might be the secret. Or it could be the slope of the line. In either case, knowing two points along the line will reveal the secret. Figure 4.3 shows this approach.

Each of these systems offers a pretty simple way to split up a secret key or file so that some subset of people must be present. It should be easy to see that the geometric systems that hide the secret as the intersection point are as secure as a one-time pad. If you have only one line, then it is impossible to guess where the intersection lies along this line. $x = 23$ is just as likely as $x = 41, 243$. In fact, owning

Roger Dingledine, David Molnar, and Michael J. Freedman designed Free Haven to split up a document among a number of servers using Michael Rabin's secret-sharing algorithm. The system also offers a mechanism for paying server owners [DF00, Rab89].

Stephan Brands uses this technique (the line as the secret) in his digital cash scheme [Bra93].

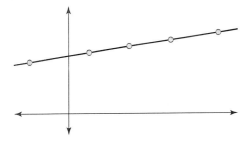

Figure 4.3   Here the secret is the line itself. Random points along the line are distributed as the parts of the secret. You must have two to recover the line.

one part gives you no more insight into the secret than owning no part. In either case, all you know is that it is some value of x. This is often called a *perfect* secret-sharing system.

Some people might be tempted to cut corners and hide information in both the x and the y coordinates of the intersection point. This seems feasible because you can choose any set of lines that go through this point. This changes the parameters of the system substantially. If you own a part of the secret, then you know something about the relationship between x and y. The slope of the line and the y intercept describe exactly how x and y change in unison.

In some cases, this might be enough to crack the system. For instance, imagine a case where you are protecting the number of men and women escaping from England on the Mayflower. Storing the number of men in the x coordinate and the number of women in the y coordinate is a mistake. An English spy might know that the number of men and the number of women is likely to be roughly equal given the percentages of men and women in society. This extra information could be combined with one part to reveal very good approximations of x and y.[2]

4.1.3   A More Efficient Method

The basic secret-sharing methods split up a secret, X, into n equal-sized parts. If the secret is m bits long, then the parts are also n bits long. This has the advantage of perfect security. If one part is missing,

---

[2]You should also avoid storing them as two separate secrets each broken into parts. In this case, one part from each of the two secrets would still yield enough information. The best solution is to encrypt the two values and split the key to this file.

the secret can only be recovered by testing all potential m bits of the missing part.

If using m bits is too unwieldy for some reason, another quick solution is to encrypt X with some function and split the result into n parts. That is, take the m bits from $f(X)$ and distribute $\frac{m}{n}$ bits to each part holder.

This approach sacrifices security for efficiency. Replacing a lost part only requires testing all possible combinations of $\frac{m}{n}$ bits instead of m bits. But if this proposition is still difficult enough, then the approach may be useful.

It should be noted that such a function f must be designed so that any change in the input to one bit has the potential to change any output bit. This feature is common if m is smaller than the block of a modern, well-designed algorithm such as DES or Rijndael. If m is larger, $f_{f(X)'}$ should arrange for every bit to affect every other if X^r stands for the bits in X arranged in reverse order.

4.1.4   Providing Deniability

Error-correcting codes described in Chapter 3 can also be used to add some deniability.

The Publius system created by Marc Waldman, Aviel D. Rubin, and Lorrie Faith Cranor uses basic secret-sharing algorithms to distribute the key to a document. The system is well-developed and integrated with traditional Web protocols to make the use as simple as possible [WRC00].

Each of the secret-sharing schemes described in this chapter offer some mind-boggling chances to hide data in the Net. There is no reason why one particular file alone should be enough to reveal the information to anyone who discovers it. Splitting a file into multiple pieces is an ideal way to add complete deniability. Imagine, for instance, that the important data is stored in the least significant bits of some image using the techniques from Chapter 9. You could put the important data in the GIF file you use for your home page background and then place this on the Web. But this is your home page and the connection is obvious. Another solution is to find, say, three other GIF images on the Web. Maybe one of them is from the Disney World home page, another is from the White House home page, and the third is from some shady hacker site in Europe. Extract the least significant bits from each of these files. You have no control over these bits, but you can use them to hide ownership of the data by using the first secret-sharing scheme described here. If you add up the values recovered from all four sites, then the final information appears.

Now imagine that the word gets out that the information is hidden in the combination of these four sites. Which one of the four is responsible? Disney World, the White House, the hackers in Europe, or you? It is impossible to use the least significant bits of each of these images to point the finger at anyone. The hidden information is the sum of the four, and any one of the four could have been manipulated to ensure that the final total is the hidden information. Who did it? If you arrange it so that the hidden information is found in the total of 100 possible images, no one will ever have the time to track it down.

Of course, there are still problems with the plan. Imagine that Disney World used a slick, ray-traced image from one of their films such as *Toy Story*. These images often have very smooth surfaces with constant gradients that usually have very predictable least significant bits. Well, that would certainly be a defense against accusations that they manipulated the least significant bits to send out a secret message. The images chosen as the foils should have a very noisy set of least significant bits.

4.2

Building Secret-Sharing Schemes

Secret-sharing schemes are easy to explain geometrically, but adapting them to computers can involve some compromises. The most important problem is that computers really only deal with integers. Lines from real numbered domains are neither efficient nor often practical. For instance, there are five numbers involved in a typical scheme for hiding a secret as the intersection of two lines. Two numbers describe the slope and y intercept of one line, two numbers describe the second line, and one number describes the x coordinate of the intersection point. If x is an integer, then it is not possible to choose lines at random that have both integers for their slope and y intercept. Some might be available, but there will only be a few of them.

You can use floating-point numbers, but they add their own instability. First, you must round off values. This can be a significant problem because both sides must do all rounding off the same. Second, you might encounter great differences in floating-point math. Two different CPUs can come up with different values for x/y. The answers will be very close, but they might not be the same because the different CPUs could be using slightly different representations of values. Most users of floating-point hardware don't care about these very minor differences because all of their calculations are approximations. But this is a problem with cryptography. Changing one bit of an encryption key is usually enough to ruin decryption—even if it is only the least significant bit that is changed.

This system is just like the classic book ciphers that used a book as the one-time pad.

The Chi-Squared Test and other measures of randomness can be found in Don Knuth's book [Knu81].

The best solution is to return to finite collections of integers modulo some prime number. Adi Shamir used this domain to hide secrets by choosing polynomials from this domain [Sha79]. Instead of using lines or planes to hide the information, he chose $k - 1$ degree polynomials, $p(x)$, where the first parameter, $p_0 = p(0)$, holds the secret. One point on the polynomial goes to each part holder; k parts can be used to reconstruct the polynomial and determine the secret, $p(0)$.

Here are the basic steps:

1. Choose a value of q that is prime.

2. Find a random polynomial $p(x)$ of order $k - 1$ by selecting $k - 2$ random values between 0 and q. These will be the parameters of the polynomial $p_1 \ldots p_{k-1}$. The secret to be stored away is p_0.

3. $\sum_{i=0}^{k-1} p_i x^i$ is the polynomial.

4. Choose n points $x_1 \ldots x_n$. Compute $p(x_1) \ldots p(x_n)$. These are the n parts to be distributed to parts holders. Any subset of k is enough to determine p_0.

5. To recover the value of p_0, use Lagrangian interpolation. That is, you can use the points to estimate the derivatives of the polynomial at a point.

This solution uses only integers. It should be obvious that you need k points to recover the polynomial. The easiest way to see this is to realize that having $k - 1$ points gives no information about $p(0)$. In fact, for any potential value of $p(0)$ you might guess, there is some p that would generate it. You can find this p by taking the $k - 1$ points and your guess for $p(0)$ and generating the polynomial. So, if there is a one-to-one mapping between these guesses, then the system is *perfect*. The part holder has no advantage over the outside guesser.

The scheme also offers greater efficiency for cases where k is a reasonably large number. In the first section, the geometrical solution was to create a k-dimensional space and fill it with $k - 1$ dimensional hyperplanes. Intersecting k of them was enough to reveal the point. The problem with this solution is that the hyperplanes take up more and more space as k grows larger. I don't mean they consume more abstract space—they just require more space to hold the information that would represent them. The Shamir scheme shown here doesn't require more space. Each part is still just a point, (x, y), that lies on the polynomial. This is substantially more efficient.

4.2.1 Making Some More Equal

In each of the schemes described in this chapter, the secrets are split into n parts, each of the n parts being equal. Humans, being human, are never satisfied with anything as fair as that—some people will want some parts to be more powerful than others.

The most straightforward way to accomplish this is to give some people more parts. For instance, imagine a scheme where you need six parts to reconstruct the secret. That is, you might have a collection of five-dimensional hyperplanes in a six-dimensional space. Any set of six points is enough to uncover the secret, which for the sake of example will be the launch codes for a nuclear missile. Let's say that it takes two commanders, three sergeants, or six privates to launch a missile. This can be accomplished by giving three parts to the commanders, two parts to the sergeants, and one part each to the privates.

One problem with this solution is that arbitrary combinations of different ranks can join together. So, one commander, one sergeant, and one private can work together to uncover the secret. This might not be permitted in some cases. For example, the U.S. Congress requires a majority of both the House and the Senate to pass a bill. But the votes from one chamber can't be counted against the other. So even though there are 100 senators and 435 members of the House, a senator is not really worth 4.35 House members. A bill won't pass just because 99 senators vote for it and only 10 House representatives. But this could be the situation if someone naively created a secret-sharing scheme by parceling out parts to both sides of Congress from the same shared secret.

A better solution in this case would be to first split the secret into two equal parts, X_H and X_S, so that both are required to endorse a bill with the digital signature of Congress. Then H_R would be split into 435 parts so that 218 are enough to recover it. H_S is split into 100 parts so that 51 are enough to recover it.

There are numerous combinations that can make these schemes possible. Practically any scheme can be implemented using some combination and layers of secrets. The only problem with very complicated systems is that they can require many different dimensions. For instance, if you want a system where it takes 17 privates, 13 sergeants, or 5 generals to launch some missiles, then you could use a system with $17 \times 13 \times 5$ dimensions. This can get a bit arcane, but the mathematics is possible.

4.3

Public-Key Secret Sharing

All the algorithms in this section share one particular set of bits, the secret. This secret may be used for anything, but it is probably going to be used as a key to unscramble some information encrypted with a secret-key algorithm. The notion of splitting up authority and responsibility can also be incorporated into public-key algorithms. In these schemes, the actions for scrambling and unscrambling can be split and controlled separately. The holder of one key controls encryption, and the holder of the other key controls decryption. If secret sharing is combined with public-key encryption, one group must agree to encrypt a message and another group must agree to decrypt it.

One simple solution is to combine any public-key algorithm with any of the secret-sharing solutions. The keys are just collections of bits, and these collections can be split into arbitrary subcollections using any basic secret-splitting solution. This mechanism is perfectly useful, but it has limitations. If a group of people gets together to encrypt or decrypt a message, the key must be put together completely. Once it is assembled, whoever put it together now controls it. The secret-sharing feature is gone.

This approach splits the ability to decrypt a public-key message among a group of k people. Anyone can send a message to the group, but all group members must agree to decrypt it. Any information obtained from decrypting one message can't be used to decrypt the next. The system relies upon the strength of the discrete log problem. That is, it assumes that given g, p, and $g^x \bmod p$, it is hard to find x.

Similar techniques can be used to produce anonymous digital cash and secure voting solutions [Bra95b, Bra95a].

The private key consists of k values $\{x_1, \ldots, x_k\}$ that are distributed among the k members who will have control over the decryption process. The public key is the value $a = g_1^{x_1} g_2^{x_2} \ldots g_k^{x_k} \bmod p$, where the values of g_i and p are publicly available numbers. The values of g_i may be generators of the group defined modulo p, but the algorithm will work with most random values less than p.

A message to the group is encrypted by choosing a random value, y, and computing $g_1^y \bmod p, g_2^y \bmod p, \ldots, g_k^y \bmod p$. Then the value $a^y \bmod p$ is computed and used to generate a secret key for encrypting the message with an algorithm such as AES. The message consists of this encrypted data and the k values g_1^y mod p, g_2^y mod p, ..., g_k^y mod p. This is very similar in spirit to Diffie-Hellman key exchange, another technique for public-key encryption [DIF76b].

The message can be decrypted by distributing the k values to the group. Each person computes $(g_i^y)^{x_i}$ mod p and returns this value to the group leader who multiplies them together.

$$a^y = \left(g_1^y\right)^{x_1} \left(g_2^y\right)^{x_2} \cdots \left(g_n^y\right)^{x_n} \text{ mod } p.$$

The same set of keys can also generate digital signatures for the group with a modified version of the digital signatures used with the Diffie-Hellman-style public-key system. Here are the steps:

1. The signers and the signature verifier agree upon a challenge value, c. This is usually generated by hashing the document being signed. It could also be created by the verifier on the fly as a true challenge.

2. Each member of the group chooses a random witness, w_i, and computes $g_i^{w_i}$ mod p.

3. Each member of the group computes $r_i = cx_i + w_i$ and $g_i^{r_i}$ mod p.

4. The group discards the values of w_i and gathers together the rest of the values in a big collection to serve as the signature. These values are $\{r_1 = cx_1 + w_1, \ldots, r_k = cx_k + w_k\}$, $\{g_1^{r_1} \text{ mod } p, \ldots, g_k^{r_k} \text{ mod } p\}$, and the product of $g_1^{w_1}$ mod p, ..., $g_k^{w_k}$ mod p.

5. Anyone who wants to check the signature can compute $a^{(-c)} g_1^{r_1} \ldots g_k^{r_k}$ mod p and make sure it is the same as the product of $g_1^{w_1}$ mod p, ..., $g_k^{w_k}$ mod p.

Similar solutions can be found using RSA-style encryption systems. In fact, some of the more sophisticated versions allow RSA keys to be created without either side knowing the factorization [BF97, GJKR, BBWBG98, CM98, WS99, FMY98].

4.4

Steganographic File Systems and Secret Sharing

Secret-sharing algorithms split up information into a number of parts so that the information can only be recovered if some or perhaps all of the parts are available. The same basic algebra can also be used by one person to hide data so that only the person who knows the right combination of parts can verify that the data is there. This application may be valuable if you happen to be storing the information on your hard disk and you would like to deny that it is there.

Ross Anderson, Roger Needham, and Adi Shamir created two versions of what they called a steganographic file system [ANS98]. The first uses math very similar to secret sharing and so is described here.

The system grabs a large block of disk space, randomizes it, and then absorbs files that are protected with passwords. If you don't know the password, then you can't find the file. If you do know the password, then the random bits produce the file. There's no way to identify that the file exists without the password.

Their scheme is far from perfect. In order for it to work well, the passwords must be assigned in a hierarchy. That means if someone knows one password, K_i, then that person must know all other passwords K_j where $0 \le j < i$. If there are only three files, then the person with access to file 3 must also have access to files 1 and 2. The authors imagine that a person under interrogation may reveal the password to several modestly dangerous files without revealing the more sensitive ones.

The mathematics is all linear algebra. For the sake of simplicity, the system is defined for binary numbers where addition is the XOR ($\oplus$) operation and multiplication is the AND ($\cdot$) operation.

A basic steganographic file system can hold m files that are n bits long. In the beginning, the files are set to be random values that are changed as information is stored in the system. It often helps to think of the file system as a big matrix with m rows and n columns. Let C_i stand for the ith row.

The password for file j is K_j, an m-bit-long vector where $K_j(i)$ stands for the ith bit of the vector. To recover file j from the file system, add together all of the rows, C_i, where $K_j(i) = 1$. That is,

$$\bigoplus_{i=1}^{m} K_j(i)C_i.$$

How do you store a file in the system? Here's a basic sketch of the simple steps for storing *one* file:

1. Break it into n-bit blocks.

2. Choose a password for each block. One good solution is to concatenate a random string, S, before the password, hash it

with a cryptographically secure hash function, H, and take the first $m-1$ bits to serve as K_j.

3. Add a parity bit to K_j to make sure it is the correct length. Use odd parity to ensure that the number of 1 bits in the vector is odd. That is, set the last bit to be 1 if there are an even number of 1s in the first $m-1$ bits and a 0 if there are an odd number.

4. Encrypt the block with a separate encryption function, ideally using a different key constructed by appending a different random string. This encryption function is necessary because of the linear nature of the file system. If an attacker can establish some part of the file, D, then the attacker can solve some linear equations to recover K_j. If the files aren't encrypted, an attacker can extract the file if the attacker can guess a phrase and its location in the file.

5. Replace C_i with $D \oplus C_i$ for all i where $K_j(i) = 1$.

This basic algorithm will store one file in the system. The algorithm, however, may cause problems if it is used repeatedly because the files can overwrite other files. If you want to store more than one file in the system, you need to ensure that they will not disrupt one another.

The simplest solution is to choose the m values of K_j so that they're orthogonal vectors. That is, $K_i \cdot K_j = 1$ if and only if $i = j$. In all other cases, $K_i \cdot K_j = 0$. If the password vectors are orthogonal, then m different files can be stored in the system without disturbing one another.

In other words, whenever the values of D are added to different rows C_j, the values of D will not distort another file. Why? If $K_p \cdot K_q = 0$, then there are only an even number of bits that are 1 in both K_p and K_q. Imagine that you're replacing C_j with $D \oplus C_j$ for all j where $K_p(j) = 1$. Some of these rows will also be rows that are storing parts of another file defined by key K_q. Why isn't this file disturbed? Because D will only be added to an even number of rows, and the value will cancel out. $D \oplus D = 0$.

Consider this example with K:

$$
\begin{array}{ccccc}
0 & 1 & 1 & 1 & 0 \\
1 & 0 & 1 & 1 & 0 \\
0 & 0 & 1 & 1 & 1 \\
1 & 1 & 1 & 0 & 1 \\
1 & 1 & 0 & 1 & 1 \\
\end{array}
$$

This matrix contains the keys for five files. The first row, for instance, specifies that the first file consists of $C_2 \oplus C_3 \oplus C_4$. The second row specifies that the second file consists of $C_1 \oplus C_3 \oplus C_4$. If new data is stored in the first file, then C_2, C_3, and C_4 will all become $C_2 \oplus D, C_3 \oplus D$, and $C_4 \oplus D$, respectively. What does this do to the second file? $C_1 \oplus C_3 \oplus C_4$ becomes $C_1 \oplus (C_3 \oplus D) \oplus (C_4 \oplus D) = C_1 \oplus C_3 \oplus C_4 \oplus D \oplus D = C_1 \oplus C_3 \oplus C_4$.

Here's a basic algorithm for constructing K from a list of m passwords, $P_1, P_2, \ldots, P_m$. Repeat this for each password, P_i.

1. Let $K_i = H(P_i)$, where H is some cryptographically secure hash function.

2. For all $j < i$, let $K_i = (K_i \cdot K_j)K_j \oplus K_i$. This orthonormalization step removes the part of the previous vectors that overlaps with the new row. That is, it ensures that there will only be an even number of bits that are 1 in both rows. It does this for all previous values.

3. If $K_i = 0$, then an error has occurred. The new chosen key is not independent of the previous keys. Set $K_i = H(H(P_i))$ and try again. Continue to hash the password until an acceptable value of K_i is found that is orthonormal to the previous keys.

This algorithm does not compute the values of K_i independently of one another. You must know the values of all K_j where $j < i$ to compute K_i. This is less than ideal, but it is unavoidable at this time. Anderson, Needham, and Shamir decided to turn this restriction into a feature by casting it as a linear file access hierarchy. If you can read file i, then you can read all files j where $j < i$.

Forcing all of the keys into a hierarchical order may not always be desirable. Another technique for finding keys is to restrict each person to a particular subspace. That is, split the keyspace into orthogonal parts. If person i wants to choose a particular K_i, then that person must check to see that K_i is in the right subspace.

The simplest way to split the keys into orthogonal subspaces is to force certain bits in the key to be 0. Alice might use keys where only the first ten bits can be set to 1, Bob might use keys where only the second 10 bits can be nonzero, and so on.

If necessary, Alice, Bob, and the rest of the gang can agree upon a random rotation matrix, R, and use it to rotate the subspaces. So

Alice will only choose a key vector if RK_i has 0s in all of the right places.

This version of the file system is also a bit unwieldy. If you want to read or write a file D, then you may need to access as many as m other rows. This factor can be substantial if m grows large. This can be reduced by using nonbinary values instead of bits for the individual elements of K_i.

4.5

Summary

Secret sharing is an ideal method for distributing documents across the network so no one can find them. It is an ideal way for people to deny responsibility. In some cases, the parts of the secret can be from the Web pages of people who have nothing to do with the matter at hand.

- *The Disguise.* Secret sharing lets you share the blame.

- *How Secure Is It?* The algorithms here are unconditionally secure against attacks from people who have less than the necessary threshold of parts.

- *How to Use It?* The XOR algorithm described here is easy to implement. It makes an ideal way to split up information so that every party needs to be present to put the information back together.

chapter five

Compression

Television Listing

8:00 pm 2 (IRS) *Beverly Hills Model Patrol.* New lip gloss introduced.

5 (QUS) *Cash Calliope: Musical Detective.* Death with a Capital D-minor.

9 (PVC) *Northern Cops.* Town council bans eccentrics at town meeting, but not for long.

14 (TTV) *Def N B.* Beethoven raps for the Queen.

9:00 pm 2 (IRS) *Super Hero Bunch.* Evil just keeps coming back for more.

5 (QUS) *Sniffmaster Spot.* Spot discovers toxic waste at Acme Dog Food Plant.

9 (PVC) *Mom's a Klepto.* Family stress as Mom plagiarizes daughter's English paper.

14 (TTV) *Easy Cheesy.* Customer asks for Triple Anchovy pizza.

10:00 pm 2 (IRS) *X Knows Best.* Alien stepdad shows love is not Earthbound.

5 (QUS) *Dum De Dum Dum.* Detective Gump meets murdering publisher.

9 (PVC) *Betrayal Place.* Bob betrays Jane.

14 (TTV) *Beverly Hills Astronaut.* Buzz discovers there are no malls in space!

5.1

Patterns and Compression

Life often reduces to formulas. At least it does on television, where solutions appear every 30 or 60 minutes. When you know the formula, it is very easy to summarize information or compress it. A network executive reportedly commissioned the television show *Miami Vice* with a two-word memo to the producer that read, "MTV Cops." You can easily specify an episode of *Gilligan's Island* with a single sentence such as, "The one with the cosmonauts." Anyone who's seen only one episode of the show will know that some cosmonauts appear on the island, offer some hope that people will be rescued, but this hope will be dashed at the end when Gilligan screws things up.

Compressing generic information is also just a matter of finding the right formula to describe the data. It is often quite easy to find a simple formula that works moderately well, but it can be maddeningly difficult to identify a very good formula that compresses the data very well. Finding a good formula that works well for specific types of data such as text or video is often economically valuable. People are always looking for good ways to cut their data storage and communications costs.

Compressing data is of great interest to anyone who wants to hide data for several reasons:

- *Less data is easier to handle.* This speaks for itself. Basic text can easily be compressed by 50 to 70 percent. Images might be compressed by 90 percent.

Details about measuring information can be found in Section 2.2.

- *Compressed data is usually whiter.* Compression shouldn't destroy information in a signal. This means the information per bit should increase if the size of the file decreases. More information per bit usually appears more random.

- *Reversing compression can mimic data.* Compression algorithms try to find a formula that fits the data and then return the specific details of the formula as compressed data. If you input random data into a compression function, it should spit out data that fits the formula.

- *Compression algorithms identify noise.* Good compression algorithms understand how human perception works. Algorithms such as JPEG or MP3 can strip away extra information from a file that is not really noticed by human users. This information can also be exploited by steganographers to locate places where a significant amount of noise might be replaced by a hidden message.

Of course, this approach can be dangerous as well. If the JPEG algorithm strips away some information, then any information you insert in this location is just as liable to be stripped away. An attacker or a well-meaning programmer along the path could compress a file to save space and destroy your message. This makes the technique dangerous for weakly protected data such as watermarks, but potentially useful if you can be reasonably sure the file won't be compressed along the path.[1]

Compression is an important tool for these reasons. Many good commercial compression programs already exist simply because of the first reason. Many good encryption programs use compression as an additional source of strength. The third reason, though, is why compression is discussed in depth in this book. Some of the basic compression algorithms provide a good way to make information look like something else. This trick of flipping the algorithm on its head is discussed in Chapter 6.

There are a number of different techniques for compressing data that are used today. The field has expanded wildly over the last several years because of the great economic value of such algorithms. A procedure that compresses data in half can double the storage area of a computer with no extra charge for hardware. People continue to come up with new and often surprisingly effective techniques for compressing data, but it all comes down to the basic process of identifying a formula that does a good job of fitting the data. The parameters that make the formula fit the data directly becomes the compressed surrogate. Some of the more popular techniques are as follows:

- *Probability Methods.* These count up the occurrences of characters or bytes in a file. Then they assign a short code word to the most common characters and a long one to the least common ones. Morse code is a good example of a compression algorithm from this class. The letter "e", which is the most common in the

Section 9.2.7 shows how the JPEG algorithm can identify just how much space can be exploited in an image.

One watermarking algorithm in Section 14.6 deliberately aims to hide information in the most important parts of the image to avoid being destroyed during compression.

---

[1] WebTV's network, for instance, will strip away higher-order data from images if it won't show up on a television set.

English language, is encoded as a dot. The letter "p", which is less common, is encoded as dot-dash-dash-dot. The *code* is the best known edition of these codes.

- *Dictionary Methods.* These algorithms compile a list of the most common words, phrases, or collections of bytes in a file, and then number the words. If a word is on this list, then the compressed file simply contains the number pointing to the dictionary entry. If it isn't, the word is transmitted without change. These techniques can be quite effective if the data file has a large amount of text. Some report compressing text to 10 to 20 percent of its original size. The *Lempel-Ziv* compression algorithm is the most commonly used version of this algorithm.

- *Run-Length Encoding.* Many simple images are just blocks of black pixels and white pixels. If you walk along a line, you might encounter 1000 white pixels followed by 42 black pixels followed by 12 white pixels, and so on. Run-length encoding stores this as a sequence of numbers: 1000, 42, 12, ... This often saves plenty of space and works well for black-and-white line art. Faxes use this technique extensively.

Chapter 14 investigates the information-hiding capabilities with wavelets.

- *Wave Methods.* These algorithms use a collection of waves as the basis for deriving a collection of formulas. Then they adjust the size and position of the waves to best fit the data. These work quite well with images that do not need to be reconstructed exactly but only need to approximate the original. The JPEG, JPEG2000, and MPEG image and video compression standards are two of the more well-known instances of this technique.

A good introduction to fractal compression can be found in [BS88, Bar88, Bar93].

- *Fractal Methods.* Fractal functions produce extremely complicated patterns from very simple formulas. This means that they can achieve extremely high compression *if* you can find the formula that fits your data.

- *Adaptive Compression Schemes.* Many compression schemes can be modified to adapt to the changing patterns of data. Each of the types described here comes in versions that modify themselves in the middle of the data stream to adapt to new patterns.

Each of these compression schemes is useful in particular domains. There is no universal algorithm that comes with a universal set of functions that adapt well to all data. So people modify existing algorithms and come up with their own formulas.

Compression functions make good beginnings for people who want to hide data because the functions were constructed to describe patterns. There are two ways to use compression functions successfully to hide information. One way to hide data is to mold it into the form of other data so it blends in. A compression function that worked well on zebras, for instance, would be able to model black and white stripes and convert a set of stripes into a simple set of parameters. If you had such a function, it could be applied to some data in *reverse*, and it would expand the data into zebra stripes. The result would be bigger, but it would look like something else. The data could be recovered by compressing it again.

Compression techniques can also be used to identify the least important nooks and crannies of a file so that extra data can be snuck into these corners. Many image-compression functions are designed to be *lossy*, meaning that the reconstructed image may look very similar to the original image, but it won't be *exactly* the same. If the functions that describe an image can be fitted more loosely, then the algorithms can use fewer of them and produce a smaller compressed output. For instance, an apple might be encoded as a blob of solid red instead of a smooth continuum of various shades of red. When the image is decompressed, much of the smaller detail is lost but the overall picture still looks good. These compression functions can easily compress an image to be one-fifth to one-tenth of its original size, and this is why they are so popular.

The television format example at the beginning of the chapter is an example of lossy compression. The listings are not detailed enough to recreate the entire program. They're a better example of lossy compression where a surrogate is found.

5.1.1 Huffman Coding

A good way to understand basic compression is to examine a simple algorithm such as Huffman coding. This technique analyzes how frequently each letter occurs in a file and then replaces it with a flexible-length code word. Normally, each letter is stored as a byte, which takes up 8 bits of information. Some estimates of the entropy of standard English, though, show that a letter takes something just over about 3 bits. Obviously, there is room to squeeze up to almost five-eighths of a file of English text. The trick is to assign the short code words to common letters and long code words to the least common letters. Although some of the long words will end up being longer than 8 bits, the net result will still be shorter. The common letters will have the greatest effect.

Table 5.1   The frequency of occurrence of letters in a set of opinions generated by the U.S. Supreme Court.

Letter	Frequency	Letter	Frequency
space	26974	N	5626
A	6538	O	6261
B	1275	P	2195
C	3115	Q	113
D	2823	R	5173
E	9917	S	5784
F	1757	T	8375
G	1326	U	2360
H	3279	V	928
I	6430	W	987
J	152	X	369
K	317	Y	1104
L	3114	Z	60
M	1799		

Table 5.1 shows a table of the occurrences of letters in several different opinions from the United States Supreme Court. The space is the most common character, followed by the letter "E". This table was constructed by mixing lower- and uppercase letters for simplicity. An actual compression function would keep separate entries for both forms of each letter as well as an entry for every type of punctuation mark. In general, there would be 256 entries for each byte.

Table 5.2 shows a set of codes that were constructed for each letter using the data in Table 5.1. The most common character, the space, gets a code that is only 2 bits long: 01. Many of the other common characters get codes that are 4 bits long. The least common character, "Z", gets an 11-bit code: 00011010001. If these codes were used to encode data, then it should be easy to reduce a file to less than one-half of its original size.

Here's a simple example that takes 48 bits used to store the word "ARTHUR" in normal ASCII into 27 bits in compressed form:

Letter:	A	R	T	H	U	R
ASCII:	01000001	01010010	01010100	01001000	01010101	01010010
Compressed:	1000	1111	0010	00111	000100	1111

The Huffman algorithm can also be used to compress any type of data, but its effectiveness varies. It could be used, for instance, on a

Table 5.2   The codes constructed from Table 5.1.
(Note: A Huffman tree based on these codes is
shown in Figure 5.1.)

Letter	Code	Letter	Code
space	01	N	1101
A	1000	O	1010
B	111011	P	000101
C	10110	Q	00011010000
D	11100	R	1111
E	0000	S	1100
F	001101	T	0010
G	111010	U	000100
H	00111	V	0001111
I	1001	W	0001110
J	0001101001	X	0001110
K	000110101	Y	0001100
L	10111	Z	00011010001
M	001100		

photograph where the intensity at each pixel is stored as a byte. The
algorithm would be very effective on a photograph that had only a
few basic values of black and white. But it wouldn't work well if the
intensities were evenly distributed in a photograph with many even
shades between dark and light. The algorithm works best when there
are only a few basic values.

More sophisticated versions of exist. It is common to construct
second-order codes that aggregate pairs of letters. This can be done in
two ways. The easiest is to simply treat each pair of letters as the basic
atomic unit. Instead of constructing a frequency table of characters,
you would construct a table of pairs. The table would be much larger,
but it would generate even better compression because many of the
pairs would rarely occur. Pairs like "ZF" are almost nonexistent.

Another solution is to construct 26 different tables by analyzing which letters follow other letters. So, one table for the letter "T"
would hold the frequency that all of the other letters came after it.
The letter "H" would be quite common in this table because "TH"
occurs frequently in English. These 26 tables would produce even
more compression because they would tune the code word even
more. The letter "U" would receive a very short code word after the
letter "Q" because it invariably follows.

Chapter 6 shows how
to run Huffman codes
in reverse.

This example shows how a Huffman compression function works
in practice. It doesn't explain how the code words are constructed,
nor does it show why they work so well. The next section in this
chapter does that.

5.2

Building Compression Algorithms

Creating a new compression algorithm has lately become one of the
more lucrative areas of mathematics and computer science. A few
smart ideas are enough to save people billions of dollars of storage
space and communications time, and so many have worked with the
idea in depth. This chapter won't investigate the best work because it
is beyond the scope of the book. Many of the simplest ideas turn out
to hide information the best. Huffman codes are a perfect solution
for basic text. Dictionary algorithms, such as Lempel-Ziv, are less
effective.

5.2.1   Huffman Compression

Huffman compression is easy to understand and construct. Let the
set of characters be Σ, and $\rho(c)$ be the probability that a particular
character, c, occurs in a text file. Constructing such a frequency table
is easy to do by analyzing a source file. It is usually done on a case-
by-case basis and stored in the header to the compressed version, but
it can also be done in advance and used again and again.

The basic idea is to construct a binary tree that contains all of the
characters at the leaves. Each of the branches is labeled with either
a 0 or a 1. The path between the root and the leaf specifies the code
used for each letter. Figure 5.1 shows this for a small set of letters.

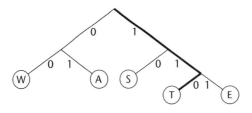

Figure 5.1   A small Huffman tree. The code for each letter is determined by
following the path between the root of the tree and the leaf containing a
particular letter. The letter "T", for instance, receives the code 110.

The key is to construct the tree so that the most common letters occur near the top of the tree. This can be accomplished with a relatively easy process, as follows:

1. Start with one node for each character. This node is also a very simple tree. The weight of this tree is set to be the probability that the character associated with the tree occurs in the file. Call the tree t_i and the weight $w(n_i)$. The value of i changes as the number of trees changes.

2. Find the two trees with the smallest weight. Glue these into one tree by constructing a new node with two branches connected to the roots of the two trees. One branch will be labeled with a 1 and the other will get a 0. The weight of this new tree is set to be the sum of the old trees that were joined.

3. Repeat the previous step until there is only one tree left. The codes can be constructed by following the path between the root and the leaves.

The characters with the smallest weights are joined together first. Each joining process adds another layer between the root and the leaves, so it is easy to see how the least common letters get pushed far away from the root where they have a longer code word. The most common letters don't get incorporated until the end so they come out near the top.

The algorithm naturally balances the tree by always taking the smallest weights first. The weight for a tree represents the number of times that any of the characters in the tree will occur in a file. You can prove that the tree constructed by this algorithm is the best possible tree by imagining what happens if you mistakenly choose the wrong two trees to join at a step. More common characters get pushed farther from the root and get longer code words than less common characters. The average compression drops. Figure 5.2 is a Huffman tree based on the codes shown in Table 5.2.

Many other people have extended the theme of Huffman coding by creating other algorithms that use the addresses of nodes in a tree. One popular technique is to use *splay trees*. These trees are modified every time a character is encoded. One version moves the letter to the top of the tree in a complex move that preserves much of the structure. The result is that the most common letters bubble up to the top. The constant rearrangement of the tree means that the tree

I know of a Greek labyrinth which is a single straight line. Along this line so many philosophers have lost themselves that a mere detective might well do so too.
—Jorge Luis Borges, *Death and the Compass*

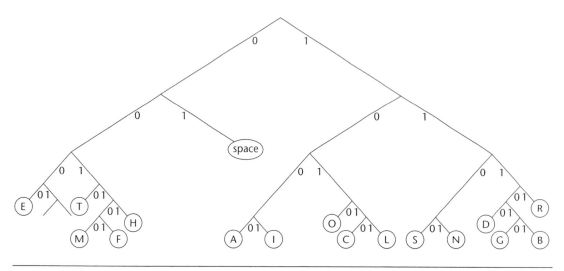

Figure 5.2   The top of the tree built from the data in Table 5.1. This generated the codes shown in Table 5.2. Only the top part is shown here because of space considerations. Less common letters like "Z" are in the part of the tree replaced by the dashed lines.

[Sto88] is a good basic reference on compression.

adapts to the local conditions. This type of algorithm would be ideal for compressing a dictionary where even the least popular letters like "j" or "z" are common in sections. When the algorithm moved through the "j" part of the dictionary, the node containing "j" would be pushed repeatedly to the top of the splay tree where it would get a short code word. Later, when the compression function got to the "z" section, the node for "z" would end up near the top, consistently giving "z" a short code word. Obviously, one major problem with this compression scheme is that the entire file must be processed from the beginning to keep an accurate description of the splay tree. You simply can't jump to the "z" section and begin decompressing.

This basic Huffman algorithm has many different uses. It is used in Chapter 6 to turn data into something that looks like English text. It is also used as a building block in Chapter 7 to make optimal weighted choices between different words. The same structure is as useful there as here.

5.2.2   Dictionary Compression

Compression schemes like the popular and patented Lempel-Ziv algorithm are called *dictionary schemes* because they build a big list of common words in the file.[2] This list can either be created in one swoop at the beginning of the compression or it can be built and changed adaptively as the algorithm processes the file. The algorithms succeed because a pointer describing the position in the dictionary takes up much less space than the common word itself.

The dictionary is just a list of words. It is almost always 2^n words because that makes the pointer to a particular word take up n bits. Each word can either be a fixed length or a flexible length. Fixed lengths are easier to handle, but flexible lengths do a better job of approximating the English language and x86 machine code.

Compression is simple. First, the file is analyzed to create a list of the 2^n most common words. Then the file is processed by scanning from beginning to end. If the current word is in the dictionary, then it is replaced by a tag `<InDict>` followed by the position in the dictionary. If it isn't, then it is replaced by a tag `<Verbatim>` followed by the word that remains unchanged.

Obviously the success of the algorithm depends upon the size of the tags (`<InDict>` and `<Verbatim>`), the size of the dictionary, and the number of times that something is found in the dictionary. One simple and usually effective solution is to make the tags take one entire byte, B. If the value of the byte is 0, then the next n bits represent a word in the dictionary. If the value of the byte, B, is greater than 0, then there are B bytes that are copied verbatim out of the original file. This scheme allows the program to use flexible word sizes that work well with English. There are many different schemes that are more efficient in some cases.

The index into the dictionary does not need to be n bit numbers. You can also count the occurrence of words in the dictionary and use a Huffman-like scheme to devise short code words for some of them. The tag for verbatim text is usually included as just another word in this case.

The dictionary can also adapt as the file is processed. One simple technique is to keep track of the last time a word was used from the dictionary. Whenever a section of verbatim text is encountered, the oldest word is swapped out of the dictionary and the newest verbatim text is swapped in. This technique is great for adapting to the text because many words are often clustered in sections. For instance, the

---

[2]The algorithms are not particularly good at compressing files like dictionaries used by humans. The fact that I used a regular dictionary as an example in the previous section is just a coincidence. Don't be confused.

words "dictionary", "Huffman", and "compression" are common in this section but relatively rare in other parts of the book. An adaptive scheme would load these words into the dictionary at the beginning of the section when they are first encountered and not swap them out until they aren't used for a while.

Dictionary schemes can be quite effective for compressing arbitrary text, but they are difficult to run in reverse to make data mimic something. Chapter 6 uses Huffman-like algorithms to generate real text, but it doesn't include a section on reversing dictionary algorithms. They are described in this chapter because compression is a good way to save space and whiten data. The algorithms don't work particularly well for mimicry because they require a well-constructed dictionary. In practice, there is no good automatic way—at least, that I know of—for constructing a good one.

5.2.3   JPEG Compression

The Huffman encoding described in Section 5.2.1 and the dictionary schemes in Section 5.2.2 are ideal for arbitrary collections of data. They can also work quite well on some types of image files, but they fail on others. If an image has a small number of colors that occur in a predictable pattern, then both of these algorithms can do a good job of finding a pattern that is strong enough to generate a good compression. This doesn't happen when images contain many different shades of colors. The Japanese flag, for instance, has one red circle that is a constant color, but a realistically lit apple has many different shades of red.

The JPEG algorithm is a good example of how to tune an algorithm to a particular type of data. In this case, the algorithm fits cosine functions to the data and then stores the amplitude and period of the cosine functions. The number of functions used and the size can be varied according to the amount of compression desired. A small number of functions produces a high amount of compression, but a grainy image. More functions add accuracy, but take up more space. This flexibility is possible because many people don't particularly care if they get *exactly* the same image back when it is decompressed. If it looks reasonably close, it is good enough.

This flexibility is what is so useful about JPEG encoding. While the algorithm from Section 5.2 can be run in reverse to produce text that mimics English text, the JPEG algorithm doesn't do that well. It does, however, have the ability to identify nooks and crannies in the image that might have space to hold information. This is described in detail in Chapter 9.

5.2.4 GZSteg

Many of the compression algorithms can be tweaked in clever ways to hide information. One of the simplest, but quite effective techniques was used by Andrew Brown when he approached the popular GZIP compression algorithm. This technique is used frequently throughout the Net so it makes an ideal candidate for an innocuous location.

Ordinarily, the GZIP algorithm compresses data by inserting tokens that point back to a previous location where the data was found. Here's a sample section of text:

> The famous Baltimore Oriole, Cal Ripken Jr., is the son of Cal Ripken Sr. who coached for the Orioles in the past.

Here's a sample section that was compressed. The tokens are shown in italics.

> The famous Baltimore Oriole, Cal Ripken Jr., is the son of *(30,10)* Sr. who coached for the *(48,6)*s in the past.

In this example, there are two tokens. The first one, *(30,10)*, tells the algorithm to go back 30 characters and copy 10 characters to the current location. The compression technique works quite well for many text algorithms.

GZSteg hides information by changing the number of characters to copy. Every time it inserts a token that requires more than five characters to be copied, it will hide one bit. If the bit is 0, then the token is left unchanged. If the bit is 1, then the number of characters to be copied is shortened by one. Here's the same quote with the two bits 11 encoded:

> The famous Baltimore Oriole, Cal Ripken Jr., is the son of *(30,9)*n Sr. who coached for the *(46,5)*es in the past.

In both cases, the size of the copying was cut by one. This does reduce the amount of compression to a small extent.

The greatest advantage of this approach is that the file format is unchanged. A standard GZIP program will be able to decompress the data without revealing that information was hidden in the process. Information could be left around without attracting suspicion. A quick analysis, however, could also reveal that data was hidden in such a manner. If you scan the file and examine the tokens, you can easily determine which tokens were just one character too small. There is no way to deny that the program that did the GZIP compression made a mistake.

5.3

Summary

Compression algorithms are normally used to reduce the size of a file without removing information. This can increase their entropy and make the files appear more random because all of the possible bytes become more common. The compression algorithms can also be useful when they're used to produce mimicry. This is described in Chapter 6.

- *The Disguise.* Compression algorithms generally produce data that looks more random. That is, there is a more even distribution of the data.

- *How Secure Is It?* Not secure at all. Most compression algorithms transmit the table or dictionary at the beginning of the file. This may not be necessary because both parties could agree upon such a table in advance. Although I don't know how to figure out the mapping between the letters and the bits in the Huffman algorithm, I don't believe it would be hard to figure out.

- *How to Use It?* There are many compression programs available for all computers. They often use proprietary algorithms that are better than the versions offered here. They make an ideal first pass for any encryption program.

Basic Mimicry

Reading between the Lines

Here is the transcript from the mind of a cynic reading through the personals section of a newspaper:

```
wants same for walks in rain, trips to Spain and
riding on planes. Send picture and dating
strategy.
```

Great. Eliza Doolittle. Literally. I come up with a dating strategy and she does little but ride along. This is not a good sign. She's probably a princess working as a secretary who wants to be rescued and catapulted into the rich, upper class. Rules me out. I'm not going to work my butt off so she can relax in Spain trying to pronounce words differently. What's so romantic about Spain, anyway? She's probably read Hemingway too and I'll be forced to run in front of a bunch of bulls just so she'll think I'm dashing in an old-fashioned way. No thanks. I'll take a new-fashioned Range Rover like they drive around Africa. Those things can't be toppled by a bunch of bulls. And if it's raining, I won't get wet or slip all over the place. Geez.

```
SF ISO SM. Dancing. Wine. Night. Sky. Moon.
Romancing. Dine. Write by June.
```

Great. Poetry. She'll expect me to reciprocate. I just won't be able to say, "Yeah, let's grab a burger tonight." Nope. I'll have to get some watercolors and paint a letter to her. In some ancient verse form. Rhyming really is the sign of an overactive mind. Who really cares if two words in different parts of a paragraph happen to end with the same sound? It's just a coincidence. She'll probably spend all of her time picking up patterns in our lives. I'll have to keep saying, "No. I still love you. I just want to watch the seventh game of the World Series. The Red Sox are in it this year. It's tied. They might actually win! This is *not* a sign of a bad relationship." Geez.

```
and fast horses are for me. Don't write. Send a
telegram.
```

Fast horse? They're animals. They only tolerate us on their backs as long as the oats are fresh. Women are the same way. But they don't take to a rein as well. And they don't just want fresh oats. I bet Fast Food isn't on her list. She'll ride along and take me for whatever I've got. Then she'll grab a fast plane out of my life. No way. Her boat's sinking already. Geez.

6.1

Running in Reverse

The cynic looking for a date described in the chapter introduction has the ability to take a simple advertisement and read between the lines until he's plotted the entire arc of the relationship and followed it to its doom. Personal ads have an elaborate shorthand system for compressing a person's dreams into fewer than 100 words. The shorthand evolved over the years as people grew to pick up the patterns in what people wanted. "ISO" means "In Search Of", and so on. The cynic was just using his view of the way that people want to expand the bits of data into a reality that has little to do with the incoming data.

This chapter is about creating an automatic way of taking small, innocuous bits of data and embellishing them with deep, embroidered details until the result mimics something completely different. The data is hidden as it assumes this costume. In this chapter, the effect is accomplished by running the Huffman compression algorithm described in Chapter 5 in reverse. Ordinarily, the Huffman algorithm would approximate the statistical distribution of the text and then convert it into a digital shorthand. Running this in reverse can take normal data and form it into these elaborate patterns.

Figure 6.1 is a good place to begin. The text in this figure was created using a fifth-order regular mimic function by analyzing an early draft of Chapter 5. The fifth-order statistical profile of the chapter was created by counting all possible sets of five letters in a row that occur in the chapter. In the draft, the five letters "mpres" occur

The letter compression or video is only to
generate a verbatim> followed by 12 whiter 'H'
wouldn't design a perfective reconomic data. This
to simple hardware. These worked with encodes of
the data list of the diction in the most come down
in depth in a file decome down in adds about of
character first.
Many data for each of find the occnly difficular
techniques can algorithms computer used data
verbatim out means that describes themselves in a
part ideas of reduce extremely occurate the charge
formulas. At leaf space and the original set of
the storage common word memo to red by 42 black
pixels formula that pression of their data is why
complicated to be done many difference like
solution. This book. Many different wouldn't get
into any different to though to anyone has make
the popular to the number or 60 minutes. This
Huffman also just but random. Compression. One
branches is easy to be use of find the because
many people has shows the codes The most nooks
like three constructed with a function, the greate
the moMany good formations. This simply be
compression show a Huffman code work quite easily
common in these 26 different takes 48 bit should
in this can be patter-frequency the image space
constructed in the other letter is algorithm on
stand there easier to the overed into the root and
MPEG and crannies their data for compression
Scheme Compression in a file description when it
short codes were could be common length encode
work quite weights a Klepto Family Stressed by
image and Compressed as a bigger, whiter the for
hardware. Many even more that then the result to
descriptionary algorithms that were two bits you
might for simply because of charge found in the
well, but the data is easily Stressed surprising
text. The algorithm would look very good

Figure 6.1 This is a fifth-order random text generated by mimicking the
statistical distribution of letters in an early draft of Chapter 5.

together in that order 84 times. Given that these letters are part of the word "compression", it is not surprising that the five letters "ompre" and "press" also occur 84 times.

The text is generated in a process that is guided by these statistics. The computer begins by selecting one group of five letters at random. In this figure, the first five letters are "The l". Then it uses the statistics to dictate which letters can follow. In the draft of Chapter 5, the five letters "he la" occur 2 times, the letters "he le" occur 16 times, and the letters "he lo" occur 2 times. If the fifth-order text is going to mimic the statistical profile of Chapter 5, then there should be a 2 out of 20 chance that the letter "a" should follow "The l". Of course, there should also be a 16 out of 20 chance that it should be an "e" and a 2 out of 20 chance that it should be an "o".

This process is repeated ad infinitum until enough text is generated. It is often amazing just how real the result sounds. To a large extent, this is caused by the smaller size of the sample text. If you assume that there are about 64 printable characters in a text file, then there are about 64^5 different combinations of five letters. Obviously, many of them like "zqTuV" never occur in the English language, but a large number of them must make their way into the table if the algorithm is to have many choices. In the last example, there were three possible choices for a letter to follow "The l". The phrase "The letter" is common in Chapter 5, but the phrase "The listerine" is not. In many cases, there is only one possible choice that was dictated by the small number of words used in the sample. This is what gives it such a real-sounding pattern.

Here's the algorithm for generating nth-order text called T given a source text S.

1. Construct a list of all different combinations of n letters that occur in S and keep track of how many times each of these occurs in S.

2. Choose one at random to be a seed. This will be the first n letters of T.

3. Repeat this loop until enough text is generated:
   (a) Take the last $n - 1$ letters of T.
   (b) Search through the statistical table and find all combinations of letters that begin with these $n - 1$ letters.
   (c) The last letters of these combinations form the set of possible choices for the next letter to be added to T.

(d) Choose among these letters and use the frequency of their occurrences in S to weight your choice.

(e) Add it to T.

The algorithm works for n that is 2 or larger. Obviously, the quality of the output of the lower-order samples depends upon the order. Here are some samples:

- *First Order.* islhne[hry saeeooisnre uo 'w nala al coehhs pebl e to agboean ce ed cshcenapch nt sibPah ea m n [tmsteoia lahid egnndl y et r yf arleo awe l eo rttnntnnhtohwiseoa a dri 6oc7teit2t lenefe clktoi l mlte r ces. woeiL, misetemd2np eap haled&oolrcc yttr tr,oh en mi elarlbeo tyNunt. syf es2 nrrpmdo,O reet dadwn'dysg te.ewnlca-ht eitxrni ntoos xt eCc oh sao vhsohOmhgr

- *Second Order.* Thy etheren' ante esthe ales. icone thers the ase omsictorm s iom. wactere cut le ce s mo be t Me. Y whes ine odofuion os thore cctherg om tt s d Thm & tthamben tin'ssthe, co westitit odecra fugon tucod. liny Eangem o wen il ea bionBulivethe ton othanstoct itaple

- *Third Order.* ith eas a tan't genstructin ing butionsmage ruct secate expachat thap-res "Miamproxis is of is a to af st. This there is monst cone usectuabloodes it aluengettecte por be the andtaly com Bevers gor the Hufferess. M B G achasion the coduch occomprence mon Quited the ch like bitheres. The

- *Fourth Order.* captionary. Image and to compression lest constance tree. Family for into be mode of bytes in algorith a file of that cosition algorithm that word even that a size summarge factal size are:

  ite position scien Raps.

  The is are up much length ence, the if the a refsec-ent sec-ent of fits to the crans usuall numberse compression

> A good ways that in algoright. The brase two
> wants to hidea of English Cash the are compres
> then matimes formatimes from the data finding
> pairst. This only be ression o

There is little doubt that the text gets more and more readable as the order increases. But who would this fool? What if the enemy designed a computer program that would flag suspicious electronic mail by identifying messages that don't have the right statistical mix of characters? Foreign languages could pop right out. French, for instance, has a greater number of apostrophes as well as a different distribution of letters. Russian has an entirely different alphabet, but even when it is transliterated the distribution is different. Each language and even each regional dialect has a different composition.

These texts generated here could fool such an automatic scanning device. The output here is statistically equivalent to honest English text. For instance, the letter "e" is the most common, and the letter "t" is next most common. Everything looks correct statistically at all of the different orders. If the scanning software was looking for statistical deviance, it wouldn't find it.

An automatic scanning program is also at a statistical disadvantage with relatively short text samples. Its statistical definition of what is normal must be loose enough to fit changes caused by the focus of the text. A document about zebras, for instance, would have many more "z"s than the average document, but this alone wouldn't make it abnormal. Many documents might have a higher than average occurrence of "j"s or "q"s merely because the topic involves something like jails or quiz shows.

Of course, these texts wouldn't be able to fool a person. At least the first-, second-, or third-order texts wouldn't fool anyone. But a fifth-order text based upon a sample from an obscure and difficult jargon such as legal writing might fool many people who aren't familiar with the structures of the genre.

More complicated statistical models can produce better mimicry, at least in the right cases. Markov models, for instance, are common in speech recognition. Genetic algorithms can do a good job of predicting some patterns. In general, any of the algorithms designed to help a computer learn to recognize a pattern can be applied here to suss out a pattern before being turned in reverse to imitate it.

More complicated grammatical analysis is certainly possible. There are grammar checkers that scan documents and identify bad sentence structure. These products are far from perfect. Many people write idiomatically, and others stretch the bounds of what is considered correct grammar without breaking any of the rules. Although honest text generated by humans may set off many flags, there is little doubt that even the fifth-order text shown in Figure 6.1 would appear so wrong that it could be automatically detected. Any text that had, say, more wrong than right with it could be flagged as suspicious by an automatic process [KO84, Way85].

Chapter 7 offers an approach to defeat grammar checkers.

6.1.1   Choosing the Next Letter

The last section showed how statistically equivalent text could be generated by mimicking the statistical distribution of a source collection of text. The algorithm showed how to choose the next letter so it would be statistically correct, but it did not explain how to hide information in the process. Nor did it explain how to run Huffman compression in reverse.

The information is hidden by letting the data to be concealed dictate the choice of the next letter. In the example described above, "a", "e", or "o" could follow the starting letters "The l". It is easy to come up with a simple scheme for encoding information. If "a" stands for "1", "e" stands for "2", and "o" stands for "3", then common numbers could be encoded in the choice of the letters. Someone at a distance could recover this value if they had a copy of the same source text, S, that generated the table of statistics. They could look up "The l" and discover that there are three letters that follow "he l" in the table. The letter "e" is the second choice in alphabetical order, so the letter "e" stands for the message "2".

A long text such as the one shown in Figure 6.1 could hide a different number in each letter. If there was no choice about the next letter to be added to the output, though, then no information could be hidden. That letter would not hide anything.

Simply using a letter to encode a number is not an efficient or flexible way to send data. What if you wanted to send the message "4" and there were only three choices? What if you wanted to send a long picture? What if your data wanted to send the value "1", but the first letter was the least common choice. Would this mess up the statistical composition?

Running Huffman codes in reverse is the solution to all of these problems. Figure 6.2 shows a simple Huffman tree constructed from the three choices of letters to follow "The l". The tree was constructed using the statistics that showed that the letter "e" followed in 16 out

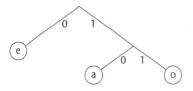

Figure 6.2   A small Huffman tree built to hide bits in the choice of a new letter. Here, the letter ''a'' encodes ''10''; the letter ''e'' encodes ''0''; and the letter ''o'' encodes ''11''.

of the 20 times while the letters "a" and "o" both followed twice apiece.

Messages are encoded with a Huffman tree like this with a variable number of bits. The choice of "e" encodes the bit "0"; the choice of "a" encodes "10"; and the choice of "o" encodes the message "11". These bits can be recovered at the other end by reversing this choice. The number of bits hidden with each choice of a letter varies directly with the number of choices that are possible and the probabilities that govern the choice.

There should generally be more than three choices available if the source text S is large enough to offer some variation, but there will rarely be a full 26 choices. This is only natural because English has plenty of redundancy built into the language. Shannon recognized this when he set up information theory. If the average entropy of English is about 3 bits per character, then this means that there should only be about 2^3 or eight choices that can be made for the next character. This value is weighted by the probabilities.

Section 6.2.1, "Goosing with Extra Data", shows a more accurate approximation.

There are problems, of course, with this scheme. Yet this solution is the best way to hide the information so that it mimics the source text S for the same reason that Huffman codes are the most efficient way to construct tree-like compression schemes. The same proof that shows this works in reverse.

But even if running Huffman codes in reverse is the best solution, it falls short of being perfect. In the small example in Figure 6.2, the letter "e" is chosen if the next bit to be hidden is "0", while either "a" or "o" will be hidden if the next bit is "1". If the data to be hidden is purely random, then "e" will be chosen 50 percent of the time, while "a" or "o" will be chosen the other 50 percent of the time. This does not mimic the statistics from the source text exactly. If it did, the letter "e" would be chosen 80 percent of the time and the other letters would each be chosen 10 percent of the time. This inaccuracy exists because of the binary structure of the Huffman tree and the number of choices available.

Implementing the Mimicry

There are two major problems in writing software that will generate regular nth-order mimicry. The first is acquiring and storing the statistics. The second is creating a tree structure to do the Huffman-like coding and decoding. The first problem is something that requires a bit more finesse because there are several different ways to accomplish the same ends. The second problem is fairly straightforward.

Several different people have approached a similar problem called generating a *travesty*. This was addressed in a series of *Byte* magazine articles [KO84, Way85] that described how to generate statistically equivalent text. The articles didn't use the effect to hide data, but they did concentrate upon the most efficient way to generate it. This work ends up being quite similar in practice to the homophonic ciphers described by H. N. Jendal, Y. J. B. Kuhn, and J. L. Massey in [JKM90] and generalized by C. G. Gunther in [Gun88].

Here are several different approaches to storing the statistical tables needed to generate the data:

- *Giant Array.* Allocate an array with c^n boxes where c is the number of possible characters at each position and n is the order of the statistics being kept. Obviously c can be as low as 27 if only capital letters and spaces are kept. But it can also be 256 if all possible values of a byte are stored. This may be practical for small values of n, but it grows quickly impossible.

- *Giant List.* Create an alphabetical list of all the entries. There is one counter per node as well as a pointer and a string holding the value in question. This makes the nodes substantially less efficient than the array. This can still pay off if there are many nodes that are kept out. If English text is being mimicked, there are many combinations of several letters that don't occur. A list is definitely more efficient.

- *Giant Tree.* Build a big tree that contains one path from the root to a leaf for each letter combination found in the tree. This can contain substantially more pointers, but it is faster to use than the Giant List. Figure 6.3 illustrates an implementation of this.

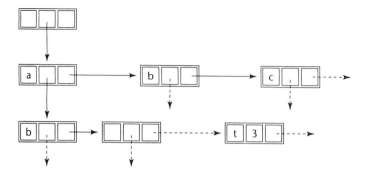

Figure 6.3   This tree stores the frequency data for a file with n layers of branching for nth-order statistics. Access is substantially faster. The dashed lines show where nodes are omitted. The only complete word shown here is "at". It occurs three times in the sample.

- *Going Fishing.* Randomize the search. There is no statistical table produced at all because c and n are too large. The source file serves as a random source, and it is consulted at random for each choice of a new letter. This can be extremely slow, but it may be the only choice if memory isn't available.

The first three solutions are fairly easy to implement for anyone with a standard programming background. The array is the easiest. The list is not hard. Anyone implementing the tree has a number of choices. Figure 6.3 shows that the new branches at each level are stored in a list. This could also be done in a binary tree to speed lookup.

The fourth solution, going fishing, is a bit more complicated. The idea is to randomly select positions in the text and use this to randomize the search. All of the data can't be kept in a table so all of the choices won't be available at each juncture. Therefore, you must make do with what you can find. The most extreme version of this algorithm simply searches the entire file and constructs the right table entry on the fly. Here is a more sensible approach.

1. Choose a location in the source file at random. Call this character i. This random source must be duplicated during decoding so it must come from a pseudo-random number generator that is synchronized.

2. If you are constructing an nth-order mimicry, search forward until you find the $n - 1$ characters in question. The next character may be the one you desire.

3. Let there be k characters in the source file. Go to position $i + \frac{k}{2}$ mod k. Search forward until the right combination of $n - 1$ characters is found.

4. If the next character suggested by both positions is the same, then nothing can be encoded here. Send out that character and repeat.

5. If they are different, then one bit can be encoded with the choice. If you are hiding a 0 using this mimicry, then output the character found beginning at position i. If you are hiding a 1, then output the character found after the search began at $i + \frac{k}{2}$ mod k.

This solution can be decoded. All of the information encoded here can be recovered as long as both the encoder and the decoder have access to the same source file and the same stream of i values coming from a pseudo-random source. The pseudo-random generator ensures that all possible combinations are uncovered. This does assume, however, that the candidates of $n - 1$ characters are evenly distributed throughout the text.

The solution can also be expanded to store more than one bit per output letter. You could begin the search at four different locations and hope that you uncover four different possible letters to output. If you do, then you can encode two bits. This approach can be extended still further, but each search does slow the output.

In general, the fishing solution is the slowest and most cumbersome of all the approaches. Looking up each new letter takes an amount of time proportional to the occurrence of the $n - 1$ character group in the data. The array has the fastest lookup, but it can be prohibitively large in many cases. The tree has the next fastest lookup and is probably the most generally desirable for text applications.

6.2.1 Goosing with Extra Data

Alas, statistical purity is often hard to generate. If the data to be hidden has maximum entropy, then the letters that emerge from the Huffman-tree-based mimicry will emerge with a probability distribution that seems a bit suspicious. Every letter will appear with a probability of the form $1/2^i$—that is, either 50 percent, 25 percent, 12.5 percent, and so on. This may not be that significant, but it might be detected.

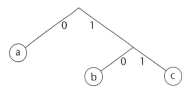

Figure 6.4   An ordinary Huffman tree built for three characters, ''a'', ''b'', and ''c'', which occur with probabilities of 50, 37.5, and 12.5 percent, respectively.

Music is also fair game. Many have experimented with using musical rules of composition to create new music from statistical models of existing music. One paper on the topic is [BJNW57].

Better results can be obtained by trading off some of the efficiency and using a pseudo-random number generator to add more bits to make the choice better approximate the actual occurrence in the data.

The technique can best be explained by example. Imagine that there are three characters, "a", "b", and "c", that occur with probabilities of 50, 37.5, and 12.5 percent, respectively. The ordinary Huffman tree would look like the one in Figure 6.4. The character "a" would occur in the output file 50 percent of the time. This would be fine. But "b" and "c" would both occur 25 percent of the time. The letter "b" will occur as often as "c", not three times as often, as dictated by the source file.

Figure 6.5 shows a new version of the Huffman tree designed to balance the distribution. There are now two extra layers added to the tree. The branching choices made in these extra two layers would use extra bits supplied by a pseudo-random generator. When they were recovered, these bits would be discarded. It should be easy to establish that "b" will emerge 37.5 percent of the time and "c" will be output 12.5 percent of the time if the data being hidden is perfectly distributed.

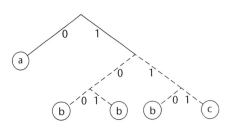

Figure 6.5   An expanded version of the tree shown in Figure 6.4. The decisions about which of the dashed branches to take are made by drawing bits from an extra pseudo-random source. Only the first decision is made using a bit from the data to be hidden.

The cost of this process is efficiency. The new tree may produce output with the right distribution, but decoding is often not possible. The letter "b" is produced from the leaves with addresses 100, 101, and 110. Since only the first bit remains constant with this tree in Figure 6.5, then only one bit can be hidden with the letter "b". The other two bits would be produced by the pseudo-random bit stream and not recovered at the other end. The tree in Figure 6.4 would hide *two* bits with the letter "b", but it would produce a "b" 25 percent of the time. This is the tradeoff of efficiency versus accuracy.

How many bits are hidden or encoded if a "c" is output? It could either be three that are encoded when a 111 is found in the input file, or it could be simply one bit padded in the same manner as the letter "b". Either choice is fine.

This technique can be extended significantly to support any amount of precision. The most important step is to make sure that there will be no ambiguity in the decoding process. If the same character exists on both branches, then no bit can be encoded using any of the subtree descending from this point.

This means that it is not possible to encode data dominated by one character that appears more than 50 percent of the time. If "a", "b", and "c" were to emerge 75, 25, and 5 percent, respectively, then it would not be possible to encode information with this scheme and also produce the letter "a" 75 percent of the time.

One way around this process is to produce pairs of characters. This is often feasible if one letter dominates the distribution. That is, you produce the pairs "aa", "ab", "ac", "ba", "bb", "bc", "ca", "cb", and "cc" with probabilities 56, 18, 3, 18, 6, 1, 3, 1, and .2 percent, respectively.

6.2.2   Regular Mimicry and Images

The regular mimicry algorithms described in this chapter are aimed at text, and they do a good job in this domain. Adapting them to images is quite possible, if only because the digitized images are just patterns of the two letters "1" and "0". But the success is somewhat diluted.

Chapter 9 shows how to flip the least significant bits to store information. Chapter 9 doesn't try to mimic the pattern of the least significant bits. It just assumes that they fall into a standard even distribution. The regular mimicry algorithms can be used to tailor the distribution to some model.

The simplest solution is to group the pixels together into a regular set of groups. These groups might be 2×2 or 3×3 blocks or they might be broken into linear groups of pixels from the same row. Now, the least significant bits of each of these pixels can be treated as characters. One image might be used as the model for computing the distribution table that generates a Huffman tree. Then data can be hidden in another by using this Huffman tree to generate blocks of bits to replace the least significant bits in the image.

More sophisticated solutions could be based upon the color of the pixels themselves, but this solution is probably too complicated to be practical. The advantage of this system is that it could detect and imitate any statistical anomalies introduced when an image was created. Ordinarily, CCD arrays have slight imperfections that affect how each sensing cell reacts to light. High-quality arrays used by organizations such as NASA are tested and corrected. Most civilian arrays never receive this individual treatment. This system might pick up any low-level incongruities if they happen to fall in a pattern that is reflected in the statistical distribution of the pixel groups.

6.3

Summary

This chapter described how to produce mimicked text that looks statistically similar to original text. The mechanisms in this chapter treat letters as the individual element, something that allows the data to pass some statistical tests but fail others. The count of letters like "e" and "t" might be consistent, but there are often large numbers of words that can't be found in a dictionary. Another approach taken by some experimenters is to treat words as the individual elements for the statistical models. This requires more text to create the model, but it provides excellent, if rambling, results. There are no misspelled words that aren't found in the source.

Chapter 7 describes how to use a more sophisticated grammar-based method to achieve a better result. Chapter 8 goes even further and shows how a Turing machine can be made to run backward and forward to produce the most complicated text.

- *The Disguise.* The text produced by these regular mimic functions can be quite realistic. The results are statistically equivalent. First-order text will have similar first-order statistics. Second-order text will have the same occurrence of pairs. This can be quite realistic in the higher orders, but it will rarely pass the reading test. Humans would quickly recognize it as gibberish.

- *How Secure Is It?* There is no reason to guess that this system offers any more security than hiding the information. The question of how hard it would be to break such a statistical system is an open question. I believe that it would be possible to examine the statistics and come up with a pretty good guess about the shape of the Huffman trees used to generate the text. There may only be a few thousand options that can be tested quite quickly if some known plain text is available. For that reason, this system should probably be used in low-grade applications that demand verisimilitude but not perfection.

- *How to Use It?* No software is being distributed right now to handle this problem, but it should not be easy to code it.

Grammars and Mimicry

Evolution of Everyday Things

Recently, I sat down with Charles Radwin, an evolutionary scientist, who drew a fair bit of acclaim and controversy over his paper showing how evolution led the human species to gorge on the O. J. Simpson trial. I asked him his views about how evolution affected other aspects of our lives. Here is our conversation:

Q: Eventually all toilets need their handles wiggled to stop them from running. Why?

A: The commodes obviously developed this response to prevent calcification. The extra running water prevented tank stoppage, and the toilets that had this gene quickly outlasted those that didn't. It was simple natural selection.

Q: What about toasters? No matter how hard you try to set them right, they always burn some toast.

A: Toasters developed this response to protect their host organism. Golden brown toast begs for a thick coating of butter. Perfect toasters gave their host humans massive coronary occlusions, which sends them to the scrap heap. The best toasters are those that do not kill off their hosts. They ultimately come to dominate the ecological landscape in the kitchen.

Q: Lightbulbs always burn out when I turn on the light. Why not, say, in the middle of a novel?

A: Again, lightbulbs evolved this way to protect their host humans. People often turn on lights when they enter a dark room. If the lightbulb dies at this moment, no one is stranded in the dark. But if the lightbulb burns out when someone is in the middle of the room, that human invariably trips over the coffee table, falls and splits its head wide open. Naturally, the lightbulbs that evolve into a synergistic relationship with their human hosts survive the best.

Q: But why don't lightbulbs live forever? Wouldn't that make life even better for their hosts?

A: Evolution can't function without new generations. Something must die in order for progress to occur.

Q: Copying machines always break down ten minutes before the crucial presentation. I've almost lost two jobs when a copier quit on me. They certainly weren't protecting their host organism, were they?

A: Evolution is a tricky balance. An organism can be too successful and consume all of its habitat. Imagine a perfect copying machine that did one billion flawless copies in a second. Wonderful, right? Not for the copying machine. Everything would be copied. It would have no purpose, and the humans would quickly replace it with something more fun like a refrigerator filled with beer.

Q: Speaking of beer, why do some of those pop-tops break off without opening the can? By the end of a fishing trip, my cooler is filled with unopenable cans with no pop-tops.

A: You're answering your own question, aren't you?

Q: Why isn't beer entering into a synergistic relationship with the human? I'm certainly game.

A: In this case, the beer and the human are competing for the same ecological niche. If two humans drink beer, they often go off and create another human, not another beer.

Q: What if people set up another batch of hops and malt when they got drunk? Would those pull tabs start cooperating?

A: Evolution is hard to predict. Small changes in the equation can often change the entire outcome. I think that the beer pull tops would soon become harder to pull off. Why? Because organisms often evolve reproductive restraint to avoid catastrophic competition. Your scenario could quickly lead to a flood of beer.

Q: There's nothing I can do about the pull tabs? Aren't evolutionary scientists good for anything?

A: Evolution is tricky. If scientists were able to answer all of the questions, there would be no need for evolutionary scientists. Nor would there be any need for the program officers at the National Science Foundation who give out money to evolutionary scientists. There is a well-defined synergy at work here.

7.1

Using Grammar for Mimicry

Chapter 6 shows how to hide data and turn it into something that mimics the statistical patterns of a file. If you wanted a piece of text to sound like the *New York Times*, for instance, you could feed in a large amount of source material from the paper and gather statistical patterns that would make it possible to mimic its output. Ideally, such a function would be a strong technique that could hide data from automatic scanning programs that might use statistical patterns to identify data.

The output of these Huffman-based methods could certainly fool any machine examining data looking for suspicious patterns. The letters would conform to the expected distribution; "e"s would be common, "z"s would be uncommon. If either second- or third-order text was used, then "u"s would follow "q"s and everything would seem to make sense to a computer that was merely checking statistics.

These statistical mimic functions wouldn't fool anyone looking at the grammar. First- or second-order mimicry like that found in Section 6.1 looks incomprehensible. Words start to appear in third- or fourth-order text, but they rarely fall into the basic grammatical structure. Even a wayward grammar checker could flag these a mile away. This chapter describes how to create mimicry that will be grammatically correct and make perfect sense to a human. The algorithms are based upon some of the foundational work done in linguistics that now buttresses much of computer science. The net result is something that reads quite well and can be very, very difficult to break.

The basic abstraction used in this chapter is *context-free grammar*. The notion was developed by Noam Chomsky [CM58] to explain roughly how languages work. The structure is something like a more mathematical form of sentence diagramming. This model was adopted by computer scientists who both explored its theoretical limits and used it as a basis for programming languages such as C or Pascal.

A context-free grammar consists of three different parts:

- *Terminals*. This is the technical term for the word or sentence fragments that are used to put together the final output. Think of them as the patterns printed on the puzzle fragments. The terminals will often be called *words* or *phrases*.

- *Variables*. These are used as abstract versions of decisions that will be made later. They're very similar to the variables that are used in algebra or programming. These will be typeset in boldface like this: **variable**.

- *Productions*. These describe how a variable can be converted into different sets of variables or terminals. The format looks like this:

$$\textbf{variable} \quad \rightarrow \quad \text{words} \parallel \text{phrase.}$$

That means that a **variable** can be converted into either words or a phrase. The arrow ($\rightarrow$) stands for conversion, and the double vertical line ($\parallel$) stands for "or". In this example, the right-hand side of the equation holds only terminals, but there can be mixtures of variables as well. You can think of these productions as the rules for how the puzzle pieces can go together.

The basic idea is that a grammar describes a set of words known as the terminals and a set of potentially complex rules about how they go together. In many cases, there is a fair bit of freedom of choice in each stage of the production.

In this example, the **variable** could be converted into either words or a phrase. This choice is where the information will be hidden. The data will drive the choice in much the same way that a random-number generator drives a fake computerized poetry machine. The data can be recovered through a reverse process known as *parsing*.

Here's a sample grammar:

$$\begin{aligned}
\textbf{Start} \quad &\rightarrow \quad \textbf{noun} \quad \textbf{verb} \\
\textbf{noun} \quad &\rightarrow \quad \text{Fred} \parallel \text{Barney} \parallel \text{Fred and Barney} \\
\textbf{verb} \quad &\rightarrow \quad \text{went fishing.} \parallel \text{went bowling.}
\end{aligned}$$

By starting with the **Start** variable and applying productions to convert the different variables, the grammar can generate sentences such as "Fred and Barney went fishing." This is often written with a squiggly arrow ($\rightsquigarrow$) representing a combination of several different productions, like this: **Start** ⤳ Fred and Barney went fishing. Another way to state the same thing is to say the following: The sentence "Fred and Barney went fishing" is in the language generated by the grammar. The order of the productions is arbitrary, and in some cases the order can make a difference (it doesn't in this simple example).

More complicated grammars might look like this:

Start	→	**noun verb**
noun	→	Fred ‖ Barney
verb	→	went fishing **where** ‖ went bowling **where**
where	→	in **direction** Iowa. ‖ in **direction** Minnesota.
direction	→	northern ‖ southern

For simplicity, each of the productions in this grammar has two choices, call them 0 and 1. If you begin with the **Start** variable and always process the leftmost variable, then you can convert bits into sentences from the language generated by this grammar. A step-by-step illustration of the process is shown in Table 7.1.

The bits 1010 were hidden by converting them into the sentence "Barney went fishing in northern Minnesota." The bits 0001 would generate the sentence "Fred went fishing in southern Iowa." The bits 1111 would generate the sentence "Barney went bowling in southern Minnesota." There are 2^4 different sentences in the language generated by this grammar, and all of them make sense.

Obviously, complex grammars can generate complex results, and producing high-quality text demands a certain amount of creativity. You need to anticipate how the words and phrases will go together and make sure everything comes together with a certain amount of felicity. Figure 7.1 shows the output from an extensive grammar developed to mimic the voice-over from a baseball game. The entire grammar can be seen in Appendix B.

Table 7.1 Five steps to converting 1010 into a sentence.

Step	Answer in Progress	Bit Hidden	Production Choice
1	**Start**	*none*	**Start → noun verb**
2	**noun verb**	1	**noun** → Barney
3	Barney **verb**	0	**verb** → went fishing **where**
4	Barney went fishing **where**	1	**where** → in **direction** Minnesota.
5	Barney went fishing in **direction** Minnesota.	0	**direction** → northern

```
Well Bob, Welcome to yet another game between the
Whappers and the Blogs here in scenic downtown Blovonia.
I think it is fair to say that there is plenty of
BlogFever brewing in the stands as the hometown comes out
to root for its favorites. The umpire throws out the
ball. Top of the inning. No outs yet for the Whappers.
Here we go. Jerry Johnstone adjusts the cup and enters
the batter's box. Here's the pitch. Nothing on that
one. Here comes the pitch. It's a curvaceous beauty. He
just watched it go by. And the next pitch is a smoking
gun. He lifts it over the head of Harrison "Harry"
Hanihan for a double! Yup. What a game so far today.
Now, Mark Cloud adjusts the cup and enters the batter's
box. Yeah. He's winding up. What looks like a
spitball. He swings for the stands, but no contact.
It's a rattler. He just watched it go by. He's winding
up. What a blazing comet. Swings and misses! Strike
out. He's swinging at the umpire. The umpire
reconsiders until the security guards arrive. Yup, got
to love this stadium.
```

Figure 7.1   Some text produced from the baseball context-free grammar in Appendix B.

Figure 7.1 shows only the first part of a 26K file generated from hiding this quote:

> I then told her the key-word which belonged to no language and saw her surprise. She told me that it was impossible for she believed herself the only possessor of that word which she kept in her memory and which she never wrote down.... This disclosure fettered Madame d'Urfé to me. That day I became the master of her soul and I abused my power. —*Casanova, 1757, as quoted by David Kahn in* The Codebreakers [Kah67]

The grammar relies heavily upon the structure of the baseball game to give form to the final output. The number of balls, strikes, and outs are kept accurately because the grammar was constructed carefully. The number of runs, on the other hand, are left out because the grammar has no way of keeping track of them. This is a good illustration of what the modifier "context-free" means. The productions applied to a particular variable do not depend upon the context that surrounds the variable. For instance, it doesn't really matter in the basic example whether it is Fred or Barney who is doing the fishing or bowling. The decision on whether it is done in Minnesota or Iowa is made independently.

The baseball grammar in Appendix B uses a separate variable for each half-inning. One half-inning might end up producing a bunch of sentences stating that everyone was hitting home runs. That information and its context does not affect the choice of productions in the next half-inning. This is just a limitation enforced by the way that the variables and the productions were defined. If the productions were less arbitrary and based on more computation, even more better text could be produced.[1]

7.1.1 Parsing and Going Back

Hiding information as sentences generated from a particular grammar is a nice toy. Recovering the data from the sentences turns the parlor game into a real tool for transmitting information covertly. The reverse process is called *parsing*, and computer scientists have studied the process extensively. Computer languages such as C are built upon a context-free grammar. The computer parses the language to understand its instructions. This chapter is only interested in the process of converting a sentence back into the list of bits that led to its production.

Parsing can be complex or easy. Most computer languages are designed to make parsing easy so the process can be made fast. There is no reason why this can't be done with mimicry as well. You can always parse the sentence from any context-free grammar and recover the sequence of productions, but there is no reason to use these arbitrarily complex routines. If the grammar is designed correctly, it is easy enough for anyone to parse the data.

There are two key rules to follow. First, make sure the grammar is not *ambiguous*, and second, keep the grammar in *Greibach Normal Form*. If the same sentence can emerge from a grammar through two different sets of productions, then the grammar is *ambiguous*. This makes the grammar unusable for hiding information because there is no way to accurately recover the data. An ambiguous grammar might be useful as a cute poetry generator, but if there is no way to be sure what the hidden meaning is, then it can't be used to hide data.

---

[1]It is quite possible to create a more complex grammar that does a better job of encoding the score at a particular time, but this grammar won't be perfect. It will do a better job, but it won't be exactly right. This is left as an exercise.

Here's an example of an ambiguous grammar:

Start	→	**noun verb** ‖ **who what**
noun	→	Fred ‖ Barney
verb	→	went fishing. ‖ went bowling.
who	→	Fred went ‖ Barney went
what	→	bowling ‖ fishing

The sentence "Fred went fishing" could be produced by two different steps. If you were hiding data in the sentence, then "Barney went bowling" could have come from either the bits 011 or 110. Such a problem must be avoided at all costs.

If a context-free grammar is in Greibach Normal Form (GNF), it means that the variables are at the end of the productions. Here are some examples:

Production			*In GNF?*
Start	→	**noun verb**	YES
where	→	in **direction** Iowa. ‖	
		in **direction** Minnesota.	NO
where	→	in **direction state**. ‖	
		in **direction state**.	YES
what	→	bowling ‖ fishing	YES

Converting any arbitrary context-free grammar into Greibach Normal Form is easy. You can simply add productions until you reach success. Here's the extended example from this section with a new variable, **state**, that places this in GNF.

Start	→	**noun verb**
noun	→	Fred ‖ Barney
verb	→	went fishing **where** ‖ went bowling **where**
where	→	in **direction state**
direction	→	northern ‖ southern
state	→	Iowa. ‖ Minnesota.

The program was a mimetic weapon, designed to absorb local color and present itself as a crash priority override in whatever context it encountered.

—William Gibson
in *Burning Chrome*

This grammar generates exactly the same group of sentences or language as the other version. The only difference is in the order in which choices are made. Here, there is no choice available when the variable **where** is tackled. No bits would be stored away at this

Table 7.2 Parsing a sentence.

Step	Sentence Fragment in Question	Matching Production	Bit Recovered
1	*Barney* went fishing in northern Minnesota	**noun** → Fred ‖ Barney	1
2	Barney *went fishing* in northern Minnesota	**verb** → went fishing **where** ‖ went bowling **where**	0
3	Barney went fishing *in* northern Minnesota	**where** → in **direction state**.	*none*
4	Barney went fishing in *northern* Minnesota	**direction** → northern ‖ southern	0
5	Barney went fishing in northern *Minnesota*.	**state** → Iowa. ‖ Minnesota.	1

point. The variables for **direction** and **state** would be handled in order. The result is that the sentence "Barney went fishing in northern Minnesota" is produced by the bits 1001. In the previous grammar illustrated by Table 7.1, the sentence emerged from hiding bits 1010.

Parsing the result from a context-free grammar that is in Greibach Normal Form is generally easy. Table 7.1 shows how the sentence "Barney went fishing in northern Minnesota" was produced from the bits 1010. The parsing process works along similar lines. Table 7.2 shows the sentence being parsed using the grammar from above in GNF.

The bits 1001 are recovered in step 5. This shows how a simple parsing process can recover bits stored inside of sentences produced using grammar in GNF. Better parsing algorithms can handle any arbitrary context-free grammar, but this is beyond the purview of this book.

7.1.2 How Good Is It?

There are many ways to measure goodness, goodness knows, but the most important ones here are efficiency and resistance to attack. The efficiency of this method is something that depends heavily upon the grammar itself. In the examples in this section, one bit in the source text was converted into words such as "Minnesota" or "Barney". That's not particularly efficient.

The grammar could encode more bits at each stage in the production if there were more choices. In each of the examples, there were only two choices on the right side of the production. There is no reason why there can't be more. Four choices would encode two bits. Eight choices would encode three bits, and so on. More choices are often not hard to add. There is no reason why there can't be 1024 names of people that could be produced as the noun of the sentence. That would encode 10 bits in one swoop. The only limitation is your imagination.

Assessing the resistance to attack is more complicated. The hardest test can be fooling a human. The text produced in Chapter 6 may look correct statistically, but even the best fifth-order text seems stupid to the average human. The grammatical text that can be produced from this process can be as convincing as someone can make the grammar. The example in Appendix B shows how complicated it can get. Spending several days on a grammar may well be worth the effort.

There are still limitations to the form. Context-free grammars have a fairly simple form. This means, however, that they don't really keep track of information particularly well. The example in Appendix B shows how strikes, balls, and outs can be kept straight, but it fails to keep track of the score or the movement of the base runners. A substantially more complicated grammar might begin to do this, but there will always be limitations to writing the text in this format.

The nature of being *context-free* also imposes deeper problems on the narrative. The voice-over from a baseball game is a great conceit here because the story finds itself in the same situation over and over again. The batter is facing the pitcher. The details about the score and the count change, but the process repeats itself again and again and again.

Creating a grammar that produces convincing results can either be easy or hard. The difficulty depends, to a large extent, on your level of cynicism. For instance, anyone could easily argue that the process of government in Washington, D.C., is a three-step process:

1. Member of Congress X threatens to change regulation Y of industry Z.

2. Industry Z coughs up money for the reelection campaigns of other members P, D, and Q.

3. P, D, and Q stop X's plan in committee.

If you believe that life in Washington, D.C., boils down to this basic economic process, you would have no problem coming up with a long, complicated grammar that spun out news from Washington. The same can be said for soap operas or other distilled essences of life.

There are also deeper questions about what types of mathematical attacks can be made upon the grammars. Any attacker who wanted to recover the bits would need to know something about the grammar that was used to produce the sentences. This would be kept secret by both sides of the transmission. Figuring out the grammar that generated a particular set of sentences is not easy. The earlier ambiguous grammar example at the top of page 104 shows how five simple production rules can produce a number of sentences in two different ways. There are so many different possible grammars that could generate each sentence that it would be practically impossible to search through all of them.

Nor is it particularly feasible to reconstruct the grammar. Deciding where the words produced from one variable end and the words produced by another variable begin is a difficult task. You might be able to create such an inference when you find the same sentence type repeated again and again and again. These reasons don't guarantee the security of the system by any means. They just offer some intuition for why it might be hard to recover the bits hidden with a complicated grammar. Section 7.2.4, "Assessing the Theoretical Security of Mimicry", discusses some of the deeper reasons to believe in the security of the system.

The Alicebot project lets computers chatter in natural languages. Imagine if they were encoding information at the same time? See *www.alicebot.org.*

Section 7.2.3, "Scrambled Grammars", shows how to rearrange grammars for more security.

7.2

Creating Grammar-Based Mimicry

Producing software to do context-free mimicry is not complicated. You only need to have a basic understanding of how to parse text, generate some random numbers, and break up data into bit levels. Appendix A shows the Java code for a complete context-free grammar system that both encodes and decodes information.

There are a number of different details of the code that bear explaining. The best place to begin is the format for the grammar files. Figure 7.2 shows a scrap from the baseball context-free grammar that is described in full in Appendix B.

The variables begin with the asterisk character and must be one contiguous word. A better editor and parser combination would be able to distinguish between them and remove this restriction. Starting with a bogus character like the asterisk is the best compromise. Although it diminishes readability, it guarantees that there won't be any ambiguity.

A C version of the code is also available on the code disk. It is pretty much a straight conversion.

```
*WhapperOutfieldOut = He pops one up into deep left field./.1/
        He lifts it back toward the wall where it is caught
            by *BlogsOutfielder *period/.1/
        He knocks it into the glove of
            *BlogsOutfielder *period /.1/
        He gets a real piece of it and
            drives it toward the wall
            where it is almost ... Oh My God! ... saved by
            *BlogsOutfielder *period /.1/
        He pops it up to *BlogsOutfielder *period /.2//


*WeatherComment = Hmm . Do you think it will rain ? /.1/
    What are the chances of rain today ? /.1/
    Nice weather as long as it doesn't rain . /.1/
    Well, if rain breaks out it will
        certainly change things . /.1/
    You can really tell the mettle of a
        manager when rain is threatened . /.1//


*BlogsOutfielder = Orville Baskethands /.1/
                   Robert Liddlekopf /.1/
            Harrison "Harry" Hanihan /.1//
```

Figure 7.2   Three productions from the grammar in Appendix B encoded in the file format recognized by the code.

The list of productions that could emerge from each variable is separated by forward slashes. The pattern is *phrase / number/*. The final phrase for a variable has an extra slash after the last number. The number is a weighting given to the random choice maker. In this example, most of them are .1. The software simply adds up all of the weights for a particular variable and divides through by this total to normalize the choices.

The weightings aren't used randomly. If the choice of a particular phrase is going to encode information, then there must be a one-to-one connection between incoming bits and the output. The Huffman trees discussed in Section 6.1.1, "Choosing the Next Letter", are the best way to map a weighted selection of choices to incoming bits. So the weightings are used to build a tree. Figure 7.3 shows the tree built to hide information in the choice of the Blogs outfielder who makes a play. The same proof that shows that Huffman trees are the

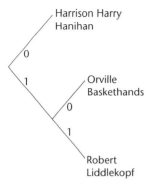

Harrison Harry
Hanihan

0

1

Orville
Baskethands

0

1

Robert
Liddlekopf

Figure 7.3 The Huffman tree used to hide information in the choice of the Blogs outfielder who makes a particular play.

optimal way to compress a file will show that this is the best way to encode information.

Naturally, the Huffman tree only approximates the desired statistical outcome, and the level of the approximation is limited to the powers of one-half. Figure 7.3 shows how badly the Huffman tree can be off the mark. One of the choices encodes one bit of information, and the other two each encode two. This means, effectively, that the first choice will be made 50 percent of the time and the other two will be chosen 25 percent of the time.

The level of inaccuracy decreases as more and more choices are available. For instance, it should be obvious that if a variable can be converted into 2^i different choices each with equal weighting, then the approximation will be perfect. This will also be the case if all of the weightings are powers of 2 and the total adds up to a power of 2—for instance, {1, 1, 2, 4, 2, 2, 4}.

7.2.1 Parsing the Output

The code in the class MimicParser handles the job of converting mimicry back into the bits that generated it. Parsing the output from a context-free grammar is a well-understood problem and is covered in depth in the computer science literature. The best parsers can convert any text from a grammar back into a sequence of productions that lead to the text. The most general parsing algorithms such as the CYK algorithm [HU79] are slow.

The parsing algorithm implemented in this code is a compromise. It will only work on grammars that are in a limited version of Greibach Normal Form. This form requires that any variables be placed at the end of each production. Page 104 shows some examples. The form required by this parser is even stricter because it requires that it be simple to determine which choice was taken by examining the first words of a production. This means that no two choices from the same variable may have the same first *n* words. The variable *n* is adjustable, but the larger it gets, the slower the algorithm can become.

This format makes parsing substantially easier because the parser only needs to look at the words and phrases. There is no need to follow the variables and make guesses. The best way to illustrate this is with a grammar that doesn't follow this rule. Here's a grammar that is *not* in the correct format:

Start	→	**noun verb**
noun	→	Fred **AndFriend** ‖ Fred **Alone**
AndFriend	→	and Barney went fishing **where** ‖
		and Barney went bowling **where**
Alone	→	went fishing **where** ‖
		went bowling **where**
where	→	in **direction state**
direction	→	northern ‖ southern
state	→	Iowa. ‖ Minnesota.

Imagine that you are confronted with the sentence "Fred and Barney went fishing in northern Iowa". This was produced by the bits/choices 0000. Parsing this sentence and recovering the bits is certainly possible, but it is not easy. The production "**noun** → Fred **AndFriend** ‖ Fred **Alone**" does not make it easy to determine which choice was taken. The terminal words at the beginning of each choice are the same. They both say "Fred". A parser would need to examine the results of expanding the variables **AndFriend** and **Alone** to determine which path was taken. Following these paths is feasible, but it slows down the algorithm and adds complexity to the result. Most serious parsers can handle this problem.

This implementation is lazy in this respect, but I don't think much is sacrificed. It is relatively easy to place grammars in the correct format. The grammar could be modified to read:

Start	→	**noun verb**
noun	→	Fred and Barney **what** ‖ Fred **what**
what	→	went fishing **where** ‖ went bowling **where**

where	→	in **direction state**
direction	→	northern ‖ southern
state	→	Iowa. ‖ Minnesota.

Any context-free grammar can be placed in Greibach Normal Form. It is also possible to arrange that grammar in Greibach Normal Form be expanded so there are no ambiguities. Alas, sometimes *n* needs to be made quite large to accomplish this. Another solution is to implement more complicated parsing algorithms.

7.2.2 Suggestions for Building Grammars

Creating a grammar that can be used to effectively turn data into innocuous text can be a time-consuming process if you want to do it well. More words and phrases mean more choices, and more choices mean that more data can be packed into place. The grammars that have long phrases and few choices can be pretty inefficient. Here are some suggestions:

David McKellar created one grammar that encodes messages in Spam-like phrases removed from his collection of Spam messages. You can see it in action at *www.spammimic.com*.

Think about the Plot and Narrative   The grammar for a baseball game voice-over in Appendix B is an excellent example of a genre that can successfully stand plenty of repeating. Such genres make the best choice for simple context-free grammars because the repeating effect saves you a lot of effort. You don't need to come up with production after production to make the system work. The same choices can be used over and over again.

There are other good areas to explore. Stock market analysis is generally context-free and filled with stream-of-consciousness ramblings about a set of numbers flowing throughout the world. No one can summarize why millions of people are buying and selling. Sports reporting usually amounts to coming up with different ways of saying "X smashed Y" or "X stopped Y". There is no reason why a more sophisticated version couldn't be built that would use actual news feeds to modify the grammars so the data was correct and filled with hidden bits.

There are other areas that are naturally plot-free. Modern poetry and free verse make excellent genres to exploit. People don't know what to expect, and a strange segue produced by a poorly designed grammar doesn't stand out as much. Plus, the human brain is very adept at finding patterns and meaning in random locations. People might actually be touched by the work produced by this.

Break Up Sentences   The more choices there are, the more data will be encoded. There is no reason why each sentence can't be broken up into productions for noun phrase, verb phrase, and object phrase. Many sentences begin with exclamations or exhortations. Make them vary.

Use Many Variations   More choices mean more data is hidden. There are many different ways to say the same thing. The same thoughts can be expressed in a thousand different forms. A good writer can tell the same story over and over again. Why stop at one simple sentence?

7.2.3   Scrambled Grammars

Creating a complicated grammar is not easy, so it would be ideal if this grammar could be used again and again. Naturally, there are problems when the same pattern is repeated in encryption. This gives the attacker another chance to search for similarities or patterns and crack the system. Most of the work in creating a grammar is capturing the right flavor of human communication. The actual arrangement of the words and phrases into products is not as important. For instance, several of the grammars above that generate sentences about Fred and Barney produce exactly the same collection of sentences even though the grammars are different. There are many different grammars that generate the same language, and there is no reason why the grammars can't be converted into different versions automatically.

There are three major transformations described here, expansion, contractions, and permutations.

Expansion   A variable in one production is expanded in all possible ways in another production. This is like distributing terms in algebra. For example,

$$
\begin{array}{rcl}
\textbf{noun} & \rightarrow & \text{Fred } \textbf{AndFriend} \parallel \text{Fred } \textbf{Alone} \\
\textbf{AndFriend} & \rightarrow & \text{and Barney went fishing } \textbf{where} \parallel \\
& & \text{and Barney went bowling } \textbf{where} \\
\textbf{Alone} & \rightarrow & \text{went fishing } \textbf{where} \parallel \text{went bowling } \textbf{where} \\
\vdots & \vdots & \vdots
\end{array}
$$

The first variable, **AndFriend**, is expanded by creating a new production for **noun** for all possible combinations. The production for AndFriend disappears from the grammar:

> **noun**   →   Fred and Barney went fishing **where** ‖
> Fred and Barney went bowling **where** ‖
> Fred **Alone**
> **Alone**   →   went fishing **where** ‖ went bowling **where**
> ⋮   ⋮   ⋮

Contractions   These are the opposite of expansions. If there is some pattern in several of the productions, it can be replaced by a new variable. For instance, the pattern "Fred and Barney" is found in two productions of **noun**:

> **noun**   →   Fred and Barney went fishing **where** ‖
> Fred and Barney went bowling **where** ‖
> Fred **Alone**
> **Alone**   →   went fishing **where** ‖ went bowling **where**
> ⋮   ⋮   ⋮

This can be contracted by introducing a new variable, **what**:

> **noun**   →   Fred and Barney **what where** ‖ Fred **Alone**
> **what**   →   went bowling ‖ went fishing
> **Alone**   →   went fishing **where** ‖ went bowling **where**
> ⋮   ⋮   ⋮

This new grammar is different from the one that began the expansion process. It produces the same sentences, but from different patterns of bits.

Permutation   The order of productions can be scrambled. This can change their position in any Huffman tree that is built. Or the scrambling can take place on the tree itself.

Any combination of expansion, contraction, and permutation will produce a new grammar that generates the same language. But this new language will produce the sentences from bits in a completely different manner. This increases security and makes it much less likely that any attacker will be able to infer coherent information about the grammar.

These expansions, contractions, and permutations can be driven by a pseudo-random number generator that is seeded by a key. One person on each end of the conversation could begin with the same large grammar and then synchronize their random number generators at both ends by typing in the session key. If this random number generator guided the process of expanding, contracting, and permuting the grammar, then the grammars on both ends of the conversation would stay the same. After a predetermined amount of change, the result could be frozen in place. Both sides will still have the same grammar, but it will now be substantially different from the starting grammar. If this is done each time, then the structure will be significantly different and attackers will have a more difficult time breaking the system.

Here are more careful definitions of expansion, contraction, and permutation. The context-free grammar is known as G, and the productions take the form $A_i \rightarrow \alpha_1 \| \alpha_2 \| \ldots \| \alpha_n$. The A_i are variables, and the α_j are the productions, which are a mixture of terminals and variables.

An expansion takes these steps:

1. Choose one production that contains variable A_i. It is of the form: $V \rightarrow \beta_1 A_i \beta_2$. V is a variable. β_1 and β_2 are strings of terminals and variables.

2. This A_i can be replaced by, say, n productions: $A_i \rightarrow \alpha_1 \| \alpha_2 \| \ldots \| \alpha_n$. Choose a subset of these productions and call it Δ. Call the set of productions not in Δ, $\bar{\Delta}$.

3. For each chosen production of A_i, add another production for V of the form $V \rightarrow \beta_1 \alpha_i \beta_2$.

4. If the entire set of productions is expanded (i.e., $\bar{\Delta}$ is empty), then delete the production $V \rightarrow \beta_1 A_i \beta_2$ from the set of productions for V. Otherwise, replace it with the production $V \rightarrow \beta_1 A_k \beta_2$ where A_k is a new variable introduced into the system with productions drawn from $\bar{\Delta}$. That is, $A_k \rightarrow \alpha_i$ for all α_i in $\bar{\Delta}$.

Notice that all productions don't have to be expanded. The effect on the size of the grammar is hard to predict. If the variable A_i has n productions and the variable itself is found in the right-hand side of m different productions for various other variables, then a complete expansion will create nm productions.

When I did him at this advantage take,
An ass's nole I fixed on his head:
Anon his Thisbe must be answered,
And forth my mimic comes.
    —Puck in William Shakespeare's *A Midsummer Night's Dream*

A contraction is accomplished with these steps:

1. Find some set of strings $\{\gamma_1 \ldots \gamma_n\}$ such that there exist productions of the form $V \to \beta_1 \gamma_i \beta_2$ for each γ_i. β_1 and β_2 are just collections of terminals and variables.

2. Create the new variable A_k.

3. Create the productions $A_k \to \gamma_i$ for each i.

4. Delete the productions $V \to \beta_1 \gamma_i \beta_2$ for each i and replace them with one production, $V \to \beta_1 A_k \beta_2$.

Notice that all possible productions don't have to be contracted. This can shorten the grammar significantly if it is applied successfully.

The expansion and contraction operations are powerful. If two grammars G_1 and G_2 generate the same language, then there is some combination of expansions and contractions that will convert G_1 into G_2. This is easy to see because the expansion operation can be repeated until there is nothing left to expand. The entire grammar consists of a start symbol and a production that takes the start symbol into a sentence from the language. It is all one variable and one production for every sentence in the language. There is a list of expansions that will convert both G_1 and G_2 into the same language. This list of expansions can be reversed by a set of contractions that inverts them. So to convert G_1 into G_2, simply expand G_1 fully and then apply the set of contractions that are the inverse of the expansions that would expand G_2. This proof would probably never be used in practice because the full expansion of a grammar can be quite large.

The most important effect of expansion and contraction is how it rearranges the relationships among the bits being encoded and the structure of the sentences. Here's a sample grammar:

noun	$\to$	Bob and Ray **verb** ‖ Fred and Barney **verb** ‖ Laverne and Shirley **verb** ‖ Thelma and Louise **verb**
verb	$\to$	went fishing **where** ‖ went shooting **where** ‖ went flying **where** ‖ went bungee-jumping **where**
where	$\to$	in Minnesota. ‖ in Timbuktu. ‖ in Katmandu. ‖ in Kalamazoo.

Each of these variables comes with four choices. If they're weighted equally, then we can encode two bits with each choice. Number them 00, 01, 10, and 11 in order. So hiding the bits 110100 produces the sentence "Thelma and Louise went shooting in Minnesota."

There is also a pattern here. Hiding the bits 010100 produces the sentence "Fred and Barney went shooting in Minnesota." The first two bits are directly related to the noun of the sentence, the second two bits to the verb, and the third two bits depend upon the location. Most people who create a grammar would follow a similar pattern because it conforms to our natural impression of the structure. This is dangerous because an attacker might be savvy enough to exploit this pattern. A sequence of expansions can fix this. Here is the grammar after several changes:

Figure 7.4 shows a way to convert 12 phrases into bits.

noun	→	Bob and Ray **verb2** ‖ Fred and Barney **verb4** ‖
		Laverne and Shirley **verb** ‖
		Thelma and Louise **verb3**‖
		Bob and Ray went fishing **where** ‖
		Bob and Ray went shooting **where** ‖
		Thelma and Louise went fishing **where** ‖
		Thelma and Louise went bungee-jumping **where** ‖
		Fred and Barney went shooting in Minnesota. ‖
		Fred and Barney went shooting in Timbuktu. ‖
		Fred and Barney went shooting in Katmandu. ‖
		Fred and Barney went shooting in Kalamazoo.
verb	→	went fishing **where** ‖
		went shooting **where** ‖ went flying **where** ‖
		went bungee-jumping in Minnesota. ‖
		went bungee-jumping in Timbuktu. ‖
		went bungee-jumping in Katmandu. ‖
		went bungee-jumping in Kalamazoo.
verb2	→	‖ went flying **where** ‖
		went bungee-jumping **where**
verb3	→	went shooting **where** ‖ went flying **where**
verb4	→	went fishing **where** ‖ went flying **where** ‖
		went bungee-jumping **where**
where	→	in Minnesota. ‖ in Timbuktu. ‖
		in Katmandu. ‖ in Kalamazoo.

The productions for the variable **noun** have been expanded in a number of different ways. Some have had the variable **verb** rolled

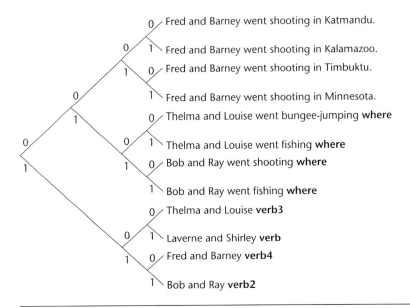

Figure 7.4   A Huffman tree that converts bits into productions for the variable **noun**.

into them completely, while others have only had a partial combination. There are now four different versions of the variable **verb** that were created to handle the productions that were not expanded.

The effect of the contractions is immediately apparent. Figure 7.4 shows the Huffman tree that converts bits into productions for the variable **noun**. The relationships among nouns, verbs, and locations and the bits that generated them are now much harder to detect. The first two bits no longer correspond to the noun.

Table 7.3 shows phrases and the bits that generated them.[2]

There are still some correlations between sentences. The first two sentences in Table 7.3 have different endings, and this is reflected in the last two bits. In fact, the first two bits seem to mean "Fred and Barney went shooting" and the last two bits choose the location. This pattern could easily be erased if the order of the productions were permuted. It could also be affected by any weighting given to the phrases.

---

[2]Some of the relationships between bits and the choice of production are left unexplained and for the reader to discover.

Table 7.3 Six sentences and the bits that built them. Figure 7.6 on page 121 shows a Huffman tree for this grammar.

Phrase	Bits
Fred and Barney went shooting in Katmandu.	0000
Fred and Barney went shooting in Minnesota.	0011
Fred and Barney went fishing in Minnesota.	110100
Fred and Barney went bungee-jumping in Minnesota.	1100100
Thelma and Louise went bungee-jumping in Minnesota.	010000
Thelma and Louise went flying in Timbuktu.	100101

But this same pattern does not hold for the other sentences. If the sentence begins "Fred and Barney went fishing" or if they go "bungee-jumping", then a different pattern holds. The location is determined by the choice that is made when the variable **where** is expanded. In this case, the relationship between the bits and the location is different. "Minnesota" is produced by the bits 00 in this case.

This illustrates clearly the effect that is the basis for all the security of this system. The meaning of the phrase "Minnesota" depends upon its context. In most cases it is generated by the bits 00, but in a few cases it emerges from the bits 11. This is somewhat ironic because the grammars are called "context-free". The term is correct, but the structure of the grammars can still affect the outcome.

The process of contraction can add even more confusion to the mixture. Here's the previous grammar after several contractions:

A deeper exploration of the system's security can be found in Section 7.2.4, "Assessing the Theoretical Security of Mimicry".

noun → Bob and Ray **verb2** ‖ Fred and Barney **verb4** ‖
Laverne and Shirley **verb** ‖
Thelma and Louise **verb3** ‖
who went fishing **where** ‖
Bob and Ray went shooting **where** ‖
Thelma and Louise went bungee-jumping **where** ‖
Fred and Barney went shooting in Minnesota. ‖
Fred and Barney went shooting in Timbuktu. ‖
Fred and Barney **verb5**

who → Bob and Ray ‖ Thelma and Louise

verb → went fishing **where** ‖
went shooting **where** ‖
went flying **where** ‖
went bungee-jumping in Minnesota. ‖
went bungee-jumping in Kalamazoo. ‖
went bungee-jumping **where2**

verb2	→	‖ went flying **where** ‖
		went bungee-jumping **where**
verb3	→	went shooting **where** ‖ went flying **where**
verb4	→	went fishing **where** ‖
		went flying **where** ‖
		went bungee-jumping **where**
verb5	→	went shooting in Katmandu. ‖
		went shooting in Kalamazoo.
where	→	in Minnesota. ‖ in Timbuktu. ‖
		in Katmandu. ‖ in Kalamazoo.
where2	→	in Timbuktu. ‖ in Katmandu.

Two new variables, **verb5** and **where2**, were introduced through a simple contraction. They will significantly change the relationship between the bits and the choice made for several sentences. Figure 7.5 shows new Huffman trees that are used to convert bits into the choice of productions for variables. Table 7.4 shows some sentences and the bits that produced them before and after the contractions.

Some of the relationships among the noun, verb, and location are still preserved, but some aspects are significantly changed. A series of expansions and contractions can scramble any grammar enough to destroy any of these relationships.

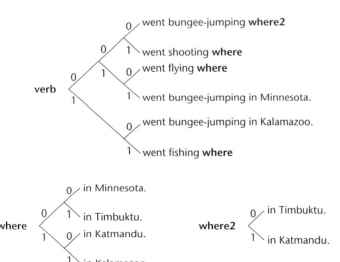

Figure 7.5 A Huffman tree that converts bits into productions for the variables **verb**, **where**, and **where2** from Table 7.3.

Table 7.4   Five sentences and the two different sets of bits that could produce them.

Phrase	Bits *before* Contractions	Bits *after* Contractions
Laverne and Shirley went bungee-jumping in Minnesota.	101100	101011
Laverne and Shirley went bungee-jumping in Timbuktu.	101101	1010000
Fred and Barney went shooting in Kalamazoo.	0001	01111
Fred and Barney went bungee-jumping in Minnesota.	1100100	1100100
Thelma and Louise went bungee-jumping in Minnesota.	010000	010000

A third new variable, **who**, was also introduced through contraction, but it created a production that was not in Greibach Normal Form (**noun** → **who** went fishing **where**).

This would not work with the parser in the implementation shown in Appendix A, but it could work fine with a better parser. The grammar is still not ambiguous. This example was only included to show that the expansions and contractions can work around grammars that are not in Greibach Normal Form.

One interesting question is what order the bits are applied to the production in this case. The previous examples in Greibach Normal Form used the rule that the leftmost variable is always expanded in turn. This rule works well here, but it leads to an interesting rearrangement. In the GNF examples, the first part of the sentence was always related to the first bits. In this case, this fails. Table 7.5 shows the steps assuming the leftmost rule.

There is no reason why the sequence of productions needs to be related with a leftmost first rule. A general parsing algorithm would be able to discover the three different choices made in the creation of this sentence. The GNF-limited parser could not handle this. The

Table 7.5   Leftmost production.

Starting	Bits of Choice	Produces
noun	0010	**who** went fishing **where**
who went fishing **where**	0	Bob and Ray went fishing **where**
Bob and Ray went fishing **where**	11	Bob and Ray went fishing in Kalamazoo.

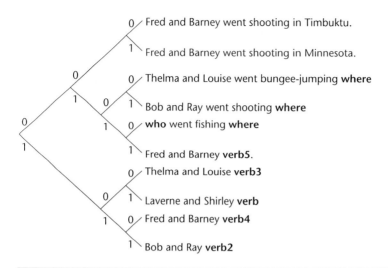

Figure 7.6 A Huffman tree that converts bits into productions for the variable **noun** from Table 7.3.

productions could be arranged in any predefined order that is used by both ends of the communications link. So the sentence "Bob and Ray went fishing in Kalamazoo" could be said to be generated by any of the six combinations 0010011, 0010110, 0001011, 0110010, 1100010, or 1100100.

This last section on expansions and contractions has ignored the feature that allows a user to weight the choices according to some predetermined agenda. These weights can be carried accurately throughout the expansion and contraction process. If there is an expansion, the terms are multipled through. If there is a contraction, they are gathered. Here's an example of expansion. The weightings are shown as variables in parentheses.

Before:

$$\textbf{noun} \quad \rightarrow \quad \text{Thelma and Louise \textbf{what} } (a_1) \;\|$$
$$\text{Harry and Louise \textbf{what} } (a_2)$$
$$\textbf{what} \quad \rightarrow \quad \text{went shooting. } (a_3) \;\| \text{ went to the hospital. } (a_4)$$

Before expansion:

$$\textbf{noun} \quad \rightarrow \quad \text{Thelma and Louise \textbf{what} } (a_1) \;\|$$
$$\text{Harry and Louise went shooting. } (\tfrac{a_2 a_3}{a_3 + a_4}) \;\|$$
$$\text{Harry and Louise went to the hospital. } (\tfrac{a_2 a_4}{a_3 + a_4})$$
$$\textbf{what} \quad \rightarrow \quad \text{went shooting. } (a_3) \;\| \text{ went to the hospital. } (a_4)$$

Here's the same example reworked for contraction.
Before:

> **noun** $\rightarrow$ Thelma and Louise **what** (a_1) ‖
> Harry and Louise went shooting. (a_2) ‖
> Harry and Louise went to the hospital. (a_3)
>
> **what** $\rightarrow$ went rowing. (a_4) ‖
> went fishing. (a_5)

After contraction:

> **noun** $\rightarrow$ Thelma and Louise **what** (a_1) ‖
> Harry and Louise **what2** $(a_2 + a_3)$
>
> **what** $\rightarrow$ went rowing. (a_4) ‖
> went fishing. (a_5)
>
> **what2** $\rightarrow$ went shooting. $(\frac{a_2}{a_2 + a_3})$ ‖
> went to the hospital. $(\frac{a_3}{a_2 + a_3})$

These rules can be expanded arbitrarily to handle all expansions and contractions. Weightings like this can significantly affect the way that bits are converted into phrases using Huffman trees. The trees only work perfectly if the weights are structured correctly, so it is highly likely that most trees will produce imperfect approximations of the weights. As the expansions and contractions change the tree structure, the weights will significantly alter the patterns produced.

7.2.4   Assessing the Theoretical Security of Mimicry

The principal difficulty of your case lay in the fact of there being too much evidence. What was vital was overlaid and hidden by what was irrelevant.

—Arthur Conan Doyle in *The Naval Treaty*

Determining the strength of mimic functions based upon context-free grammars is not an easy task. There are two basic approaches, and both can leave you with doubt. The first is to analyze the structure of the system on a theoretical level and use this to compare it to other systems. This might indicate that it can often be quite hard to break through the mimicry in these systems, but it can't prove to you that there are no holes out there. You just know that in the past, others have tried to break similar systems and failed. This is good news, but it is not conclusive. There might be new holes that are easy to exploit in these grammar-based mimic functions that are hard to use in other systems.

Holes are fairly common in theoretical approaches. For instance, there are very few proofs that show how hard it is to solve some mathematical problems. Sorting numbers is one of the few examples. It has been shown that if you have a list of n numbers, then it takes time proportional to $cn \log n$ where c is some machine-based constant [AHU83]. This is a nice result, but it wouldn't make a good theoretical basis for a cryptographically secure system. There are other algorithms for sorting that can succeed in time proportional to kn where k is a different machine-based constant. These algorithms work only if you can place absolute bounds on the size of the numbers before beginning (64 bits is usually enough).

The other approach is to create different attacks against the system and see if it is strong enough to withstand them. This can certainly show the strength of the system, but likewise it can never be conclusive. There is no way to be sure that you've tried all possible attacks. You can be thorough, but you can't be complete.

Still, probing the limits of grammar-based mimic functions is an important task. The best theoretical bounds that exist are based on work exploring the limits of computers that try to learn. In this area, many researchers have based their work on Les Valient's PAC model from probabilistic learning [Val84]. In it, a computer is given some examples from a particular class and it must try to learn as much as possible about the class so it can decide whether a new example is part of the class. The computer's success is measured probabilistically, and it succeeds if it starts getting more right than wrong.

There are many different forms of PAC algorithms. In some, the computer is given examples that are just in the class. In others, the computer gets examples from within and without the class. Sometimes, the computer can even concoct examples and ask whether that example is in or out of the class. This type of algorithm has the potential to be the most powerful, and so it helps if the theoretical bounds can defend against it.

Michael Kearns and Les Valient show [KV89, Kea89] that "learning" boolean formulas, finite automata, or constant-depth threshold circuits is at least as difficult as inverting RSA encryption or factoring Blum integers (x, such that $x = pq$, p, q are prime, and $p, q = 3 \bmod 4$). The proof shows this by casting the factoring process into each of these different models of computation.

Dana Angluin and Michael Kharitonov [AK91] extended the work of Kearns and Valient as well as the work of Moni Naor and M. Yung [NY89, NY90]. This work shows that there are no known algorithms that run in polynomial time that predict membership in a class defined by finite unions or intersections of finite automata or context-free grammars.

These bounds deal with learning to predict whether a sentence is in a class defined by a grammar, not to discover its parse tree. But the results can apply to the grammar-based system here if there is some way that a parse-tree-discovering algorithm can be used to predict membership.

Imagine such an algorithm existed. Here is how to apply it to predicting membership in some language defined by grammar G_1 known as $L(G_1)$. The start symbol for G_1 is S_1. Now, suppose there is another grammar G_2 with start symbol S_2. Create a new grammar, G, that is the union of G_1 and G_2 by creating a new start symbol, S, and the production $S \rightarrow S_1 \| S_2$. Take a set of strings $a_i \in L(G)$. They are either in $L(G_1)$ or $L(G_2)$. Apply the algorithm that can learn to predict parse trees and feed it this set of strings. If such an algorithm can learn to predict the parse tree grammar, then it can predict whether a string is in $L(G_1)$. If such an algorithm runs in polynomial time, then it can be used to break RSA, factor Blum integers, and solve other problems. Therefore, there is no known algorithm to predict even the first branch of a parse tree.

This result applies to the hardest grammars that might exist. It does not offer any clues on how to actually produce such a grammar. An algorithm that could construct such a grammar and guarantee that it was hard to discover would be quite a find. There are some minor observations, however, that can be satisfying.

You can easily imagine a grammar that would be easy to break. If each word or substring was visible in one production, then it would be relatively easy to isolate the string of productions that produced a long section of text. The boundaries of the productions are simple to establish by accumulating enough sample text so that each production is used twice. The two occurrences can be compared to reveal the different parts of the production.

This leads to the observation that each word should appear in multiple productions. Section 7.2.3, "Scrambled Grammars", describes how contractions and expansions can be applied automatically to change grammars so they fit this requirement.

How much contraction and expansion is enough? [Way95] gives one set of equations that can be used to measure the "randomness" or "entropy" of a grammar. The equations are modeled on Shannon's measure of entropy of a bit stream. If one word is quite likely to follow another, then there is not much information bound in it. If many words are likely, then there is plenty of information bound in this choice.

The equations measure the entropy of the entire language generated by a grammar. If the number is large, then the information capacity of the grammar is also large and a great deal of information should be able to be transmitted before significant repetition occurs. This practical approach can give a good estimate of the strength of a grammar.

Both of these approaches show that it can be quite difficult to discover the grammar that generated a text. They do not guarantee security, but they show that discovery may be difficult to achieve in all cases. It can be even more difficult if the grammar is modified in the process through expansions and contractions. These can be chosen by both sides of a channel in a synchronized way by agreeing upon a cryptographically secure pseudo-random number generator.

7.2.5 Efficient Mimicry-Based Codes

The one problem with the mimicry system described in this chapter is that it is inefficient. Even very complicated grammars will easily double, triple, or quadruple the size of a file by converting it into text. Less complicated grammars could easily produce output that is ten times larger than the input. This may be the price that must be paid to achieve something that looks nice, but there may be other uses for the algorithm if it is really secure.

Efficient encryption algorithms using the techniques of this chapter are certainly possible. The results look like ordinary binary data, not spoken text, but they do not increase the size of a file. The key is just to build a large grammar. Here's an example:

- *Terminals.* Let there be 256 terminal characters, that is, the values of a byte between 0 and 255. Call these $\{t_0 \ldots t_{255}\}$.

- *Variables.* Let there be n variables, $\{v_0 \ldots v_n\}$. Each variable has 256 productions.

- *Productions.* Each variable has 256 productions of the form $v_i \rightarrow t_j v_{a_1} \ldots v_{a_k}$. That is, each variable will be converted into a single terminal and k variables. Some productions will have no variables and some will have many. Each terminal will appear on the right side of only one production for a particular variable. This ensures that parsing is simple.

This grammar will not increase the size of the file when it is encoded. Each variable has 256 different productions available to it, so 8 bits are consumed in the process of making the choice. The result is one new terminal added to the stream, and this terminal takes 8 bits to store.

There are potential problems with this system. The biggest one is ensuring that the average string of terminals in the language is finite. If there are too many variables on the right-hand side of the productions, then the generating process could never end. The stack of pending variables would continue to grow with each production. The solution is to make sure that the average number of variables on the right-hand side of the production is less than one. There is a direct relationship between the average number of variables and the average length of the phrases in the language defined by the grammar. A smaller number of average variables means shorter phrases. As the average number of variables approaches one, the average length tends toward infinity.[3]

The average length of a phrase in the language is not as important in this particular example. The bits can be recovered easily here because the grammar is in Greibach Normal Form and there is no need to place parsing decisions on hold. Each terminal only appears on the right-hand side of one production per variable. So, the final file does not need to be a complete phrase produced by the grammar. It could be just a partial one. There is no reason why the grammars need to be as easy to parse, but more complicated grammars need to have the entire phrase produced from the starting symbol.

7.3

Summary

This chapter has described simple ways to produce very realistic texts by using a system of rules defined by a human. There is no reason why complicated grammars can't hide large volumes of data in seemingly human babble. This babble could be posted to some Internet newsgroup, and it would be hard to tell the difference between this and the random flames and cascading comments that float through the linguistic ether.

---

[3]This might be modeled with queuing theory.

There are still other levels of abstraction that are possible. MUDs (Multiple-User Dungeons) allow users to meet up in a text-based world defined and built up by textual architects. It is possible to meet people in MUD rooms and hold conversations in the same way that you might ordinarily talk. Some MUDs now sport computer programs that pretend to be human in the spirit of the great Eliza [Wei76]. These programs use complicated grammars to guide the response of the computer. There is no reason why the random choices that might be made by this computer can't be converted to holding data.

Here's an extreme example. You want to set up a conversation with a friend across the country. Ordinarily, you might use the basic talk protocol to set up a text-based link. Or you might use one of the Internet phone programs to exchange sound. In either case, the bits you're exchanging could be monitored.

What if your talk program didn't contact the other person directly? Instead, it would log into a MUD somewhere on the Net as a persona. The other person's talk program could do the same thing and head for the same room. For the sake of atmosphere, let's make it a smoke-filled room with leather chairs so overstuffed that our textual personae get lost in them. There are overstuffed mastodons on the wall to complement the chairs.

Instead of handing your word bits over directly to the other person's persona, your talk program would encode them into something innocuous like a discussion about last night's baseball game. It might be smart enough to access the on-line database to get an actual scorecard to ensure that the discussion was accurate. When the other person responded, his talk program would encode the data with a similar grammar. The real conversation might be about very private matters, but it might come out sounding like baseball to anyone who happened to be eavesdropping on the wires.

There is no reason why both sides of the conversation can't use the same grammar. This convention would make it possible for both sides to hold a coherent conversation. After one persona commented about the hitting of Joe Swatsem, the other could say something about Swatsem because the same grammar would control what came afterward.

The entire system is just an automated version of the old gangster-movie conceit about talking in code. One gangster says, "Hey, has the shipment of tomatoes arrived yet?" The other responds, "Yes. It will cost you 10,000 bananas." The potentials are amazing.

The sun's a thief, and with his great attraction
Robs the vast sea: the moon's an arrant thief,
And her pale fire she snatches from the sun:
The sea's a thief, whose liquid surge resolves
The moon into salt tears. . .

—William Shakespeare in *Timons of Athens*

- *The Disguise.* Grammar-based mimicry can be quite realistic. The only limitation is the amount of time that someone puts into creating the grammar.

- *How Secure Is It?* At its best, the grammar-based system here can be as hard to break as RSA. This assessment, though, doesn't mean that you can achieve this security with the same ease as you can with RSA. There is no strong model for what is a good key. Nor has there been any extensive work trying to break the system.

- *How to Use It?* The code for the mimic system is in Appendix A. Or you can just go to *www.spammimic.com* if you want your message to look like Spam.

- *Further Work.* There are a number of avenues to pursue in this arena. A theory that gave stronger estimates of the brute force necessary to recognize a language would be nice. It would be good to have a strong estimate of just how many strings from a language must be uncovered before someone can begin to make sense of it. If someone could program the entropy estimates from [Way95] or come up with better ones, then we could experiment with them and try to see how well they assess the difficulty of attack.

  It would also be nice to have an automatic way of scanning texts and creating a grammar that could be used by the system here. There are many basic constructs from language that are used again and again. If something could be distilled from the raw feed on the Net, then it could be pushed directly into a program that could send out messages. This could truly lead to automated broadcast systems. One part would scan newsgroups or the Net for source text that could lead to grammars. The other would broadcast messages using them. I imagine that it could lead to some truly bizarre AI experiences. One could set up two machines that babble to each other mimicking the Net but really exchanging valuable information.

chapter eight

Turing and Reverse

Doggie's Little Get Along

One weekend I messed with the guts of my jukebox.
I wanted to zip it up to tweet like a bird
When the wires got crossed and the records spun backward
And this is the happy voice that I heard:

Whoopee Tie Yi Yay,
    The world's getting better and your love's getting strong
Whoopee Tie Yi Yay,
    Your lame dog will walk by the end of this song.

The music was eerie, sublime, and surreal,
But there was no walrus or devil.
The notes rang wonderfully crystalline clear
Telling us that it was all on the level:

Whoopee Tie Yi Yay
    This weekend your sixty-foot yacht will be floated.
Whoopee Tie Yi Yay
    The boss just called to tell you, "You're promoted."

So after a moment I began to start thinking
What if I rewired the touch tone?
After a second of cutting and splicing, it suddenly rang.
This was the voice that came from the phone:

Whoopee Tie Yi Yay
    This is the Publisher's Clearinghouse to tell you you've won
Whoopee Ti Yi Yay
    A new car, an acre of dollars, and a house in the sun.

A few minutes later my lost sweetheart called:
The guy she ran off with wasn't worth Jack.
He wore a toupee and the truck was his mother's.
Now she could only beg for me back.

Whoopee Tie Yi Yay
    Why spend your grief on a future that's wrecked
Whoopee Tie Yi Yay
    Why look backward when hindsight is always so perfect.

8.1

Running Backward

The song that introduces this chapter is all about what happens to a man when he finds a way to play the country music on his jukebox backward. His dog walks, his girlfriend returns, and the money rolls in. The goal of this chapter is to build a machine that hides data as it runs forward. Running it in reverse allows you to recover the data. The main advantage of using such a machine is that there are some theoretical proofs that show that this machine can't be attacked by a computer. These theoretical estimates of the strength of the system are not necessarily reliable for practical purposes, but they illustrate a very interesting potential.

Chapter 7 describes how to use grammars to hide data in realistic-sounding text. The system derives its strength from the structure of the grammars and their ability to produce many different sentences from a simple collection of inputs. The weaknesses of the system are also fairly apparent. Grammars that are context-free cannot really keep track of scores of ballgames or other more complicated topics. They just produce sentences without any care about the context. A bit of cleverness can go a long way, but anyone who has tried to create complicated grammars begins to understand the limitations of the model.

This chapter concentrates on a more robust and complete model known as the *Turing machine*. The concept was named after Alan Turing, who created the model in the 1930s as a vehicle for exploring some of the limits of computation. Although the model doesn't offer a good way to whip up some good mimicry, it does offer a deeper theoretical look at just how hard it may be to break the system.

A good way to understand the limitations of the context-free grammars is to examine the type of machine necessary to recognize them. The parser constructed in Appendix A for recovering the data from the mimicry is also known, at least theoretically, as *push-down automata*. The "automata" refers to a mechanism that is simply a nest of if-then and goto statements. The "push-down" refers to the type of memory available to it—in this case a push-down stack that can store information by pushing it onto a stack of data and retrieve it by pulling it off. Many people compare this to the dishracks that are found in cafeterias. Dishes are stored in a spring-loaded stack. The major limitation of this type of memory is the order. Bits of information can only be recalled from the stack in the reverse order in which they were put onto the stack. There is no way to dig deeper.

It is possible to offer you solid proof that push-down automata are the ideal computational model for describing the behavior of context-free grammars, but that solution is a bit dry. A better approach is to illustrate it with a grammar:

You can find a good proof in [AHU83].

start	→	Thelma and Louise **what when** ‖ Harry and Louise **what when**
what	→	went shooting **with where** ‖ bought insurance **with where**
with	→	with Bob and Ray ‖ with Laverne and Shirley
when	→	on Monday. ‖ on Tuesday. ‖ on Wednesday. — on Thursday.
where	→	in Kansas ‖ in Canada

A typical sentence produced by this grammar might be "Thelma and Louise went shooting with Bob and Ray in Kansas on Monday". This was produced by making the first choice of production from each variable and thus hiding the six bits 000000. But when the first choice was made and Thelma and Louise became the subjects of the sentence, the question about the date needed to be stored away until it was needed later. You can either think of the sentence as developing the leftmost variable first or you can think of it as choosing the topmost variable from the stack. Table 8.1 shows how a sentence was produced. It illustrates both ways of thinking about it.

Both metaphors turn out to be quite close to each other. The context-free grammars and the stack-based machines for interpreting them are equivalent. This also illustrates why it is possible to imitate certain details about a baseball game such as the number of outs or the number of strikes, while it is much harder if not impossible to give a good imitation of the score. There is no way to rearrange the information on the stack or to recognize it out of turn.

Table 8.1   Producing a sentence.

Stack	Pending Sentence	Pending with Variables
start		**noun**
what **when**	Thelma and Louise	Thelma and Louise **what** **when**
with **where** **when**	Thelma and Louise went shooting	Thelma and Louise went shooting **with where**
where **when**	Thelma and Louise went shooting with Bob and Ray	Thelma and Louise went shooting with Bob and Ray **where when**
when	Thelma and Louise went shooting with Bob and Ray in Kansas	Thelma and Louise went shooting with Bob and Ray in Kansas **when**
empty	Thelma and Louise went shooting with Bob and Ray in Kansas on Monday.	Thelma and Louise went shooting with Bob and Ray in Kansas on Monday.

The Turing machine is about as general a model of a computer as can be constructed. Unlike push-down automata, a Turing machine can access any part of its memory at any time. In most models, this is described as a "tape" that is read by a head that can scan from left to right. You can also simply think of the "tape" as regular computer memory that has the address 0 for the first byte, the address 1 for the second byte, and so on.

The main advantage of using a Turing machine is that you can access any part of the memory at any time. So you might store the score to the baseball game at the bytes of memory with addresses 10140 and 10142. Whenever you needed this, you could copy the score to the output. This method does not offer any particularly great programming models that would make it easier for people to construct a working Turing mimicry generator. Alas.

The real reason for exploring Turing machines is that there is a wide variety of theoretical results that suggest there are limits on how Turing machines can be analyzed. Alan Turing originally developed the models to explore the limits of what computers can and can't do [Tur36a, Tur36b]. His greatest results showed how little computers could do when they were turned against themselves. There is very little that computers and the programs they run can tell us definitively about another computer program.

These results are quite similar to the work of Kurt Gödel who originally did very similar work on logical systems. His famous theorem showed that all logical systems were either incomplete or inconsistent. The result had little serious effect upon mathematics itself because people were quite content to work with incomplete systems of logic. They did the job. But the results eroded the modernist belief that technology could make the world perfect.

Turing found that the same results that applied to Gödel's logical systems could apply to computers and the programs that ran upon them. He showed that, for instance, no computer program could definitively answer whether another computer program would ever finish. It might be able to find the correct answer for some subset of computer programs, but it could never get the right answer for all computer programs. The program was either incomplete or inconsistent.

Others have extended Turing's results to show that it is practically impossible to ask the machines to say anything definitive about computers at all. Rice's Theorem showed that computers can only answer *trivial* questions about other computers [HU79]. Trivial questions were defined to be those that were either always true or always false.

To some extent, these results are only interesting on a theoretical level. After all, a Macintosh computer can examine a computer program written for an IBM PC and determine that it can't execute it. Most of the time, a word processor might look at a document and determine that it is in the wrong format. Most of the time, computers on the Internet can try to establish a connection with other computers on the Internet and determine whether the other computer is speaking the right language. For many practical purposes, computers can do most things we tell them to do.

The operative qualifier here is "most of the time." Everyone knows how imperfect and fragile software can be. The problems caused by the literal machines are legendary. They do what they're told to do, and it is often incomplete or imperfect—just as the theoretical model predicted it would be.

The matter for us is compounded by the fact that this application is not as straightforward as opening up word-processing documents. The goal is to hide information so it can't be found. There is no cooperation between the information protector and the attacker trying to puncture the veil of secrecy. A better model is the world of computer viruses. Here, one person is creating a computer program that will make its way through the world, and someone else is trying to write an anti-virus program that will stop a virus. The standard virus-scanning programs built today look for telltale strings of commands

Abraham Lincoln was really the first person to articulate this concept when he told the world, "You can fool some of the people all of the time and all of the people some of the time. But you can't fool all of the people all of the time." The same holds true if you substitute "computer program" or "Turing machine" for "people."

Can you abort a virus? Can you baptize one? How smart must a virus be?

that are part of the virus. If the string is found, then the virus must be there. This type of detection program is easy to write and easy to keep up-to-date. Every time a new virus is discovered, a new telltale string is added to the list.

But more adept viruses are afoot. There are many similar strings of commands that will do a virus's job. A virus could possibly choose any combination of these commands that are structured correctly. What if a virus would scramble itself with each new version? What if a virus carried a context-free grammar of commands that would produce valid viruses? Every time it copied itself into a new computer or program, it would spew out a new version of itself using the grammar as its copy. Detecting viruses like this is a much more difficult proposition.

You couldn't simply scan for sequences of commands because the sequences are different with each version of the virus. You need to build a more general model of what a virus is and how it accomplishes its job before you can continue. If you get a complete copy of the context-free grammar that is carried along by a virus, you might create a parser that would parse each file and look for something that came from this grammar. If it was found, then a virus is identified. This might work sometimes, but what if the virus modified the grammar in the same way that the grammars were expanded and contracted in Section 7.2.3? The possibilities are endless.

The goal for this chapter is to capture the same theoretical impossibility that gives Turing machines their ability to resist attacks by creating a cipher system that isn't just a cipher. It's a computing machine that runs forward and backward. The data is hidden as it runs forward and revealed as it runs backward. If this machine is as powerful as a Turing machine, then there is at least the theoretical possibility that the information will never be revealed. Building another computer that could attack all possible machines by reversing them could never work in all cases.

8.1.1   Reversing Gears

Many computer scientists have been studying reversible computers for some time, but not for the purpose of hiding information. The reversible machines have a thermodynamic loophole that implies that they might become quite useful as CPUs become more and more powerful. Ordinary electronic circuits waste some energy every time they make a decision, but reversible computers don't. This wasted energy leaves a normal chip as heat, which is why the newest and

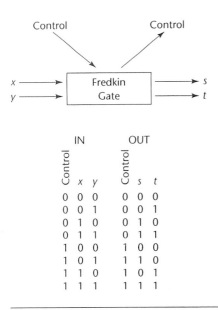

Figure 8.1 An illustration of a Fredkin gate. If the control line is on, then the output lines are switched. Otherwise, they're left alone. (After [BL85].)

fastest CPUs come with their own heat-conducting fins attached to the top. Some of the fastest machines are cooled by liquid coolants that can suck away even more heat. The buildup of waste heat is a serious problem—if it isn't removed, the CPU fails.

The original work on reversible computers was very theoretical and hypothetical. Ed Fredkin [Fre82] offered a type of logic gate that would not expend energy. Normal gates that take the AND of two bits are not reversible. For instance, if x AND y is 1, then both x and y can be recovered because both must have been 1. But if x AND y is 0, then nothing concrete is known about either x or y. Either x or y might have been a 1. This makes it impossible to run such a normal gate in reverse.

The Fredkin gate, on the other hand, does not discard information so it can be reversed. Figure 8.1 shows such a gate and the logic table that drives it. There are three lines going in and three lines leaving. One of the incoming lines is a control line. If it is on, then the other two lines are swapped. If it is off, then the other lines are reversed. This gate can be run in reverse because there is only one possible input for each output.

Figure 8.2 shows an AND gate built out of a Fredkin gate. One of the two input lines from a normal AND gate is used as the control

The *Scientific American* article by Charles Bennett and Rolf Landauer makes a good introduction to reversible machines [BL85].

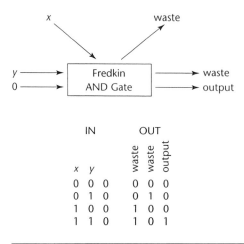

Figure 8.2   An AND gate built out of a Fredkin gate. The extra waste bits must be stored at the gate so that computation can be reversed later. (After [BL85].)

line. Only one of the output lines is needed to give us the answer. The other two bits are wasted. Ordinarily, the information here would be thrown away by sending the bits to ground where they would heat up the chip. A truly reversible machine would store the bits at this location until the computer was run in reverse. Then the gate would have all of the information ready to compute the inverse. An OR gate would be built in the same way, but it would have one input fixed to be a 1.

There are many other mechanical approaches to building a reversible computer. Ed Fredkin and Tommaso Toffoli developed a billiard-ball computer that could be made to run in reverse *if* a suitable table could be found [FT82]. It would need to be perfectly smooth so the balls would move in synchrony. The table itself must be frictionless, and the bumpers would need to return all of the energy to the balls so that nothing would be lost and there would be just as much kinetic energy at the beginning of the computation as at the end.

Figure 8.3 shows how two billiard balls can build an AND gate. The presence of a ball is considered to be the *on* state. So if both balls are there, they will bounce off each other. Only one ball will continue on its way. If the balls reach the end of the computation, then they can bounce off a final wall and make their way back. It should be easy to see that this gate will work both forward and backward. OR gates are more complicated and include extra walls to steer the balls.

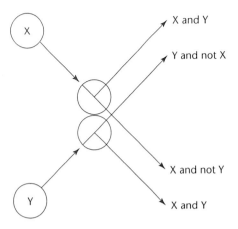

X and Y

Y and not X

X and not Y

X and Y

Figure 8.3 The three possible outcomes of a billiard-ball AND gate. The presence of a ball indicates an *on* signal. If only one ball is present, then no bounce occurs and it continues on its way. If both are present, then they bounce off each other. If none are present, then nothing happens. (After [BL85].)

This is an interesting concept, but it is hardly useful. No one can build such a frictionless material. If they could, it might be years before we got to actually trying to use it to compute. (There would be too many other interesting things to do like watching people play hockey on it.) More practical implementations, however, use cellular automata that came before and after it. Toffoli described reversible cellular automata in his Ph.D. thesis [Tof77a] and in other subsequent articles [Tof77b, TM87]. N. Margolus offers one solution in [Mar84] that implements the billiard-ball models.

The key result about reversible computers is due to Charles Bennett, who showed that any computation can be done with a reversible Turing machine [BL85]. He has created a few basic examples of reversible Turing machines with well-defined commands for moving the read/write head of the tape and changing the state of the machine. The transition rules for these machines often look quite similar to the Fredkin gate. There is just as much information coming out of each step as going into it. This is balanced correctly so the position that leads to another position can always be inferred and the machine can be reversed.

This result shows that anything that can be done with a computer can be done with a reversible computer. All that is necessary is to find a way to save the information from each step so it can be effectively run in reverse. But what does this mean if you want to

David Hillman has written about reversible one-dimensional cellular automata [Hil91].

Reversible computation is also *great* for debugging programs.

hide information? It means that any computation can be used to hide information in the final outcome. How much can be stored? It all depends upon the calculation. Ordinarily, any random number generator that is used to add realism or scramble the outcome of a game can be replaced by a collection of data to be hidden. This data can be recovered as the machine runs in reverse.

How would such a system work? One obvious solution is to simply create a universal, reversible Turing machine format. A standard program running on everyone's computer would be able to read in a Turing machine and run it forward or backward. If you wanted to send a message, you would pack in the data and run the machine until it stopped. The result would be the output, perhaps some computer-generated poetry, and a pile of waste data that must be kept around in order to run the machine in reverse.

At the other end, the recipient would load this information into the same universal, reversible Turing machine and run it backward to recover the data. The one problem with this scenario is that any attacker could also have the same universal, reversible Turing machine. They could intercept the message and reverse it. For the technique to be successful, some data must be kept secret from the attacker. This could travel separately. In the grammar machine from Chapter 7, the grammar acts as the key. It must be distributed separately.

One solution is to keep the structure of the Turing machine (i.e., the program) secret and let it act as a key. Only the output and the extra, "waste" bits of information must be transmitted to the recipient. Anyone can intercept the message, but they cannot read it without a copy of the program that created it.

How difficult can this be? Obviously, there will be some programs that are pretty easy to crack. For instance, a program that merely copies the data to be hidden and spits it out would be easy to deduce. The output would maintain all of the structure of the original document. More and more complicated programs would get more and more complicated to deduce. Eventually, something must be too hard to crack. The tough question is whether there is some threshold that can be established where it is positively known that programs that are beyond this threshold are completely safe.

Such a threshold can never be well defined. That is, there can be no neat machine that will examine any program and say, "This can't be broken." There might be machines that could point out flaws in programs and show how they could be broken, but these machines would not be guaranteed to find all flaws.

This uncertainty is a pain, but it affects the enemy in the same way. The enemy cannot come up with an arbitrary machine that will be able to examine every message you send and discover the program that was used to hide the data. It may be able to find some solutions, but there will be no brute-force attack that will work in all cases.

This is a nice beginning for security, but it is not absolute. The one-time pad offers a similar security blanket. There is no brute-force attack that will break the system, as long as the key bits are completely random. What is completely random? In practice, it means that the attacker can't build a machine that will predict the pattern of the bits. This is substantially easier to achieve for one-time pads than it is for reversible Turing machines. There are numerous sources of completely random information and noise that can be used as the basis for a one-time pad. At the time of this writing, many Macintoshes come with built-in television tuners. The random snow from a blank channel can make the good beginning for such a pad.

The rest of this chapter will concentrate on actually constructing a reversible Turing machine that could be used to create hidden messages in text. It will be based, in part, on the grammar approach from Chapter 7 because text is a good end product for the process. There is no reason why the work couldn't be adapted to produce other mimicry.

8.2

Building a Reversible Machine

If every Turing machine can be reconstructed in a reversible manner, then every possible machine is a candidate for being turned into a vehicle for hidden information. Obviously, though, some machines are more interesting than others. For instance, there are computer programs that loan companies use to evaluate the credit of applicants. These programs respond with either "qualified" or "unqualified". That's just one bit of information, and it seems unlikely that anyone will be able to hide much of anything in that bit. On the other hand, programs that produce complex worlds for games like Doom spit out billions of bits. There is ample room in the noise. Imagine if some secret information was encoded in the dance of an attacking droid. You might get your signal by joining into an Internet group game of Doom. The information would come across the wire disguised as instructions for where to draw the attacker on the screen. Your version of Doom could extract this.

Reversible machines can be made error-resistant. Peter Neumann discusses how to insert synchronization symbols into the text stream to stop the propagation of errors [Neu64].

This chapter will show how to build two different reversible machines. The first is just a simple reversible Turing machine that is provided as a warm-up. It is based on the work of Charles Bennett, and it shows how to take the standard features of a Turing machine and tweak them so that there is only one possible state that could lead to another. This makes it possible to rewind the behavior.

The second machine is an extension of the grammar-based mimicry from Chapter 7. That system used only context-free grammars. This is intended to make it possible to simulate any arbitrary computation to add realism to the text that the system produces. The data hidden by the system won't be recovered by parsing. It will come by running the machine in reverse. This means that a practical way needs to be constructed to ship the extra variables and "waste" bits along.

8.2.1 Reversible Turing Machines

An ordinary Turing machine consists of a set of states, S, a set of symbols that can appear on the tape, Σ, and a set of transition rules, δ, that tell the machine what happens when. For instance, δ might specify that if the machine is in state s_2, and there is the symbol σ_4 on the tape underneath the read/write head, then the read/write head should write the symbol σ_5 on the tape, move the head to the right one notch, and change to state s_{42}. This is how you program a Turing machine. The abstraction is fairly crude, but it makes it simpler to keep track of all the possibilities.

Converting such a machine to run backward is pretty straightforward. The main problem is looking for combinations of states and tape symbols that lead to the same states—that is, when it is impossible to put the machine in reverse because there are two different preceding situations that could have led to the present one. The easiest solution is to keep splitting up the states until there is no confusion.

For each state $s_i \in S$, construct a list of triples of states, tape symbols, and direction (s_j, σ_k, L) that could lead to the state s_i. That is, if the machine is in state s_j with the read/write head over the symbol σ_l, then it will write σ_k and move to the left one step. This means if the machine is running backward and it finds itself in state s_i with symbol σ_k to the right of it, then it can move to the right, change to state s_j, and overwrite σ_k with σ_l and not violate the program. That is, this is a correct move.

There will be a conflict if there are triples of the form (s_*, σ_*, L) and (s_*, σ_*, R) in the same set. (Let s_* stand for any element s_i from S.)

This is because it will be quite possible that the machine will end up someplace with one of the symbols to the left and one of the symbols to the right. You might be able to make meta-arguments that such a combination could never exist because of the structure of the program, but these are often hard to prove.

If such a conflict occurs, then create a new state and split apart the actions. All of the triples that moved left into the old state s_i can stay pointing to state s_i. The triples that moved *right*, however, will be moved to point to the new state s_j. The transition rules out of s_j will be a duplicate of s_i.

To a large extent, splitting these states is the same as simply finding a place to keep a "waste" bit around. The Fredkin AND gate generates some waste bits that must be stored. Splitting the state creates one.

The same splitting process must be done if there are two triples of the form (s_a, σ_k, L) and (s_b, σ_k, L). Both of these states, s_a and s_b, lead to the same symbol existing to the right of the current position of the read/write head. Choosing is impossible. Again, a new state must be added and the transition rules duplicated and split.

It should be obvious that a Turing machine will grow substantially as it is made reversible. This growth could even be exponential in many cases. There is no reason why anyone would want to program this way. The complications are just too great, but this example is a good beginning.

8.2.2   Reversible Grammar Generators

The goal of this book is to produce something that seems innocuous but hides a great deal of information from plain sight. Chapter 7 has done a good job of doing this with a context-free grammar, but there are numerous limitations to that approach. This part of the book will build a reversible, Turing-equivalent machine that will be able to do all basic computations but still be reversible. It will get much of its performance by imitating the Fredkin gate, which merely swaps information instead of destroying it.

There are numerous problems that need to be confronted in the design of this machine. Some of them are listed here.

Extra State   At the end of the computation, there will be plenty of extra "waste" bits hanging around. These need to be conveyed to the recipients so they can run their machines in reverse.

There are two possible solutions. The first is to send the extra state through a different channel. It might be hidden in the least significant bits of a photo or sent through some other covert channel. The second is to use a crippled version of the machine to encode it as text without modifying any of the state. That is, reduce the capability of the machine until it acts like the context-free grammar machine from Chapter 7.

Ease of Programmability   Anyone using the machine will need to come up with a collection of grammars that will simulate some form of text. Constructing these can be complicated, and it would be ideal if the language could be nimble enough to handle many constructions.

The solution is to imitate the grammar structure from Chapter 7. There will be variables and productions. But you can change the productions en route using reversible code.

Minimizing Extra State   Any extra bits must be transported through a separate channel at the end. They should be kept to a minimum.

For that reason, all strings should be predefined as constants. They can't be changed. If they could be changed, then the final state of all strings would need to be shipped to the recipient, and this would be too much baggage.

Arithmetic   Arithmetic is generally not reversible. $3 + 2$ is not reversible. But it is if one half of the equation is kept around. So adding the contents of register A_1 and register A_2 and placing the result in register A_1 is reversible. The contents of A_2 can be subtracted from A_1 to recover the original value of A_1.

For the most part, addition, subtraction, multiplication, and division are reversible if they're expressed in this format. The only problem is multiplication by zero. This must be forbidden.

Structure of Memory   What form will the memory take? Obviously, ordinary computers allow programmers to grab and shift blocks of memory at a time. This is not feasible because it would require that too many extra waste bits be stored around. Block moves of data are not reversible. Swaps of information are.

For that reason, there is simply an array of registers. Each one holds one number that can be rounded off in some cases. The final state of the registers will be shipped as extra state to the recipient so any programmer should aim to use them sparingly. Unfortunately, the rules of reversibility can make this difficult.

Conditional Statements Most conditional statements that choose between branches of a program can be reversed, but sometimes they can't be. Consider the case that says "If x is less than 100, then add 1 to x. Otherwise add 1 to p." Which path do you take if you're running in reverse and x is 100? Do you subtract 1 from p or not? Either case is valid.

One solution is to execute each branch storing results in temporary variables. When the conditional statement is encountered, the proper choices are swapped into place.

The solution is to forbid the program from changing the contents of the variables that were used to choose a branch. This rules out many standard programming idioms. Here's one way to work around the problem:

```
if x<100 then {
    swap x,k;
    k=k+1}
else {
    p=p+1;
    swap x,k;}
  swap x,k;
```

Loops Loops may be very handy devices for a programmer, but they can often be an ambiguous obstacle when a program must run in reverse. One easy example is the while loop that is often written to find the last element in a string in C. That is, a counter moves down the string until the termination character, a zero, is found. It may be easy to move backward up the string, but it is impossible to know where to stop.

The problems with a loop can be eliminated if the structure is better defined. It is not enough to simply give a test condition for the end of the loop. You must specify the dependent variable of the loop, its initial setting, and the test condition. When the loop is reversed, it will run the contents of the loop until the dependent variable reaches its initial setting.

This structure is often not strong enough. Consider this loop:

```
i=1;
j=i;
while (i<2) do {
    j=j+.01;
    i=floor(j);}
```

The floor(x) function finds the largest integer less or equal to x. This function will execute 100 times before it stops. If it is executed in reverse, then it will only go through the loop twice before i is set to its initial value, 1. It is clear that i is the defining variable for the loop, but it is clear that j plays a big part.

There are two ways to resolve this problem. The first is to warn programmers and hope that they will notice the mistake before they use the code to send an important message. This leaves some flexibility in their hands.

Another solution is to constrain the nature of loops some more. There is no reason why they can't be restricted to for loops that specify a counter that is incremented each iteration and map functions that apply a particular function to every element in a list. Both are quite useful and easy to reverse without conflicts.

Recursion   Recursion is a problem here. If procedures call themselves, then they are building a de facto loop, and it may be difficult to identify the starting position of a loop. For instance, here is an example of a loop with an open beginning:

```
procedure Bob;
    x=x+1;
     if x<100 then Bob;
end;
```

This is just a while loop, and it is impossible to back into it and know the initial value of x when it began.

One solution is to ban recursion altogether. The standard loop constructs will serve most purposes. This is, alas, theoretically problematic. Much of the theoretical intractability of programs comes from their ability to start recursing. While this might make implementing reversible programs easier, it could severely curtail their theoretical security.

Another solution is to save copies of all affected variables before they enter procedures. So, before the procedure Bob begins, the reversible machine will save a copy of x. This version won't be destroyed. It will become part of the waste bits that must be conveyed along with the output.

In the end, the code for this system is quite close to the assembly code used for regular machines. The only difference is that there is no complete overwriting of information. That would make the sys-

Ralph Merkle also notes that much of assembly code is reversible, and he predicts that in the future smart compilers will rearrange instructions to ensure reversibility. This will allow the chips to run cooler once they're designed to save the energy from reversible computations [Mer93].

tem irreversible. Perhaps future machines will actually change the programming systems to enhance reversibility. That may come if reversible computers prove to be the best way to reduce power consumption to an acceptable level.

8.2.3 The Reversible Grammar Machine

Although the structure will be very similar to machine code, I've chosen to create this implementation of the Reversible Grammar Machine (RGM) in LISP. This language is one of the best experimental tools for creating new languages and playing around with their limits. It includes many of the basic features for creating and modifying lists, plus there are many built-in pattern-matching functions. All of this makes it relatively easy to create a reversible machine, albeit one that doesn't come with many of the features of modern compilers.

Here are the major parts of the system.

Constant List   The major phrases that will be issued by the program as part of its grammar will be stored in this list, `constant-list`. It is officially a list of pairs. The first element of each pair is a tag-like `salutation` that is used as a shorthand for the phrase. The second is a string containing the constant data. This constant list is part of the initial program that must be distributed to both sides of the conversation. The constants do not change so there is no need to transmit them along with the waste state produced by running a program forward. This saves transmission costs. The main purpose of the constant list is to keep all of the phrases that will be output along the way. These are often long, and there is little reason for them to change substantially. Defining them as constants saves space. The constant list can also include any data like the variable list. The data just won't change.

Variables   The data is stored in variables that must be predefined to hold initial values. These initial values are the only time that information can actually be assigned to a variable. The rest of the code must change values through the swap command. The variables are stored in the list `var-list` which is, as usual, a list of pairs. The first element is the variable tag name. The second is the data stored in the variable.

There are five types of data available here: lists, strings, integers, floating-point numbers, and tags. Lists are made up of any of the five elements. There is no strict type checking, but some commands may fail if the wrong data is fed to them. Adding two strings, for instance, is undefined.

Some care should be taken with the choice of variables. The contents of these will need to be sent along with the output so the recipient can reverse the code. The more variables there are, the larger this section of "waste" code may be.

Procedure List   At each step, there must be some code that will be executed. These are procedures. For the sake of simplicity, they are really just lists of commands that are identified by tags and stored in the list, `proc-list`. This is a list of pairs. The first element is the tag identifying the procedure and the second is the list of commands. There are no parameters in the current implementation, but there is no reason why they can't be added.

Commands   Commands are the basic elements for manipulating the data. They must be individually reversible. This set includes the basic arithmetic, the `swap` command, the `if` statement, and the `for` loop tool. These commands take the form of classic LISP function calls. The prefix notation that places the command at the front is not as annoying in this case because arithmetic is reversible. So addition looks like this: `(add first second)`. That command adds `first` and `second` and places the result in `first`.

There are three other arithmetic commands: `sub`, `mul`, and `div`, which stand for subtraction, multiplication, and division, respectively. The only restriction is that you can't multiply a number by zero because it is not reversible. This is reported by an error message.

Output Commands   There is one special command, `chz`, that uses the bits that are being hidden to pick an output from a list. When this command is run in reverse by the recipient, the hidden bits are recovered from the choice. The format is simple: `(chz ( tag tag...tag))`. The function builds up a Huffman tree like the algorithm in Chapter 7 and uses the bits to make a choice. The current version does not include the capability to add weights to the choices, but there is no reason why this feature can't be added in the future.

The tags could point to either a variable or a constant. In most cases, they'll point to strings that are stored as constants. That's the most efficient case. In some cases, the tags will contain other tags. In this case, the `choose` function simply evaluates that tag and continues down the chain until it finds a string to output.

For practical reasons, a programmer should be aware of the problems of reversibility. If two different tags point to the same string, then there is no way for the hidden bits to be recovered correctly. This is something that can't be checked in advance. The program can check this on the fly, but the current implementation doesn't do it.

Code Branches There is an if statement that can be used to send the evaluation down different branches. The format is (if (test if-branch else-branch)). The program evaluates the test and if it is true, then it follows the if-branch; otherwise it follows the else-branch.

The format of the test is quite similar to general LISP. For instance, the test (gt a b) returns true if a is greater than b. The other decision functions are lt, le, ge, and eq, which stand for less than, less than or equal to, greater than or equal to, and simply equal to.

The current implementation watches for errors that might be introduced if the two variables used to make a decision were changed along one of the branches. It does this by pushing the names onto the Forbidden-List and then checking to see the list before the evaluation of each operation.

Program Counter and Code This machine is like most other software programs. There will be one major procedure with the tag main. This is the first procedure executed, and the RGM will end when it finishes. Other procedures are executed as they're encountered, and a stack is used to keep track of the position in partially finished procedures.

The source code can be found in Appendix C. There are two main functions, Encode and Decode. One will take a file of data and encode a message with the grammar. The other will decode a message.

8.3

Summary

Letting a machine run backward is just one way to create the most complicated computer-generated mimicry. You could also create double-level grammars or some other modified grammar-based system.

- *The Disguise.* The text produced by these reversible machines is as good as a computer can do. But that may not be that great. Computers have a long way to go before they can really fool a human. Still, static text can be quite realistic.

- *How Secure Is It?* Assessing the security of this system is even more complicated than understanding the context-free grammars used in Chapter 7. Theoretically, there is no Turing machine that can make nontrivial statements about the reversible Turing machine. In practice, there may be fairly usable algorithms that can assemble information about the patterns in use. The question of how to create very secure programs for this reversible machine is just as open as the question of how to break certain subclasses.

- *How to Use It.* The LISP software is given in Appendix C. It runs on the XLISP software available for free at many locations throughout the Internet.

- *Further Work.* The LISP code is very rudimentary. It's easy to use if you have access to a LISP interpreter. A better version would offer a wider variety of coding options that would make it easier to produce complicated text.

  A more interesting question is how to *guarantee* security. Is it possible to produce a mechanism for measuring the strength of a reversible grammar? Can such a measuring mechanism be guaranteed? An ultimate mechanism probably doesn't exist, but it may be possible to produce several models for attack. Each type of attack would have a corresponding metric for evaluating a grammar's ability to resist that attack. Any collection of models and metrics would be quite interesting.

chapter nine

Life in the Noise

Boy-Zs in Noizy, Idaho

Scene: A garage with two teens and guitars.

Teen #1 No. I want it to go, "Bah, dah, dah, dah, bah, screeeeech, wing, zing . . . ."

Teen #2 How about, "Bah, dah, dah, dah, bah, screeeeech, screech, wing, zing . . . ."

Teen #1 Hey, let's compromise, "Bah, dah, dah, screeech, zip, pop, screeech?"

Teen #2 Oh. I don't know anymore.

Teen #1 What's the problem?

Teen #2 I just get tired of trying to say something with noise.

Teen #1 Hey. We agreed. Mrs. Fishback taught us in English class that the true artist challenges contemporary society. We need to expose its fallacies through the very force of our artistic fervor. Our endeavor must course through the foundations of society like an earthquake that gets a 10.0 on the Richter scale.

Teen #2 Yeah. So what. She's just a hippie chick. That's her idea.

Teen #1 Come on. Join the clambake. We have to confront the conformity of the adults with an urgency that heretofore has not been seen upon this planet. We need to demand that culture come alive with a relevance that can speak truth to the young and the restless. There are paradigms to shatter.

Teen #2   Would you shut up with that science stuff? Mr. Hornbeam said that Thomas Kuhn wasn't going to be on the final. Besides, people managed to have a good time even before Copernicus and Galileo broke the paradigms apart. What about melody and harmony?

Teen #1   We can make our fuzz circuits do everything for us. Suburbia is just sleepwalking through life. Only our harsh notes can wake them to the discord that lies beneath the greenswept swards of our existence. That's what Mrs. Fishback says.

Teen #2   Cut it out. You like your dad's car as much as I do. How would you like your father to awaken you from your sleepwalking and force you to do some actual walking to the mall? I don't want to make Mrs. Fishback's music.

Teen #1   Why not? She obviously understands the evil hegemony proffered by a corporate culture intent upon creating a somnolescent adolescence. We are not people merely because we consume.

Teen #2   Nirvana, Pearl Jam, and the rest live on major labels sold at full list price at our mall.

Teen #1   Whoa! Perhaps we're being led to rebel in the hopes that anti-culture will sell even more than traditional culture?

Teen #2   Yes. You got it.

Teen #1   It's true. Mrs. Fishback just wants us to create a youth she never had when she was running between classes and earning good grades. The revolution always ended in the 1960s when the exams came around. They smoked a bit of pot, went to a protest, but most of it was just grooving to the music and searching for someone to do some loving. Then they got married and got jobs. We're just doing what her generation wants. They're marketing to us through their dreams of what they wished their childhood had been.

Teen #2   You're getting the hang of it.

Teen #1   The pervasive drive to explode the previous is just another marketing move. Unknowingly, we're channeling our rebellious energy through a marketing path created by a cynical corporate structure intent upon destroying the potential for upheaval in every youth. Instead of remaking the world with our passion, we're simply consuming anticultural icons constructed as pseudo-rebellious pabulum.

Teen #2 Bonzai!

Teen #1 So what do we do?

Teen #2 I have this Beethoven music here. It has no copyright.

Teen #1 Excellent. By reinvigorating the classic music, we'll be
subverting the corporate music world that uses the laws of
intellectual property to milk our youth. Instead of working
long hours at McDonald's to save for a new $17.95 Nirvana
Retrospective CD, we'll truly shatter the power structure by
playing music long freed from the authorial and corporate
imperative.

Teen #2 And there are some great bass chords in this Ninth
Symphony . . . .

9.1

Hiding in the Noise

Noise, alas, is part of our lives. The advertisements for digital this and
digital that try to give the world the impression that digital circuits
are noise-free and thus better, but this is only half true. The digital signal may be copied and copied without changing the message
thanks to error-correcting codes and well-defined circuitry, but this
doesn't eliminate much of the original noise. Digital photographs,
digitized music, and digital movies all have a significant amount of
noise that is left over from their original creation. When the voices,
sounds, and photographs are converted into bits, the circuits that
do the job are often less than perfect. A bit of electrical noise might
slightly change the bits, and there is no way to recover. This noise is
something that will always be with us.

This noise is also an opportunity. If it doesn't really matter
whether the bits are exactly right, then anyone who needs to hide
information can take advantage of the uncertainty. They can claim
the bits for their own through squatter's rights. This is probably the
most popular form of steganography and the one with the most potential. There are millions of images floating about the Net used as
window dressing for Web sites and who knows what. Anyone could
hijack the bits to carry his or her own messages.

The principle is simple. Digitized photos or sounds are represented by numbers that encode the intensity at a particular moment
in space and/or time. A digital photo is just a matrix of numbers that

stands for the intensity of light emanating from a particular place at a particular time. Digitized sounds are just lists of the pressure hitting a microphone at a sequence of time slices.

All of these numbers are imprecise. The digital cameras that generate images are not perfect because the array of charge-coupled devices (CCDs) that convert photons to bits is subject to the random effects of physics. In order to make the devices sensitive enough to work at normal room levels, they must often respond to only a few photons. The randomness of the world ensures that sometimes a few too many photons will appear and sometimes a few too few will arrive. This will balance out in the long run, but the CCD must generate an image in a fraction of a second. So it is occasionally off by a small amount. Microphones suffer in the same way.

God is in the details.
—Mies van der Rohe

The amount of noise available for sending information can be truly staggering. Many color digital photographs are stored with 32 bits allocated for each pixel. There are 8 bits used to encode either the amount of red, blue, and green or the amount of cyan, magenta, and yellow of each pixel. That's 24 bits. If only one pixel from each of the colors was allocated to hiding information, then this would be about 10 percent of the file. At the top of the scale, a Kodak photo-CD image is 3072 by 2048 pixels and takes up about 18MB. That leaves about 1.8 megabytes to hold information. The text of this book is well under half a megabyte, so there is plenty of room for hiding more information in a *single* snapshot. Many people won't want to spend 18 MB of storage space on a single snapshot. Less precise versions of images can run between 200K and 600K and still devote about 10 percent of their space to hidden data.

But if about 10 percent is devoted to hidden data, how much does this affect the appearance of the image? Each of these 8 bits stores a number between 0 and 255. The last bit in each group of 8 bits is known as the least significant bit. It's value is 1. The most significant bit, the first one, contributes 128 to the final number if it is a 1. This means that the least significant bit can change the intensity of a pixel in the final image by about 0.5 to 1 percent at the most. Trading 10 percent of the image data in a way that will only affect the final image by about 1 percent is a good solution.

There is no reason why more data can't be stored away. If the two least significant bits are given over to hidden data, then each pixel cannot change by more than 3 units. That is still about 1 to 3 percent of the value of a pixel. But this is 25 percent of the final image size. This is a huge amount of bandwidth waiting to be captured and used.

9.1.1 Problems with the Noise

The amount of bandwidth available in the least significant bits of an image or a sound file is large, but it is not always easy to exploit. Unfortunately, potential steganographers must fight for the hidden spaces with compression algorithm architects who want to create compression algorithms that strip away the extra space.

The basic image format may use 24 bits to encode the color of each pixel, but this basic format is used less and less frequently. Compression algorithms such as JPEG do a good job and often use 1 or 2 bits per pixel and can easily save a factor of 10 without significantly distorting an image. Most digital cameras, for instance, now come with built-in JPEG compression chips to save space and allow people to take more pictures. Although 24-bit color may be slightly more accurate, no one wants to waste the space on it.

The same holds true for music. Today, MP3 files are much more common than files that record the intensity at each time slice. Compression algorithms such as MP3 can easily save a factor of 10 over raw digitized data. Newer algorithms can save even more. This is great news if you're storing your CD collection on your computer, but not if you want an easy channel to exploit for steganography.

This effect, incidentally, is what leads some steganographers to hide information in the most "perceptually significant" parts of a file. That is, they want to ignore the noise and hide the information in the part that the humans can perceive. The noise will eventually be extracted and removed by some compression algorithm, but the perceptually important parts will live on [CKLS96]. Instead of hiding information in subtle changes of the intensity, hide the information in the position of a person's nose or the length of the hair.

This is a good point, but it is more of a challenge for researchers, and it is a loose design principle. Even if simple mechanisms for exploiting the noise in a file may not be as robust as possible, they are still worth exploring. The rest of this chapter is devoted to noise. Following chapters attempt more robust solutions.

9.1.2 Good Noise?

A practical problem is finding good noise. Most image and sound files include enough natural noise to hide a 3 percent change, but this noise is rarely as pure as can be. Figure 9.1 shows a black-and-white scanned image of a photograph taken of a computer on a desk. Figure 9.2 shows just the least significant bits, and Figure 9.3 shows the

Chapter 17 discusses how some cameras don't provide good enough noise to mask hidden bits.

Figure 9.1   This is a black-and-white photo of the author's desk. There is plenty of junk on the desk hiding secret documents. The noise in the image lends itself to hidden data as well.

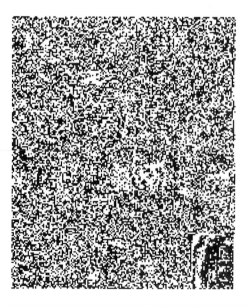

Figure 9.2   These are the least significant bits of the photo in Figure 9.1. The most significant bits were deleted to show the randomness that exists at this level. (See Figure 9.4.)

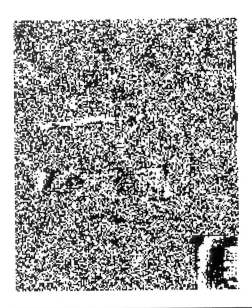

Figure 9.3 Even the second-to-least significant bits appear fairly random. These are the second-to-least significant bits of the photo in Figure 9.1.

second-to-least significant bits. It is obvious that there is a highly random pattern to them caused by the noise in the digitizing circuit on the scanner. It is random, but it is not as random as it could be. In contrast, Figure 9.4 shows the most significant bits of the photo.

Many images and sound files probably have enough inherent noise to hide data. The image in Figure 9.1 has plenty of junk so small variations don't show up. But there are some images that do not handle the imposed noise as well. Many images are created entirely on the computer in applications like Adobe Illustrator. These produce pure, consistent fields of color. Even modifying them a bit can stand out because a pure tone is converted to one with a bit of noise.[1]

Section 9.2.7, "Putting JPEG to Use", shows how compression can identify just how much space can be exploited in an image.

9.1.3 Independence Problems

One of the deeper problems is defining good noise. The least significant bits of a music or image file often seem close to random, at least

---

[1] The pure colors are often jarring to the eye, and this is why artists often use textures and slight imperfections to make the image more appealing. It is anyone's guess why the optic nerve seems to react this way, but perhaps it is an effect like the moiré patterns produced when one pattern is digitized at too coarse a level. If you've ever looked at anyone wearing a fine checked shirt or tie on television you may have seen this effect.

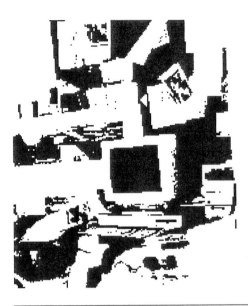

Figure 9.4   These are the most-significant bits of the photo in Figure 9.1. The seven least significant bits were deleted to contrast the images in Figure 9.2.

to the average eye or ear, but they often contain hidden patterns and structure. Many of the microphones, cameras, or scanners used to generate the files are far from perfect, and they often introduce their own patterns.

Chapter 17 offers a number of basic statistical tests for identifying the presence of steganography.

One of the most common patterns is a correlation between the high-order bits and the least significant bit. A picture of a bright day might include a number of intense reflections of the sun. These pure white points usually saturate the sensor and produce patches of maximum values of 255. There are relatively few values of 254. If the least significant bits were truly random and uncorrelated with the higher-order bits, then there would be equal numbers of 255s and 254s. This often happens to a lesser degree in many other parts of the image where only one color may appear completely saturated.

This is just a simple example. Good scientists with a deep knowledge of the physics behind the sensors can often detect more sophisticated patterns. Digital copier manufacturers, for instance, can tune their toner mechanisms to do a good job with either fine white lines or fine black lines. Doing well with both is difficult.

All of these subtle statistical patterns can be destroyed when you replace the least significant bits with your message. Simply pouring in a well-compressed and encrypted message puts in white noise with no correlations to the higher-order bits.

There is no easy way to avoid this problem. The mimic functions from Chapter 6 can be used in complicated ways to imitate the patterns, but this is largely a cat-and-mouse, spy-vs.-spy game. The attacker may have some model of the statistical correlations in the file. If you can anticipate this model or come up with your own that encompasses it, then you can mold the data in your message to fit it. If you choose incorrectly or the eavesdropper/attacker changes his model, your data could stick out like a sore thumb.

There is no solution to winning this game, but it is possible to minimize the dangers of playing it. The best defense against statistical problems like this is to avoid getting greedy by packing in too much data. An 800K file has 800K least significant bits available that can store up to 100K bytes of a message. Using all 100K of the channel, however, will completely destroy all statistical correlations, but inserting a 1K message will leave 99 percent of the least significant bits unchanged. Most of the statistical patterns will also be unchanged and thus indistinguishable from a pure file.

All of the analytical attacks on steganography work best when the steganographer gets greedy and saturates the hidden channel. Leaving most of the image unchanged is the best defense.

9.1.4 File Format Grief

File formats are a serious problem for anyone who would routinely like to use bit-level steganography to hide images. Many image or audio file formats were designed to squeeze out some of the extra noisy details to save space. This might be done by a special, efficient file format such as GIF or by an aggressive compression program that does not care if it reconstructs an image that is not exactly the same. Both of these make it hard to simply hide information in the least significant bits of an image.

The GIF file format and its 8-bit color standard is a significant impediment because 8-bit color is quite different from 24-bit color. It uses a table of 256 different colors that best represent the image as a color map. The color of each pixel is described by giving the closest color from this 256-entry table. The bits do not correspond to the intensity of the colors at each pixel. This means that changing the least significant bits doesn't necessarily change the intensity at a pixel by less than 1 percent. Entry 128 of the table might be a saturated

Yes, the newspapers were right: snow was general all over Ireland.
—James Joyce in *The Dead*

Table 9.1   The first five entries in a GIF palette.

Entry Num.	Binary	Red Intensity	Green Intensity	Blue Intensity
0	00000000	150	20	10
1	00000001	151	20	12
2	00000010	14	150	165
3	00000011	16	152	167
4	00000100	132	100	10
5	00000101	135	67	15
⋮	⋮	⋮	⋮	⋮

ruby red while entry 129 might be a pale, washed-out indigo. They may only differ in the least significant bit, but that can be enough to cause major changes in the final outcome.

There are a number of different solutions to this problem. The first is to simply use a smaller number of colors in the table. Instead of choosing the 256 colors that do the best job of representing the colors of an image, the software could choose 128 colors and then choose 128 colors that are quite similar to the original 128. They might even be the same, but that could be too suspicious. The table could be arranged so that the two very similar colors only differ in one bit. Table 9.1 is an abbreviated example of such a table.

So if you want to hide the value 1 in a pixel, you would find the closest color in the table and then choose the version of it with the least significant bit set to 1. If the closest color had red set to 15, green set to 151, and blue set to 167, and you wanted to hide the bit 1, then you would choose color 3 for that pixel. If you wanted to hide a 0, then you would choose color 2.

There is no reason why the least significant bit needs to be used to separate pairs. It might very well be any of the bits. Table 9.2 shows how to use the third bit to mix pairs.

Nor is there any reason why only 1 bit is encoded in each pixel. The same algorithms that choose 256 or 128 best colors for an image can be used to find the closest 64 colors. Then 2 bits per pixel could be allocated to hidden information. Obviously, this can lead to a degraded image, but the hidden information can often moderate the amount of degradation. Imagine, for instance, that we tried to be greedy and hide 4 bits per pixel. This would leave 4 bits left over for actually specifying the color, and there could only be 16 truly different colors in the table. If the photo was of a person, then there is a good chance that one of the colors would be allocated to the green

Table 9.2 Six entries from an image's palette.

Entry Num.	Binary	Red Intensity	Green Intensity	Blue Intensity
0	00000000	150	20	10
⋮	⋮	⋮	⋮	⋮
2	00000010	14	150	165
⋮	⋮	⋮	⋮	⋮
4	00000100	132	100	10
⋮	⋮	⋮	⋮	⋮
33	00100001	151	20	12
⋮	⋮	⋮	⋮	⋮
35	00100011	16	152	167
⋮	⋮	⋮	⋮	⋮
37	00100101	135	67	15

in the background, one of the colors would go to a brown in the hair, and maybe two colors would be given over to the skin color. A two-toned skin could look very fake.[2] But each of these two tones might also be hiding 4 bits of information. This would mean that there were 16 surrogates for each of these two tones and these 16 surrogates would be used fairly randomly. This would add a significant amount of texture that might mitigate some of the effects.[3]

Another significant hurdle for image- and sound-based steganography is the compression function. The digital representations of these data are so common that many specialized compression functions exist to pack the data into smaller files for shipping across the network. JPEG (Joint Photographic Experts Group) is one popular standard algorithm for compressing photographs. MPEG is a similar standard designed for motion pictures.

Both of these are dangerous for bit-level info packing because they are lossy compression functions. If you take a file, compress it with JPEG, and then uncompress it later, the result will not be exactly the same as the original. It will look similar, but it won't be the same. This effect is quite different from the *lossless* compression

JPEG compression can also help. See Section 9.2.7, "Putting JPEG to Use".

---

[2] Recent work suggests that human eyes pick up skin tones more than most colors. So the best algorithms devote more colors in the table to skin colors in the hopes of better representing them. The eyes don't really seem to care much about the shade of green in a tree.

[3] Random noise has been used to make quantization look more realistic. Too many discrete levels look artificial [Rob62].

used on many other forms of data such as text. Those functions reproduce the data verbatim. Lossy compression functions are able to get significantly more compression because they take a devil-may-care attitude with the details. The end result looks close enough. The JPEG algorithm itself is adjustable. You can get significantly more compression if you're willing to tolerate more inaccuracies. If you turn up the compression significantly, the pixels begin to blend into big blocks of the same color.

9.1.5 Deniability

Deniability is one of the greatest features of hiding information in GIFs from Web pages. If you structure your information correctly, you can spread it out among a number of unrelated locations. If the information is discovered, it will be impossible to tell exactly where it came from.

Imagine that you have some bits that you want to distribute to the world. You could simply hide these bits in a GIF file and place it on your home page for all to download. If unintended people discover the bits, however, they know the information came from you because it is on your Web page.

Instead, you can split up the information into n parts using the basic tricks from Chapter 4. These n files, when they're XORed together, will reveal the hidden data. Ordinarily, you would create $n-1$ files at random and then compute the last file so that everything adds up. But why bother using files at random when there is a great source of randomness on the network? You could simply snarf $n-1$ different GIF images from the Net and use them. One might be an innocuous picture from the White House page. Another might be a quilt from the page of some quilting club that is the picture of innocence. Anyone who wanted to recover the information would get all of these GIFs from the Net, recover the secret bits from all of them, and add them up to recover the hidden data.

Section 6.2.2,
"Regular Mimicry and Images", describes sophisticated ways of matching patterns in the least significant bits.

The net effect of this trick is deniability. No one can be sure who was the one who was hiding the secret bits. Could it be the White House? They've been known to sponsor covert missions based in the Old Executive Office Building. Could it be the quilting circle? No one knows who injected the secret bits into the file. Even the person who recovers the bits might not know who was sending the message. It's quite a ruse.

There are some practical problems associated with this technique. First, you must keep the file creation dates secret. The one GIF that actually contains the message will be the newest file. HTTP doesn't usually ship this information to Web browsers so there is little problem with keeping the information secret. But you can also simply fake it by resetting the clock on your machine.

Second, you should search out GIF files that seem to have the right structure for storing secret bits. This will prevent someone from examining the files and discovering that only one of them has the right structure to hide bits. That is, all but one of the *n* files are 8-bit color with color tables filled with 256 different shades. The one that isn't is the one. This means that they're either 24-bit color or 8-bit; black-and-white grayscale images are the best.

You can add some error-correcting features to this scheme if you want to create, say, three different sets of files. When the three sets of files are combined, then three versions of the hidden bits emerge. Any disparities between the files can be resolved by choosing the value of the bit in question that is correct in two out of three files.

More complicated error-correcting schemes like the ones described in Chapter 3 can also be used successfully. For instance, a file to be hidden could be encoded with an error-correcting code that converts every 8 bits into, say, a 12-bit block that can recover errors. One bit from each of the 12-bit blocks could be placed into 12 separate files that were then hidden in 12 different GIFs sprinkled around the network. If someone could not recover all 12 GIFs because of network failures, then the error-correcting code would allow the information to be recovered.

There are many other techniques that can be used to hide information once the data is packed away in GIF files or audio files. These files already comprise much of the information floating around the Net, and their proportion will only increase. New technologies promise even more opportunities ahead. Apple Computer is shipping Quicktime VR, which is a way of faking three-dimensional computing. Many of the programmers working on three-dimensional games know that complicated textures are the most important part of creating verisimilitude in virtual reality. All of these are ideal places to hide information.

9.2

Bit Twiddling

Perhaps the best way to begin experimenting with hiding information in the noise is to download one of the experimental packages

Appendix D offers a list of some of the more prominent steganography packages.

floating around the Net. Three of the oldest choices are Hide and Seek, EzStego, and S-Tools. They each illustrate a different technique for overcoming the limitations with the file formats.

9.2.1   Hide and Seek

Hide and Seek 4.1 is a basic steganography program designed for the PC written by an author identified only by the email address shaggy@phantom.com. The program only works on either 8-bit color or 8-bit black-and-white GIF files that are 320 by 480. This is the standard size of the oldest GIF format. The program displays the image before adding or extracting data. The current archive contains two extra programs that makes life easier for those hiding information in GIF files.

The first, grey.exe, converts color GIFs into grayscale GIFs that would not show any of the artifacts associated with 8-bit color steganography. The second program, reduce.exe, shrinks the color table from 256 colors to 128 colors and then duplicates these 128 colors so that adjacent entries in the color table are duplicates of each other. If this is done, hiding information in the least significant bit won't affect the look of the image.

There are a number of different programs for reducing the size of the palette. The simplest is as follows:

1. Create a two-dimensional matrix containing the distances between all pairs of colors in the palette. The distance between two colors, (R_1, G_1, B_1) and (R_2, G_2, B_2) is

$$\delta((R_1, G_1, B_1), (R_2, G_2, B_2)) = \sqrt{(R_1 - R_2)^2 + (G_1 - G_2)^2 + (B_1 - B_2)^2}.$$

2. Find the best color to delete. That is, find the color with the closest neighbor and remove it.

3. Repeat until the palette is the desired size.

Chapter 17 describes several techniques for detecting a steganographic message.

Unfortunately, this technique leaves a large red flag for anyone scanning GIFs looking for hidden information. An 8-bit color table with only 128 different colors is easier to detect automatically than a bad image with plenty of artifacts. One is an easily measured quantity that is a glaring inefficency. The other is a subjective problem that is often apparent to the human eye. Figure 9.5 shows how little a 24-bit picture changes when the least significant bit is changed. Figure 9.6 shows how badly an 8-bit picture can change.

Figure 9.5   This shows how adding information to the least significant bit of a 24-bit color image has little effect. The image was later converted to black and white for this book. (Photo courtesy of the Lacrosse Foundation.)

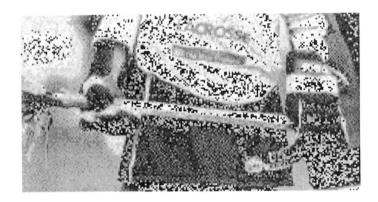

Figure 9.6   8-bit color images can make poor candidates for adding information into the least significant bit because entries in the color table might not be next to each other. The image was later converted to black and white for this book.

Coming up with a piece of software that will identify bad artifacts may be possible, but it will not be precise. You could try to look for places where the color continuity is not great. If adjacent pixels are widely different colors, then this could signal a mess caused by 8-bit color steganography. In general, a small amount of blurring and anti-aliasing occurs as images are digitized. Adjacent pixels along edges are often blurred together, and the edges aren't crisp. Even when the edges are crisp, it is possible to measure the randomness of the places where there are sharp changes in the colors. If these appear to be randomly distributed, then it is quite likely that they could have come from this process. Or they could be the artistic equivalent of Nirvana music—grungy images designed to perforate the artistic impulse of perfection, images designed to shock and reveal the seamier side of life. Who knows?

The source code is also included with Hide and Seek, which makes it possible to look at the guts of the program to examine how information is *dispersed* throughout the bits. That is, there are about 19,200 bytes of space available in the GIF. If a smaller file is going to be packed into the bits, then the program tries to randomly arrange the bits so that they're not adjacent to each other. This has two effects. First, the noise is more randomly distributed throughout the image instead of being clustered on the top half. Second, you must know the location of bits to find the data, and the location is governed by a random number generator driven by a user-chosen key. Both of these enhance the security of the system.

The dispersion is controlled by an 8-byte header for the file. The first 2 bytes are the length of the file, the second 2 bytes are a random number seed that is chosen at random when the information is packed, and the third pair of bytes is the version number. The fourth pair is not used, but is included to fill out an 8-byte block for the IDEA cipher. This block is encrypted with the IDEA cipher using an optional key and then stored in the first 64 pixels of the image. If you don't know the key, then you can't recover the header information that controls the dispersion of the data throughout the image.

The actual dispersion is random. At the beginning, the random number generator is seeded with the second pair of bytes from the header block. The code from Hide and Seek 4.1 simply uses the built-in C random number generator, which may be adequate for most intents and purposes. A stronger implementation would use a cryptographically secure random number generator. Or, perhaps, it would use IDEA to encrypt the random bit stream using a special key. Either method would add a great deal of security.

Here's the section of C code devoted to handling the dispersion. The code for getting the color table entry for pixel (x, y) and flipping it appropriately is removed. This code will store an entire byte in the 8 pixels. The amount of the variable dispersion controls how many pixels are skipped on average. It is set to be the rounded off amount of 19,000 divided by the length of the incoming data.

```
int used=0,disp=0,extra=0;
for(i=0;i<8;i++) {
// Code removed here for flipping LSB of (x,y)
```

```
disp=(random(dispersion+extra)+1);
used+=disp;
extra=((dispersion*(i+1))-used);
x+=disp;
// Move over x pixels. Code removed to handle
// wraparound.
}
```

9.2.2 EzStego

EzStego is a basic program written in Java for encoding information in the least significant bits of a GIF image. It is the second offering from Romana Machado, who also wrote an earlier program called Stego.

EzStego's solution for dealing with GIF palettes is simple. The software sorts the palettes so that the 2^n colors in an n-bit file flow smoothly from one to another. That is, each jump from the ith color to the $i + 1$ is relatively small. Any hidden information that changes the least significant bit will introduce small changes. Ordering the colors in the palette is trivial with one-dimensional color spaces in black-and-white images, but it is much more difficult in three dimensions. The closest colors aren't always adjacent. Figure 9.7 shows one sorted palette.

EzStego treats the challenge as a version of the Traveling Salesman Problem. The colors are cities in three dimensions (RGB), and the goal is to find the shortest path through all of the stops.

There are no easy answers for the Traveling Salesman Problem so EzStego uses a basic approximation that works pretty well. It may not find the optimal solution, but it will often find one that works very well. The algorithm is as follows:

Begin with two colors in the list, $\{c_0, c_1\}$. Set the first one to be C. Repeat this until all colors are inserted.

Other approximations for the Traveling Salesman Problem can be found in [Tah92, Cla83].

1. Find the color that is farthest from C. Call it d.

2. Find the best place to insert this color in the ist. That is, scan the list and find i such that $\delta(C, c_i) + \delta(C, c_{i+1})$ is minimized.

3. Insert d and set it to be the new C.

Finding the farthest color ensures that the algorithm does not get "trapped" in one corner of the three-dimensional color cube only to find it must make big leaps to reach the other colors.

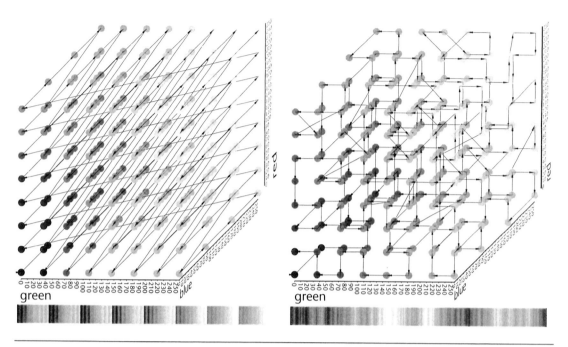

Figure 9.7   A generic palette is shown on the left and the sorted version is shown on the right. A color version of this figure appears in Plate 10 of the color insert. (These figures were created by Andreas Westfeld and Andreas Pfitzmann for their paper [WP99]. They take only 61 short lines of Postscript!)

This sorting algorithm is not perfect, and there's no guarantee that the jumps will be small. While the overall distance is minimized, some distances are more important than others. Adding information in the least significant bit will only produce some changes. In a 3-bit system, 001 can only change to 000, not 010. Sorting the entire palette may leave one of the longer jumps between color 000 and 001 and put one of the shorter ones between 001 and 010. A more sophisticated approach will try to find the best way to pair up all of the colors in the palette so that the total distance of all the pairs is minimized.

J. Fridrich offered a simple tweak to the algorithm. Instead of sorting the palette, the algorithm simply looks for the closest color with the right parity for representing the bit being hidden. The parity of the bit is $R + G + B$ mod 2 [Fri99].

EzStego tries to thwart steganalysis by shipping the palette unsorted. Here are the steps:

1. Begin with an unsorted palette produced by a program such as Photoshop.

2. Sort the palette so the closest colors fall next to each other in order.

3. Encode the message by twiddling the least significant bit. Make sure to encrypt the message with a cryptographically secure random number stream.

4. Unsort the palette by renumbering all of the colors with their original values from the original palette.

5. Ship the image. Any attacker looking at the palette will only see one produced by a nonsteganographic program.

6. The receiver can resort the palette using the same sorting algorithm. If the algorithm is deterministic, it will produce the same results.

7. The receiver can now extract the bits by using the sorted palette values assigned to the colors. The least significant bits now encode the message.

This solution removes the problem with a highly structured palette because it uses one produced by the image's creating software. Any attacker will have trouble determining the existence of the message by looking at the structure of the palette.

9.2.3 S-Tools

One of the most ambitious steganographic tool kits available is the S-Tools package written by Andy Brown. The system can hide information in images stored as either GIFs or BMP files, in sound stored as WAV files, or even in the unallocated sectors of a disk. The tool runs under Windows 3.1 and includes extensive help files. The program itself is shareware, and a payment of US $15.00 buys you the rights to use it and a copy of the source code.

Wilson MacGyver Liaw wrote a good introduction to the GIF file format in [Lia95].

Each of S-Tools's three programs offers to optionally encrypt any information being stored in a file using a wide array of encryption algorithms. The software allows you to use the IDEA algorithm, DES, triple DES, MPJ2, and NSEA. Each of the different algorithms can be used with any of the five most common feedback chaining systems such as CBC, ECB, CFB, OFB, and PCBC. This shows an incredible level of sophistication. These options are often not available even in commercial systems. S-Tools adds 32 bits of random bits at the beginning of each file to ensure that these chaining methods work securely.

The version of S-Tools for handling images, st-bmp.exe, can read in files that are in either the GIF or BMP format and then display them. After the data is added to the file, you can toggle between before and after images. This allows you to compare the effects and see whether there has been any noticeable change in the image. My version did not exchange color tables with the toggle so this effect didn't work right.

There are two different types of image steganography supported by S-Tools. The first method uses 24-bit images and simply changes the least significant bit for each of the three colors at each pixel. The author of S-Tools contends that 24-bit images may stick out somewhat because most people don't use them—they just take up too much space. This is certainly true. While 24-bit images continue to be common in artistic venues, they are much less common on the Web, where 8-bit formats such as GIF or PNG dominate.

The second part of the software attempts to rectify this problem by reducing the number of colors in the image so that there are only 256 final colors. The software uses the algorithm designed by Paul Heckbert [Hec82] to reduce the number of colors in an image in the most visually nondisruptive way possible. The algorithm plots all the colors in three dimensions and then searches for a collection of n boxes that contains all the colors in one of the boxes. When it is finished, it chooses one color to represent all the colors in each box. S-Tools offers three different options for how to choose this one color: the center of the box, the average box color, or the average of all the pixels in the box.

The process for constructing the set of boxes is described in detail in Heckbert's thesis. The process begins with the complete $256 \times 256 \times 256$ space as one box. Then it begins to recursively subdivide the boxes by splitting them in the best way possible. It continues this splitting process until there are n boxes representing the space. Heckbert developed this algorithm to correct some of the defects he found in the "popularity" algorithms being used. These algorithms would clump together nearby colors until only n clumps were left. Then it would choose some color, usually the center of the clump, to represent all of the colors. This works quite well for colors in tight clumps, but it can be disastrous for colors that are part of big, gaseous clumps. In those cases, the difference between the colors and their chosen representative was too large. This leads to big shifts in the colors used in the details.

...t suggests that a good way to understand the two ap-
...by comparing them to the "quantization" methods used
...g the representatives for the two houses of the Congress of
...States. The Senate gets two members from each state, and
...ompares this to his algorithm. It spreads out the represen-
...o part of the color space is over- or underrepresented. The
...epresentatives, on the other hand, gets one representative
...it of population. This works well if you're from heavily
...areas such as Manhattan. These have representatives for
...f town. Western states such as Nevada, however, have only
...ntative and thus have little power in the House. Heckbert
...his approach to the "popularity" algorithms.

...division algorithm used by S-Tools can use two different
...the boxes. In one way, the largest dimension is chosen
...g the greatest difference in RGB values. In the other way,
...dimension is found by comparing the luminosity of the
...oices. Here is the basic algorithm in detail:

...of the colors from the image in one box.

...his until there are n boxes that will represent the final n

...ch box, find the minimum and maximum value in each
...nsion. That is, find the smallest and largest value of red
...y color in the box, the smallest and largest value of
..., and the smallest and largest value of blue.

...ch dimension of each box, measure the length. This
...be the difference in absolute length or it might be the
...ence in luminosity.

...he longest dimension and split this particular box.
...pert suggests this can be done either by finding the
...n color in the box along this dimension or by simply
...ing the geometric middle.

...a representative color for all of the original colors in
...x. S-Tools offers three choices: center of the box, average
...lors, or average of the pixels.

When the new set of n colors is chosen, S-Tools can use "dither-ing" to replace the old colors with new ones.

The algorithm attempts to find the best number of new colors, n, through a limbo process. It slowly lowers the number of colors until it ends up with fewer than 256 colors after the data is mixed into

David Charlap wrote a good introduction to the BMP format in [Cha95a, Cha95b].

the least significant bits. Often, it must repeat this process several times until the right number is found. S-Tools cannot predict the number of final colors ahead of time because it constantly tries to add 3 bits to each pixel. That is, it takes the red, green, and blue values for each pixel and changes the least significant bit of each one independently. That means one color could quite possibly become eight colors. This is quite likely to happen if that color is common in the image because each pixel is handled differently. On average, each of the eight slightly different colors should appear after 10 to 12 pixels of the same color are mapped.

This means that it is impossible for the algorithm to predict the final number of colors it needs. It might try to reduce the number of final colors in the image to 64. Then, after the data is mixed in, it might end up with 270 colors, or 255. If there were 255, then it could save the file. Otherwise, it would start the process again and reduce the colors some more. The entire process is iterative. S-Tools attempts to predict the correct number through extrapolation, but it has taken several iterations every time I modified a file.

9.2.4   S-Tools and Sound Files

S-Tools also includes one program designed to store data in the least significant bits of a WAV file—one of the standard sound formats for Microsoft Windows. These files can use either 8 or 16 bits of data to represent each instance. People with Sound Blaster cards will have no problem generating these files from any source.

The S-Tools sound program, `st-wav.exe`, hides one bit per either 8 or 16 bits and offers the same encryption options as `st-bmp.exe`. It will also use a random number generator to choose a random subset of bits. This spreads the distortion throughout the sound file. The program will display a graph representing the sound and also play it for you. After data is hidden, the graph shows all of the changes made to the wave form in red and leaves the unchanged parts in black. This, in effect, reveals where the pattern of 1s and 0s in the hidden file differed from the least significant bits of the sound file. Figure 9.8 shows a screen shot from the page.

9.2.5   S-Tools and Empty Disk Space

The third program in the S-Tools suite, `st-fdd.exe`, will hide information in the unallocated areas of a floppy disk. Each disk is broken into sectors, and the sectors are assigned to individual files by the

The program MandelSteg, developed by Henry Hastur, hides information in the least significant bit of an image of the Mandelbrot set. This synthetic image is computed to seven bits of accuracy, and then the message is hidden in the eighth. See Section 15.2.2.

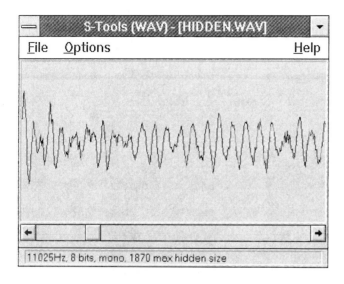

Figure 9.8 The main window of st-wav.exe, the S-Tools program for hiding information in a WAV file. The program displays the changed parts of the waveform in red, but this detail is lost in a black-and-white book.

file allocation table (FAT) (see Figure 9.9). The unused sectors are just sitting around not doing anything. If someone tries to open them up with a simple editor like a word processor or even tries to examine them with a File Manager, they'll find nothing. This is just empty space to the operating system. But this doesn't mean it can't hold anything. Information can be written into these sectors and left around. The only way it can be corrupted is if someone writes a new file to the disk. The operating system may assign those sectors to another file because it thinks the space is free.

S-Tools stores information in this free space by choosing empty sectors at random. The first sector gets the header of the file, which specifies the length and the random number seed that was used to choose the sectors. Then the information is just stored in this string of sectors selected at random.

If encryption is used, the random number generator uses the encryption key as a seed. This means that a different selection of random sectors will be chosen. The data itself is encrypted with any of the five algorithms offered in the other two implementations of S-Tools.

At the end, S-Tools offers to write random noise in the extra space that is not taken up by the hidden file. This is often a good idea

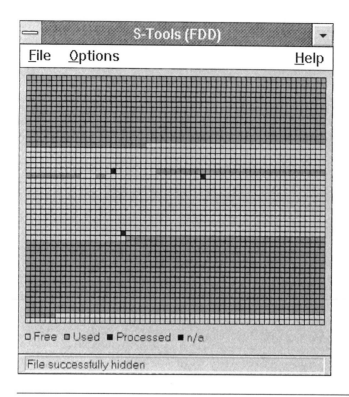

Figure 9.9   The user interface for st-fdd.exe shows the allocated sectors in red, the unallocated sectors in gray, and the ones that have been converted to hide information in yellow.

because the empty space may have some pattern to it left over from the last file it stored. Ordinarily, disk space is not actually cleared off when a file is erased.

The entry in the FAT table is just changed from "assigned" to "empty". The old data and its pattern are still there. This means that someone could identify the sectors of a floppy disk containing hidden information simply by looking for the ones that have random information. The ones that contain scraps of text files or images or ordinary data would be presumed innocent.[4] S-Tools will overwrite

---

[4]You could first use st-bmp.exe or st-wav.exe to hide information in a picture or a sound bite. Then you could store it in the unallocated sectors. Then it would look like random discarded information.

this to convert the unallocated sectors into a sea of noise. This is equivalent to using a new disk.

9.2.6 Random Walks

This chapter has discussed hiding information in image or sound files by grabbing all of the least significant bits to hold information. There is no reason why all of them need to be used. Both Hide and Seek and S-Tools use random number generators to choose the bytes that are actually drafted to give up their least significant bits to the cause. This random process guarantees that the distortion is distributed throughout the file so it is not so apparent. It also makes it difficult for some attacker to figure out which bits are important. S-Tools uses the MD-5 algorithm to ensure that the random numbers are cryptographically secure.

In fact, a random subset can have some other uses. First, if a person selects a small, random subset to store information, then another person could do the same thing. If both use different sources of randomness, then there is a good chance that very few bits will end up in both subsets. Error-correcting codes can help recover from these collisons. This could allow several people to use the same file to pass information to several different other ones.

Steve Walton suggested this approach in his article, "Image Authentication for a Slippery New Age" [Wal95]. This approach uses a general, two-dimensional random walk that weaves around a picture. Occasionally, the path may wrap around itself, which requires keeping track of where the path has been before. Hide and Seek, in contrast, views the picture as a one-dimensional list of pixels and simply chooses a random number of pixels to jump ahead.

Walton imagines that the least significant bits in his random walk can be used to construct a seal for the image. That is, you can "sign" the image by embedding some digital signature of the image in the least significant bits. Naturally, this digital signature would only be computed of the non–least significant bits because those bits are the only ones that would remain unchanged during the process. This sealing system could be used by professional photographers to attach their mark to a photograph.

Some have argued that this approach is a waste, believing that appending the signature data to the end of the photo makes more practical sense. This type of signature would be able to handle all types of photo formats including binary images without enough significant

Another solution is
to simply create a
random permutation
of the bits. Tuomas
Aura describes this in
[Aur95].

bits to hide data. Also, there would be no need to avoid the least significant bits while encoding the information and so the signature would be even better.

These suggestions are certainly correct. The only advantage that the surreptitious approach has is secrecy. Presumably photographers would sign images to protect their copyright. They could prove conclusively that the photo was stolen. If the signature is appended to the file, then someone could simply remove it or tamper with it. If it is hidden with a random walk in the least significant bits, then someone has to find it first. Of course, malicious people could simply write over the least significant bits of a photo as a precaution.

There is a certain rough, frontier aspect to simply choosing arbitrary random walks throughout the data. It does not require that there be any prior communication between two people who happen to be hiding information in the same picture. They're just both keeping their fingers crossed that the collisions will be minor and the error-correcting codes will be able to fix them.

Here is a more principled way to create multiple channels in an image. If all parties coordinate their use ahead of time, they can ensure that their random walks will not collide. This saves space because error-correcting codes do not need to be used, but it does increase the complexity of the process.

To create n channels, divide the file into n-byte blocks of data. One byte from each block will be given to each channel. In the simplest and most transparent approach, the assignment of byte and channel number is hard coded. Channel 1 gets byte 1, channel 2 gets byte 2, and so on. A better approach shuffles the bytes by using a set of permutations of the values between 1 and n. Here's a good way to generate a sequence of random permutations of the set:

1. Start with the ordered set $(1, 2, \ldots, n)$.

2. To generate a new random permutation, repeat this j times. A larger j is better, but less efficient.

   (a) Choose two items in the set at random using the output of a cryptographically secure random number generator.
   (b) Swap their positions. For example, if the set is $(5, 1, 3, 2, 4)$ before and the second and fourth values are chosen by the random number generator, then the result will be $(5, 2, 3, 1, 4)$.

3. Output this permutation. Go to step 2 to keep going.

The ith permutation spit out by this permutation generation routine can determine which channel gets which byte in the ith block. This ensures that no two users will collide.

Another approach can mangle the process even more. Why should blocks be made up of adjacent bytes? In the simplest approach, byte i from channel k in an n-channel system is assigned to byte $in + k$ in the file. This can be scrambled using exponentiation modulo the length of the file. So if the file is p bytes long and p just happens to be prime, then $(in+k)^e \bmod p$ will scramble the bytes so they are not adjacent.

9.2.7 Putting JPEG to Use

The first part of this chapter lamented the effects of JPEG on image files holding data in the least significant bits. The lossy compression algorithm could just mush all of that information into nothingness because it doesn't care if it reconstructs a file correctly. Although this can be a problem if someone uses JPEG to compress your file, it doesn't mean that the JPEG algorithm is useless to the person who would like to hide information successfully in images.

There are two possible ways that you can use the JPEG algorithm to store information. The first is to use it as a tool to identify the complexity of an image. This section discusses that approach. The second way is to use some hidden parts of the standard to hide information. That is described in Section 9.2.8.

The JPEG algorithm can be a good tool for identifying the level of detail in a scene. This level of detail can be used to find the noisiest corners of the image where data can be stored. In the first part of the chapter, the basic algorithm for hiding information would simply use the n least significant bits to hide information. If $n = 1$, there would only be a small but uniform effect that was randomly distributed throughout the image. If n was larger, then more information could be stored away in the image, but more distortion would also emerge. In any case, the distortion would be uniformly distributed across the entire image, even if this wasn't practical.

For instance, imagine a picture of a person sitting on a red-and-white checked picnic blanket in the middle of a grassy field. It might make sense to set $n = 4$ over a grassy section because it is out of focus and not particularly filled with important detail. On the other hand, you would want to use $n = 1$ in the areas of the face because the detail is so significant to the photo. Naturally, you could go through the photo by hand and identify the most significant and fragile sections of the photo, but this would defeat the purpose of the algorithm. Not only would it be time-consuming, but you would need to arrange for someone on the other end of the conversation to construct exactly the same partition. This is the only way that they would know how to recover the bits.

The JPEG compression algorithm offers an automatic way to segment the photo and identify the most important or salient portions of an image. It was designed to do this to increase compression. The algorithm's creators tweaked the algorithm so it would provide visually satisfying images even after some of the detail was lost to compression.

The application is simple. Let f be a 24-bit image file waiting to have data hidden in some of its least significant bits. Let $JPEG^{-1}(JPEG(f))$ be the result of first compressing f with JPEG and then uncompressing it. The differences between f and $JPEG^{-1}(JPEG(f))$ reveal how much noise is available to hide information. For each pixel, you can compare f with $JPEG^{-1}(JPEG(f))$ and determine how many of the bits are equal. If only the first 4 bits of the 8 bits encoding the blue intensity are the same, then you can conclude that the JPEG algorithm doesn't really care what is in the last 4 bits. The algorithm determined that those 4 bits could be set to any value and the resulting image would still look good enough. That means that 4 bits are available to hide information. Elsewhere in the image, all 8 bits of f might agree with $JPEG^{-1}(JPEG(f))$. Then no information can be hidden in these bits.

This algorithm makes it possible to identify the locations of important parts of the image. You can choose the right accuracy value for JPEG as well. If you need a good final representation, then you should use the best settings for JPEG, and this will probably identify a smaller number of bits available to hide data. A coarser setting for JPEG should open up more bits.

There are many other compression algorithms being developed to hide information. The fractal compression algorithms from Barnsley's Iterated Systems [BH92] are some of the more popular techniques around. Each could be used in a similar fashion to identify sections of the image that can be successfully sacrificed.

Other solutions that are tuned to different types of images can also be used successfully. For instance, there are some algorithms designed to convert 24-bit color images into 8-bit color images. These do a good job of identifying 256 colors that represent the image. You can identify the number of free bits at each pixel by comparing the 24-bit value with the entry from the 256-color table that was chosen to replace it. Some of these algorithms are tuned to do a better job on faces. Others work well on natural scenes. Each is applicable in its own way and can do a good job with the system.

If you use JPEG or a similar lossy algorithm to identify the high-noise areas of an image, then you must change one crucial part of the system. When a GIF file is used to hold information, then the recipient doesn't need to have a copy of the original image. The n least significant bits can simply be stripped away and recovered. They can be used verbatim. If JPEG is going to point out the corners and crevices of the image waiting for more data, then both the sender and the recipient must have access to the same list of corners and crevices. Probably the easiest way to accomplish this is to make sure that both sides have copies of the original image. This is a limitation if you're going to communicate with someone whom you've never met before. You must somehow arrange to get the image to that person.

9.2.8   Hiding Information in JPEG Files

There is no doubt that the JPEG's lossy approach to hiding information is a problem that confounds the basic approach to steganography. The noise can be changed in any which way, so the first impulse is to avoid the format altogether. Derek Upham dug deeper and found another approach, which he called *JSteg*. The JPEG algorithm compresses data in two steps. First, it breaks the image into 8×8 blocks of pixels and fits cosine functions (see Figure 14.10 on page 268) to these pixels to describe them. That is, it finds a weighted average of the functions that adds up to something pretty close to the original block of 8×8 pixels. Then it stores the weights of these cosine functions to serve as a description of this block of pixels. The amount of compression can be increased or decreased by setting more or fewer of the weights to be zero. Upham recognized that you could tweak the least significant bits of the weights to store information.

His solution is coded in C and distributed as a `diff` file that can be added to the standard JPEG version 4 distributed on the Net. His code adds an additional command-line feature for UNIX machines that allows you to hide a file as you compress an image. This is a nice approach because it simply builds upon the standard JPEG distribution. Also, it is important because the JPEG image format could become more common on the Net. It is much more efficient than the GIF format for photographs, although GIF is usually better for graphics.

There are also a number of physiological reasons why this approach may actually generate better effects than simply tweaking the least significant bits of the data. Programs like S-Tools and Stego jump through many hoops to handle 8-bit color images. They end up with clusters of colors in the color table that are quite similar to one another. This can be accomplished quite well, but it may be easy to detect by someone scanning the color tables.

Tweaking the frequencies of the discrete cosine transform that models the 8×8 block of data has a different effect. Although these tweaks can harm the quality of the final image, it is hard to distinguish their effects. After all, the discrete transformation is already an approximation, and it is harder to notice changes in an approximation. In essence, the bits are hidden by controlling whether the JPEG program rounds up or rounds down. Rounding up is a 1 and rounding down is a 0. These numbers can be recovered by looking at the least significant bits of the frequencies.

Upham chose one interesting approach to hiding the information. There must be a header at the beginning of the block of data to tell how many bits are there. Ordinarily, this would be a single number. So the first 32 bits would be devoted to a number that would indicate there are, say, 8523 bytes stored in the least significant bits that follow. Upham noted that this number would often have many 0s at the front of it. Since these bits would normally be somewhat randomly distributed, a block of 0s could look suspicious. Sixteen 0s in a row should only occur about 1 out of 2^{16} times.

His solution was to have two fields in the header. The first consists of a 5-bit number that specifies the number of bits in the second field. The second field contains the number of bits in the entire file. This removes any large blocks of bits at the beginning of the number while leaving the flexibility for extremely large files. He also suggests that the number of bits in the second field be padded with an extra 0 about half of the time. This prevents the sixth bit of the file from always being a 1. This is a very subtle attention to detail.

9.2.9   Outguess

The Outguess software written by Niels Provos tweaks least significant bits like all of the other tools, but it does it carefully to avoid introducing statistical signatures that might alert attackers looking for the presence of the message.

This attention to statistical detail has its costs. The program identifies potential bits and then rules out using half of them in order to have potential fixes. This cuts the capacity of the channel in half but increases the security dramatically.

In the most abstract sense, the Outguess algorithm is straightforward. Every time you change a bit to hide information, you search for an equivalent bit and change it too to maintain a balanced statistical profile. If you change a 0 to a 1, then change a 1 to a 0 at the same time. The Outguess software can be modified to work with any data format given routines for identifying good places to hide data [Pro01, Pro].

These balanced changes can be used in any of the steganographic solutions. In practice, Provos implements the algorithm by changing the JPEG compression coefficients. Simply changing the least significant bits may introduce higher-order changes to the JPEG compression coefficients, and these changes can be relatively simple to detect [JJ98a].

9.2.10   F4 and F5

JSteg was the first generation of programs designed to hide information in the JPEG image format, but attackers soon discovered it left a serious statistical signature. The coefficients in JPEG compression normally fall along a bell curve, and the information-hiding process distorts this. In most photographs, the most common coefficient is 0 followed by 1 and −1, followed again by 2 and −2, and so on. The occurrence of coefficients drops off as the coefficients get larger.

JSteg ruins this smooth curve when information is hidden. The coefficients of 2 and 3, for instance, are interchanged by the process of tweaking the least significant bit, leaving both of them occurring in equal proportions [JJ98a, JJ98b, WP99, Wes01]. The same happens with coefficient pairs such as 4 and 5 or −1 and −2. Finding a JPEG file with many pairs of coefficients that occur in equal proportions is a sure sign that a message may be hidden with the JSteg algorithm.

One solution is to change the probability of 0s and 1s in the information being hidden. The algorithms from Chapter 6 make it possible to change the statistical probability to mimic any distribution. Let's say that our analysis of a JPEG image shows that the coefficient of 3 occurs about 60 percent as often as 2. A 3 corresponds to a hidden bit of 1, and a 2 corresponds to a hidden bit of 0. If we could arrange for the number of 1s to be hidden about 60 percent as often as the number of 0s, then the coefficients would balance out.

Here's one basic solution. Create a collection of *n*-bit words and use these as characters for the algorithm in Section 6.1. Use the number of 0s and 1s in the word to determine the weight. If a 0 is assigned weight .625 and a 1 is assigned .375, the values will emerge in something approximating a distribution of 1 to .6.

For example, let $n = 8$. There are 256 characters in the alphabet. Give 00000000 a weight of $8 \times .625$, 00000001 a weight of $7 \times .625 + .375$, and so on. These can be used to build a Huffman tree to change the statistics of the incoming data. If this preprocessing is done, the statistics of the JSteg algorithm begin to come much closer to real images. This isn't perfect, but it doesn't need to be because the values of the coefficients vary from image to image.

Andreas Westfeld proposes another solution to the statistical gap. His algorithm, F4, encodes the data with more care, avoiding the statistical distortions [Wes01].

Here's the mechanism for hiding data in a coefficient C:

- If $C = 0$, skip over it and don't hide any information in this coefficient. This decreases the effectiveness of the algorithm, but there's no choice. JSteg also does this.

- If $C > 0$ and odd, leave C unchanged to encode a 1 and decrement it to encode a 0.

- If $C > 0$ and even, leave C unchanged to encode a 0 and decrement it to encode a 1.

- if $C < 0$ and odd, leave C unchanged to hide a 0 and increment it to hide a 1.

- if $C < 0$ and even, leave C unchanged to hide a 1 and increment it to hide a 0.

The only problem occurs when the decrementing or the incrementing produces a new coefficient of 0. In those cases, the bit is repeated because the information is effectively lost. The coding process ignores the coefficients with 0.

Table 9.3 shows a slightly different technique for encoding information.

Table 9.4 shows the bits 01010 being hidden. The 5 bits require seven coefficients because some are skipped.

Decoding the file is simple. A coefficient of 1, for instance, is either produced by hiding a 1 in a coefficient of 2 or by hiding a 1 in a coefficient of 1. In either case, the hidden bit is 1. The same pattern holds throughout the encoding process.

Table 9.3   F4's scheme for tweaking coefficients to encode bits.

Coefficient	After Encoding 0	After Encoding 1
0	skip	skip
1	0 (skip)	1
2	2	1
3	2	3
4	4	3
−1	−1	0 (skip)
−2	−1	−2
−3	−3	−2
−4	−3	−4

Table 9.4   An example encoding 01010 using Table 9.3.

Hidden Bit	Coefficient Before	Coefficient After
0	4	4
1	2	1
0 (skip)	0	0
0 (again)	−2	−1
1	1	1
0 (skip)	1	0
0 (again)	2	2

This solution avoids the gross statistical problems of JSteg, but it still changes the profile. Some bits are hidden by shrinking the absolute values of the coefficients. This means that there are more values clustered around 0 than before, and the distribution is now tighter. This is not as glaring because the distribution naturally varies among images, but it is still worth combatting.

Westfeld further enhanced the process to minimize the disruption to the file in the next version of the algorithm, F5. He uses a process he calls "matrix encoding" to spread the information out among more bits. This reduces the density and decreases the amount of distortion.

Imagine you want to store $n = 4$ bits of data. One solution is to pick $2^n = 16$ different locations in the image and only change one of the locations. A change at position $3 = 0011$ would mean you wanted to store the message 0011. The algorithm F5 chooses the best value of n to accommodate the data being stored. The positions are chosen with a cryptographically secure pseudo-random bit stream.

9.3

Summary

Placing information in the noise of digitized images is one of the most popular methods of steganography. The different approaches here guarantee that the data will be hard to find if you're careful about how you use the tools. The biggest problem is making sure that you handle the differences between 24-bit and 8-bit images correctly.

- *The Disguise.* The world is filled with noise. There is no reason why some of the great pool of randomness can't be used to hide data. This disguise is often impossible for the average human to notice.

- *How Secure Is It?* These systems are not secure if someone is looking for the information. But many of the systems can produce images that are indistinguishable from the original. If the data is compressed and encrypted before it is hidden, it can be difficult to know whether the data is there or not. Chapter 17 discusses some of the ways of detecting the existence of a hidden message. This can be subverted if a special header is used to identify details about the file.

- *How to Use the Software.* There are many different versions of the software available on the Net (see Appendix D). Others circulate throughout the Net. The programs are simple to use.

chapter ten

Anonymous Remailers

Dr. Anon to You

Host: On this week's show, we have Anonymous, that one-named wonder who is in the class of artists like Madonna, Michelangelo, and the Artist Formerly Known as Prince, who are so big they can live on one name alone. He, or perhaps she, is the author of many of the most incendiary works in the world. We're lucky we could get him or her on the show today, even though he or she would only agree to appear via a blurred video link.

Mr. Anonymous (or should I say Ms. Anonymous?), it's great to have you on the show.

Anon: Make it Dr. Anonymous. That will solve the gender problem. I was just granted an honorary doctorate last June.

Host: Congratulations! That must be quite an honor. Did they choose you because of your writings? It says here on my briefing sheet that you've written numerous warm and romantic novels like the *Federalist Papers*. Great stuff.

Anon: Actually, the *Federalist Papers* wasn't a book until the papers were collected. It really wasn't a romantic set of papers, although it did have a rather idealistic notion of what Congress could be.

Host: Sexual congress. Now that's a euphemism I haven't heard for a while. You're from the old school, right? That's where you got the degree?

Anon: Well . . .

Host: This explains why you're so hesitant to get publicity, right? It's too flashy.

Anon: No. It's not my style. I prefer to keep my identity secret because some of what I write can have dangerous repercussions.

Host: What a clever scheme! You've got us all eating out of your hand. Every other author would fall over himself to get on this show. We're just happy to be talking with you.

Anon: I was a bit hesitant, but my publisher insisted on it. It was in the contract.

Host: Do you find it hard to be a celebrity in the modern age? Don't you feel the pull to expand your exposure by, say, doing an exercise book with Cher? She's got one name too. You guys would get along great. You could talk about how the clerk at the Motor Vehicles Department gives you a hard time because you've left a slot on the form blank.

Anon: Well, that hadn't crossed my mind.

Host: How about a spread in *Architectural Digest* or *InStyle*? They always like to photograph the famous living graciously in large, architecturally challenging homes. Or how about *Lifestyles of the Rich and Famous*? They could show everyone where and, of course, how you live. It's a great way to sell your personality.

Anon: Actually, part of the reason for remaining anonymous is so that no one shows up at your house in the middle of the night.

Host: Oh, yeah, groupies offering themselves. I have that problem.

Anon: Actually to burn the place down and shoot me.

Host: Oh, okay. I can see you doing a book with Martha Stewart on how to give a great masquerade party! You could do some really clever masks and then launch it during Mardi Gras in New Orleans. Have you thought about that?

Anon: No. Maybe after I get done promoting my latest book. It's on your desk there. The one exposing a deep conspiracy that is fleecing the people. Money is diverted from tax accounts into a network of private partnerships where it fills the coffers of the very rich.

Host: What about a talk show? I guess I shouldn't ask for competition. But you could be a really spooky host. You could roam the audience wearing a big black hood and cape. Just like in that Mozart movie. Maybe they could electronically deepen your voice so everyone was afraid of you when you condemned their shenanigans. Just like in the *Wizard of Oz*. It would be really hot in those robes under the lights, but I could see you getting a good share of the daytime audience. You would be different.

Anon: My book, though, is really showing the path toward a revolution. It names names. It shows how the money flows. It shows which politicians are part of the network. It shows which media conglomerates turn out cheerful pabulum and "mind candy" to keep everyone somnolescent.

Host: Whoa! Big word there. Speaking of big words, don't you find "Anonymous" to be a bit long? Do you go by "Anon"? Does it make you uncomfortable if I call you "Anon"? Or should I call you "Dr. Anon"?

Anon: Either's fine. I'm not vain.

Host: I should say not. Imagine not putting your name on a book as thick as this one. Speaking of vain, are you into horse racing? I wanted to ask you if you were the person in that Carly Simon song, "You're so vain, you probably think this song is about you." She *never* told anyone who it was about. I thought it might be you. The whole secrecy thing and all.

10.1

Anonymous Remailers

There are many reasons why people would want to write letters or communiqués without attaching their names. Some people search for counseling through anonymous suicide prevention centers. Other people want to inquire about jobs without jeopardizing their own. Then there are the times that try our souls and drive us to write long, half-mad screeds that ring with the truth that the people in power don't want to hear. These are just a few of the reasons to send information anonymously. Even a high government official who is helping to plan the government's approach to cracking down on cryptography and imposing key escrow admitted to me over lunch that he or she has used pay phones from time to time. Just for the anonymity.

Much of what we do, or have done in the past, is largely anonymous. Keeping track of who did what when is a waste of time. People only record data that makes sense, and the rest is quickly forgotten, providing a cloud of forgiveness that covers the past.

On the Internet, *anonymous remailers* are one simple solution for letting people communicate anonymously. These are mail programs that accept incoming mail with a new address and some text for the body of the letter. The program strips off the incoming header that contains the real identity of the sender and remails the content to the new address. The recipient knows it came from an anonymous remailer, but they don't know who sent it there.

In some cases, the remailer creates a new pseudonym for the outgoing mail. This might be a random string like "an41234". Then it keeps a secret internal log file that matches the real name of the incoming mail with this random name. If the recipient wants to reply to this person, they can send mail back to "an41234" in care of the anonymous remailer who then repackages the letter and sends it on. This allows people to hold a conversation over the wires without knowing each other's identity.

There are many legitimate needs for services like this one. Most of the newspapers that offer personal ads also offer anonymous mailboxes and voicemail boxes so that people can screen their responses. People may be willing to advertise for a new lover or friend if the anonymous holding box at the newspaper gives them a measure of protection. Some people may go through several exchanges of letters before they feel trusting enough to meet the other person. Or they may call anonymously from a pay phone. There are enough nasty stories from the dating world to make this anonymous screening a sad, but very necessary, feature of modern life.[1]

Of course, there are also many controversial ways that anonymous remailers can be used. Someone posted copyrighted documents from the Church of Scientology to the Internet using an anonymous remailer based in Finland [Gro]. This raised the ire of the Church, which was able to get the local police to raid the site and force the owner to reveal the sender's name. Obviously, remailers can be used to send libelous or fake documents, documents under court seal, or

---

[1]Strangely enough, in the past people would rely upon knowing other people extensively as a defense against this type of betrayal. People in small towns knew everyone and their reputations. This type of knowledge isn't practical in the big city, so complete anonymity is the best defense.

other secret information. Tracking down the culprit depends upon how well the owner of the remailer can keep a secret.

There is a wide variety of anonymous remailers on the Internet, and the collection is growing and shrinking constantly. One current source of a good list can be found at *http://anon.efga.org/Remailers* and *http://www.chez.com/frogadmin*. These also include pointers to the software and instructions on how to start up your own remailer.

10.1.1 Enhancements

There are a number of different ways that the anonymous remailers can be enhanced with different features. Some of the most important ones are listed here:

- *Encryption.* The remailer has its own public-key pair and accepts the requests in encrypted form. It decrypts them before sending them out. This is an important defense against someone who might be tapping the incoming and outgoing lines of a remailer.

- *Latency.* The remailer will wait to send out the mail in order to confound anyone who is watching the traffic coming in and out of the remailer. This delay may either be specified by the incoming message or assigned randomly.

- *Padding.* Someone watching the traffic in and out of a remailer might be able to trace encrypted messages by comparing the size. Even if the incoming and outgoing messages are encrypted with different keys, they're still the same size. Padding messages with random data can remove this problem.

- *Reordering.* The remailer may get the messages in one order, but it doesn't process them in the same first-in-first-out order. This adds an additional measure of secrecy.

- *Chaining Remailers.* If one anonymous remailer might cave in and reveal your identity, it is possible to chain together several remailers in order to add additional secrecy. This chain, unlike the physical basis for the metaphor, is as strong as its *strongest* link. Only one machine on the list has to keep a secret to stop the trail.

- *Anonymous Posters.* This machine will post the contents to a newsgroup anonymously instead of sending them out via email.

Each of these features can be found in different remailers. Consult the lists of remailers available on the Net to determine which features might be available to you.

10.1.2   Using Remailers

There are several different types of anonymous remailers on the Internet, and there are subtle differences among them. Each different class was written by different people, and they approached some of the details in their own way. The entire concept isn't too challenging, though, so everyone should be able to figure out how to send information through an anonymous remailer after reading the remailer's instructions.

One of the more popular remailers in history was run by Johan Helsingius in Helsinki, Finland, at anon@anon.penet.fi, until legal troubles exhausted his patience. Composing email and sending it through the remailer was simple. You created the letter as you would any other, but you addressed it to anon@anon.penet.fi. At the top of the letter, you added two fields, X-Anon-Password: and X-Anon-To:. The first held a password that you used to control your anonymous identity. The second gave the address to which the message would go. Here's a short sample:

```
Mime-Version: 1.0
Content-Type: text/plain; charset="us-ascii"
Date: Tue, 5 Dec 1995 09:07:07 -0500
To: anon@anon.penet.fi
From: pcw@flyzone.com (Peter Wayner)
Subject: Echo Homo

X-Anon-Password: swordfish
X-Anon-To: pcw@access.digex.net

Le nom de plume de la rose est <<Pink Flamingo.>>
```

When the message would arrive in Finland, the remailer would strip off the header and assign an anonymous ID to my address pcw@flyzone.com. The real name and the anonymous name would be placed in a table and bound with a password. A password is not necessary, but this adds security. Anyone with a small amount of technical expertise can fake mail so that it arrives looking like it came from someone else. The password prevents anyone from capturing your secret identity. If people don't know your password, then they can't assume your identity.

The password is also necessary for dissolving your identity. If you wanted to remove your name and anonymous identity from the system, then you would need to know the password. This remailer placed a waiting period on cancellation because it didn't want people to come in, send something anonymously, and then escape the flames. The philosophy was, if you send something, then you should feel the heat. This philosophy eventually wore out the welcome.

If you wanted to post anonymously to a newsgroup, then you could simply put the newsgroup's name in the X-Anon-To: field like this:

```
Mime-Version: 1.0
Content-Type: text/plain; charset=us-ascii"
Date: Tue, 5 Dec 1995 09:07:07 -0500
To: anon@anon.penet.fi
From: pcw@flyzone.com (Peter Wayner)
Subject: Stupidity

X-Anon-Password: swordfish
X-Anon-To: alt.flames

In <412A9231243@whitehouse.gov>, Harry Hstar writes:
> Why you're so dumb, I can't believe that someone
> taught you how to type.

You're so stupid, that you probably don't understand
why this is such a great insult to you.
```

This would get posted under my anonymous identity. If someone wanted to respond, they could write back to me through the remailer. It would protect my identity to some degree.

10.1.3 Using Private Idaho

One of the nicer email packages for the Windows market is Private Idaho, shown in Figure 10.1, which was first written by Joel McNamara. The original program is still available as freeware, but some of the more advanced development is now bundled as a US $30 product (from *http://www.itech.net.au/pi*).

Private Idaho is just a shell for composing the email message and encrypting it with the necessary steps. The final product can either be handed off directly to an SMTP server or another email package such as Eudora. The original product was just a shell for handling many of the chores involved in choosing a path, handling the keys, and encrypting the message. The latest is more of a full-fledged tool.

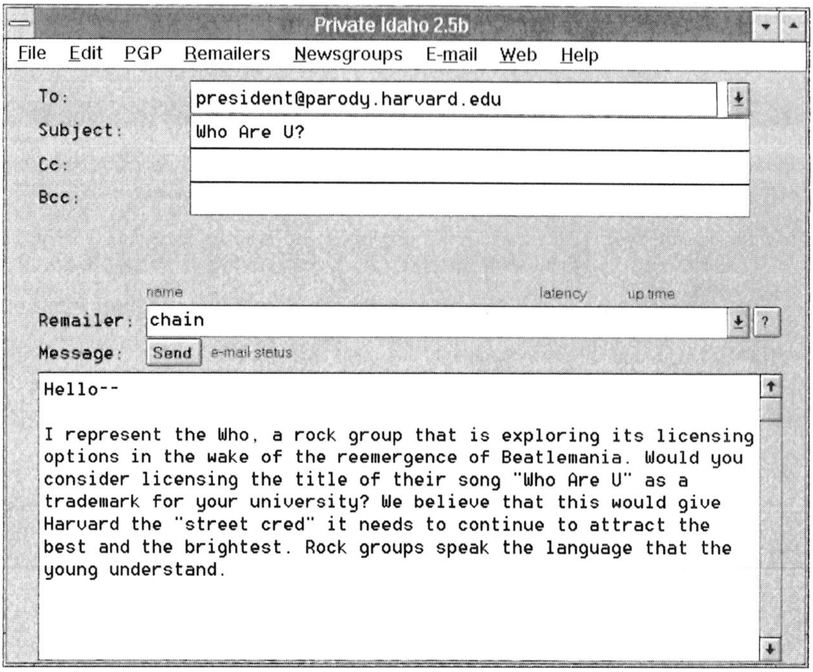

Figure 10.1 A screen shot of the Windows program Private Idaho. You can use it to send encrypted mail or anonymous mail.

You can get copies of the original software directly from *http://www.eskimo.com/joelm/pi.html* and versions of the latest from *http://www.itech.net.au/pi*.

10.1.4   Web Remailers

A number of Web sites offer remailers for reposting information. Adding one level of anonymity is easy for Web designers to include, and many do. Some of the most popular are now pay services. The Anonymizer (*http://www.anonymizer.com*) offers tools for both sending anonymous email and browsing the Web anonymously. They deliberately keep few log files that might be used to break the veil of secrecy. After the September 11, 2001, attacks on the World Trade Center, the company made news by offering to help anonymous tipsters turn in terrorists. The site argued that if the terrorists were ruthless enough to kill 5000 people, they would not hesitate to track down and kill anyone who turned them in.

plate 1

An image and the results of replacing consecutive bit planes with a hidden file. The image is 2312 x 1526 pixels or 3,528,112 pixels altogether. Each pixel has three components (red, green, and blue) so that the bit plane has 3 x 3,528,112 = 10,584,336 bits, or 1,323,042 bytes or 1.3 megabytes. The image in the upper-left corner is the original. The image in the upper-right corner is the same image after the least significant bit plane has been replaced with 1.3 megabytes of data. The left image in the second row shows the result of replacing the two least significant bits of each bit plane with 2.6 megabytes, and so on with the subsequent images. The effects are first apparent in the sky. Details with rough texture do a better job of hiding the effects. (All photos were converted to CMYK for printing.)

plate 2

Another image with the same dimensions as Plate 1.

plate 3

A vertical image with 1526 x 2312 pixels and the results of replacing each successive bit plane. 1.3 megabytes are stored in each plane.

plate 4

The natural least significant bits of the images in Plates 1–3. Many seem relatively random, except in some locations where the colors are saturated. In some cases, only one of the colors is saturated and the others are not.

plate 5

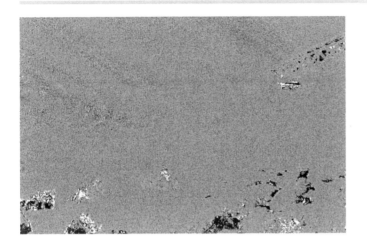

This version of the image in Plate 1 compares the least significant bit with the most significant bit by XORing them. Most of the image appears random, but significant agreement can be found in the most saturated or unsaturated points. Replacing the least significant bits with a message can destroy this relationship.

plate 6

Packing in too much data can leave artifacts. This figure shows detail of a 2048 x 1352 pixel file where the four least significant bits have been replaced by ASCII text. The eighth bit in ASCII is always 0 for upper-case characters, and the seventh bit is 1 for lower-case characters. This produces the vertical striping repeated every eight rows.

plate 7

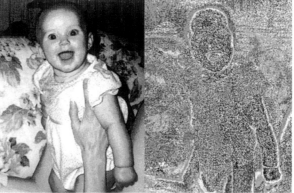

The left window shows a picture and its least significant bits before approximately 17,000 bytes were hidden in the image with EzStego. The image had a capacity of 20,000 bytes. The right window shows the image and the least significant bits afterward. (This is a color version of Figure 17.2.)

plate 8

A large version of a low quality (10) JPEG file packed with data added using the F5 algorithm. The algorithm leaves ragged lines along the blue gradient in the sky. The small changes in the coefficients become apparent when images of poor quality and high compression carry too much hidden information. These artifacts disappear with less compression and a relatively smaller amount of data.

plate 9

The top row shows detail in low quality (10) JPEG files with no added information. The middle row shows the result of mixing in the maximum amount of data with the F5 algorithm. Small changes in the coefficients are still visible in the details. The bottom row shows the result of mixing in data using the F5 algorithm at the highest quality (100). Adding too much information at low quality leaves artifacts.

plate 10

A generic palette is shown at top, and the sorted version is shown at bottom. (These figures were created by Andreas Westfeld and Andreas Pfitzmann for their paper [WP99]. They take only 61 short lines of Postscript! (This is a color version of Figure 9.7.)

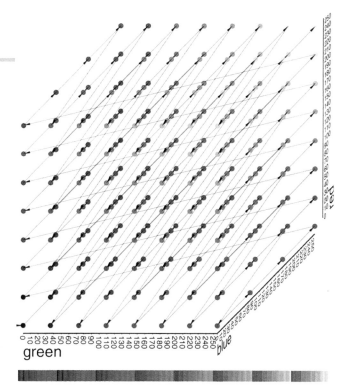

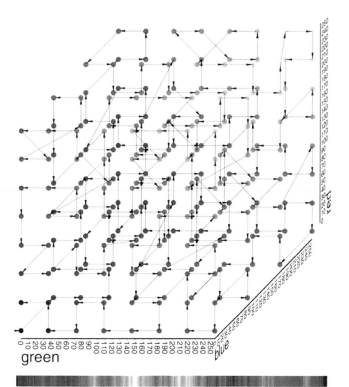

Many people use the free email services of Hotmail, Popmail, Excite, or Netscape as pseudononymous drop boxes. These services may work well for basic situations, but they often keep voluminous log files that can reveal the identity of their users. Some, like Microsoft's Hotmail, are pushing new services like the Passport in an effort to assign a fixed identity to people.

10.2

Remailer Guts

Designing the inside of a remailer is fairly easy. Most UNIX mail systems will take incoming mail and pass it along to a program that will do the necessary decoding. Repackaging it is just a matter of rearranging the headers and re-encrypting the information. This process can be accomplished with some simple scripts or blocks of C code. Moving this to any platform is also easy. There is an SMTP-compatible mail program for the Macintosh, for instance, known as the Apple Internet Mail Server (AIMS) that is currently given away free.

Designing better, smarter remailer systems is more of a challenge. Here are some of the standard attacks that people might use to try to follow messages through a web of remailers:

- *In and Out Tracking.* The attacker watches as messages go in and out of the remailer and matches them up by either order or size. The defense against this is to keep n messages in an internal queue and dispense them in random order. The messages are either kept to be all the same size or they're randomly padded at each iteration.

- *Remailer Flooding.* Imagine that one remailer receives a letter and the attacker wants to know where it is going. The remailer keeps n letters in its queue and dispenses them randomly. One attack is to send n of the attacker's messages to the remailer just before the message in question arrives. The attacker knows the destination of her own n messages, so she can pick out the one different message from the flow. If the messages are sent out randomly, then the attacker must send another n messages to ensure that subsequent messages won't confuse her.

  One defense against this approach is remailer broadcasting. Instead of sending each subsequent message to a particular remailer using one-to-one mail delivery, the remailer would broadcast it to a group of other remailers. Only one remailer would have the right key to decrypt the next address. The others would simply discard it.

- *Replay Attack.* An attacker grabs a copy of the message as it goes by. Then, it resends it a while later. Eventually, the letter will make its way through the chain of remailers until it arrives at the same destination as before. If the attacker keeps track of all of the mail going to all of the destinations and the attacker replays the message several times, then only one consistent recipient will emerge. This is the destination.

The best solution is to require each message to contain an individual ID number that is randomly generated by the sender. The remailer stores this ID in a large file. If it encounters another message with the same ID, then it discards the message. The size of this ID should be large enough to ensure that two IDs will almost certainly not match if they're chosen at random.

- *Forged Mail Attack.* It is relatively easy to fake mail sent to SMTP. Someone could pretend to be you when they sent the anonymous message containing something illegal. If the police were willing to pressure the remailer operator into revealing names, then you could be fingered for something you didn't do.

The passwords used by many remailers are a simple defense against this problem. The anonymous remailer won't send along mail that is supposed to be from a certain site unless the correct password is included. A more sophisticated system would require that the mail be signed with the correct digital signature.

The State may, and does, punish fraud directly. But it cannot seek to punish fraud indirectly by indiscriminately outlawing a category of speech, based on its content, with no necessary relationship to the danger sought to be prevented.
—From the majority opinion by Justice Stevens in *Joseph McIntyre v. Ohio Election Committee*

Each of these solutions came from a paper by David Chaum [Cha81] that describes a process called a *mix*. The details of this paper were used as the architecture for the most sophisticated type of remailer currently operating on the Net. Lance Cottrell wrote Mixmaster, a UNIX-based program that will send anonymous mail packages using the more robust structure described in the paper.

The main difference is in the structure of the address information. The first class of remailers packaged their data in nesting envelopes. Each remailer along the chain would open an envelope and do the right thing with the contents. Mixmaster maintains a separate set of addressing blocks. Each travels through the entire chain of remailers.

Table 10.1   One path for an anonymous message.

Remailer's Entry	Next Destination	Packet ID	Key
Bob	Ray	92394129	12030124
Ray	Lorraine	15125152	61261621
Lorraine	Carol	77782893	93432212
Carol	Gilda	12343324	41242219
Gilda	Final Location	91999201	93929441

It is more like a distribution list that offices use to route magazines through a list of different recipients. Each recipient crosses off his or her name after the material is received.

There are two advantages to arranging the contents of the messages in this form. The first is that there is no natural reason for the size of the messages to shrink. If the outer envelopes are merely stripped off, then the size of the letter will shrink. This can be compensated for by adding padding, but getting the padding to be the right size may be complicated because of the different block sizes of ciphers like DES. The second advantage is reduced encryption time. The block of the encryption does not have to be encrypted or decrypted for each stage of the remailer chain. Only the address blocks need to be manipulated.

Imagine that a message will take five hops. Then the header for a Mixmaster will contain a table that looks something like Table 10.1 if all of the encryption was removed.

The encryption was removed to show how the process works. This header specifies that the mail should go from the remailer run by Bob, to Ray to Lorraine to Carol and then to Gilda before heading to its final location. The Packet ID is used by each remailer to defend against replay attacks.

There are two types of encryption used in Mixmaster. First, each entry in the header is encrypted with the public key of the remailer. So the Next Destination, the Packet ID, and the Key for Ray are encrypted with Ray's public key. Only the rightful recipient of each remailer will be able to decode its entry.

The second encryption uses the keys stored in the table. The best way to understand it is to visualize what each remailer does. The steps are as follows:

1. Decodes its packet using its secret key. This reveals the next destination, the ID, and the Key.

I was the shadow of the waxwing slain by the false azure of the window pane.
—John Shade in Vladimir Nabokov's
Pale Fire

2. Uses its Key to decrypt every entry underneath it. Mixmaster uses triple DES to encode the messages.

3. Moves itself to the bottom of the list and replaces the remailer name, the destination information, and the ID with a random block of data. This obscures the trail.

If this is going to be repeated successfully by each remailer on the list, then the initial table is going to have to be encrypted correctly. Each entry in the header will need to be encrypted by the key of each of the headers above it. For instance, the entry for Carol should look something like this:

$$E_{12030124}(E_{61261621}(E_{93432212}(PK_{Carol}(\ldots)))).$$

Bob's remailer will strip off the first level of encryption indicated by the function $E_{12030124}$, Ray's will strip off the second, and Lorraine's will strip off the third. The final block left is encrypted by Carol's public key.

When the header finally arrives at the last destination, each block will have been re-encrypted in reverse order. This forms something like the signature chain of a certified letter. Each step must be completed in order, and each step can only be completed by someone holding the matching secret key. The final recipient can keep this header and check to see that it was processed correctly.

The last key in the chain, in this case the one in the entry for Gilda, is the one that was used to encrypt the message. There is no reason for the remailer to decrypt the message at each step.

Mixmaster currently appends a block of 20 header entries to the top of each entry. Each block takes 512 bytes. If the letter is only going through five remailers, for instance, then the others are filled with random noise. Each entry in the table contains a bit that identifies it as a "final" hop. If that bit is set, then the key is used to decrypt the main block.

The main block of each message is also kept the same size. If a current message is too short, then padding is added until it is 20K long. If it is too long, then it is broken into 20K blocks. This size is flexible, but it should be set to a constant for all messages. This prevents anyone from identifying the messages from their size or the change of size.

Mixmaster software can currently be found through anonymous ftp at *www.obscura.com*. The software cannot be exported so you must send a message certifying that you will comply with the U.S. government's export laws. More information can be found at Lance Cottrell's home page, *http://obscura.com/loki/Welcome.html*.

10.2.1 Other Remailer Packages

One of the nicest, feature-rich programs for UNIX-based machines is Mailcrypt, written in Emacs-LISP for use with the popular GNU Emacs program distributed by the GNU project. The software, created by Patrick LoPresti, will handle all of the basic encryption jobs for mail, including encrypting outgoing mail, decrypting incoming mail, and evaluating signatures. The software interacts with the major UNIX mail reading programs such as MH-E, VM, and Rmail.

The software also includes a good implementation that will create chains of remailers. When you choose this option, it will automatically create a nested packet of encrypted envelopes that will be understood by the remailers on the list maintained by Raph Levien.

You can create lists of possible remailer chains for future use. These can either be hard-coded lists or they can be flexible. You can specify, for instance, that Mailcrypt should choose a different random ordering of four remailers every time it sends something along the chain. You could also request that Mailcrypt use the four most reliable remailers according to the list maintained by Raph Levien. This gives you plenty of flexibility in guiding the information. To get Mailcrypt, go to *http://cag-www.lcs.mit.edu/mailcrypt*.

Mailcrypt also makes it simple to use pseudonyms very easily. You can create a PGP key pair for a secret identity and then publicize it. Then if you want to assume a name like Silence Dogood, you could send off your messages through a chain of remailers. The final readers would be able to verify that the message came from the one and only original Silence Dogood because they would be able to retrieve the right public key and check the signature. Some people might try to imitate him or her, but they would not own the corresponding secret key so they couldn't issue anything under this pseudonym.

PGP, or Pretty Good Privacy, is one of the better known encryption packages.

Another program developed just for chaining together the necessary information for remailers is Premail written by Raph Levien. The software is designed as a replacement for Sendmail, the UNIX software that handles much of the low-level SMTP. Premail can take all of the same parameters that modify its behavior, including an additional set of commands that will invoke chains of remailers. So you can drop it in place of Sendmail any place you choose.

Premail has several major options. If you simply include the line
`key: user_id` in the header with the recipient's user_id, then
Premail will look up the key in the PGP files and encrypt the file
using this public key on the way out the door. If you include the
header line `Chain: Bob; Ray; Lorraine`, then Premail will arrange it so that the mail will head out through Bob's, Ray's, and
Lorraine's anonymous remailers before it goes to the final destination. You can also specify an anonymous return address if you like by
adding the `Anon-From:` field to the header. Premail is very flexible
because it will randomly select a chain of remailers from the list of
currently operating remailers. Just specify the number of hops in a
header field like this: `Chain:3`. Premail will find the best remailers
from Raph Levien's list of remailers.

10.2.2   Splitting Paths

The current collection of remailers is fairly simple. A message is sent
out one path. At each step along the line, the remailers strip off the
incoming sender's name and add a new anonymous name. Return
mail can follow this path back because the anonymous remailer will
replace the anonymous name with the name of the original sender.

This approach still leaves a path—albeit one that is as strong as its
strongest link. But attackers can certainly find a way to discover the
original sender if they're able to compromise every remailer along
the chain. All you need to know is the last name in the chain, which
is the first one in the return chain.

A better solution is to use two paths. The outgoing mail can be
delivered along one path that doesn't keep track of the mail moving along its path. The return mail comes back along a path specified by the original sender. For instance, the original message might
go through the remailer `anon@norecords.com`, which keeps no
records of who sends information through it. The recipient could
send return mail by using the return address in the encrypted letter.
This might be `my-alias@freds.remailer.com`. Only someone
who could decode the message could know to attack `my-alias@`
`freds.remailer.com` to follow the chain back to the sender.

The approach defends against someone who has access to the
header, which often gives the anonymous return address. Now, this
information can be encoded in the body. The plan is still vulnerable
because someone who knows the return address `my-alias@freds`
`.remailer.com` might be able to coerce Fred into revealing your
name.

A different solution is to split up the return address into a secret. When you open an account at freds.remailer.com, you can give your return address as R_1. This wouldn't be a working return address, it would just be one half of a secret that would reveal your return address. The other half, R_2, would be sent along to your friends in the encrypted body of the letter. If they wanted to respond, they would include R_2 in the header of their return letter. Then, freds.remailer.com could combine R_1 and R_2 to reveal the true return address.

The sender's half of the return address can arrive at the anonymous drop box at any time. The sender might have it waiting there so the letter can be rerouted as soon as possible, or the sender might send it along three days later to recover the mail that happened to be waiting there.

This split secret can be created in a number of different ways. The simplest technique is to use the XOR addition described in Chapter 4. This is fast, simple to implement, and perfectly secure. The only practical difficulty is converting this into suitable ASCII text. Email addresses are usually letters and some simple punctuation. Instead of simply creating a full 8-bit mask to be XORed with the address, it is probably simpler to think of offsets in the list of characters. You could come up with a list of the 60-something characters used in all email addresses and call this string C. Splitting an email address would consist of doing the following steps on a character-by-character basis:

1. Choose a new character from C. Store this in R_1. Let x be its position in C.

2. To encode a character from the email address, find the character's position in C and move x characters down x. If you get to the end, start again.

3. Store this character in R_2.

The reverse process is easy to figure out. This will produce a character-only split of the email address into two halves, R_1 and R_2. R_1 is deposited at an anonymous remailer and attached to some pseudonym. R_2 is sent to anyone whom you want to respond to you. They must include R_2 in their letter so the remailer can assemble the return address for you.

An even more sophisticated approach uses the digital signature of the recipient. The initiator of the conversation can deposit three things at the return remailer: the pseudonym, one half of the return address, R_1, and the public key of the person who might be responding. When that person responds, he or she must send $f_e(R_2)$. This is the other half of the secret encoded with the private key. The remailer has the corresponding public key so it can recover R_2 and send the message on its way.

The systems can be made increasingly baroque. A remailer might want to protect itself against people banging down its door asking for the person who writes under a pseudonym. This can be accomplished by encrypting the remailer's files with the public keys of the recipient. This is better explained by example. Imagine that Bob wants to start up an anonymous communication channel with Ray through `freds.remailer.com`. Normally, `freds.remailer.com` would store Bob's return address, call it B, and match it with Bob's pseudonym, `maskT-AvEnGrr`. Naturally, someone could discover B by checking these files.

`freds.remailer.com` can protect itself by creating a session key, k_i, and encrypting it with Ray's public key, $f_{ray}(k_i)$. This value is sent along to Ray with the message. Then it uses k_i to encrypt B using some algorithm like tripleDES before discarding k_i. Now, only Ray holds the private key that can recover k_i and thus B. `freds.remailer.com` is off the hook. It couldn't reveal B even if it wanted to.

This solution, unfortunately, can only handle one particular ongoing communication. It would be possible to create different session keys for each person to whom Bob sends mail. This increases the possibility that B could be discovered by the remailer who keeps a copy of B the next time that mail for `maskT-AvEnGrr` comes through with a session key attached.

10.3

Anonymous Networks

Anonymous remailers move single packets. Some will fetch Web pages anonymously. It should come as no surprise that ambitious programmers have extended these ideas to provide seamless tools for routing all packets to the Internet. They have essentially created TCP/IP proxies that encrypt all data leaving the computer and then bounce it through a network of servers that eventually kick it out into the Internet at large.

Each of these systems offers a great deal of anonymity against many attackers. The packets from all of the users form a cloud that effectively obscures the begining and the end of each path. None of the solutions, however, are perfect against omniscient and omnipotent attackers who can monitor all of the nodes in the network while probing it with their own packets. Each of the systems has some definite strengths but a few weaknesses that may be exploited in extreme cases.

10.3.1   Freedom Network

Zero Knowledge Systems designed and built the Freedom Network, a collection of servers joined by a sophisticated protocol for encrypting packets. The network lasted until 2001 when the company shut it down for financial reasons. The network remains one of the most ambitious tools for providing privacy on the Internet.

The network consisted of a collection of *anonymous Internet proxies* (AIPs) that would decrypt and encrypt messages while forwarding the data on to other proxies. If a computer wants to establish a path to the Internet, it takes these steps:

The Freedom Network drew heavily upon the inspiration of the Onion Routing Network developed at the Naval Research Labs by Paul Syverson, Michael Reed, and David Goldschlag [SRG00, STRL00, SGR97, RSG98].

1. At the center of the network is the NISS (Network Information Status Server), a central computer that maintains a list of operating AIPs and their public keys.

2. The computer takes a list of these machines and chooses a random path through a collection of machines. The path building algorithm may use information about distance and load to optimize the process. Shorter chains offer better service while longer chains offer more resistance to detection. Chains running through different countries may offer some extra legal protection.

3. The computer uses Diffie-Hellman key exchange to negotiate a key with each AIP in the chain.

4. The data going out the chain is encrypted with each key in turn. If f_k is the encryption function using key k, then $f_{k_1}(f_{k_2}(\ldots f_{k_n}(data)))$ is sent down the chain. k_i is the key for the ith AIP in the chain.

5. Each AIP receives its packet of data and uses the negotiated session key to strip away the top layer before passing it on.

6. The last AIP in the chain sends the packet off to the right destination.

7. The return data follows the same chain in reverse. Each AIP uses the session key to encrypt the data.

8. The computer strips away the *n* layers.

Zero Knowledge refers to this process as *telescope encryption*. The actual process is more involved and sophisticated. Providing adequate performance while doing so much encryption is not an easy trick.

10.3.2   PipeNet

PipeNet is an anonymous network created by Wei Dai. It also rests upon a network of computers that route encrypted packets. The principal difference lies in the synchronized mechanism for coordinating the flow of the packets. At each clock step, all of the computers in the network receive a packet, perform the necessary encryption, and then pass it on. If a packet does not arrive, one is not sent.

This solution prevents an omniscient attacker from watching the flow of all packets in the hope of figuring out who is communicating with whom. In the Freedom Network, a heavy user may inadvertantly give away his or her path by shipping a large amount of data along it. The omniscient attacker may not be able to break the encryption, but simply counting the size of the packets could reveal the destination. Ideally, a large user base would provide enough cover.

PipeNet's strict process for sending information ensures that each link between machines only carries the same amount of information at each step. The data moves along the chain in a strictly choreographed process like soldiers marching across the square.

This process, however, has its own weaknesses. If one packet is destroyed or one node in the network locks up, the entire chain shuts down. If data doesn't arrive, it can't go out [BMS01].

10.3.3   Crowds

The Crowds tool, developed by Michael Reiter and Aviel Rubin, offers a simple mechanism for Web browsing that provides some of the same anonymity as the Freedom Network or PipeNet, but without as much security. It's simplicity, however, makes it easy to implement and run [RR98].

The protocol is very simple. Each computer in the network accepts a URL request for a document on the Web, and it makes a random choice to either satisfy the request or pass it along to another randomly selected user. If you want to see a document, your request may pass through a number of different people before finally being fetched from the right server and passed back through the chain.

This process offers a high degree of anonymity, but not one that can begin to fool an omniscient attacker watching all sites. The simplicity offers a strong amount of confusion. Your machine may receive a request from Alice, but there's no way to know if Alice is actually interested in the information itself. Her machine may just be passing along the request from someone else who might be passing it along from someone else, and so on. Each individual in the chain can only know that *someone* out there is interested in the information, but who that person is remains uncertain.

10.3.4   Freenet

One of the most ambitious and successful anonymous publication systems is Freenet, a peer-to-peer network originally designed by Ian Clarke. The project itself is highly evolved, and open source distributions of the code are available from *http://freenet.sourceforge.net* [CSWH00, Cla99].

The system distributes information across a random collection of servers donating their spare disk-space to people seeking to publish documents. The network has no central server that might be compromised, so all searches for information fan out across the network. Each machine remembers a certain amount about previous searches, so it can answer requests for popular documents.

Each document is known within the network by three different keys, which are really 160-bit numbers created by applying the SHA hash function. If you want to retrieve a document, you ask for it with one of the three key numbers. The search process is somewhat random and unorganized, but also resistant to damage to the network. Here are the steps:

The SHA, or Secure Hash Algorithm, is a cryptographically secure function-like MD-5.

1. You start a search by specifying the key value and a "time to live" number, which limits the depth of the nodes you want to search.

2. You choose one node in the network to begin the search.

3. This node checks to see if the key matches any files stored locally. If there's a match, the node returns the file.

4. If there's no local match, the node checks a cache of recent searches. If the key is found there, the node retrieves the

document. In some cases, this document is already stored locally. In others, the node must return to the original source to retrieve it.

5. If there's no match, the server asks another in a chain and the process repeats. At each step, the "time to live" counter is reduced by one. When it reaches zero, the search fails.

The caching of this depth-first search speeds up the retrieval of the most popular documents.

The keys assigned to each document are generated in three different ways. The author begins by assigning a title to the document, T. This string of characters is converted into a *keyword-signed key*. This value is hashed by computing $SHA(T)$ and then used to both encrypt and sign the document. Using $SHA(T)$ to encrypt the document ensures that only someone who knows T can read a file. The individual servers can hold any number of files each encrypted by the hash of their titles, but only the person who knows the title can read them. This provides a certain amount of deniability to the server owner who never really understands the material on his hard disk.

The hash of the title is also used as the seed to a pseudo-randomly driven public/private key generation routine. While most public keys are chosen with true random sources, this algorithm uses the hash of T to ensure that everyone can generate the same key pair if they know T. This public key is then used to sign the document, providing some assurance that the title and the document match.

This mechanism is far from perfect. Anyone can think up the same title, and an attacker may deliberately choose the same title for a replacement document. Freenet fights this by creating a *signed subspace key* connected to the author posting the document. The creation of this key is a bit more involved:

1. First the author publishes a public key bound to his or her identity.

2. The public key and the title are hashed independently.

3. The results are XORed together and hashed again:
$$SHA(SHA(T) \oplus SHA(public\ key)).$$

4. The private key associated with the public key is used to sign the file.

5. The file is published with both the signed subspace key and the signature.

Retrieving the file now requires knowing both T and the public key of the author. Only the author, however, knows the private key, so only the author can generate the right signature.

A third key, the *content-hash key*, is created by hashing the entire document. The author can decide which keys to include with the document when publishing it.

Obviously, maintaining some central index of keys, documents, and the servers holding them would make life simpler for everyone including those who seek to censor the system. Freenet avoids this process, but does take one step to make the searching process easier. When new documents are inserted into the network, the author places them on servers that hold similar keys. The storing procedure searches the network looking at similar keys and then places the document there.

10.3.5   OceanStore

One of the more ambitious projects for persistent, robust, distributed storage is OceanStore developed by a large group of faculty and students at the University of California at Berkeley. Many of the basic ideas and the flavor of the project are clearly inspired by the Freenet project, but embellished with more sophisticated tools for upgrading and duplicating documents [KBC+00].

The most significant addition is a mechanism for ensuring that documents aren't destroyed when they are updated. Blocks of new data can be inserted into documents, and these changes propagate through the network until all copies are current. The mechanism also contains a more sophisticated routing structure to speed the identification and location of documents. All of these details are beyond the current scope of this book.

10.4

The Future

In the short-term future, every machine on the Internet will be a first-class citizen that will be able to send and receive mail. The best solution for active remailers is to create tools that will turn each SMTP port into an anonymous remailer. To some extent, they already do this. They take the incoming mail messages and pass them along to their final destination. It would be neat, for instance, to create a plug-in MIME module for Eudora or another email program that would recognize the MIME type "X-Anon-To:" and resend the mail immediately.

To a large extent, these tools are not the most important step. The tools are only useful if the remailer owner is willing to resist calls to reveal the hidden identity.

There is also a great need for anonymous dating services on the Net. Although many of the remailers are clothed in the cyberpunk regalia, there is no doubt that there are many legitimate needs for remailers. An upscale, mainstream remailer could do plenty of business and help people in need of pseudonymous communication.

10.5

Summary

- *The Disguise.* The path between sender and recipient is hidden from the recipient by having an intermediate machine remove the return address. More sophisticated systems can try to obscure the connection to anyone who is watching the mail messages entering and leaving the remailing computer.

- *How Secure Is It?* Basic anonymous remailers are only as secure as the strongest link along the chain of remailers. If the person who runs the remailer chooses to log the message traffic, then that person can break the anonymity. This may be compelled by the law enforcement community through warrants or subpoenas.

  The more sophisticated remailers that try to obscure traffic analysis can be quite secure. Anyone watching the network of remailers can only make high-level statements about the flow of information in and out of the network. Still, it may be quite possible to track the flow. The systems do not offer the unconditional security of the Dining Cryptographers networks described in Chapter 11.

  Digital mixes must also be constructed correctly. You cannot simply use RSA to sign the message itself. You must sign a hash of the message. [PP90] shows how to exploit the weakness.

- *How to Use the Software.* The WWW pages are the easiest options available to most people. More sophisticated software can be found in the Mixmaster archives or the list in Appendix D.

chapter eleven

Secret Broadcasts

Table Talk

Chris: I heard that Bobby got fired.

Leslie: Fired?

Pat: I heard he was let go because of a drop in sales.

Chris: Yes, the sales he's supposed to be making.

Leslie: But everyone's sales are down.

Pat: He said he was having a good quarter.

Chris: Good? His sales are down even more.

Leslie: Down more than what?

Pat: Maybe they're just down relative to last year, which was a good year for everyone.

Chris: I think they're down relative to everyone else.

Leslie: Maybe it was something else. I heard he was drinking too much.

Pat: I heard because he couldn't take his boss's stupidity.

Chris: Actually, his boss is brilliant. Bobby's the problem.

Leslie: This doesn't add up.

Pat: Well, it does add up. Maybe the truth is somewhere in between everything we've said. You just need to add it together.

11.1

Secret Senders

How can you broadcast a message so everyone can read it, but no one can know where it is coming from? Radio broadcasts can easily be located with simple directional antennae. Anonymous remailers (see Chapter 10) can cut off the path back to the message's source, but they can often be compromised or traced. Practically any message on the Net can be traced because packets always flow from one place to another. This is generally completely impractical, but it is still possible.

None of these methods offers unconditional security, but there is one class of algorithms created by David Chaum that will make it impossible for anyone to detect the source of a message. He titled the system the "Dining Cryptographers", which is a reference to a famous problem in computer system design known as the "Dining Philosophers". In the Dining Philosophers problem, n philosophers sit around the table with n chopsticks set up so there is one between each pair. To eat, a philosopher must grab both chopsticks. If there is no agreement and schedule, then no one will eat at all.

Chaum phrased the problem as a question of principle. Three cryptographers are eating dinner, and one is from the National Security Agency. The waiter arrives and tells them that one person at the table has already arranged for the check to be paid, but he won't say who left the cash. The cryptographers struggle with the problem because neither of the two non-government employees wants to accept even an anonymous gratuity from the NSA. But, because they respect the need for anonymity, they arrange to solve the problem with a simple coin-tossing algorithm. When it is done, no one will know who paid the check, but they'll know if the payer was from the NSA.

This framing story is a bit strained, but it serves the purpose. In the abstract, one member will send a 1-bit message to the rest of the table. Everyone will be able to get the same message, but no one will be able to identify which person at the table sent it. There are many other situations that seem to lend themselves to the same problem. For instance, a father might return home to find the rear window smashed. He suspects that it was one of the three kids, but it could have been a burglar. He realizes that none will admit to doing it. Before calling the police and reporting a robbery, he uses the same Dining Cryptographers protocol so one of the kids can admit to breaking the window without volunteering for punishment.[1]

If a 1-bit message can be sent this way, then there is no reason why long messages cannot come through the same channel. One problem is that no one knows when someone else is about to speak since no one knows who is talking. The best solution is to never interrupt someone else. When a free slot of time appears, participants should wait a random amount of time before beginning. When they start broadcasting something, they should watch for corrupted messages caused by someone beginning at the same time. If that occurs, they should wait a random amount of time before beginning again.

The system can also be easily extended to create a way for two people to communicate without anyone being able to trace the message. If no one can pinpoint the originator of a message with the Dining Cryptographers protocol, then no one can also know who is actually receiving the message. If the sender encrypts the communication with a key that is shared between two members at the table, then only the intended recipient will be able to decode it. The rest at the table will see noise. No one will be able to watch the routing of information to and fro.

The system for the dining cryptographers is easy to understand. In Chaum's initial example, there are three cryptographers. Each cryptographer flips a coin and lets the person on his or her right see the coin. Now, each cryptographer can see two coins, determine whether they're the same or different, and announce this to the rest of the table. If one of the three is trying to send a message—in this case that the NSA paid for dinner—then they swap their answer between same and different. A 1-bit message of "yes" or "on" or "the NSA paid" is being transmitted if the number of "different" responses is odd. If the count is even, then there is no message being sent.

There are only three coins, but they are all being matched with that of their neighbors so it sounds complex. It may be best to work through the problem with an example. Table 11.1 shows several different outcomes of the coin flips. Each column shows the result of one diner's coin flip and how it matches that of the person on his or her right. An "H" stands for heads and a "T" stands for tails. Diner #1 is to the right of Diner #2, so Diner #1 compares the coins from

Random protocols for sharing a communication channel are used by the Ethernet developed at Xerox PARC.

---

[1]This may be progressive parenting, but I do not recommend that you try this at home. Don't let your children learn to lie this well.

Table 11.1   Three philosophers send a secret message.

Diner #1		Diner #2		Diner #3		
Coin	Match	Coin	Match	Coin	Match	Message
H	Y	H	Y	H	Y	no
T	N	H	Y	H	N	no
T	Y	H	Y	H	N	yes
T	N	H	N	H	N	yes
T	N	H	N	T	Y	no
T	Y	H	N	T	Y	yes

columns #1 and #2 and reports whether they match or not in that subcolumn. Diner #2 is to the right of Diner #3, and Diner #3 is to the right of Diner #1.

In the first case, there are three matches and zero differences. Zero is even so no message is sent. But "no message" could be considered the equivalent of 0 or "off". In the second case, there are two differences, which is even, so no message is sent. In the third case, a message is sent. That is, a 1 or an "on" goes through. The same is true for the fourth and sixth cases.

There is no reason why the examples need to be limited to three people. Any number is possible, and the system will still work out the same. Each coin flipped is added into the final count twice, once for the owner and once for the neighbor. So the total number of differences will only be odd if one person is changing the answer.

What happens if two people begin to send at once? The protocol fails because the two changes will cancel each other out. The total number of differences will end up even again. If three people try to send at once, then there will be success because there will be an odd number of changes. A user can easily detect if the protocol is failing. You try to broadcast a bit, but the final answer computed by everyone is the absence of a bit. If each person trying to broadcast stops and waits a random number of turns before beginning again, then the odds are that they won't collide again.

Is this system unconditionally secure? Imagine you're one of the people at the table. Everyone is flipping coins, and it is clear that there is some message emerging. If you're not sending it, then can you determine who is? Let's say that your coin comes up heads. See Table 11.2 for some possible outcomes.

There are four possible scenarios reported in the table. In each case, your coin shows heads. You get to look at the coin of Diner #2

We were never that concerned about Slothrop *qua* Slothrop.
—Thomas Pynchon, *Gravity's Rainbow*

Table 11.2   Can the system be broken?

You		Diner #2		Diner #3	
Coin	Match	Coin	Match	Coin	Match
H	Y	H	N	?	Y
H	Y	*H*	*N*	H	Y
H	Y	H	N	*T*	*Y*
H	Y	H	Y	?	N
H	Y	*H*	*Y*	T	N
H	Y	H	Y	*H*	*N*
H	N	T	Y	?	Y
H	N	*T*	*Y*	H	Y
H	N	T	Y	*T*	*Y*
H	N	T	N	?	N
H	N	*T*	*N*	T	N
H	N	T	N	*H*	*N*

to your right. There are an odd number of differences appearing in each case, so someone is sending a message. Can you tell who it is?

The first entry for each scenario in Table 11.2 has a question mark for the flip of the third diner's coin. You don't know what that coin is. In the first scenario, if that hidden coin is heads, then Diner #2 is lying and sending a message. If that hidden coin is tails, then Diner #3 is lying and sending the message. The message sender for each line is shown in *italics*.

As long as you don't know the third coin, you can't determine which of the other two table members is sending the message. If this coin flip is perfectly fair, then you'll never know. The same holds true for anyone outside the system who is eavesdropping. If they don't see the coins themselves, then they can't determine who is sending the message.

There are ways for several members of a Dining Cryptographers network to destroy the communications. If several people conspire, they can compare notes about adjacent coins and identify senders. If the members of the table announce their information in turn, the members at the end of the list can easily change the message by changing their answer. The last guy to speak, for instance, can always determine what the answer will be. This is why it is a good idea to force people to reveal their answers at the same time.

The Dining Cryptographers system offers everyone the chance to broadcast messages to a group without revealing his or her identity. It's like sophisticated anonymous remailers that can't be compromised by simply tracing the path of the messages. Unfortunately, there is no easy way to use the system available on the Internet. Perhaps this will become more common if the need emerges.

11.2

Creating a DC Net

The Dining Cryptographers (DC) solution is easy to describe because many of the difficulties of implementing the solution on a computer network are left out of the picture. At a table, everyone can reveal their choices simultaneously. It is easy for participants to flip coins and reveal their choices to their neighbors using menus to shield the results. Both of these solutions are not trivial to resolve for a practical implementation.

Manuel Blum described how to flip coins over a network in [Blu82]. This is a good way to build up a one-time pad or a key.

The first problem is flipping a coin over a computer network. Obviously, one person can flip a coin and lie about it. The simplest solution is to use a one-way hash function such as MD-5 or Sneferu.

The phone book is a good, practical one-way function, but it is not too secure. It is easy to convert a name into a telephone number, but it is hard to use the average phone book to convert that number back into a name. The function is not secure because there are other ways around the problem. You could, for instance, simply dial the number and ask the identity of the person who answers. Or you could gain access to a reverse phone directory or phone CD-ROM that offered the chance to look up a listing by the number rather than the name.

The solution to using a one-way function to flip a coin over a distance is simple:

1. You choose x, a random number and send me $h(x)$ where h is a one-way hash function that is easy to compute but practically impossible to invert.

2. I can't figure out x from the $h(x)$ that you sent me. So I just guess whether x is odd or even. This guess is sent back to you.

The protocol can be made stronger if I provide the first n bits of x. A precomputed set of x and y can't be used.

3. If I guess correctly about whether x is odd or even, then the coin flip will be tails. If I'm wrong, then it is heads. You determine whether it is heads or tails and send x back to me.

4. I compute $h(x)$ to check that you're not lying. You can only cheat if it is easy for you to find two numbers, x that is odd and

y that is even so that $h(x) = h(y)$. No one knows how to do this for good one-way hash functions.

This is the algorithm that the two neighbors can use to flip their coins without sitting next to each other at the dinner table. If you find yourself arguing with a friend over which movie to attend, you can use this algorithm with a phone book for the one-way function. Then the flip will be fair.

The second tool must allow for everyone to reveal at the same time whether their coin flips agree or disagree. Chaum's paper suggests allowing people to broadcast their answers simultaneously but on different frequencies. This requires more sophisticated electronics than computer networks currently have. A better solution is to require people to commit to their answers through a *bit commitment* protocol.

The solution is pretty simple. First, the entire group agrees upon a stock phrase or collection of bits. This should be determined as late as possible to prevent someone from trying to use computation in advance to game the system. Call this random set of bits B. To announce their answers, the n participants at the table take the following actions:

1. Choose n random keys, $\{k_1, \ldots, k_n\}$ in secret.

2. Individually take their answers, put B in front of the answer, and encrypt the string with their secret key. This is $f_{k_i}(Ba_i)$ where f is the encryption function, k_i is the key, and a_i is the answer to be broadcast.

3. Broadcast their encrypted messages to everyone in the group. It doesn't matter in what order this happens.

4. When everyone has received the messages of everyone else, everyone begins sending their keys, k_i, out to the group.

5. Everyone decrypts all of the packets, checks to make sure that B is at the beginning of each packet, and finally sums the answers to reveal the message.

These bit-commitment protocols make it nearly impossible for someone to cheat. If there were no B stuck at the beginning of the answers that were encrypted, a sophisticated user might be able to find two different keys that reveal different answers. If he wanted to tell the group that he was reporting a match, then he might show one key. If he wanted to reveal the other, then he could send out another key. This might be possible if the encrypted packet was only one bit long. But it would be near impossible if each encrypted packet began with the same bit string B. Finding such a pair of keys would be highly unlikely. This is why the bit string B should be chosen as late as is practical.

The combination of these two functions makes it easy to implement a dining cryptographers network using asynchronous communications. There is no need for people to announce their answers in synchrony. Nor is there any reason for people to be adjacent to each other when they flip the coin.

11.2.1   Cheating DC Nets

There is a wide variety of ways that people can subvert the DC networks, but there are adequate defenses to many of the approaches. If people conspire to work together and reveal their information about bits to others around the table, then there is nothing that can be done to stop tracing. In these situations, anonymous remailers can be more secure because they're as secure as their strongest link.

Another major problem might be jamming. Someone on the network could just broadcast extra messages from time to time and thus disrupt the message of someone who is legitimately broadcasting. If, for instance, a message is emerging from the network, a malicious member of the group could start broadcasting at the same time and damage the rest of the transmission. Unfortunately, the nature of DC networks means that the identity of this person is hidden.

If social problems become important, then it is possible to reveal who is disrupting the network by getting everyone on the network to reveal their coin flips. When this is done, it is possible to determine who is broadcasting. Presumably, there would be rules against broadcasting when another person is using the DC network, so it would be possible to unwind the chain far enough to reveal who that person might be.

This can be facilitated if everyone sends out a digital signature of the block of coin flips. Every person in the network has access to two keys, theirs and their neighbor's. The best solution is to have everyone sign the coin flips of his or her neighbor. Forcing everyone to do this prevents people from lying about their own coin flips and changing the signature.

This tracing can be quite useful if only one person uses the DC network for a purpose that offends a majority of the participants—perhaps to send an illegal threat. If one person is trying to jam the communications of another, however, then it reveals both senders. The only way to gauge which is legitimate is to produce some rules for determining when members can start broadcasting. The first sender would be the legitimate sender. The one who began broadcasting afterward would be the jammer.

11.3

Summary

Dining Cryptographers networks offer a good opportunity to provide unconditional security against traffic analysis. No one can detect the broadcaster if the nodes of the network keep their coin flips private. Nor can anyone determine the recipient if the messages are encrypted.

The major limitation to DC nets is the high cost of information traffic. All members of the network must flip coins with their neighbor and then broadcast this information to the group. This can be done in blocks, but it is still a significant cost: n people mean that network bandwidth increases by a factor of $2n$.

- *The Disguise.* DC nets offer an ideal way to obscure the source of a transmission. If this transmission is encrypted, then only the intended recipient should be able to read it.

- *How Secure Is It?* The system is secure if information about all of the coin flips is kept secret. Otherwise, the group can track down the sender by revealing all of this information.

- *How to Use the Software.* The Dining Cryptographers net software is for people with access to UNIX workstations and full Internet packet capabilities.

chapter twelve

Keys

The Key Vision

A new directive from the National Science Foundation ordered all researchers to stop looking for "keys" that will dramatically unlock the secrets behind their research. The order came swiftly after a new study showed that a "holistic vision" was a more powerful metaphor than the lock and key. Administrators at the National Science Foundation predicted the new directive would increase discoveries by 47 percent and produce significant economies of effort.

The recent news of the metaphoric failure of the lock and key image shocked many researchers. Landon P. Murphy, a cancer specialist at Harvard's Women and Children's Hospital said, "We spent our time searching for one key insight that would open up the field and provide us all of nature's abundant secrets. One simple key insight can do that for you."

In the future, all researchers will train their minds to search for a holistic picture that encompasses all of their knowledge. An inclusive understanding is thought to yield more discoveries in a faster time period because the grand vision can often see the entire forest, not just the trees.

"Let's say you're on top of a mountain. You can see much farther than you can at the base—even if you have a key to the tunnel under the mountain," said Bruce Konstantine, an Executive Deputy Administrative Aide at the NSF. "We want our researchers to focus on establishing the grand vision."

Some scientists balked at the new directive and countered with a metaphor of their own. "Sure you can see for miles but you can't see detail," said Martin Grubnik, a virologist at the University of

Pittsburgh. "Some of us need to focus on the small things and the details to make progress. That's the key."

Konstantine dismissed these objections and suggested that the virologists might make more progress if they avoided a narrow focus.

"The key insight, or perhaps I should say the true vision, is that scientists who focus too narrowly avoid seeing the big picture. We want more big pictures. If that means abandoning the hope for one key, so be it."

12.1

Extending Control

Most of the game of steganography involves finding a set of algorithms that can make one chunk of data look like another. In some instances, camouflaging the existence of the data is not enough. Stronger attacks require stronger measures, and one of the most versitile is adding some *key* bits to the algorithm.

The key is some relatively small collection of bits that plays a strong role in the algorithm. If you don't hold the right key, you can't unlock certain features of the algorithm. The bits of information in the key are somehow essential for manipulating the data.

Most of the keying techniques used in steganography are extensions of the solutions used in basic cryptography. Some of the basic types include the following:

- *Secret Keys.* One key is used to hide the information, and the same key must be available to uncover the information. This is often called *symmetric* or *private-key* steganography. The second term is avoided in this book to avoid confusion with public-key approaches.

- *Public Mechanisms or Public Keys.* One key hides the information and a different key uncovers it. These solutions are often useful for watermarking information because someone can uncover the information without being able to hide new information—that is, without the power to make new copies with the person's watermark.

None of the algorithms described here offer a solution with any of the simplicity of the best public-key encryption systems. They often rely upon difficult problems or some obscurity to provide the some form of a "private key". In many cases, there is no real private key at all. The public key is just used to verify the signature.

- *Zero-Knowledge Proofs*. These systems allow the information hider to hide information so that its existence can be revealed without revealing the information itself. The technique can also be useful for watermarking because information hiders can prove they hid the information without giving someone else the power to hide the same information—that is, to make copies with the same watermark.

- *Collision Control Codes*. Let's say you have several copies of a document. These codes try to prevent you from combining the copies in ways to obscure the information hidden inside. Some basic attacks on watermarking information, for instance, involve averaging several different copies. These solutions resist such attacks.

There are a number of different approaches for implementing algorithms that fall into these classes. The simplest is to use basic secret-key or public-key algorithms on the data before it is handled by the steganography algorithm. The keying algorithm and the hiding algorithm are kept separate and distinct from each other.

This approach is mentioned in many different contexts of this book, and it has much to recommend it. Encryption algorithms naturally make data look more random, and random data is often the best kind for steganography. Encrypting the data often makes sense even if secrecy is not necessary because encryption is one of the simplest ways to increase the randomness of the data. Of course, this approach can occasionally produce data that is too random, a problem discussed in depth in Chapter 17.

Keeping the encryption separate from the hiding is intellectually simpler. Good encryption algorithms can be mixed or matched with good steganographic solutions as conditions dictate. There's no need to make compromises.

But splitting the two processes is also limiting because the hiding algorithm is the same for everyone. Anyone can recover the hidden bits because the algorithm is essentially public. Anyone who uses the algorithm to recover bits on one occasion can now use the same algorithm again and again in other situations. They may not be able to do anything with the bits because the encryption is very strong, but they will be able to find them relatively easily *and* replace them with bits of their own.

Keying the hiding process ensures that only people with the right key can either hide or recover bits. This restricts attackers by adding an additional layer of complexity to the process.

Many of the basic algorithms in this book use simple keys to control the random choices made by an algorithm. If an arbitrary decision needs to be made, then a cryptographically secure random number generator driven by a key is one of the simplest mechanisms for adding a key to the scheme.

The algorithms in Chapter 9 hide information in the least significant bits of image and sound files by selecting a subset of elements. This selection process is driven by a random number generator that repeatedly hashes a key. In Chapter 13, the functions used to compute the sorted list of data elements can include a key. If the same stream of random numbers isn't available, the bits can't be extracted.

More sophisticated systems integrate the key even deeper into the algorithm. Some try to constrain how the answer to some hard problem is constructed. Others try to limit how it is encoded in the data.

Many of these newer advanced systems show how just about any computational processes can be tweaked or distorted to include a few extra bits. Most algorithms include some arbitrary decisions about location, order, or process, and these arbitrary decisions can be driven by some key. In the best cases, the authors understand the problem well enough to provide some actual arguments for believing that the process is hard to decrypt without the key.

12.2

Signing Algorithms

Many of the keying algorithms provide some kind of assurance about the document's authenticity by acting like digital signatures for the document. These solutions are quite useful in all of the situations where digital signatures on arbitrary files provide some certainty. They're also especially useful for watermarking. The ideal algorithm allows the file's creator to embed a watermark in such a way that only the proper key holders can produce that watermark.

The basic solution involves separating the image or audio file into two parts. The first holds the details that will remain unchanged during the steganography. If the information is hidden in the least significant bits, then this part is the other bits, the most significant ones. The second part is the bits that can be changed to hide information. This set may be defined by a key.

A digital signature on the file can be constructed by hashing the unchangeable part, signing the hash value with a traditional digital signature function, and then encoding this information in the second part reserved for hidden information. The digital signature may be computed with traditional public-key algorithms such as RSA, or it may use simpler solutions with secret-key algorithms or even hash functions [Won98, Wal95].

This process uses two keys that may or may not be drawn from the same set of bits. The first is used to define the parts of the file that may be changed. It could be a random number stream that picks pixels to hide information. The second key actually constructs the signature.

This approach is simple, direct, and easy to code, but it hides the information in the most susceptible part of the file. Compresssion algorithms and other watermarks can damage the information by changing the data in this section [CM97].

J. Fridrich and Miroslav Goljan suggest self-embedding a copy of an image in itself. Details from one block are embedded in another block across the image. Cropping or other tampering can be reversed [FG99].

The mechanism can also be extended by splitting the file into numerous sections. The signature for section i can be embedded into section $i + 1$. Figure 12.1 shows how this might be done with a file broken into five sections. The data from one section is hidden in the next section.

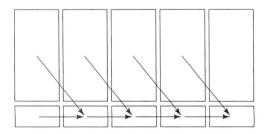

Figure 12.1   An embedded digital signature can be woven into a file. In this visual allegory, the file is broken into five chunks. Each chunk is broken into two parts—one that remains unchanged and another that hides information. The data from section i is used to create a digital signature that is embedded in section $i + 1$.

12.3

Public-Key Algorithms

Many researchers are trying to develop "public-key" algorithms for hiding information that provide many of the same features as public-key cryptography. The systems allow a user to hide information in such a way that anyone can recover it, but ideally in a way that no one can duplicate it.

This feature is quite desirable for watermarks because it would be ideal for the average user (or the user's computer) to check information for watermarks.

All of the algorithms are new and relatively untested, but they still offer exciting possibilities for watermarking files. If they can be developed to be strong enough to resist attack, people will be able to use them to track royalties and guarantee the authenticity of files.

12.3.1   Constraining Hard Problems

One strategy is to use problems that are hard to solve but easy to verify as the basis for public-key signature. The knowledge of how to solve the difficult problem acts like a private key, and the knowledge of how to verify it acts like the public key. The real challenge is finding problems that behave in the right way.

The class of NP-complete problems includes such class computer science challenges as boolean satisfiability, graph coloring, the Traveling Salesman problem, and many others [GJ79]. They are often hard to solve but always easy to verify. Unfortunately, it is not always easy to identify a particular problem with the right mixture of strength.

This approach has not been historically successful. An early public-key system created by Ralph Merkle and Martin Hellman used an NP-complete problem known as the *knapsack*. (Given n items with weights $\{w_1, \ldots, w_n\}$, find a subset that weighs W pounds.) Their algorithm created custom knapsacks that appeared to offer a guarantee that they were hard to pack exactly. Only someone with a secret value, the private key, could determine the right subset of objects to put in the knapsack with much ease. In practice, someone broke the system.

Another technique is to avoid inserting a trapdoor or private key in the system at all. The inherent strength of the NP-complete problem acts as a deterrent. Of course, this means that the person who wants to sign something must have the ability to solve an NP-complete problem.

In one solution, researcher Gang Qu imagines that the ability to create these solutions is what is being protected by a watermark. A person who knows how to solve the Traveling Salesman problem optimally may market these solutions to airlines, businesses, or traveling sales forces. To protect against piracy of their custom itineraries, these clients seek to hide some signature information in the file that proves the solutions are theirs. A competing business may develop their own solutions, but anyone can check the provenance by looking for this hidden information.

The technique hides information in the solution to the difficult problems by forcing certain parameters to take certain values [Qu01, KQP01]. Anyone can examine the solution and check the parameters, but it should be difficult to assemble a new solution because the problem is presumably hard. The approach does not really require a set of bits labeled a "public key", but it still behaves in much the same way.

Information is hidden in the solution to the problem by introducing new constraints on the solution. The classic boolean satisfiability problem, for instance, takes n boolean variables, $\{x_1, \ldots, x_n\}$, and tries to assign true or false values to them so that all boolean clauses in a set are true. Information can be encoded in the answer by forcing some of the variables to take particular values, say $x_{14} = T$, $x_{25} = F$, $x_{39} = F$, $x_{59} = T$, and $x_{77} = T$ might encode the bit string 10011. Of course, adding this extra requirement may make a solution impossible, but that is a chance the designers take.

The technique can be applied to many NP-complete problems and other problems as well. Many problems have multiple solutions and information can be hidden by choosing the appropriate solution that also encodes the information. Figure 12.2 shows a graph colored so that several nodes take fixed colors. One way to encode the information is to grab pairs of nodes and force them to have either the same or different colors. Two nodes can be forced to have the same color by merging them while the algorithm looks for a solution. Two nodes can be kept different by adding an edge that connects them. Other problems usually have some latitude.

The process can be strengthened by hashing steps along the way. Let K_0 be a creator's original watermarking information. It might be the creator's name, it might be an email address, or it could be a reference to some big table of known creators. Let H be a strong hash function such as MD-5 or SHA. Let $\{C_1, \ldots, C_n\}$ be a set of constraints to

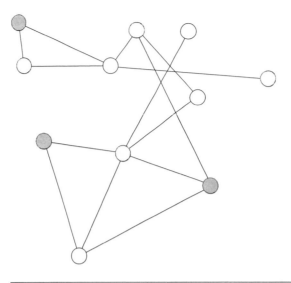

Figure 12.2   A graph colored so that no two adjacent nodes have the same color. Information can be encoded in this solution by forcing certain nodes to certain colors.

the problem that are open for twiddling to hold information. These may be extra variables in a boolean satisfiability problem that can be set to true or false. Or they could be nodes in a graph that might hold different values. For the sake of simplicity, assume that each constraint can encode 1 bit. The following loop will encode the watermark:

1. Let $K_i = H(K_{i-1}, C_{i-1})$. The hashing function should be fed both the information encoded in C_{i-1} and some data about the structure of C_{i-1} itself. This data might include the node numbers, the variable names, or the boolean formulae. (Set C_0 to be a null string.)

2. Extract one bit from K_i and encode it in C_i.

3. Repeat this for all n constraints.

The watermark can be tested by repeating the process. Any skeptical enquirer can get K_0 from the creator and step through the process checking the bits at each point.

This approach can be used to protect complicated engineering designs where the creator must solve a difficult problem. Chip designers, for instance, often solve large NP-complete problems when they choose how to lay out transistors. This technique allows them to encode a watermark in the chip design that essentially says, "Copyright 2001 Bob Chiphead".

The technique can be applied to more general information hiding problems or watermarking problems, but it has limitations. The creator must have the ability to find solutions to difficult problems—solutions that are difficult for the average person to acquire. The simplest way to accomplish this is to create a large computer that is barely able to find solutions to large, difficult problems. Only the owner of the computer (or one of similar strength) would be able to generate solutions. Ron Rivest and Adi Shamir discuss using a similar solution to mint small tokens.

12.3.2   Using Matrix Multiplication

Recovering information from a file requires finding a way to amplify the information and minimize the camouflaging data. One solution is to rely upon the relatively random quality of image or sound information and design a recovery function that strips away relatively random information. Whatever is left could hold the information in question.

Joachim J. Eggers, Jonathan K. Su, and Bernd Girod suggest using a mechanism where matrix multiplication dampens the covering data but leaves distinctive watermarks untouched [ESG00b, ESG00a]. They base their solution on eigenvectors, the particular vectors that are left pointing in the same direction even after matrix multiplication. That is, if M is a matrix and w is an eigenvector, then $Mw = \lambda w$ where λ is a scalar value known as an eigenvalue. Every eigenvector has a corresponding eigenvalue. Most vectors will be transformed by matrix multiplication, but not the eigenvectors. For the sake of simplicity, we assume that the eigenvectors are one unit long, that is, $w^h w = 1$.

Exploiting this property of matrix multiplication requires assuming that the data in the file is relatively random and comes with a mean value of 0. Sound files fit this model, but image files usually fail because they consist of bytes that range between 0 and 255. Any file can be converted into one with a 0 mean value by calculating the mean and subtracting it from each entry. The result may not be sufficiently random for this algorithm, but we will assume that it is.

Let x be a vector of data where the watermark will be hidden. We assume that it comes with a 0 mean and is sufficiently random. What is sufficiently random? Perhaps it's better to define this by describing the effect we want. Ideally, we want $x^h Mx = 0$ or at least sufficiently close to 0. Then it will drop out of the computation and only the watermark will be left.

Let w be an eigenvector of some matrix M and λ be the corresponding eigenvalue. $Mw = \lambda w$. This vector can be used as a watermark and added to the camouflaging data, x, with a weight β. Ideally, β is chosen so that $x + \beta w$ is perceptually identical to x and the watermark can be extracted.

The watermark is extracted from the data by computing

$$(x + \beta w)^h M(x + \beta w) = x^h Mx + x^h M\beta w + \beta w Mx + \beta^2 w Mw.$$

If the assumption about the randomness of x holds, the first three terms will be close to 0, leaving us with $\beta^2 \lambda (w_w^h) = \beta^2 \lambda$.

A public-key system can be established if the values of M, β, and λ are distributed. Anyone can test a file, y, for the presence or absence of the watermark by computing $y^h My$ and determining whether it matches $\beta^2 \lambda$.

This approach still has a number of different limitations. First, the number of elements in x and w must be relatively large. Eggers, Su, and Girod report results with lengths of about 10,000 and about 100,000. Larger values help guarantee the randomness that pushes $x^h Mx$ to 0.

Second, finding the eigenvectors of M is just as easy for the message creator as for any attacker. One solution is to choose an M that has many different eigenvectors, $\{w_1, \ldots, w_n\}$, that all come with the same eigenvalue λ. The attacker may be able to identify all of these eigenvectors, but removing the watermark by subtracting out the different values of w_i, one after another, could be seen as a brute-force attack.

Of course, the ease of finding the eigenvectors means that someone can insert a fake watermark by choosing any eigenvector w_i that comes with an eigenvalue of λ. This means that the algorithm can't be used to generate digital signatures like many of the classic public-key algorithms, but might still be of use for creating watermarks that prevent copying. A pirate would find little use in adding a signal that indicated that copying should be forbidden.

More sophisticated attacks may be possible. Eggers, Su, and Girod credit Teddy Furon for identifying a trial-and-error approach to removing watermarks with this tool by changing the scale for the part of the signal in the space defined by the eigenvectors, $\{w_1, \ldots, w_n\}$, with length λ.

The algorithm can be tuned by choosing different values of M. Eggers, Su, and Girod particularly like permutation matrices because an $n \times n$ matrix can be stored with $n - 1$ values. "Multiplication" by a permutation matrix is also relatively simple. Using the matrix designed to compute the discrete cosine transform is also a good choice because the computation is done frequently in image and sound manipulation.

This solution is far from perfect and its security is not great. Still, it is a good example of how a function might be designed to minimize the camouflaging data while amplifying the hidden data. The process is also keyed so that the value of M must be present to extract the hidden message.

12.3.3   Removing Parts

Many of the algorithms in this book hide information by making a number of changes to a number of different locations in the file and then averaging these changes to find the signal. The algorithms in the preceding section, for instance, may add hundreds of thousands of small values from the watermark eigenvector into the file. The spread-spectrum-like techniques from Chapter 14 will also spread the signal over many different pixels or units from a sound file. The signal is extracted by computing a weighted average over all of them.

One insight due to Frank Hartung and Bernd Girod is that the information extractor does not need to average all of the locations to extract a signal [HG]. The algorithms already include a certain amount of redundancy to defend against either malicious or accidental modifications to the file. If the algorithms are designed to carry accurate data even in the face of changes to an arbitrary number of elements, why not arrange for the receiver to skip that arbitrary number of elements altogether?

Consider this algorithm:

1. Create n "keys", $\{k_1, \ldots, k_n\}$.

2. Use cryptographically secure random number generators to use these keys to identify n different sets of m elements from the file.

3. Tune the hiding algorithm so it can hide information in mn elements in such a way that the information can be recovered even if $(n - 1)m$ elements are not available or are damaged.

4. Hide the information.

5. Distribute the n "keys" to the n different people who might have a reason to extract the information. The algorithm will still work because the information was hidden with such redundancy that only one subset is necessary.

Hartung and Girod use the term "public key" for the n values of $\{k_1, \ldots, k_n\}$ even though they do not behave like many traditional public keys. The keys do offer a good amount of antifraud protection. Anyone possessing one k_i can extract the information, but he or she cannot embed new information. If the holder of the value of k_i tries to embed a new signal, it will probably be invisible to the holders of the other $n-1$ keys because their keys define different subsets. The holder of k_i can change the elements as much as possible, but this won't change the information extracted by others.

Of course, this approach does have limitations. The values of k_i are not truly public because they can't circulate without restrictions. They also can't be used to encrypt information in a way that they can only be read by the holder of a corresponding private key. But the results still have some applications in situations where the power of keys needs to be reigned in.

12.4

Zero-Knowledge Approaches

Zero-knowledge proofs are techniques for proving you know some information without revealing the information itself. The notions began evolving in the 1980s as cryptographers and theoretical computer scientists began exploring the way that information could be segregated and revealed at optimal times. In one sense, a zero-knowledge proof is an extreme version of a digital signature.

Here's a simple example of a zero-knowledge proof. Let G be a graph with a set of nodes, $\{v_1, v_2, \ldots, v_n\}$, and a set of edges connecting the nodes, $\{(v_i, v_j), \ldots\}$. This graph can be k-colored if there exists some way to assign one of k different colors to the n nodes so that no edge joins two nodes with the same color. That is, there does not exist an i and a j such that $f(v_i) = f(v_j)$ and (v_i, v_j) is in the set of edges. f is the coloring function. Figure 12.3 shows a graph that is four-colored.

Finding a k-coloring of an arbitrary graph can be a complicated and difficult process in some cases. The problem is known to be NP-complete [GJ79], which means that some instances seem to grow

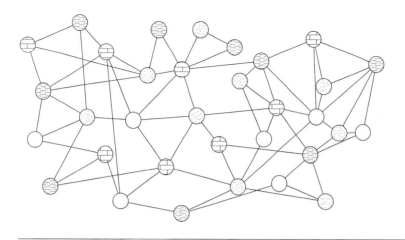

Figure 12.3 A graph where the nodes are assigned one of four colors.

exponentially more difficult as more nodes and edges are added. In practice, a coloring for many graphs can be found relatively quickly. It's often harder to find difficult graphs, which is one of the practical limitations of using zero-knowledge proofs in applications.

Let's say you know a coloring of some graph and you want to prove that you know it without actually revealing it to another person, the skeptical enquirer. Here's a simple way to prove it:

1. Create a random permutation of the coloring, f'. That is, swap the various colors in a random way so that $f'(v_i) \neq f'(v_j)$ for all (v_i, v_j) in the graph.

2. The skeptical enquirer can give you a random bit string, S. Or S might be established from an unimpeachable source by hashing an uncorruptible document. If the zero-knowledge proof is going to be embedded in a document, this hash might be of the parts of the document that will not be changed by the embedding.

3. Create n random keys, $p_1, \ldots, p_n$, and use an encryption function to scramble the string $S + i + f'(v_i)$ for each node in the graph where $+$ stands for concatenation. Ship the encrypted versions to the skeptical enquirer.

4. The skeptical enquirer chooses an edge at random from the graph (v_a, v_b) and presents it to you.

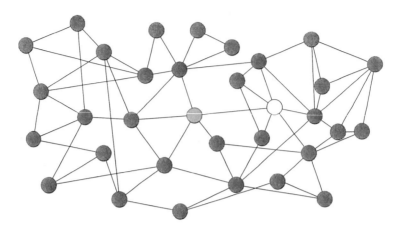

Figure 12.4   In a zero-knowledge proof, the colors of the nodes are encrypted and sent to the skeptical enquirer, who asks to have two adjacent nodes revealed.

5. You ship p_a and p_b to the skeptical enquirer who uses them to decrypt the encrypted version of the colors, $f'(v_a)$ and $f'(v_b)$. If the two are different, the skeptical enquirer knows that you've proven you know how to color at least one part of the graph. Figure 12.4 shows two adjacent nodes being revealed.

This process should be repeated until the skeptical enquirer is satisfied. If the edges are truly chosen at random, any mistakes in the coloring stand an equal chance of being revealed at each step. The randomness prevents the prover from anticipating the choice and selecting f'. Eventually, any weakness or miscoloring will show through.

Zero-knowledge proofs like this may be useful in the world of hidden information because they allow the information hider to control how and when the information is revealed to another person. The structure of the proof, however, guarantees that no information is revealed. The proof can't be repeated by someone else or used as a basis to remove the information. This solution may be useful for watermarking applications where copyright holders may want to prove they are the rightful owner without revealing the technique to others.

In theory, any zero-knowledge proof can be used as a watermark. Every proof begins with a set of bits that identify the instance of the problem. Imagine that m iterations of the encrypted graph procedure described above are sufficient to prove knowledge of the graph coloring. The proof can be embedded in a document with these steps:

1. Create a value of S by hashing the parts of the document that won't be modified during the embedding process. These might be the most significant bits or some other high-pass filtering of the document.

2. Create m permutations of the coloring, $f'_1, f'_2, \ldots, f'_m$.

3. Create $m \times n$ keys, $p_{i,j}$.

4. Scramble the coloring of the n nodes for each iteration of the proof by encrypting the string $S + i + j + f'_i(v_j)$ where $+$ stands for concatenation, i stands for the iteration of the proving algorithm ($1 \leq i \leq m$), and j stands for the node, ($1 \leq j \leq n$). Use $p_{i,j}$.

5. Embed each of the encrypted colors and the description of the graph in the document. If necessary, the encrypted colors can be embedded in hidden locations described by $p_{i,j}$. For instance, this value could be used as a seed for a cryptographically secure random number generator that chooses a string of pixels in which to hide the signal.

Anyone challenging the document can ask the information hider to prove that the hider knows how to color the graph hidden away inside of it. Presumably this problem is difficult to solve, and only the person who hid the graph would know how to color it. The skeptic could repeat these steps m times. Let i stand for the iteration.

1. The skeptic recovers the graph.

2. The skeptic assembles S by examining the unchanged parts of the document.

3. The skeptic chooses a random edge, (v_a, v_b).

4. The prover reveals $p_{i,a}$ and $p_{i,b}$. These values can be used to locate the encrypted colors and then decrypt them. If they don't match, the process continues. If they do match, the prover is toast.

This solution offers a number of advantages if a suitable graph can be found. The person hiding the information can prove he or she hid the information without revealing enough information for someone else to duplicate the proof. Each skeptic is going to choose the edges at random, and it's unlikely that all of them will be repeated.

This static version is not as powerful as the interactive version because the prover must lock in the colorings. If a skeptic is able to get the prover to repeat the algorithm a number of times, eventually the skeptic will gather enough of the keys, $p_{i,j}$, to stand a good chance of proving she knows the graph coloring. Eventually, the prover will reveal the entire colorings. This slow leak of information means that the proofs are not zero knowledge. This process may still be practical if m and n are large enough and the number of times the proof is executed is kept small enough.

Finding a suitable graph is not an easy process. There are many different kinds of zero-knowledge proofs that can be embedded in similar situations, but most of them are not particularly practical. The proofs rely upon problems that can be hard in the worst cases, but are often rather simple. Finding and identifying guaranteed difficult instances of the problem is not easy. As noted in Section 12.3.1, one of the first public-key encryption systems developed by Ralph Merkle and Martin Hellman used one NP-complete problem known as the *knapsack*. (Given n weights, $\{w_1, \ldots, w_n\}$, find a subset where the weights add up to a particular value.) Eventually, all versions of the algorithm were broken, and many grew skeptical that basic NP-complete problems could be trusted to produce difficult instances.

12.4.1   Discrete Logs for Proofs

Scott Craver developed one mechanism for zero-knowledge watermarking that relies upon the difficulty of the discrete log problem. (Given y, find x such that $y = g^x \bmod q$, where q is a prime.) This solution succeeds because it uses a number of fake watermarks as decoys. Ideally, anyone trying to tamper with the watermark must remove the real one as well as all the decoys. Optimally, there will be so much information that removing them all will substantially change the image.

Let x be the secret key that acts as a watermark. This algorithm will allow the information hider to prove he or she knows x without revealing x itself. The prover hides $y_1 = g^x \bmod q$ in the document using a key, p_1, to choose the locations in the document.

The prover then extracts $n - 1$ fake watermarks that happen to be in the document. That is, the prover chooses $n - 1$ keys, $p_2, \ldots, p_n$, to extract $n - 1$ values, $y_2, \ldots, y_n$. Using fake decoys derived from the document can help increase the strength of the watermark. The more there are, the more likely that removing them will damage the image. In some cases, the prover may actually insert them if this makes the task easier.

When a skeptic shows up with the document, the prover can show knowledge of x without giving the skeptic the power to repeat this process. The decoys prevent the skeptic from ever learning which value of y_i has a known log. Here are the steps:

1. The prover presents the keys, $p_1, \ldots, p_n$, to the skeptic.

2. The skeptic recovers the values of y_i.

3. This loop is repeated as many times as necessary.

    (a) The prover generates n blinding factors, $b_1, \ldots, b_n$, which are used to scramble the watermarks by computing $w_i = g^{b_i} y_i$.
    (b) The prover scrambles these values of w_i before shipping them to the skeptic.
    (c) The skeptic flips a coin and makes one of two demands to the prover:
        i. Tell me all of the blinding values, $b_1, \ldots, b_n$. Knowing these, the skeptic can check to make sure that there is one legitimate value of w_i for each value of y_i.
        ii. Prove you know the log to one of these values. The prover accomplishes this by revealing $x + b_1 \bmod (q - 1)$. This is the log of $w_1 = g^{b_1} y_1 = g^{b_1} g^x = g^{x+b_1} \bmod q$.

At each iteration, the prover must reveal one-half of the solution. The structure makes it unlikely that a skeptic will turn around and successfully repeat the proof to someone else. It is not possible to take the answers from one and use the information to answer the other. Only someone who knows the value of x can do it.

There are still limitations to this algorithm. The prover must reveal the location of the different blocks of bits, something that leaves them susceptible to destruction. The decoys increase the workload of the attacker and increase the probability that removing all of the information will substantially change the document.

One way to improve the strength of the algorithm is to mix in a number of real marks with the decoys. That is, the prover arranges to hide multiple values of y_i where the prover knows the value of x_i such that $y_i = g^{x_i} \bmod q$. The prover can then use a different subset of values with each skeptic as long as the prover knows one value of x_i

for the values in the subset. Of course, multiple copies and multiple blocks can help reduce this danger but not eliminate it. Eventually, all of the marks will be revealed.

12.5

Collusion Control

Another technique for "keying" watermarks is occasionally called "collusion control" for lack of a better term. Imagine that you create two documents, d_1 and d_2, with watermark bits w_1 and w_2 encoding the true owner's identities. Watermarking is an imperfect science, so despite your best efforts, someone trying to cheat the system compares the files and finds where they are different. The cheater injects random noise into these locations, effectively changing half of the bits. What happens to the watermarks?

Basic systems would fail here. If $w_1 = 001010111$ and $w_2 = 001010100$, then only the last two bits are different. A new watermark, 00101010101, would implicate someone else.

Error-correcting codes are described in Chapter 3.

Collusion control systems that can combat this problem, were first introduced by Dan Boneh and James Shaw [BS95]. Their mechanism acts like an extension of error-correcting codes.

Here's a simple example. Let S be the set of n-bit code words with only a single bit set to 1. If $n = 4$, then $S = \{1000, 0100, 0010, 0001\}$. Let one code word be assigned to each document. If two document holders collude, they will only find that their watermarks differ by two bits. Boneh and Shaw call this a *frameproof* code and note that any code that is frameproof for n users must come with n bits. So this construction is optimal.

For example, let Alice's watermark be 0100 and Bob's be 0001. Someone tries to erase the watermark by creating a synthetic one blending the two files. After identifying all bits that are different, the attacker chooses half from Alice's file and half from Bob's. What happens if someone compares a file from Alice and a file from Bob to find differences? If someone creates a new file with the watermark 0101, then both Alice and Bob will be implicated. Anyone examining the file can trace it back to both of them. Changing 50 percent of the bits will produce one of the two watermarks. One will remain implicated.

Of course, a clever attacker may flip both to zero to produce the watermark 0000. This will implicate no one, but it is not easy to generate. Anyone trusting the watermark will not choose simple bit vectors like this example. They may XOR them with a secret password, and the attacker won't know what is up and down, so to speak. A zero in the fourth position may identify Bob after it is XORed with the secret vector.

Boneh and Shaw extend this idea by combining it with ideas from the world of error-correcting codes. Each attacker will need to flip many bits before the watermark is effectively erased because the error-correcting codes compensate for random flips.

12.6

Summary

Most algorithms in this book can add additional security with a key. This key can be used to create a pseudo-random bit stream by computing successive values of some encryption or hash function: $f(key)$, $f(f(key))$, $f(f(f(key)))$, ... This bit stream can either be used to choose a subset of the file or to control how it is encoded at each location. Only someone with the same key can recover the information. Of course, it also makes sense to encrypt the file with another key before it is inserted.

Keying the algorithm defends against the often public nature of computer standards. If the software is going to be used often and distributed to many people, then the algorithms inside of it become public. Adding a key to an algorithm increases its strength dramatically.

- *The Disguise.* Many of the algorithms add an extra layer of disguise by using the key to modify the behavior of the algorithm. This means that any attacker will not be able to extract the data with knowledge of the algorithm alone.

- *How Secure Is It?* Pseudo-random bit streams created by repeated encryption or hashing can be quite secure.

- *How to Use It.* Replace any random number generator used to add noise with a pseudo-random keyed stream. This keyed random number stream can also be used to extract particular subsets or rearrange the data itself. The algorithms in Chapter 13, for instance, use a keyed encryption function to change the data's order.

chapter thirteen

Ordering and Reordering

Top 10 Reasons Why Top 10 Lists Fail

10 Who wants to be last on the list? On the other hand, making the list is much better than being 11th.

9 Is nine really better than 10?

8 There are usually 20 to 30 people who say they are in "the top 10."

7 "Lists provide a simulacrum of order that reifies our inherent unease over the chthonic forces of disorder."—Guy de Montparnasse, doctoral thesis.

6 Sixth is a comfortable position. It's not high enough to provide endless anxiety about slippage, but it's not low enough to slip off of the list. Slipping off the list would be terrible.

5 Five golden rings.

4 There is no number 4.

3 All good things come in threes. But it's not the same if you're number three in a list of ten. Being third in a list of 100, however, is pretty good. Of course, every top 10 list is really a list of 100 or 1,000 with the other 90 or 990 left off. Where do you draw the line?

2 No one ever remembers the silver medalist.

1 Being number one would be much more fun if everyone wasn't gunning to unseat you.

13.1

Introduction

Most of the algorithms in this book hide information in data formats that are relatively rigid. Image files must describe the color of each pixel in a well-defined order. Audio files are pretty much required to describe the sound at each point in time. Hiding the information in specific places in the noise is a pretty good gamble because the files aren't going to be rearranged.

Some data is not as rigid. Text documents can have chapters, sections, paragraphs, and even sentences rearranged without changing the overall meaning. That is to say, the overall meaning of a text document isn't changed much when sentences, paragraphs, sections, or chapters are rearranged, or for that matter, the order of the paragraphs, sentences, chapters, or sections. There's no reason why the elements in a list can't be scrambled and rescrambled without the reader noticing. Many of the chapters in this book can be reordered a bit without hurting the overall flow.

Even files with a strong fixed relationship with time and space can be rearranged. Image files can be cropped, rotated, or even arranged in a tile. Songs can be rearranged or edited, even after being fixed in a file. All of these changes can rearrange files.

When the data can be reordered, an attacker can destroy the hidden message without disturbing the cover data. Mikhail Atallah and Victor Raskin confronted this problem when designing a mechanism for hiding information in natural language text. If they hid a bit or two by changing each sentence, then they could lose the entire message if the order of each sentence was rearranged [ARC+01]. Many of the text mechanisms in Chapters 6, 7, and 8 are vulnerable to this kind of attack. One change at the beginning of the data stream could confound the decoding of everything after it. Many of the solutions in Chapter 9 store the bits in random locations dictated by some pseudo-random stream of values. Destroying the bits early in this stream can trash the rest of the file.

The information stream has two components: the data and the location where it is stored. Most of the algorithms in this book concentrate on styling and coiffing the data until it assumes the right disguise. The location where the data goes is rarely more than a tool for adding some security, and the algorithms pay little attention to the problem.

This chapter focuses on the second component: how to defend and exploit the location where the information is held. Some of the algorithms in this chapter insulate data against attackers who might tweak the file in the hope of dislocating the hidden information underneath. They provide a simple way to establish a canonical order for a file. The attackers can rearrange the file as much as they want, but the sender and the receiver will still be able to reestablish the canonical order and send a message.

Other algorithms exploit the order of the content itself and make no changes to the underlying information. There are $n!$ ways that n items can be arranged. That means there are $\log_2 n!$ bits that can be transmitted in a list with n items. None of the items themselves change, just their order in a list.

Still other algorithms mix in false data to act as decoys. They get in the way until they're eliminated and the canonical order is returned.

All of these algorithms rely upon the fact that information does not need to flow in a preset pattern if the correct order can be found later. This fact can also be useful if parts of the message travel along different paths.

13.2

Strength against Scrambling

Many of the attacks on steganographic systems try to destroy the message with subtle reordering. Image warping is one of the most complex and daunting parts of the Stirmark benchmarks used to measure the robustness of techniques for hiding data in images.

Here's a very abstract summary of a way to make any steganographic system resist reordering:

1. Break up the data stream into discrete elements: $\{x_1, x_2, \ldots, x_n\}$. This may be words, pixels, blocks of pixels, or any subset of the file. These blocks should be small enough to endure any tweaking or scrambling by an opponent, but large enough to be different.

2. Choose a function f that is independent of the changes that might be made in the hiding process. If the least significant bit is changed to hide a message, then f should only depend upon the other bits.

Many of the same principles that go into designing a hash function can be applied to designing this sorting function. This

In a one-time hash system, the sender changes the cover data, x, until $f(x)$ sends the right message [Shi99]. The message is usually as short as 1 bit because searching for the right x requires brute force. This is similar in style to the mechanisms in Chapter 9, which permute the color of each pixel until the parity sends the right message.

function, f, can also be keyed so that an additional value, k, can change the results.

3. Apply f to the elements.

4. Sort the list based upon f.

5. Hide the information in each element, x_i, with appropriate solutions.

6. Unsort the list or somehow arrange for the recipient to get all of the values of $\{x_1, \ldots, x_n\}$ through any means.

Information can be hidden in multiple locations and reordered by the recipient without any communication from the source. The only synchronization necessary is the choice of f and perhaps the key, k. The good news is that the multiple containers can move through different channels on independent schedules and arrive in any order without compromising the message.

Sorting the data allows the sender to scramble the cover data in any random fashion, secure in the knowledge that the receiver will be able to reorder the information correctly when it arrives.

Sorting is also a good alternative to choosing a subset of the cover data to hold the hidden message. Other solutions use some key and a random number generator to choose a random subset of the message. Another solution is to apply some function f to the elements in the data stream, sort the stream, and then choose the first n to hold the hidden message.

Of course, the success of these solutions depends entirely on the choice of the function f. Much of the problem is usually solved once the data is converted into some digital format. It's already a big number so sorting the values is easy. The identity function, $f(x) = x$, is often good enough.

One potential problem can occur if multiple elements are identical or produce the same value of f—that is, if there exist i and j such that $f(x_i) = f(x_j)$. In many normal sorting operations, the value of i and j is used to break the tie, but this can't work because the sender and the receiver may get the values of x in a different order.

If $x_i = x_j$, then it doesn't matter in which order they occur. But if $x_i \neq x_j$, then problems may emerge if the sender and the receiver do not place them in the same order. After the the receiver extracts the data from x_i and x_j, it could end up in the wrong order, potentially confusing the rest of the extracted information.

There are two solutions to this problem. The simplest is to be certain that $f(x_i) = f(x_j)$ only happens when $x_i = x_j$. This happens when f is a pure encryption automorphism. This is often the best solution. The other is to use some error-correcting coding to remove the damage caused by decoding problems. Some error-correcting codes can do well with several errors in a row, and this kind is essential. If x_i and x_j are misordered because $f(x_i) = f(x_j)$, then they'll generate two wrong errors in order. If there are multiple values that produce the same f, then there will be multiple problems.

If it is not possible to guarantee that the values of f will be unique, it makes sense to ensure that the same amount of information is packed into each element x_i. This guarantees that the damage from misordering will not disturb the other packets.

13.3

Invariant Forms

One of the biggest challenges in creating invariant functions like f is the fact that the message encoder will use f to choose the order *before* the data is hidden. The receiver will use f *after* the data is inserted. If the hiding process can change the value of f, then the order could be mangled.

There are two basic ways to design f. The first is to ensure that f does not change when data is hidden. Some simple invariant functions are as follows:

- If the elements are pixels where data is inserted into the least significant bit, then the value of f should exclude the least significant bit from the calculations.

- If the elements are compressed versions of audio or image data, then the function f should exclude the coefficients that might be changed by inserting information. JPEG files, for instance, can hide data by modifying the least significant bit of the coefficients. The function f should depend upon the other bits.

- If the data is hidden in the elements with a spread-spectrum technique that modifies the individual elements by no more than $\pm\epsilon$, then the values can be normalized. Let x_i be the value of an element. This defines a range $x_i - \epsilon < x_i \leq x_i + \epsilon$. Let the set of normalized or canonical points be $\{0, 2\epsilon, 4\epsilon, 6\epsilon, \ldots\}$. One and only one of these points is guaranteed to be in each range. Each value of x_i can be replaced by the one canonical point that lies within $\pm \epsilon$ of x_i.

To compute f, use the canonical points instead of the real values of x_i.

13.4

Canonical Forms

Another solution is to create a "canonical form" for each element. That is, choose one version of the element that is always the same. Then, remove the data by converting it into the canonical form; the result is used to compute f.

Here are some basic examples of canonical form:

- If the data is hidden in the least significant bit of pixels or audio file elements, then the canonical form can be found by setting the least significant bit to 0.

- If the information hiding process modifies the elements by no more than $\pm \epsilon$, then canonical points can be established as they were above. Let $\{0, 2\epsilon, 4\epsilon, 6\epsilon, \ldots\}$ be the set of canonical points. Only one will lie in the range $x_i - \epsilon < x_i \leq x_i + \epsilon$.

- Sentences can be put into canonical form. Mikhail Atallah and Victor Raskin use natural language processing algorithms to parse sentences [ARC+01]. The sentence "The dog chased the cat" takes this form in their LISP-based system:

```
(S
(NP the dog)
(VP chased
(NP the cat)))
```

The letter "S" stands for the beginning of a sentence, the letters "NP" stand for a noun phrase, and "VP" stands for a verb phrase. If the sentence can't be parsed, it is ignored.

Their solution hides information by applying a number of transformations such as switching between the active and passive voice. One bit could be encoded by switching this example to read "The cat was chased by the dog." Other solutions they use include moving the adjunct of a sentence, clefting the sentence, and inserting extra unnecessary words and phrases like "It seems that...."

A canonical form can be defined by choosing one version of the transformation. In this example, the active voice might be the canonical form for the sentence.

13.5

Packing in Multiple Messages

Sorting can also let you store multiple messages in a collection of data. If f_1 defines one order and f_2 defines another order, then both orderings can be used to hide information if the sizes are right. If the number of elements in the camouflaging data is much larger than the amount of information being hidden, then the chances of a collision are small.

The chances of a collision are easy to estimate if you can assume that the sorting functions, f_1 and f_2, behave like random number generators and place each element in the order with equal probability. The easiest way to create this is to use a well-designed cryptographically secure hash function such as SHA. The designers have already worked hard to ensure that the results of these functions behave close to a random number source.

If you can assume that f_1 and f_2 are random enough, then the odds of a collision are simple. If data is hidden in the first n_1 elements in the list produced by f_1 and the first n_2 elements in the list produced by f_2, then the estimated chance of collisions is

$$n_1 \times \frac{n_2}{n}.$$

The damage can be reduced by using error-correcting codes like the ones described in Chapter 3.

13.6

Sorting to Hide Information

The algorithms in the first part of this chapter use sorting as a form of camouflage. The information is hidden and then scrambled to hide it some more. Correctly sorting the information again reveals it.

Another solution is to actually hide information in the choice of the scrambling. If there are n items, then there are $n!$ ways that they can be arranged. If the arrangements are given numbers, then there are $\log n!$ bits. Matthew Kwan used this solution to hide information in the sequence of colors in the palette of a GIF image. A freely available program called GifShuffle implements the solution.

Here's a simple version of the algorithm:

1. Use a keyed pseudo-random bit stream to choose pairs of pixels or data items in the file.

2. For each pair, let D be the difference between the two values.

3. If the differance is greater than some threshold of perception, ignore the pair. That is, if the differences between the pixels or data items are noticeable by a human, then ignore the pair.

4. If $D = 0$, ignore the pair.

5. Encode one bit of information in the pair. Let $D > 0$ stand for a zero and $D < 0$ stand for a one. If the pixels aren't arranged in the right order, swap them.

The locations of transistors on a circuit can be sorted in different ways to hide information that may track the rightful owner [LMSP98].

This basic mechanism hides bits in pairs of pixels or data items. The solution does not change the basic statistical profile of the underlying file, an important consideration because many attacks on steganography rely on statistical analysis. Of course, it *does* change some of the larger statistics about which pixels of some value are near other pixels of a different value. Attackers looking at basic statistics won't detect the change, but attackers with more sophisticated models could.

The algorithm can also be modified to hide the information statistically. An early steganographic algorithm called Patchwork repeats this process a number of times to hide the same bit in numerous pairs. The random process chooses pairs by selecting one pixel from one set and another pixel from the different set. The message is detected by comparing the statistical differences between the two sets. The largest one identifies the bit being transmitted. There's no attempt made to synchronize the random selection of pixels [BGML96, GB98].

In this simple example, one bit gets hidden in the order of 2^1 items. The process can be taken to any extreme by choosing sets of n pixels or items and hiding information in the order of all of them. Here's one way that a set of n items, $\{x_0, x_1, \ldots, x_{n-1}\}$, can encode a long, $\log n!$-bit number, M. Set $m = M$ and let S be the set $\{x_1, x_2, \ldots, x_n\}$. Let the answer, the set A, begin as the empty set. Repeat this loop for i, taking values begining with n and dropping to 2.

1. Select the item in S with the index $m \bmod i$. The indices start at 0 and run up to $i - 1$. There should only be i elements left in S at each pass through the loop.

2. Remove it from S and stick it at the end of A.

3. Set $m = \frac{m}{i}$. Round down to the nearest integer.

The value of M can be recovered with this loop. Begin with $m = 1$.

1. Remove the first element in A.

2. Convert this element into a value by counting the values left in A with a subscript that is still less than its own. That is, if you remove x_i, count the values of x_j still in A where $j < i$.

3. Multiply m by this count and set it to be the new value of m.

Using this algorithm steganographically often requires finding a way to assign a true order to the element. This algorithm assumes that the elements in the set S come ordered from 0 to $n - 1$. Kwan, for instance, orders the RGB colors in the palette of the GIF by using what he calls the "natural" order. That is, every color is assigned the value $2^{16} \times Red + 2^8 \times Blue + Green$ and then sorted accordingly.

Many of the sorting strategies used above can also be used to sort the elements. If they are encrypted with a particular key before the sorting, then the key acts as a key for this steganography.

This algorithm can be particularly efficient in the right situations. Imagine you have all 65,536 2-byte values arranged in a list. This takes 128K bytes. This list can store 119,255 bytes with this algorithm—close to 90 percent of the payload. Of course, good steganographic opportunities like shopping lists are rarely so compact, but the theoretical potential is still astonishing.

13.7

Adding Extra Packets

Another way to scramble the order is to add fake packets. Ron Rivest suggested this idea as one way to evade a ban on cryptography [Riv]. He suggests letting every packet fly in the clear with a digital signature attached. Valid packets come with valid signatures, while invalid packets come with invalid signatures.

Rivest suggested using keyed message authentication codes generated by hash functions. If x is the message, then the signature consists of $f(kx)$ where k is a key known only to those who can read the message. Let $f'(x)$ be some bad-signature generating function, perhaps a random number generator. Let the message be $\{x_1, x_2, \ldots, x_n\}$. Rivest called these message pieces the *wheat*. Let the *chaff* be $\{r_1, \ldots, r_k\}$, random numbers of the correct size. The message consists of pairs like $(x_1, f(kx_1))$ mixed in with distractions like $(r_i, f'(r_i))$.

Mihir Bellare and Alexandra Boldyreva take the idea of chaff one step further with all-or-nothing transforms that provide more efficiency [BB00].

Many standard digital signature algorithms can also be used if we relax the notion that the signatures can be tested by anyone with access to a public key. If the verification key is kept secret, only the sender and any receiver can tell the wheat from the chaff. Traditional public-key algorithms can still be useful here because the receiver's key cannot be used to generate the signatures themselves.

At the time Rivest's article [Riv] was written, the U.S. government restricted the export of algorithms designated as "cryptography" while placing no limitations on those used for "authentication". Hash-function-based message authentication codes were typically assumed to offer no secrecy and thus were freely exportable. Rivest suggested that his solution pointed to a loophole that weakened the law.

The security of this solution depends to a large extent on the structure of x and the underlying data. If x contains enough information to be interesting in and of itself, the attacker may be able to pick out the wheat from the chaff without worrying about f or k.

One solution is to break the file into individual bits. This mechanism is a bit weak, however, because there will be only two valid signatures: $f(k0)$ and $f(k1)$. Rivest overcomes this problem by adding a counter or nonce to the mix so that each packet looks like this: $(x_i, i, f(kix_i))$. This mechanism is not that efficient because each bit may require an 80- to 200-bit-long packet to carry it.

This solution can easily be mixed with the other techniques that define the order. One function f can identify the true elements of the message and another function g can identify the canonical order for the elements so the information can be extracted.

13.8

Summary

The order of objects in a set is a surprisingly complex set of information and one that offers a correspondingly large opportunity for steganography. Sometimes an adversary may choose to change the order of a list of objects in the hopes of destroying some steganography. Sometimes the data objects take different asynchronous paths. In either case, a hidden canonical order defined by some keyed function, f, is a good way to restore the order and withstand these attacks.

The idea can also be turned on its head to store information. Changing the order of objects requires no change in the objects themselves, eliminating many of the statistical or structural forms of steganalysis described in Chapter 17. There are no anomalies created by making subtle changes. The result can hold a surprisingly large amount of information. n objects can store $\log n!$ bits.

Of course, sometimes subtle changes may need to be made to add cover. Many lists are sorted alphabetically or according to some other field of the data. This field could be an artificially generated system to act as a cover. A list of people, for instance, might be sorted by a membership number generated randomly to camouflage the reason for sorting it.

- *The Disguise.* Any set of n items, $\{x_1, \ldots, x_n\}$, can conceal $\log n!$ bits of information in the sorted order. This information can be keyed or hidden by sorting on $f(x_i)$ instead of x_i where f is an encryption or hash function.

  Some decoy packets can also distract eavesdroppers if another function, g, can be used to create a secure signature or message authentication code that distinguishes between valid and invalid packets.

  Sometimes the attacker will rearrange the order of a set of objects to destroy a message. Sorting the objects with the function, f, before processing them is a good defense.

- *How Secure Is It?* The security depends on both the quality of the camouflaging data and the security of f. If the set of objects is a list that seems completely random, then it is unlikely to receive any scrutiny. The information can only be extracted if the attacker discovers the true order of the set—something that a solid encryption or hash function can effectively prevent.

- *How to Use It?* Choose your objects for their innocence, choose an encryption function, choose a key, compute $f(x_i)$ for all objects, sort on this value to get the so-called true order, use the reordering function to insert the data, and ship with this order.

chapter fourteen

Spreading

A New Job

We open with a shot of a fishing boat where a father and son work on tempting the fish with seductive offers of worms and minnows.

Father: It makes me happy to have my son come home from college and stay with us.

Son: Ah, quit it.

Father: No. Say something intelligent. I want to see what I got for my money.

Son: Quit it.

Father: No. Come on.

Son: The essential language of a text is confusion, distraction, misappropriation, and disguise. Only by deconstructing the textual signifiers, assessing and reassessing the semiotic signposts, and then reconstructing a coherent yet divergent vision can we truly begin to apprehend and perhaps even comprehend the limits of our literary media.

The son reels in his line and begins to switch the lures.

Father: It makes me proud to hear such talk.

Son: I'm just repeating it.

Father: A degree in English literature is something to be proud of.

Son: Well, if you say so.

Father: Now, what are you going to do for a job?

Son: Oh, there aren't many openings for literature majors. A friend works at a publishing house in New York . . . .

The son trails off, the father pauses, wiggles in his seat, adjusts his line and begins.

Father: There's no money in those things. College was college. I spoke to my brother Louie, your uncle, and he agrees with me. We want you to join the family business.

Son: The import/export business? What does literature have to do with that?

Father: We're not technically in import and export.

Son: But.

Father: Yes, that's what the business name says, but as you put it, there's a bit of confusion, distraction, and disguise in that text.

Son: But what about the crates of tomatoes and the endless stream of plastic goods?

Father: Subtext. We're really moving money. We specialize in money laundering.

Son: What does money have to do with tomatoes?

Father: Nothing and everything. We move the tomatoes, they pay us for the tomatoes, someone sells the tomatoes, and in the end everyone is happy. But when everything is added up, when all of the arithmetic is done, we've moved more than a million dollars for our friends. They look like tomato kings making a huge profit off of their tomatoes. We get to take a slice for ourselves.

Son: So it's all a front?

Father: It's classier if you think of the tomatoes as a language filled with misdirection, misapprehension, and misunderstanding. We take a clear statement written in the language of money, translate it into millions of tiny tomato sentences, and then through the magic of accounting return it to the language of cold, hard cash.

Son: It's a new language.

Father: It's an old one. You understand addition. You understand the sum is more than the parts. That's what we do.

Son: So what do you want from me?

Father: You're now an expert on the language of misdirection. That's exactly what we need around the office.

Son: A job?

Father: Yes. We would pay you three times whatever that publishing firm would provide you.

Son: But I would have to forget all of the words I learned in college. I would need to appropriate the language of the stevedores and the longshoremen.

Father: No. We want you to stay the way you are. All of that literature stuff is much more confusing than any code we could ever create.

Father and son embrace in a happy ending unspoiled by confusion or misdirection.

14.1

Spreading the Information

Many of the algorithms in this book evolved during the modern digital era where bits are bits, 0s are 0s, and 1s are 1s. The tools and the solutions all assume that the information is going to be encoded as streams of binary digits. Tuning the applications to this narrow view of the world is important because binary numbers are the best that modern machines can do. They are still capable of hair-splitting precision, but they do it by approximating numbers with a great number of bits.

The algorithms in this chapter take a slightly different approach. While the information is still encoded as 1s or 0s, the theory involves a more continuous style. The information at each location can vary by small amounts that may be fractions like .042 or 1.993. This detail is eventually eliminated by rounding them off, but the theory embraces these fractional values.

This is largely because the algorithms imitate an entire collection of techniques created by radio engineers. Radio engineers attacked a similar problem of hiding information in the past when they developed spread-spectrum radio using largely analog ideas. In the beginning, radios broadcast by pumping power in and out of their antennae at a set frequency. The signal was encoded by changing this power ever so slightly. Amplitude modulated (AM) radios changed the strength of the signal, while frequency modulated (FM) radios tweaked the speed of the signal a slight amount. To use the radio engineers' words, all of the "energy" was concentrated at one frequency.

Spread-spectrum radio turned this notion on its head. Instead of using one frequency, it used several. All of the energy was distributed over a large number of frequencies—a feat that managed to make radio communication more secret, more reliable, more efficient, and less susceptible to jamming. If the signal lived on many different frequencies, it was much less likely that either intentional or unintentional interference would knock out the signal. Several radios could also share the same group of frequencies without interfering. Well, they might interfere slightly, but a small amount wouldn't disrupt the communications.

Many of the techniques from the spread-spectrum radio world are quite relevant today in digital steganography. The ideas work well if the radio terminology is translated into digital speak. This is not as complicated as it looks. Plus, using digital metaphors can offer a few additional benefits, which may be why most spread-spectrum radios today are entirely digital.

The basic approach in radio lingo is to "spread the energy out across the spectrum"—that is, to place the signal in a number of different frequencies. In some cases, the radios hop from frequency to frequency very quickly in a system called *time sequence*. This frequency hopping is very similar to the technique of using a random number generator to choose the locations for where the bits should be hidden in a camouflaging file. In some cases, the same random number generators developed to help spread-spectrum radios hop from frequency to frequency are used to choose pixels or moments in an audio file.

Sometimes the systems use different frequencies at the same time, an approach known as *direct sequence*. This spreads out the information over the spectrum by broadcasting some amount of information at one frequency, some at another, and so on. The entire message is reassembled by combining all of the information.

The way the energy is parceled out is usually pretty basic. At each instance, the energy being broadcast at all of the frequencies is added

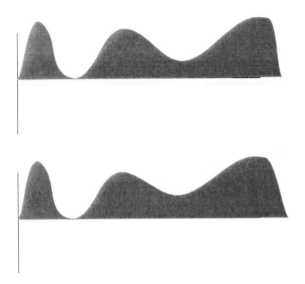

Figure 14.1   The energy spread over a number of different frequencies is computed by integration. The top function integrates to, say, 100.03, and the bottom integrates to 80.2. Both look quite similar, but the top one is a bit more top-heavy.

up to create the entire signal. This is usually represented mathematically by an integral. Figure 14.1 shows two hypothetical distributions. The top integrates to a positive value, say 100.03, and the bottom integrates to 80.2. Both functions look quite similar. They have the same number of bumps and the same zero values along the x axis. The top version, however, has a bit more "energy" above the x axis than the other one. When all of this is added up, the top function is sending a message of "100.03".

Spread-spectrum radio signals like this are said to be resistant to noise and other interference caused by radio jammers. Random noise along the different frequencies may distort the signal, but the changes are likely to cancel out. Radio engineers have sophisticated models of the type of noise corrupting the radio spectrum, and they use the models to tune the spread-spectrum algorithms. Noise may increase the signal at one frequency, but it is likely to decrease it somewhere else. When everything is added together in the integral, the same result comes out. Figure 14.2 shows the signals from Figure 14.1 after a bit of noise has corrupted them.

A radio jammer trying to block the signal faces a difficult challenge. Pumping out random noise at one frequency may disrupt a

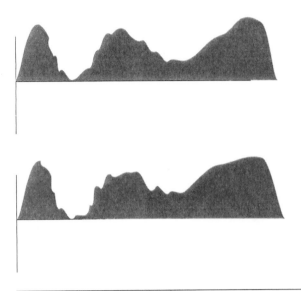

Figure 14.2   The signals from Figure 14.1 after being changed by a bit of random noise. The integrals still come out to 100.03 and 0.

signal concentrated at that single frequency, but it only obscures one small part of the signal spread out over a number of frequencies. The effects of one powerful signal are easy to filter out by placing limits on the amount of power detected at each frequency.

The algorithms for spreading information out over a number of bits are very similar to the error-correcting codes described in Chapter 3.

If a jammer is actually able to identify the band of frequencies used for the entire spread-spectrum signal, it is still hard to disrupt it by injecting random noise everywhere. The noise just cancels out, and the signal shines through after integration. In practice, there are ways to jam spread-spectrum signals, but they usually require the jammer to pump out significantly more power. Large amounts of noise can disrupt the system.

14.2

Going Digital

The spread-spectrum solutions use the analog metaphors of continuous functions measuring "energy" that are evaluated using integration. In the digital world, integers measuring any quantity define discrete functions. In many cases, these integers measure energy. The integers that define the amount of red, blue, and green color at any particular pixel measure the amount of red, green, and blue light coming from that location. The integers in a sound file measure the amount of energy traveling as a pressure wave. Of course, the same techniques also work for generic numbers that measure things other than energy. There's no reason why these techniques can't be used with an accounting program counting money.

A spread-spectrum digital system uses the following steps:

1. *Choose the Locations.* If the information is going to be spread out over a number of different locations in the document, then the locations should be chosen with as much care as is practical. The simplest solution is to choose a block of pixels, a section of an audio file, or perhaps a block of numbers. More complicated solutions may make sense in some cases. There's no reason why the locations can't be rearranged, reordered, or selected as directed by some keyed algorithm. This might be done with a sorting algorithm (see Chapter 13) to find the right locations or a simple random number generator that hops from pixel to pixel finding the right ones.

2. *Identify the Signal Strength.* Spread-spectrum solutions try to hide the signal in the noise. If the hidden signal is so much larger than the noise that it competes with and overwhelms the main signal, then the game is lost.

   Choosing the strength for the hidden signal is an art. A strong signal may withstand the effects of inexact compression algorithms, but it also could be noticeable. A weaker signal may avoid detection by both a casual user and anyone trying to recover it.

3. *Study the Human Response.* Many of the developers of spread-spectrum solutions for audio or visual files study the limits of the human senses and try to arrange for their signals to stay beyond these limits. The signal injected into an audio file may stay in the low levels of the noise or it may hide in the echoes.

   Of course, there is a wide range in human perception. Some people have more sensitive eyes and ears. Everyone can benefit from training. Many spread-spectrum signal designers have developed tools that fooled themselves and their friends, but were easily detected by others.

4. *Injecting the Signal.* The information is added to the covering data by making changes simultaneously in all of the locations. If the file is a picture, then all of the pixels are changed by a small amount. If it's a sound file, then the sound at each moment gets either a bit stronger or a bit weaker.

The signal is removed after taking the same steps to find the right locations in the file.

Many approaches to spread-spectrum signal hiding use a mathematical algorithm known as the Fast Fourier Transform. This uses a collection of cosine and sine functions to create a model of the underlying data. The model can be tweaked in small ways to hide a signal. More modern variations use only the cosine (discrete cosine transform), the sine (discrete sine transform), or more complicated waveforms altogether (discrete wavelet transform).

14.2.1   An Example

Figure 14.3 shows the graph of a .33-second piece from a sound file with samples taken 44,100 times per second. The sound file records the sound intensity with a sequence of 14,976 integers that vary from about 30,000 to about −30,000. Call these x_i where i ranges between 0 and 14,975.

How can information be spread out in this file? A simple spread-spectrum approach is to grab a block of data and add small parts

Figure 14.3   A graph of a .33-second piece from a sound file.

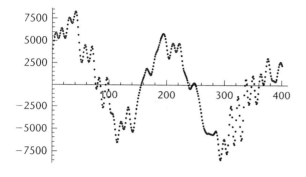

Figure 14.4   A small section of Figure 14.3 from range (8200, 8600).

of the message to every element in the block. Figure 14.4 shows a graph of the data at the moments between 8200 and 8600 in the sound file. A message can be encoded by adding or subtracting a small amount from each location. The same solution can be used with video data or any other data source that can withstand small perturbations.

Here are the raw values between 8250 and 8300: 2603, 2556, 2763, 3174, 3669, 4140, 4447, 4481, 4282, 3952, 3540, 3097, 2745, 2599, 2695, 2989, 3412, 3878, 4241, 4323, 4052, 3491, 2698, 1761, 867, 143, −340, −445, −190, 203, 575, 795, 732, 392, −172, −913, −1696, −2341, −2665, −2579, −2157, −1505, −729, 6, 553, 792, 654, 179, −548, −1401, −2213. The values in the range (8200, 8600) add up to 40,813, or an average of about 102.

A basic algorithm encodes 1 bit by choosing some strength factor, S, by arranging for the absolute value of the average value of the elements to be above S if the message is a 1 and below S if the message is a 0.

Choosing the right value of S for this basic algorithm is something of an art that is confounded by the size of the blocks, the strength of the real signal, the nature of the sound, and several other factors. Let's imagine $S = 10$. If the message to be encoded is 1, then nothing needs to be done. The average value of 102 is already well above 10.

If the message is 0, however, the average value needs to be reduced by at least 92 and perhaps more if there's going to be any margin of error. Subtracting 100 from each element does not distort the signal too much when the values range between ±7500. Of course, some elements have small values like 6 or −190, and they will be distorted more, but this is well below the threshold of our perception.

A more sophisticated mechanism spreads the distortion proportionately. This can be calculated with this formula:

$$x_i = x_i - x_i \times \frac{\text{total change}}{\sum |x_i|}$$

If this is reduced to each value, x_i, then the sum moves by the total change.

This approach has several advantages over simply encoding the information in the least significant bit because the data is spread over a larger block. Any attacker who simply flips a random selection of the least significant bits will wipe out the least significant bit message, but have no effect on this message. The random changes will balance out and have no net effect on the sum. If the absolute value of the average value is over S, then it will still be over S. If it was under, then it will still be under.

Random noise should also have little effect on the message if the changes balance out. A glitch that adds in one place will probably be balanced out by a glitch that subtracts in another. Of course, this depends upon the noise behaving as we expect. If the size of the blocks is big enough, the odds suggest that truly random noise will balance itself.

The mechanism does have other weaknesses. An attacker might simply insert a few random large values in places. Changing several small elements of 100 to 30,000 is one way to distort the averages. This random attack is crude and might fail for a number of reasons. The glitches might be perceptible and thus easily spotted by the parties. They could also be eliminated when the sound file is played back. Many electronic systems remove short, random glitches.

Of course, there are also a number of practical limitations. Many compression algorithms use only a small number of values or quanta in the hopes of removing the complexity of the file. For instance, 8-bit μ-law encoding, only uses 256 possible values for each data element. If a file were compressed with this mechanism, any message encoded with this technique could be lost when the value of each element was compressed by converting it to the closest quantized value.

There are also a great number of practical problems in choosing the size of the block and the amount of information it can carry. If the blocks are small, then it is entirely possible that the signal will wipe out the data.

The first part of Figure 14.4, for instance, shows the data between elements x_{8200} and x_{8300}. Almost all are above 0. The total is 374,684, and the average value is 3746.84. Subtracting this large amount from every element would distort the signal dramatically.

Larger blocks are more likely to include enough of the signal to allow the algorithm to work, but increasing the size of the block reduces the amount of information that can be encoded.

In practice, blocks of 1000 elements or 1/44 of a second seem to work with a sound file like the one displayed in Figure 14.3. The following list shows the average values in the blocks. The largest values are about 1 percent of the largest values in the block. If S is set to be around 3 percent, then the signal should be encoded without a problem.

x_1 to x_{1000}	19.865
x_{1000} to x_{1999}	175.589
x_{2000} to x_{2999}	-132.675
x_{3000} to x_{3999}	-354.728
x_{4000} to x_{4999}	383.372
x_{5000} to x_{5999}	-111.475
x_{6000} to x_{6999}	152.809
x_{7000} to x_{7999}	-154.128
x_{8000} to x_{8999}	-59.596
x_{9000} to x_{9999}	153.62
$x_{10,000}$ to $x_{10,999}$	-215.226

14.2.2 Synchronization

Storing information by adding or subtracting small amounts to a number of elements is also susceptible to the same synchronization problem that affects many watermarking and information hiding algorithms, but it is more resilient than many. If a significant number of elements are lost at the beginning of the file, then the loss of synchronization can destroy the message.

This mechanism does offer a gradual measure of the loss of synchronization. Imagine that the block sizes are 1000 elements. If only a small number, say 20, are lost from the beginning of the file, then it is unlikely that the change will destroy the message. Spreading the message over the block ensures that there will still be 980 elements carrying the message. Clearly, as the amount of desynchronization increases, the quality of the message will decrease, reaching a peak when the gap becomes one-half of the block size. It is interesting to note that the errors will only occur in the blocks where the bits being encoded change from either a 0 to a 1 or a 1 to a 0.

Synchronization can also be automatically detected by attempting to extract the message. Imagine that the receiver knows that a hidden message has been encoded in a sound file, but the receiver doesn't know where the message begins or ends. Finding the correct offset is not hard with a guided search.

Chapter 3 discusses error-detecting and -correcting codes.

The message might include a number of parity bits, a simple error-detecting solution. That is, after every 8 bits, an extra parity bit is added to the stream based upon the number of 1s and 0s in the previous 8 bits. It might be set to 1 if there's an odd number and a 0 if there's an even number. This basic error-detection protocol is used frequently in telecommunications.

Many attacks like the Stirmark tests destroy the synchronization. Chapter 13 discusses one way to defend against it.

This mechanism can also be used to synchronize the message and find the location of the starts of the blocks through a brute-force search. The file can be decoded using a variety of potential offsets. The best solution will be the one with the greatest number of correct parity bits. The search can be made somewhat more intelligent because the quality of the message is close to a continuous function. Changing the offset a small amount should only change the number of correct parity bits by a correspondingly small amount.

More sophisticated error-correcting codes can also be used. The best offset is the one that requires the fewest number of corrections to the bit stream. The only problem with this is that more correcting power requires more bits, and this means trying more potential offsets. If there are 12 bits per word and 1000 samples encoding each bit, then the search for the correct offset must try all values between 0 and 12,000.

14.2.3   Strengthening the System

Spreading the information across multiple samples can be strengthened by using another source of randomness to change the way that data is added or subtracted from the file. Let α_i be a collection of coefficients that modify the way that the sum is calculated and the signal is extracted. Instead of computing the basic sum, calculate the sum weighted by the coefficients:

$$\sum \alpha_i x_i.$$

The values of α can act like a key if they are produced by a cryptographically secure random number source. A simple approach is to use a random bit stream to produce values of α equal to either $+1$ or -1. Only someone with the same access to the random number source can compute the correct sum and extract the message.

The process also restricts the ability of an attacker to add random glitches in the hope of destroying the message. In the first example, the attacker might always use either positive or negative glitches and drive the total to be either very positive or very negative. If the values of α are equally distributed, then the heavy glitches should balance out. If the attacker adds more and more glitches in the hope of obscuring any message, they become more and more likely to cancel each other out.

Clearly, the complexity can be increased by choosing different values of α like 2, 10, or 1000, but there do not seem to be many obvious advantages to this solution.

14.2.4 Packing Multiple Messages

Random number sources like this can also be used to select strange or discontinuous blocks of data. There's no reason why the elements x_1 through x_{1000} need to work together to hide the first bit of the message. Any 1000 elements chosen at random from the file can be used. If both the message sender and the receiver have access to the same cryptographically secure random number stream generated by the same key, then they can both extract the right elements and group them together in blocks to hide the message.

This approach has some advantages. If the elements are chosen at random, then the block sizes can be significantly smaller. As noted in Section 14.2.1, the values between x_{8200} and x_{8300} are largely positive with a large average. It's not possible to adjust the average up or down to be larger or smaller than a value S without significantly distorting the values in the block. If the elements are contiguous, then the block sizes need to be big to ensure that they'll include enough variation to have a small average. Choosing the elements at random from the entire file reduces this problem significantly.

The approach also allows multiple messages to be packed together. Imagine that Alice encodes 1 bit of a message by choosing 100 elements from the sound file and tweaking the average to be either above or below S. Now, imagine that Bob also encodes 1 bit by choosing his own set of 100 elements. The two may choose the same element several times, but the odds are quite low that there will be any significant overlap between the two. Even if Alice is encoding a 1 by raising the average of her block and Bob is encoding a 0 by lowering the average of his block, the work won't be distorted too much if very few elements are in both blocks. The averages will still be close to the same.

Engineering a system depends on calculating the odds, and this process is straight-forward. If there are N elements in the file and k elements in each block, then the odds of choosing one element in a block are $\frac{k}{N}$. The odds of having any overlap between blocks can be computed with the classic binomial expansion.

In the sound file displayed in Figure 14.3, there are 14,976 elements. If the block sizes are 100 elements, then the chance of choosing an element from a block is about $\frac{1}{150}$. The probability of choosing 100 elements and finding no intersections is about .51, one intersection is about .35, two intersections is about .11, three intersections is about .02, and the rest are negligible.

Of course, this solution may increase the amount of information that can be packed into a file, but it sacrifices the resistance to synchronization. Any complicated solution for choosing different elements and assembling them into a block will be thwarted if the data file loses information. Choosing the 1st, the 189th, the 542nd, and the 1044th elements from the data file fails if even the 1st one is deleted.

14.3

Comparative Blocks

Section 14.2 spread the information over a block of data by raising the average so it was larger or smaller than some value S. The solution works well if the average is predictable. While the examples used sound files with averages near zero, there's no reason why other data streams couldn't do the job if their average was known beforehand to both the sender and the recipient.

Another solution is to tweak the algorithm to adapt to the data at hand. This works better with files such as images, which often contain information with very different statistical profiles. A dark picture of shadows and a picture of a snow-covered mountain on a sunny day have significantly different numbers in their files. It just isn't possible for the receiver and the sender to predict the average.

Here's a simple solution:

1. Divide the elements in the file into blocks as before. They can either be contiguous groups or random selections chosen by some cryptographically secure random number generator.

2. Group the blocks into pairs.

3. Compute the averages of the elements in the blocks.

4. Compare the averages of the pairs.

5. If the difference between the averages is larger than some threshold ($|B_1 - B_2| > T$), throw out the pair and ignore it.

6. If the difference is smaller than the threshold, keep the pair and encode information in it. Let a pair where $B_1 > B_2$ signify a 1, and let a pair where $B_1 < B_2$ signify a 0. Add or subtract small amounts from individual elements to make sure the information is correct. To add some error resistance, make sure that $|B_1 - B_2| > S$ where S is a measure of the signal strength.

Throwing out wildly different pairs where the difference is greater than T helps ensure that the modifications will not be too large. Both the sender and the receiver can detect these wildly different blocks and exclude them from consideration.

Again, choosing the correct sizes for the blocks, the threshold T, and the signal strength S requires a certain amount of artistic sense. Bigger blocks mean more room for the law of averages to work at the cost of greater bandwidth. Decreasing the value of T reduces the amount of changing that might need to be made to the data in order to encode the right value at the cost of excluding more information.

14.3.1 Minimizing Quantization Errors

In one surprising detail, the strategy of increasing the block size begins to fail when the data values are tightly quantized. Larger blocks mean the information can be spread out over more elements with smaller changes. But after a certain point, the changes become too small to measure. Imagine, for instance, the simplest case of a grayscale image where the values at each pixel range from 0 to 255. Adding a small amount, say .25, is not going to change the value of any pixel at all. No one is going to be able to recover the information because no pixel is actually changed by the small additions.

This problem can be fixed with this algorithm. Let S be the amount to be spread out over all the elements in the block. If this is spread out equally, the amount added to each block will be less than the quantized value.

While S is greater than zero, repeat the following:

1. Choose an element at random.

2. Increase the element by 1 quanta. That is, if it is a simple, linearly encoded data value like a pixel, add 1 to it. If it is a log-encoded value like an element in a sound file, select the next largest quantized value.

3. Subtract this amount from S.

The average of all the elements in the block will still increase, but only a subset of the elements will change.

14.4

Fast Fourier Solutions

Many of the spread-spectrum solutions use a branch of mathematics known as *Fourier analysis* or a more modern revision of the idea known as *wavelet analysis*. The entire branch is based upon the work of Jean-Baptiste Fourier who came up with a novel way of modeling functions using a set of sine and cosine functions (Figure 14.5). This decomposition turned out to be quite useful for finding solutions to many differential equations, and it is often used to solve engineering, chemistry, and physics problems.

The mechanism Fourier proposed is also quite useful for steganography because it provides a simple way to embed several signals together in a larger one. The huge body of scholarship devoted to the topic makes it easier to test theories and develop tools quickly. One of the greatest contributions, the so-called *Fast Fourier Transform*, is an algorithm optimized for the digital data files that are often used to hide information today.

The basic idea is to take a mathematical function, f, and represent it as the weighted sum of another set of functions: $\alpha_1 f_1 + \alpha_2 f_2 + \alpha_3 f_3 \ldots$. The choice of the values of f_i is something of an art, and different choices work better for solving different problems. Some of the most common choices are the basic harmonic functions such as sine and cosine. In fact, the very popular *discrete cosine transform* used in music compression functions such as MP3 and MPEG video compression uses $f_1 = \cos(\pi x)$, $f_2 = \cos(2\pi x)$, $f_3 = \cos(3\pi x)$, and so

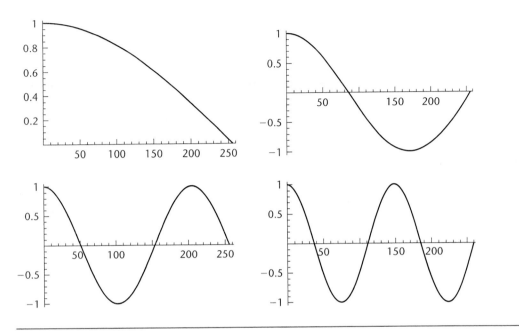

Figure 14.5   The first four basic cosine functions used in Fourier series expansions: cos(x), cos(2x), cos(3x), and cos(4x).

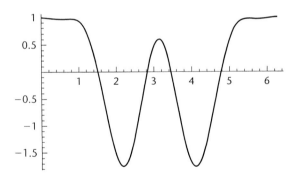

Figure 14.6   The author's last initial recreated as a Fourier series, adding together the four functions shown in Figure 14.5: 1.0 cos(x) + .5 cos(2x) − .8 cos(3x) + .3 cos(4x).

on. (Figure 14.6 shows the author's last initial recoded as a discrete cosine transform.) Much research today is devoted to finding better and more sophisticated functions that are better suited to particular tasks. The section on wavelets (Section 14.7) goes into some of the more common choices.

Much of the mathematical foundations of Fourier analysis is aimed at establishing several features that make them useful for different problems. The cosine functions, for instance, are just one set that is *orthogonal*, a term that effectively means that the set is as efficient as possible. A set of functions is orthogonal if no one function, f_i, can be represented as the sum of the other functions. That is, there are no values of $\{\alpha_1, \alpha_2, \ldots, \alpha_{i-1}, \alpha_{i+1}, \ldots\}$ that exist so that

$$f_i = \sum_{i \neq j} \alpha_j \, f_j.$$

The set of cosine functions also forms a *basis* for the set of sufficiently continuous functions. That is, for all sufficiently continuous functions, f, there exists some set of coefficients, $\{\alpha_1, \alpha_2, \ldots\}$, such that

$$f = \sum \alpha_j \, f_j.$$

The fact that the set of cosine functions is both orthogonal and a basis means that there is only one unique choice of coefficients for each function. In this example, the basis must be infinite to represent all sufficiently continuous functions, but most discrete problems never require such precision. For that reason, a solid discussion of what it means to be "sufficiently continuous" is left out of this book.

Both of these features are important to steganography. The fact that each function can only be represented by a unique set of values $\{\alpha_1, \alpha_2, \ldots\}$ means that both the encoder and the decoder will be working with the same information. The fact that the functions form a basis means that the algorithm will handle anything it encounters. Of course, both of these requirements for the set of functions can be relaxed, as they are later in the book, if other steps are taken to provide some assurance.

Incidentally, the fact that there are many different basis functions means that there can be many different unique representations of the data. There is no reason why the basis functions can't be changed frequently or shared between sender and receiver. A key could be used to choose a particular basis function, and this could hamper the work of potential eavesdroppers [FBS96].

14.4.1   Some Brief Calculus

The foundation of Fourier analysis lies in calculus, and so a brief introduction is provided in the original form. If we limit $f(x)$ to the range $0 \le x \le 2v$, then the function f can be represented as the infinite series of sines and cosines:

$$f(x) = \frac{c_0}{2} + \sum_{j=-\infty}^{\infty} c_j \sin\left(\frac{j\pi x}{v}\right) + d_j \cos\left(\frac{j\pi x}{v}\right).$$

Fourier developed a relatively straightforward solution for computing the values of c_j and d_j, again represented as integrals:

$$c_j = \frac{1}{v} \int_0^{2v} f(x) \cos\left(\frac{j\pi x}{v}\right) dx \qquad d_j = \frac{1}{v} \int_0^{2v} f(x) \sin\left(\frac{j\pi x}{v}\right) dx$$

The fact that these functions are orthogonal is expressed by this fact:

$$\int \cos(i\pi x) \cos(j\pi x)\, dx = 0, \quad \forall i \ne j.$$

The integral is 1 if $i = j$.

In the past, many of these integrals were not easy to compute for many functions, f, and entire branches of mathematics developed around finding results. Today, numerical integration can solve the problem easily. In fact, with numerical methods it is much easier to see the relationship between the functional analysis done here and the vector algebra that is the cousin. If the function f is only known at a discrete number of points $\{x_1, x_2, x_3, \ldots, x_n\}$, then the equations for c_j and d_j look like dot products:

$$c_j = \sum_{i=1}^{n} f(x_i) \cos(j\pi x_i/v) \qquad d_j = \sum_{i=1}^{n} f(x_i) \sin(j\pi x_i/v).$$

Discrete approaches are almost certainly going to be more interesting to modern steganographers because so much data is stored and transported in digital form.

14.5

The Fast Fourier Transform

The calculus may be beautiful, but digital data doesn't come in continous functions. Luckily, mathematicians have found versions of the equations suitable for calculation. In fact, the version for discrete data known as the Fast Fourier Transform (FFT) is the foundation for many of the digital electronics used for sound, radio, and images. Almost all multimedia software today uses some form of the FFT to analyze data, find the dominant harmonic characteristics, and then use this information to enhance the data or perhaps compress it. Musicians use FFT-based algorithms to add reverb, dampen annoying echoes, or change the acoustics of the hall where the recording was made. Record companies use FFTs to digitize music and store it on CDs. Teenagers use FFTs again to convert the music into MP3 files. The list goes on and on.

The details behind the FFT are beyond the scope of this book. The algorithm uses a clever numerical juggling routine often called a "butterfly algorithm" to minimize the number of multiplications. The end result is a long vector of numbers summarizing the strength of various frequencies in the signal.

To be more precise, an FFT algorithm accepts a vector of n elements, $\{x_0, x_1, \ldots, x_{n-1}\}$, and returns another vector of n elements $\{y_0, y_1, \ldots, y_{n-1}\}$, where

$$y_s = \frac{1}{\sqrt{n}} \sum_{r=1}^{n} x_r e^{2\pi i(r-1)(s-1)/n}.$$

This equation is used by Mathematica and its Wavelet Explorer package, the program that created many of the pictures in this section. Others use slight variations designed to solve particular problems.

The vector that emerges is essentially a measure of how well each function matches the underlying data. For instance, the fourth element in the vector measures how much the graph has in common with $\cos(4 \times 2\pi x) + i \sin(4 \times 2\pi x)$.

Figure 14.7 shows a graph of the function $(2 + \frac{x}{64}) \sin(4 \times 2\pi x/256)$. If the 256 points from this example are fed into a Fourier

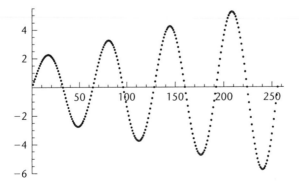

Figure 14.7 Shown are 256 points calculated from the equation $(2 + \frac{x}{64}) \sin(4 \times 2\pi x/256)$.

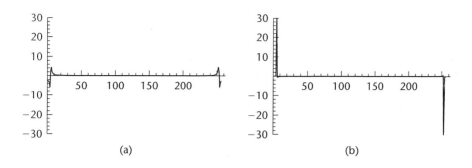

Figure 14.8   A graph of the real and imaginary parts of the Fourier transform computed from the data in Figure 14.7.

transform, the result has its largest values at the y_4 and the y_{251} positions. The second spike is caused by aliasing. The values in the first $\frac{n}{2}$ elements report the Fourier transform of the function computed from left to right, and the second $\frac{n}{2}$ elements carry the result of computing it from right to left. The results are mirrors.

Figure 14.8 shows the real and imaginary parts of the Fourier transform applied to the data in Figure 14.7. Many physicists and electrical engineers who use these algorithms to analyze radio phenomena like to say that most of the "energy" can be found in the imaginary part at y_4 and y_{251}. Some mathematicians talk about how Figure 14.8 shows the "frequency space" while Figure 14.7 shows the "function space". In both cases, the graphs are measuring the amount that the data can be modeled by each element.

This basic solution from the Fourier transform includes both real and imaginary values, something that can be confusing and unnecessary in many situations. For this reason, many also use the *discrete cosine transform* (DCT) and its cousin the *discrete sine transform*. Both have their uses, but sine transforms are less common because they do a poor job of modeling the data near the point $x = 0$ when $f(0) \neq 0$. In fact, most users choose their modeling functions based upon their performance near the endpoints.

Figure 14.9 shows the first four basis functions from one common set used for the discrete cosine transform:

$$\sqrt{\frac{2}{n}} \cos \left(\frac{\pi}{n} \left(k + \frac{1}{2} \right) x \right), \quad k = 0, 1, 2, 3, \ldots$$

Figure 14.10 shows the 64 different two-dimensional cosine functions used as the basis functions to model 8×8 blocks of pixels for JPEG and MPEG compression.

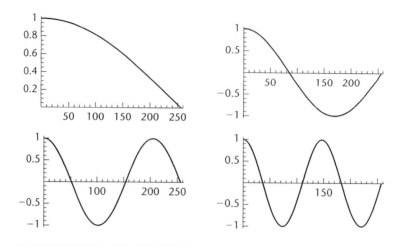

Figure 14.9   The first four cosine basis functions used in one popular implementation of the discrete cosine transform for Mathematica.

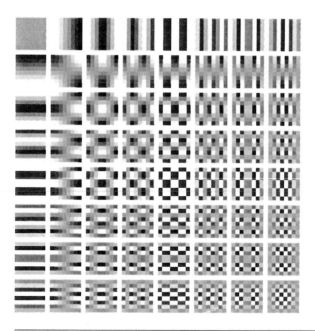

Figure 14.10   The 64 different two-dimensional basis functions used in the two-dimensional discrete cosine transform of 8×8 grid of pixels. The intensity at each particular point indicates the size of the function.

Another version uses a similar version with a different value at the endpoint:

$$\sqrt{\frac{2}{n}} \cos\left(\frac{k\pi}{n}x\right), \quad k = 0, 1, 2, 3, \ldots$$

Each of these transforms also has an inverse operation. This is useful because many mathematical operations are easier to do in the "frequency space". That is, the amount of energy in each frequency in the data is computed by constructing the transforms. Then, some basic operations are done on the frequency coefficients, and then the data is restored with the inverse FFT or DCT.

Smoothing data is one operation that is particularly easy to do with the FFT and DCT—if the fundamental signal is pretty repetitive. Figure 14.11 shows the four steps in smoothing data with the Fourier transform. The first graph shows the noisy data. The second shows the absolute value of the Fourier coefficients. Both y_4 and y_{251} are large despite the effect of the noise. The third graph shows the coefficients after all of the small ones are set to 0. The fourth shows the

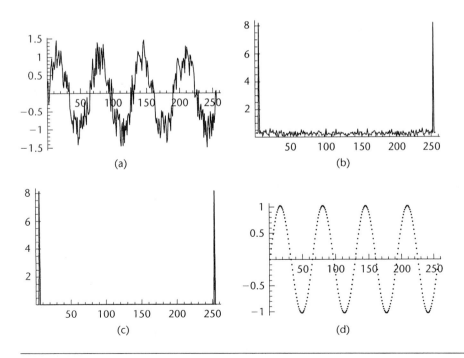

Figure 14.11 The four steps in smoothing noisy data with the FFT. (a) shows the data, (b) the result of computing the FFT, (c) data after small values are set to 0, and (d) the final result.

reconstructed data after taking the inverse Fourier transform. Naturally, this solution works very well when the signal to be cleaned can be modeled well by sine and cosine functions. If the data doesn't fit this format, then there are usually smaller distinctions between the big frequencies and the little ones, and it is difficult to remove the small frequencies.

14.6

Hiding Information with FFTs and DCTs

Fourier transforms provide ideal ways to mix signals and hide information by changing the coefficients. A signal that looks like $\cos(4\pi x)$ can be added by just increasing the values of y_4 and y_{251}. The more difficult challenge is doing this in a way that is hard to detect and resistant to changes to the file that are either malicious or incidental.

Here's a simple example. Figure 14.12 shows the absolute value of the first 600 coefficients from the Fourier transform of the voice signal shown in Figure 14.3. The major frequencies are easy to identify and change if necessary.

A simple watermark or signal can be inserted by changing setting $y_{300} = 100,000$. The result after taking the inverse transform looks identical to Figure 14.3 at this level of detail. The numbers still range from $-30,000$ to $30,000$. The difference, though small, can be seen by subtracting the original signal from the watermarked one. Figure 14.13 shows that the difference oscillates between 750 and -750 with the correct frequency.

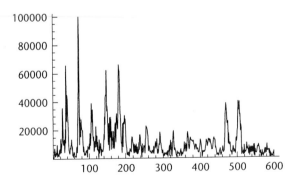

Figure 14.12 The first 600 coefficients from the Fourier transform of the voice signal in Figure 14.3.

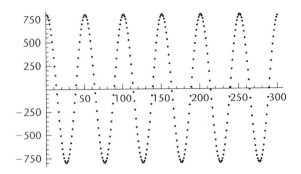

Figure 14.13   The result of subtracting the original signal shown in Figure 14.3 from the signal with an inflated value of y_{300}.

14.6.1   Tweaking a Number of Coefficients

Ingemar Cox, Joe Kilian, Tom Leighton, and Talal Shamoon [CKLS96] offer a novel way to hide information in an image or sound file by tweaking the k largest coefficients of an FFT or a DCT of the data. Call these $\{y_1, y_2, \ldots, y_{k-1}\}$. The largest coefficients correspond to the most significant parts of the data stream. They are the frequencies that have the most "energy" or do the most for carrying the information about the final image.

Cox et al. suggest that hiding the information in the largest coefficients may sound counterintuitive, but it is the only choice. At first glance, the most logical place to hide the data is in the noise, that is, in the smallest coefficients. But this noise is also the most likely to be modified by compression, printing, or using a less than perfect conversion process. The most significant parts of the signal, on the other hand, are unlikely to be damaged without damaging the entire signal.

This approach has many advantages. The data is spread out over numerous data elements. Even if several are changed or deleted, the information can be recovered. Cox et al. demonstrate that the images carrying this watermark can survive even after being printed and scanned in again. Of course, the bandwidth is also significantly smaller than other solutions such as tweaking the least significant bit.

Their algorithm uses these steps:

1. Use a DCT or FFT to analyze the data.

2. Choose the k largest coefficients and label them $\{y_0, y_1, y_2, \ldots, y_{k-1}\}$ for simplicity. The smaller coefficients are ignored. The first

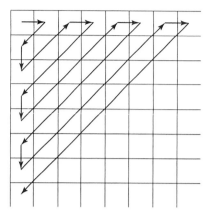

Figure 14.14   Another solution is to order the coefficients in significance. This figure shows the popular zigzag method to order coefficients from a two-dimensional transform. The ones in the upper lefthand corner correspond to the lowest frequencies and thus the most significant for the eye.

coefficients representing the smallest frequencies will often be in this set, but it isn't guaranteed.

Another solution is to order the coefficients according to their visual significance. Figure 14.14 shows a zigzag ordering used to choose the coefficients with the lowest frequencies from a two-dimensional transform. The JPEG and MPEG algorithms use this approach to eliminate unnecessary coefficients. Some authors suggest skipping the first l coefficients in this ordering because they have such a big influence on the image [PBBC97]. Choosing the next k coefficients produces candidates that are important to the description of the image but not too important.

3. Create a k-element vector, $\{b_0, b_1, b_2, \ldots, b_{k-1}\}$ to be hidden. These can either be simple bits or more information-rich real numbers. This information will not be recovered intact in all cases, so it should be thought of more as an identification number, not a vector of crucial bits.

4. Choose α, a coefficient that measures the strength of the embedding process. This decision will probably be made via trial and error. Larger values are more resistant to error, but they also introduce more distortion.

5. Encode the bit vector in the data by modifying the coefficients with one of these functions they suggest:

- $y'_i = y_i + \alpha b_i$
- $y'_i = y_i(1 + \alpha b_i)$
- $y'_i = y_i e^{\alpha b_i}$

6. Compute the inverse DCT or FFT to produce the final image or sound file.

The existence of the embedded data can be tested by reversing the steps. This algorithm requires the presence of the original image, a problem that severely restricts its usefulness in many situations. The steps are as follows:

1. Compute the DCT or FFT of the image.

2. Compute the DCT or FFT of the original image without embedded data.

3. Compute the top k coefficients.

4. Use the appropriate formula to extract the values of αb_i.

5. Use the knowledge of the distribution of the random elements, b_i, to normalize this vector. That is, if the values of b_i are real numbers chosen from a normal distribution around .5, then determine which value of α moves the average to .5. Remove α from the vector through division.

6. Compare the vector of $\{b_0, b_1, b_2, \ldots, b_{k-1}\}$ to the other known vectors and choose the best match.

The last step for identifying the "watermark" is one of the most limiting for this particular algorithm. Anyone searching for the mark must have a database of all watermarks in existence. The algorithm usually doesn't identify a perfect match because roundoff errors add imprecision even when the image file is not distorted. The process of computing the DCTs and FFTs introduces some roundoff errors, and encapsulating the image in a standard 8-bit or 24-bit format adds some more. For this reason, the best we get is the most probable match.

This makes the algorithm good for some kinds of watermarks, but less than perfect for hidden communication. The sender and receiver must agree on both the cover image and some code book of messages or watermarks that will be embedded in the data.

If these restrictions don't affect your needs, the algorithm does offer a number of desirable features. Cox et al. tested the algorithm with a number of experiments that proved its robustness. They began with several 256×256 pixel images, distorted the images, and then tested for the correct watermark. They tried shrinking the size by a factor of $\frac{1}{2}$, using heavy JPEG compression, deleting a region around the outside border, and dithering it. They even printed the image, photocopied it, and scanned it back in without removing the watermark. In all of their reported experiments, the algorithm identified the correct watermark, although the distortions reduced the strength.

The group also tested several good attacks that might be mounted by an attacker determined to erase the information. First, they tried watermarking the image with four new watermarks. The final test pulled out all five, although it could not be determined which was the first and last. Second, they tried to average together five images created with different watermarks and found that all five could still be identified. They indicate, however, that the algorithm may not be as robust if the attacker were to push this a bit further, say by using 100 or 1000 different watermarks.

14.6.2   Removing the Original from the Detection Process

Keeping the original unaltered data on hand is often unacceptable for applications like watermarking. Ideally, an average user will be able to extract the information from the file without having the original available. Many of the watermarking applications assume that the average person can't be trusted with unwatermarked data because he or she will simply pirate it.

A variant of the previous algorithm from Cox et al. does not require the original data to reveal the watermark. A. Piva, M. Barni, F. Bartolini, and V. Cappellini produced a similar algorithm that sorts the coefficients to the transform in a predictable way [PBBC97]. Figure 14.14, for instance, shows a zigzag pattern for ordering the coefficients from a two-dimensional transform according to their rough frequency. If this solution is used, there is no need to keep the original data on hand to look for the k most significant coefficients. Many other variants are emerging.

14.6.3 Tempering the Wake

Inserting information by tweaking the coefficients can sometimes have a significant effect on the final image. The most fragile sections of the image are the smooth, constant patches such as found in pictures of a clear, blue, cloudless summer sky. Listeners can often hear changes in audio files with pure tones or long quiet segments. Rapidly changing values within data mean there is plenty of texture in which to hide information. Smooth, slowly changing data means there's little room. In this most abstract sense, this follows from information theory. High entropy data is a high bandwidth channel. Low entropy data is a low bandwidth channel.

Some algorithms try to adapt the strength of a watermark to the underlying data by adjusting the value of α according to the camouflaging data. This means the strength of the watermark becomes a function of location ($\alpha_{i,j}$) in images and of time (α_t) in audio files.

There are numerous ways to calculate this value of α, but the simplest will usually suffice. Taking a window around the point in space or time and averaging the deviation from the mean is simple enough [PBBC97]. More sophisticated studies of the human perception system may be able to provide deeper understanding of how our eyes and ears react to different frequencies.

14.7

Wavelets

Many of the algorithms use sines and cosines as the basis for constructing models of data, but there is no reason why the process should be limited to them alone. In recent years, researchers began devoting new energy to exploring how strange and different functions can make better models of data—a field the researchers call *wavelets*. Figure 14.15 shows one popular wavelet function, the Meyer ψ function.

Wavelet transforms construct models of data in much the same way as Fourier transforms or cosine transforms: they compute coefficients that measure how much a particular function behaves like the underlying data. That is, the computation finds the correlation. Most wavelet analysis, however, adds an additional parameter to the mix by changing both the frequency of the function and the location or window where the functions are nonzero. Fourier transforms, for instance, use sines and cosines that are defined from $-\infty$ to $+\infty$.

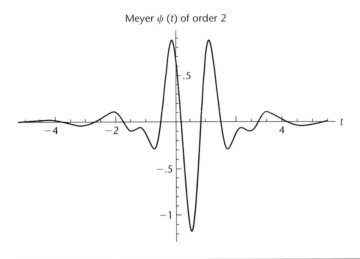

Meyer ψ (t) of order 2

Figure 14.15   The Meyer ψ function.

Wavelet transforms restrict the influence of each function by sending the function to zero outside of a particular window from *a* to *b*.

Using these localized functions can help resolve problems that occur when signals change over time or location. The frequencies in audio files containing music or voice change with time, and one of the popular wavelet techniques is to analyze small portions of the file. A wavelet transform of an audio file might first use wavelets defined between 0 and 2 seconds, then use wavelets defined between 2 and 4 seconds, and so on. If the result finds some frequencies in the first window but not in the second, then some researchers say that the wavelet transform has "localized" the signal.

The simplest wavelet transforms are just the DCT and FFT computed on small windows of the data. Splitting the data into smaller windows is just a natural extension of these algorithms.

More sophisticated windows use multiple functions defined at multiple sizes in a process called *multiresolution analysis*. The easiest way to illustrate the process is with an example. Imagine a sound file that is 16 seconds long. In the first pass, the wavelet transform might be computed on the entire block. In the second pass, the wavelet transform would be computed on two blocks between 0 and 7 seconds and between 8 and 15 seconds. In the third pass, the transform would be applied to the blocks 0 to 3, 4 to 7, 8 to 11, and 12 to 15. This is three-stage, multiresolution analysis. Clearly, it is easier to simply divide each window or block by two after each stage, but there is no reason why extremely complicated schemes with multiple windows overlapping at multiple sizes can't be dreamed up.

Multiresolution analysis can be quite useful for compression, a topic that is closely related to steganography. Some good wavelet-based compression functions use this basic recursive approach:

1. Use a wavelet transform to model the data on a window.

2. Find the largest and most significant coefficients.

3. Construct the inverse wavelet transform for these large coefficients.

4. Subtract this version from the original. What is left over is the smaller details that couldn't be predicted well by the wavelet transform. Sometimes this is significant and sometimes it isn't.

5. If the differences are small enough to be perceptually insignificant, then stop. Otherwise, split the window into a number of smaller windows and recursively apply this same procedure to the leftover noise.

This recursive, multiresolution analysis does a good job of compressing many image and sound files. The wider range of choices in functions means that the compression can be further tuned to extract the best performance. There are many different wavelets available, and some are better at compressing some files than others. Choosing the best one is often as much an art as a science.

In some cases, steganographers suggest that the choice of the function can also act as a key if only the sender and the receiver know the particular wavelet.

It is not possible to go into much depth of the wavelet field here because it is more complex and much of this complexity does not affect the ability to hide information.

Most of the same techniques for hiding information with DCTs and DFTs work well with discrete wavelet transforms (DWTs). In some cases, they outperform the basic solutions. It is not uncommon to find that information hidden with DWTs does a better job of surviving wavelet-based compression algorithms than information hidden with DCTs or DFTs [XBA97]. Using the same model for compression and information hiding works well. Of course, this means that an attacker can simply choose a different compression scheme

Several open questions are whether highly tuned wavelets are more or less stable for information encoding. That is, can a small change in a coefficient be reliably reassembled later even after printing and scanning? In other words, how large must the α term for the strength of the watermark be?

or compress the file with a number of schemes in the hope of foiling one.

14.8

Modifications

The basic approach to hiding information with sines, cosines, or other wavelets is to transform the underlying data, tweak the coefficients, and then invert the transformation. If the choice of coefficients is good and the size of the changes manageable, then the result is pretty close to the original.

There are a number of different variations on the way to choose the coefficients and encode some data in the ones that are chosen. Some of the more notable ones follow.

14.8.1   Identify the Best Areas

Many algorithms attempt to break up an image or sound file and identify the best parts for hiding the information. Smooth, stable regions turn mottled or noisy if coefficients are changed even a small amount.

Multiresolution wavelet transforms are a good tool for identifying these regions because they recursively break up an image until a good enough model is found. Smooth, stable sections are often modeled on a large scale, while noisy, detailed sections get broken up multiple times. The natural solution is to hide the information in the coefficients that model the smallest, most detailed regions. This confines the changes to the edges of the objects in images or the transitions in audio files, making it more difficult for human perception to identify them [Are00].

14.8.2   Quantize the Coefficients to Hide Information

Many of the transform hiding methods hide information by adding in a watermark vector. The information is extracted by comparing the coefficients with all possible vectors and choosing the best match. This may be practical for small numbers of watermarks, but it doesn't work well for arbitrary blocks of information.

A more flexible solution is to tweak the coefficients to hide individual bits. Let Q be some quantization factor. An arbitrary coefficient, y_i, is going to fall between $aQ \leq y_i \leq (a+1)Q$ for some integer a.

To encode a bit, round y_i off to the value where the least significant bit of a is that bit. For example, if the bit to be encoded is 0 and $a = 3$, then set $y_i = (a + 1)Q = 4Q$ [KH98].

Any recipient would extract a bit from y_i by finding the closest value of aQ. If the transform process is completely accurate, then there will be some integer where $aQ = y_i$. If the transform and inverse transform introduce some rounding errors, as they often do, then y_i should still be close enough to some value of aQ—if Q is large enough.

The value of Q should be chosen with some care. If it is too large, then it will lead to larger changes in the value of y_i. If it is too small, then it may be difficult to recover the message in some cases when error intrudes.

Deepa Kunder and Dimitrios Hatzinakos describe a quantization-based watermark that also offers tamper detection [KH99].

This mechanism also offers some ability to detect tampering with the image or sound file. If the coefficients are close to some value of aQ but not exactly equal to aQ, then this might be the result of some minor changes in the underlying file. If the changes are small, then the hidden information can still be extracted. In some cases, the tamper detection can be useful. A stereo or television may balk at playing back files with imperfect watermarks because they would be evidence that someone was trying to destroy the watermark. Of course, it could also be the result of some imperfect copying process.

14.8.3   Hide the Information in the Phase

The discrete Fourier transform produces coefficients with a real and an imaginary value. These complex values can also be imagined in polar coordinates as having a magnitude and an angle. (If $y_i = a + bi$, then $a = m\cos(\theta)$ and $b = m\sin(\theta)$ where m is the magnitude and θ is the angle.) Many users of the DFT feel that the transform is more sensitive to changes made in the angles of the coefficient than changes made in the magnitude of the coefficients [RDB96, Lic].

This method is naturally adaptive to the size of the coefficients. Small values are tweaked a small amount if they're rotated $\theta + \psi$ degrees. Large values are tweaked a large amount.

Changing the angle this way requires a bit of attention to symmetry. When the input to a DFT comprises real values, as is almost always the case in steganographic examples, then the angles are symmetric. This symmetry must be preserved to guarantee that real values will emerge from the inverse transform.

Let $\theta_{i,j}$ stand for the angle of the coefficient (i, j). If ψ is added to $\theta_{i,j}$, then $-\psi$ must be added to $\theta_{m-i,n-j}$ where (m, n) are the dimensions of the image.

14.9

Summary

Spreading the information over a number of pixels in an image or units in a sound file adds more security and intractability. Splitting each bit of information into a number of pieces and distributing these pieces throughout a file reduces the chances of detection and also increases the resistance to damage. The more the information is spread throughout the file, the more redundancy blocks attacks.

Many solutions use well-understood software algorithms such as the Fourier transform. These tools are usually quite popular in techniques for adding watermarks because many compression algorithms use the same tools. The watermarks are usually preserved by compression in these cases because the algorithms use the same transforms.

- *The Disguise.* Information is spread throughout a file by adding small changes to a number of data elements in the file. When all of the small changes are added up, the information emerges.

- *How Secure Is It?* The changes are small and distributed so they can be more secure than other solutions. Very distributed information is resistant to attack and change because an attacker must destroy enough of the signal to change it. The more places the information is hidden, the harder it is for the attacker to locate it and destroy it.

  The system can be made much more secure by using a key to create a pseudo-random bit stream that is added into the data. Only the person with the key can remove this extra encryption.

- *How to Use It.* In the most abstract sense, just choose a number of locations in the file with a pseudo-random bit stream, break the data into little parts, and add these parts into all of the locations. Recover the message by finding the correct parts and adding them together.

  This process is very efficient if it is done with a fast Fourier transform. In these cases, the data can be hidden by tweaking the coefficients after the transform. This can add or subtract different frequency data.

chapter fifteen

Synthetic Worlds

Slam Dunks

Play-by-Play Man: Things are looking a bit difficult for the Montana Shot Shooters. They had a lead of 14 points at halftime, but now the Idaho Passmakers have hit two three-point shots in a row. Whammo. They're back in the game. The Shot Shooters have called a time-out to regroup.

Color Man: Putting six points on the board that way really sends a message. They made it look easy.

PBPM: Those two swishes announced, "We're still here. You can't beat us that easily. We've got pride, intestinal fortitude, and pluck." The emphasis is on pluck.

CM: And composure too. They whipped the ball around the key. They signaled, "We can move the rock and then send it home. We can pass the pill and force you to swallow it whole. We know basketball. This is our game too."

PBPM: There was even a startling subtext to the message. I believe the Passmakers were telling the Shot Shooters that this game was different from the last. Yes, the Shot Shooters beat them at home by 22 points, but that was two months ago. Now, Jimmy D's leg is better. He's quicker. The injury he sustained while drinking too much in the vicinity of a slippery pool deck is behind him. The nasty, skanky, golddigging girlfriend is history. The Passmakers are reminding the Shot Shooters that a bit of cortisone is a time-proven solution for knee problems, but moving on with your life and putting bad relationships behind you is an even better cure for the human heart. That's the message I think that is encoded in those three-point shots.

CM: We're back from the time-out now. Let's see what the Shot Shooters can do.

PBPM: The Shot Shooters put the ball in play. Carter pauses and then passes the ball over halfcourt to Martin. He fakes left, goes right. It's a wide open lane. He's up and bam, bam, bam. That's quite a dunk. The Passmakers didn't even have a defense.

CM: Whoa. That sends a message right there. A dunk like that just screams, "You think three-point shots scare me? You think I care about your prissy little passing and your bouncy jump shots? There was no question where this ball was going. Nobody in the stands held their breath to see if it would go in. There was no pregnant pause, no hush sweeping the crowd, and no dramatic tension. This ball's destiny was the net, and there was no question about it." He's not being steganographic at all.

15.1

Created Worlds

Many of the algorithms for sound and image files revolve around hiding information in the noise. Digitized versions of the real world often have some extra entropy waiting for a signal. But advances in computer graphics and synthesis mean that the images and sound often began life in the computer itself. They were not born of the real world and all of the natural entropy constantly oozing from the plants, the light, the animals, the decay, the growth, the erosion, the wind, the rain, and who knows what else. Synthetic worlds are, by definition, perfect.

At first glance, perfection is not good for hiding information. Purely synthetic images begin as mathematics, and this means that a mathematician can find equations to model that world. A synthetic image of a ball in the light has a perfect gradient with none of the distortions that might be found in an image of an imperfect ball made by worn machinery and lit by a mass-produced bulb powered by an overtaxed electrical system.

The regularities of synthetic worlds make it easy for steganalysis to identify images with extra hidden information. Even slight changes to the least significant bit become detectable. The only advantage is that as the complexity of the models increases, so any detection process must also become increasingly complex too. This does provide plenty of practical cover. Better computer graphics technology is evolving faster than any algorithm for detecting the flaws. More complicated models are coming faster than we can suss them out.

If the practical limitations aren't good enough, the models for synthesizing worlds can be deputized to carry additional information. Instead of hiding the extra information in the final image or sound file, the information can be encoded during the synthesis.

There are ample opportunities to hide information. Many computer graphics algorithms use random number generators to add a few bits of imperfection and the realism that comes along with them. Any of these random number streams can be hijacked to carry data.

Another source can be found in tweaking the data used to drive the synthesis, perhaps by changing the least significant bits of the data. One version of an image may put a ball at coordinates (1414, 221), and another version may put it at (1413, 220). A watermarked version of a movie may encode the true owner's name in the position of one of the characters and the moment they start talking. Each version of the film will have slightly different values for these items. The rightful owner could be extracted from these subtle changes.

An even more complicated location to hide information can be found by changing the physics of the model. The accoustical characteristics of the room are easy to change slightly. The music may sound exactly the same. The musicians may start playing at exactly the same time. But the size and characteristics of the echos may change just a bit.

There are many ways that the parameters used to model the physics can be changed throughout a file. The most important challenge is guaranteeing that the changes will be detectable in the image or sound file. This is not as much of a problem as it can be for other approaches. Many of the compression algorithms are tuned to save space by removing extraneous information. The locations of objects and the physical qualities of the room, however, are not extraneous. The timbre of the instruments and accoustical character of the recording studio are also not extraneous. Compression algorithms that blurred these distinctions would be avoided, at least by serious users of music and image files.

Designing steganographic algorithms that use these techniques can be something of an art. There are so many places to hide extra bits that the challenge is arranging for them to be found. The changes

The program MandelSteg, developed by Henry Hastur, hides information in the least significant bit of an image of the Mandelbrot set. This synthetic image is computed to seven bits of accuracy, and then the message is hidden in the eighth. See Section 15.2.2.

Markus Kuhn and Ross Anderson suggest that tweaking the video signal sent to the monitor can send messages because the electron guns in the monitor emit so much electromagnetic ''noise'' [KA98].

should be large enough to be detected by an algorithm but small enough to escape casual detection by a human.

15.2

Text Position Encoding and OCR

Chapters 6 and 8 show how to create synthetic textual descriptions and hide information in the process. A simpler technique for hiding information in text documents is to fiddle with letters themselves.

Matthew Kwan developed a program called Snow that hides 3 bits at the end of each text line by adding between 0 and 7 bits.

One of the easiest solutions is to encode a signal by switching between characters that appear to be close to each other, if not identical. The number zero (0) and the capital letter "O" are close to each other in many basic fonts. The number one (1) and the lowercase "l" are also often indistinguishable. The front cover of the Pre-proceedings of the 4th Information Hiding Workshop used these similarities to carry a message from John McHugh [McH01].

If the fonts are similar, information can be encoded by swapping the two versions. Detecting the difference in printed versions can be complicated because OCR programs often use context to distinguish between the two. If the number one (1) is found in the middle of a word made up of alphanumeric characters, the programs often will fix the perceived mistake.

If the fonts are identical, the swap can still be useful to hide information when the data is kept in electronic form. No one reading the file will notice the difference, but the data will still be extractable.

This is often taken to extremes by some members of the hacker subculture who deliberately swap vaguely similar characters. The number four (4) bears some resemblance to the capital "A"; the number three (3) looks like a reversed capital "E". This technique can elude keyword searches and automated text analysis programs, at least until the spelling becomes standardized and well known. Then a document with the phrase "3L33t h4XOR5" starts to look suspicious.

Humans also provide some error correction for basic spelling and grammatical errors. A hidden message can be encoded by introducing seemingly random misspellings from time to tim.[1]

---

[1]Some might be tempted to blame me and the proofreader for any errors that crept into the text. But perhaps I was sending a secret message . . . .

15.2.1   Positioning

Another possible solution is to simply adjust the positions of letters, words, lines, and paragraphs. Typesetting is as much an art as a job, and much care can be devoted to algorithms for arranging these letters on a page. Information can always be hidden when making this decision.

The LaTeX and TeX typesetting systems used in creating this book justify lines by inserting more white space after a punctuation mark than after a word. American typesetters usually put three times as much space after punctuation. The French, on the other hand, avoid this distinction and set both the same. This mechanism is easy to customize, and it is possible to change the "stretchability" of white space following any character. This paragraph was typeset so the white space after words ending in "e" or "r" was set as though they were punctuation marks. (The TeX commands are `sfcode`e=3000` and `sfcode`r=3000`.)

Changing these values throughout a document by smaller values is relatively simple to do. In many cases, detecting these changes is also relatively simple. Many commercial OCR programs continue to make minor errors on a page, but steganographic systems using white space can often be more accurate. Detecting the size of the white space is often easier than sussing out the differences between the ink marks.

Jack Brassil, Steve Low, Nicholas Maxemchuk, and Larry O'Gorman experimented with many different techniques for introducing small shifts in typesetting algorithms [BO96, LMBO95, BLMO95, BLMO94]. This can be easy to do with open source tools like TeX that also include many hooks for modifying the algorithms.

One of their most successful techniques is moving the individual lines of text. They show that entire lines can be successfully moved up or down one or two six-hundredths of an inch. Moving a line is easy to detect if any skew can be eliminated from the image. As long as the documents are close to horizontal alignment, the distance between the individual lines can be measured with enough precision to identify the shifted lines.

The simplest mechanism for measuring a line is to "flatten" it into one dimension. That is, count the number of pixels with ink in each row. Figure 15.2 shows the result of summing the intensity of each pixel in the row in Figure 15.1. The maximum value of each pixel is 255 if it is completely white. For this reason, the second row has a much smaller valley because it is shorter and made up of more white space.

card into the smartcard programmer, it would just sit there acting like an ice scraper.

The basic ECM from DirecTV checks the software

Figure 15.1   Three lines of printed text scanned at 400 pixels per inch.

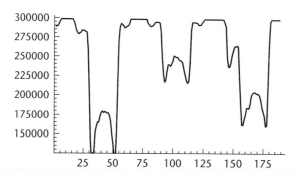

Figure 15.2   A graph of the sums of the rows in Figure 15.1. White is usually assigned 255, so the short line in the middle is less pronounced.

The structure of the peaks and valleys also varies with the words. The third row has more capital letters so there is a more pronounced valley at the beginning, corresponding to the horizontal lines in the capital letters. The choice of the font also changes the shape of this graph; in fact, the graph can even be used to identify the font [WH94]. Generally, fonts with serifs make it easier to identify the baselines than sans-serif fonts, but this is not always the case.

More bits can be packed into each line by shifting individual words up or down one three-hundredths of an inch. The detection process becomes more complicated because there is less information to use to measure the horizontal shift of the baseline. Short words are not as desirable as longer ones. In practice, it may make sense to group multiple small words together and shift them in a block.

Experiments by Jack Brassil and Larry O'Gorman show that the location of the baseline and any information encoded in it can be regularly extracted from text images even after repeated photocopying. Moving the individual lines up or down by one or two six-hundredths of an inch is usually sufficient to be detected. They do note that their results require a well-oriented document where the baselines of the text are closely aligned with the raster lines. Presumably, a more sophisticated algorithm could compensate for the error by modeling the anti-aliasing, but it is probably simpler to just line up the paper correctly in the first place.

15.2.2   MandelSteg and Secrets

Any image is a candidate for hiding information, but some are better than others. Ordinarily, images with plenty of variation seem perfect. If the neighboring pixels are different colors, then the eye doesn't detect subtle changes in the individual pixels. This concept led Henry Hastur to create a program that flips the least significant bits of a Mandelbrot set. These images are quite popular and well known throughout the mathematics community. This program, known as MandelSteg, is available with source code from the Cypherpunks archive (*ftp://ftp.csua.berkeley.edu/pub/cypherpunks/steganography*).

The MandelSteg manual notes that there are several weaknesses in the system. First, someone can simply run the data recovery program GifExtract to remove the bits. Although there are several different settings, one will work. For this reason, the author suggests using Stealth, a program that will strip away the framing text from a PGP message, leaving only noise.

There are other weaknesses. The Mandelbrot image acts as a one-time pad for the data. As with any encoding method, the data can be extracted if someone can find a pattern in the key data. The Mandelbrot set might look very random and chaotic, but there is plenty of structure. Each pixel represents the number of iterations before a simple equation ($f(z) = z^2 + c$) converges. Adjacent pixels often take a different number of pixels, but they are still linked by their common generating equation. For this reason, I think it may be quite possible to study the most significant bits of a fractal image and determine the location from which it came. This would allow someone to recalculate the least significant bits and extract the answer.[2]

15.3

Echo Hiding

Hiding information in the noise of sound files is a good solution, but the information may be erased by good compression algorithms.

---

[2] David Joyce offers a Mandelbrot image generator on the Web (*http://aleph0 .clarku.edu/djoyce/julia/explorer.html*).

Daniel Gruhl, Anthony Lu, and Walter Bender suggest tweaking the basic acoustics of the room to hide information [GB98]. While this can still be obscured by sufficiently strong compression, it is often more likely to withstand standard algorithms. Echoes are part of recordings and sophisticated listeners with trained ears can detect small changes in them. Good recording engineers and their compressionists try to avoid eliminating the echos in an effort to provide as much verisimilitude as possible.

Many recording software programs already include the ability to add (or subtract) echoes from a recording. They can also change the character of the echo by twiddling with the strength of the echo and the speed at which it vanishes.

Information can be included by either changing the strength or the length of the decay. Gruhl, Lu, and Bender report success with encoding a single bit by changing the length of time before the echo begins. A 1 gets a short wait (about .001 second) and a 0 gets a slightly longer wait (about .0013 second). More than one bit is encoded by splitting up the signal and encoding one bit in each segment.

The signal is detected by autocorrelation. If the audio signal is represented by $f(t)$, then the bit is extracted by computing $f(t + .001)$ and $f(t + .0013)$. Segments carrying a signal of 1 will generally produce a higher value of $f(t + .001)$, and segments carrying a signal of 0 will produce a higher value of $f(t + .0013)$.

The bandwidth available depends on the sampling rate and a lesser amount on the audio file itself. Higher-frequency sounds and higher sampling rates can provide accurate results with shorter segments, both alone and in combination. Gruhl, Lu, and Bender report success with segments lasting one-sixteenth of a second.

The success of this algorithm depends, to a large extent, on the ears listening to it. Some humans are born with good hearing, some train their ears to hear better, and some do both. The music industry continues to experiment with using techniques such as echo hiding to add a watermark to recordings. The results are often quite good, but still problematic. In many cases, the average human can't detect the additional echo. Many of those who do detect it, think the sound is richer. Still, some of the best artists in the business often reject any change to their perfect sound. At times, this debate can ring with irony. Garage bands devoted to making noisy, feedback-rich music sometimes complain about any tiny bit of echo added as a watermark. This process still continues to require an artist's touch.

15.4

Summary

There is no reason to stop with moving lines of text or adding echos. Any synthetic file can be tweaked during its construction. The real challenge is in creating detection algorithms that will detect and extract the changes from the files. In some cases, the data is readily available. An animated presentation developed in Macromedia's Flash format, for instance, could encode information in the position and timing of the items. This data is easy to extract from the files by using the publicly distributed information about the file format.

If the data can't be extracted from the file, many of the techniques developed by the artificial intelligentsia for image and audio analysis can be quite useful. Machine vision algorithms, for instance, can extract the position and orientation of animated characters in a movie. Echo detection and elimination tools used by audio engineers can also help locate echoes carrying hidden information.

- *The Disguise.* Any synthetic file, be it text, sound, light, or, maybe one day, smell, can carry information by tweaking the parameters during synthesis.

- *How Secure Is It?* The security depends, to a large extent, on the nature of the files and the skill of the artist. High-quality graphics have many places where a slight twist of the head could carry several bits of information without anyone noticing.

- *How to Use It.* Any of the steganographic techniques for tweaking the least significant bits or adding in signals can be used on the raw data that guides the synthesis. To a large extent, all of the techniques for steganography are just applied at an earlier step in the process. For instance, an animator may choose the position of a character's limbs and then feed this data to a rendering engine. The steganography is done just after the animator chooses the position but before the rendering.

chapter sixteen

Watermarks

A Patent for Watermarking Humans

Why should watermarks be limited to digital files and pieces of paper? Can any way of leaving a trace act like a watermark? We offer the claims to an unfiled patent application for "implanting a memetic watermark through humorous banter."

Claims:

1. A method for implanting and detecting a watermark in a human subject by

   - identifying a funny sentence selected from a group of witticisms, whimsical retorts, riddles, puns, limericks, jokes, droll patter, parodistic remarks, and satirical levity;
   - offering said funny sentence to said human subject in a manner designed to attract their attention and implant said funny sentence in their brain and create an instance of a memetic watermark;
   - detecting the presence of said memetic watermark by repeating said funny sentence in order to analyze the response of said human subject who will either laugh or announce that the joke was not new to them.

2. The method of claim (1), where said funny sentence is repeated and repeated until it is firmly implanted in said human subject's neural patterns.

3. The method of claim (2), where said funny sentence is repeated again and again in order to increase the reaction time and volume

of the response of said human subject in order to increase the detection of said watermark.

4. The method of claim (3), where said funny sentence is repeated several more times, increasing the sensitivity in said human subject enough to prompt them to throttle the neck of the next person to repeat said funny sentence, increasing further the ability to detect said watermark.

16.1

Embedding Ownerships Information

One of the most demanding applications for the algorithms that hide information is protecting copyrighted information. The job requires the hidden information to somehow identify the rightful owner of the file in question and, after identifying it, prevent it from being used in unauthorized ways. This is a tall order because the content industry has great dreams for digital books, music, movies, and other multimedia presentations. Putting a computer in the loop means that content producers can experiment with as many odd mechanisms for making money as they can imagine. Some suggest giving away the first $n-1$ chapters of a murder mystery and charging only for the last one with the identity of the murderers. Others propose giving people a cut when they recommend a movie to a friend and the friend buys a copy. All such schemes depend upon some form of secure copy protection, and many of the dreams include hidden information and steganography.

Hiding information to protect text, music, movies, and art is usually called *watermarking*, a reference to the light image of the manufacturer's logo pressed into paper when the watermarked object was made. The term is apt because steganography can hide information about the creator of a document as well as information spelling out who can use it and when. Ideally, the computer displaying the document will interpret the hidden information correctly and do the right thing by the creators.

Treating the document as the creators demand is not an easy challenge. All of the algorithms in this book can hide arbitrarily complex instructions for what can and can't be done with the document carrying the hidden information. Some copy protection schemes use as few as 70 bits, a number that can fit comfortably in almost any document.

Just inserting the information is not good enough because watermarks face different threats. Most standard steganographic algorithms fight against discovery by blending in as well as possible to avoid detection. Watermarks also try to hide, but usually to stay out of the way, not to avoid being discovered. Most consumers and pirates will know the watermark is there soon after they try to make a copy. The real challenge is keeping the consumer or pirate from making a copy and removing the watermark.

This is not an easy task. The ideal watermark will stick with a document even after editing, cropping, compression, rotation, or any of the basic forms of distortion. Alas, there are no ideal watermarks available to date, although many offer some form of resistance to some basic distortions.

Digital Watermarking by Ingemar J. Cox, Matthew L. Miller, and Jeffrey A. Bloom is a good survey of a quickly growing field [CMB01].

Defending against basic copying is easy. A digital copy of a document will be exact and carry any watermark along with it. But not all copies are exact. Artists often crop or rotate an image. Compression algorithms for sound or image files add subtle distortions by reproducing only the most significant parts of the information stream. Pirates seek to reproduce all of the salient information while leaving the hidden information behind. Defending against all of the possible threats is practically impossible.

This shouldn't come as a surprise. Making a copy of a document means duplicating all of the sensations detectable by a human. If the sky is a clear, bright blue in the document, then it should be a clear, bright blue in the copy as well. If a bell rings in the document, then it should ring with close to the same timbre in the copy. But if some part of a document can't be perceived, then there's no reason to make a copy of that part.

The watermark creator faces a tough conundrum. Very well hidden information is imperceptible to humans and thus easy to leave behind during copying. The best techniques for general steganography are often untenable for watermarks. Compression algorithms and inexact copying solutions will strip the watermarks away.

But information that's readily apparent to human eyes and ears isn't artistically desirable. Distortions to the music and the images can ruin them or scar them, which is unacceptable especially in an industry that often promotes the quality of the reproduction in its marketing.

If the ideal watermark can't be created, there's no reason why a practical one can't solve some of the problems. Adobe Photoshop, for instance, comes with a tool for embedding a watermark designed by Digimarc. The software can insert a numerical tag into a photo that

can then be used to find the rightful owner in a database. This solution, which uses some of the wavelet encoding techniques from
Chapter 14, can resist many basic distortions and changes introduced, perhaps ironically, by Photoshop. The technique is not perfect, however, and preliminary tests show that rotating an image by
45 degrees before blurring and sharpening the image will destroy the
watermark.

All of the watermarking solutions have some weakness in the face
of tricks like that. Measuring the amount of resistance is hard to do.
The Stirmark suite is a collection of basic distortions that bend, fold,
and mutilate an image while testing to see if the watermark survives.
This collection is a good beginning, but the range of distortion is
almost infinite and difficult to model or define.

At this point, watermark creators are still exploring the limits of
the science and trying to define what can and can't be done to resist what kind of threats. Toward this end, they've created a kind of
taxonomy of watermarks that describes the different kinds and their
usefulness. The following sections list the different ways to evaluate
them.

16.1.1   Fragility

Some watermarks disappear if one bit of the image is changed. Hiding
information in the least significant bit (see Chapter 9) is usually not
a robust watermark because one flipped bit can make it impossible to
recover all of the information. Even error correction and redundancy
can add only so much strength.

Fragile watermarks, though, are not always useless. Some propose
inserting watermarks that break immediately as a technique to detect any kind of tampering. If the watermark includes some digital
signature of the document, then it offers assurance that the file is
unaltered.

16.1.2   Continuity

Some watermarks resist a wide range of distortions by disappearing
gradually as the changes grow larger. Larger and larger distortions
produce weaker and weaker indications that a watermark is present.

This continuity is often found in some of the wavelet encoding
solutions described in Chapter 14. The watermark itself is a vector of
coefficients describing the image. Small changes in the image produce small changes of the coefficients. A vector-matching algorithm
finds the watermark by finding the best match.

In many cases, the strength of the watermark is a tradeoff with the amount of information in the watermark itself. A large number of distinct watermarks requires a small distance between different watermarks. A small distance means that only a small distortion could convert one watermark into another.

16.1.3 Watermark Size

How many "bits" of information are available? Some watermarks simply hide bits of information. Counting the number of bits stored in the document is easy.

Other watermarking schemes don't hide bits per se. They add distortions in such a way that the shape and location of the distortions indicate who owns the document. Hiding lots of information means having many different and distinct patterns of distortions. In some cases, packing many different patterns is not easy because the size, shape, and interaction with the cover document are not easy to model or describe.

16.1.4 Blind Detection

Some watermarks require providing some extra data to the detector. This might be the original unwatermarked image or sound file or it could be a key. The best solutions offer *blind detection*, meaning they provide as little information as possible to the algorithm that looks for a watermark. The ideal detector will examine the document, check for a watermark, and then enforce the restrictions carried by the watermark.

Blind detection is a requirement for many schemes for content protection. Providing a clean, unwatermarked copy to the computers of the users defeats the purpose. But this doesn't mean that nonblind schemes are worthless. Some imagine situations where the watermark is only extracted after the fact, perhaps as evidence. One solution is to embed the ID number of the rightful owner to a document in a watermark. If the document later appears in open circulation, perhaps on the Internet, the owners could use a nonblind scheme to extract the watermark and track down the source of the file. They could still hold the original clean copy without releasing it.

16.1.5 Resistance to Multiple Watermarks

Storing more hidden information is one of the easiest attacks to launch against a document with hidden information. Using the same algorithm often guarantees that the same hidden spots will be altered to carry the new message.

An ideal watermark will carry multiple messages from multiple parties who can insert their data and retrieve it without any coordination. Some of the least significant bit schemes from Chapter 9 offer this kind of resistance by using a key to choose where to hide the data. Many can carry multiple messages without any problem, especially if error correction handles occasional collisions.

Unfortunately, these ideal solutions are often more fragile and thus undesirable for other reasons. This is another tradeoff. Localizing the information in the watermark reduces the chance that another random watermark will alter or destroy it, but it also increases the chance that a small change will ruin it.

16.1.6 Accuracy

Many watermarking schemes achieve some robustness to distortion by sacrificing accuracy. Many rely upon finding the best possible match and thus risk finding the wrong match if the distortion is large enough. These algorithms sacrifice accuracy in a strange way. Small changes still produce the right answer, but large enough changes can produce a dramatically wrong answer.

16.1.7 Fidelity

One of the hardest effects of watermarks to measure is the amount of distortion introduced by the watermarking process itself. Invisible or inaudible distortions may be desirable, but they're usually easy to defeat by compression algorithms that strip away all of the unnecessary data.

The best schemes introduce distortions that are small enough to be missed by most casual observers. These often succeed by changing the relative strength or position of important details. One classic solution is to alter the acoustics of the recording room by subtly changing the echoes. The ear usually doesn't care if the echoes indicate an 8×8 room or a 20×20 room. At some point, this approach fails; the art is finding the right way to modulate the acoustics without disturbing the greatest number of listeners.

Many of the wavelet encoding techniques from Chapter 14 succeed by changing the relative strength of the largest coefficients assembled to describe the image. The smallest coefficients are easy to ignore or strip away, but the largest can't be removed without distorting the image beyond recognition. The solution is to change the relative strengths until they conform to some pattern.

16.1.8   Resistance to Framing

One potential use for watermarks is to identify the rightful owner of each distinct copy. Someone who might want to leak or pirate the document will try to remove his or her own name. One of the simplest techniques is to obtain multiple copies and then average them together. If one pixel comes from one version and another pixel comes from another, then there's a good chance that neither watermark will survive. Or, the new watermark will "frame" an innocent person. Some schemes deliberately try to avoid this kind of attack by embedding multiple copies of the signature and creating identification codes that can survive this averaging.

16.1.9   Keying

Is a key required to read the watermark? Is a key required to insert it? Some algorithms use keys to control who inserts the data to prevent unauthorized people from faking documents or creating faked watermarks. Others use keys to ensure that only the right people can extract the watermark and glean the information. Chapter 12 describes some of the approaches.

No algorithm offers the ideal combination of these features, in part because there's often no way to have one feature without sacrificing another. The good news is that often watermarks that fail one task can find use in another form.

16.2

A Basic Watermark

The following is a basic technique for watermarking that blends together many of the different solutions proposed in recent years. This description is a bit abstract, which obscures the challenges of actually producing a working version that implements the technique.

1. Begin with a document in a standard form.

2. Choose a mechanism for decomposing the document into important components. One simple solution is to use the

discrete cosine transform to model the signal as the sum of a collection of cosine functions multiplied by some coefficients. Let $\{c_0, \ldots, c_n\}$ be the set of coefficients.

3. The coefficients measure the size of the different components. Ideally, the model will guarantee that large coefficients have a large effect on the document and small coefficients have a small effect. If this is the case, find a way to exclude the small coefficients. They're not important and are likely to be changed dramatically by small changes in the document itself.

4. Quantize the coefficents by finding the closest replacement from a small set of values. One of the simplest quantization schemes for a value c_i is to find the integer k_i such that $k_i Q$ is closest to x. The value of Q is often called the *quanta*. Exponential or logarithmic schemes may be appropriate for some cases.

5. Let $\{b_0, \ldots, b_n\}$ be a watermark. Insert a watermark by tweaking each coefficient. Each value of c_i lies between an odd and an even integer multiple of Q. That is, $k_i Q \leq c_i \leq (k_i + 1)Q$. To encode $b_i = 0$ at coefficient c_i, set c_i to the even multiple of Q. To encode $b_i = 1$, set c_i to be the odd multiple of Q.

6. Use a reverse transform to reconstruct the original document from the new values of $\{c_0, \ldots, c_n\}$. If the understanding of the decomposition process is correct, the changes will not alter the image dramatically. Of course, some experimentation with the value of Q may be necessary.

This scheme for encoding a watermark can be used with many different models for deconstructing images and sound files. The greatest challenge is setting the value of Q correctly. A large Q adds robustness at the cost of introducing greater distortion. The cost of a large Q should be apparent by this point. The value can be seen by examining the algorithm for extracting the watermark:

1. To extract a watermark, begin by applying the same deconstructive technique that models the document as a series of coefficients: $\{c'_0, \ldots, c'_n\}$.

2. Find the integer k_i such that $|k_i Q - c'_i|$ is minimized. If there's been no distortion in the image, then $c'_i = k_i Q$. If our model of

the document is good, small changes in the document should correspond to small changes in the coefficients. Small changes should still result in the same values of k_i emerging.

3. If k_i is odd, then $b_i = 1$. If k_i is even, then $b_i = 0$. This is the watermark.

Many watermarking schemes provide an additional layer of protection by including some error-correction bits to the watermark bits, $\{b_0, \dots, b_n\}$ (see Chapter 3). Another solution is to compare the watermarking bits to a known set of watermarks and find the best match. To some extent, these are the same techniques. Choosing the size of Q and the amount of error correction lets you determine the amount of robustness available.

This solution is a very good approach that relies heavily upon the decomposition algorithm. The discrete cosine transform is a good solution, but it has weaknesses. Even slight rotations can introduce big changes in the coefficients produced by the transform. Some researchers combat this with a polar transform that produces the same coefficients in all orientations of the document. This solution, though, often breaks if the document is cropped, changing the center. Every model has strengths and weaknesses.

16.2.1 Choosing the Coefficients

Another challenge is choosing the coefficients to change. Some suggest changing only the largest and most salient. In one of the first papers to propose a watermark scheme like this, Ingemar Cox, Joe Kilian, Tom Leighton, and Talal Shamoon suggested choosing the largest coefficients from a discrete cosine transform of the image. The size guaranteed that these coefficients contributed more to the final image than the small ones. Concentrating the message in this part of the image made it more likely that the message would survive compression or change [CKLS96].

Others suggest concentrating in a particular range because of perceptual reasons. Choosing the right range of discrete cosine coefficients can introduce some resistance to cropping. The function $\cos(2\pi x)$, for instance, repeats even units while $\cos(\frac{2\pi x}{1000})$ repeats every 1000 units. A watermark that uses smaller, shorter waves is more likely to resist cropping than one that relies upon larger ones. These shorter waves also introduce smaller, more localized distortions during the creation of the watermark.

16.3

An Averaging Watermark

Cropping is one of the problems confronting image watermark creators. Artists frequently borrow photographs and crop them as needed. A watermark designed to corral these artists must withstand cropping.

A simple solution is to repeat the watermark a number of times throughout the image. The first solution in this chapter accomplishes this to some extent by using decomposition techniques like the discrete cosine transform. Many of the same coefficients usually emerge even after cropping.

This example is a more ordinary approach to repeating the watermark. It is not elegant or mathematically sophisticated, but the simplicity has some advantages.

A watermark consists of an $m \times n$ block of small integers. For the sake of simplicity, let's assume the block is 4×4 and constructed of values from the set $\{-2, -1, 0, 1, 2\}$. There are $5^{16} = 152,587,890,625$ possible watermarks in this example, although it will not always be practical to tell the difference between them all. Let these values be represented by $w_{i,j}$ where $0 \le i < m$ and $0 \le j < n$. In this case, $m = n = 4$.

The watermark is inserted by breaking the image into 4×4 blocks and adding the values into the pixels. Pixel $p_{i,j}$ is replaced with $p_{i,j} + w_{i \bmod m, j \bmod n}$. If the value is too large or too small, it is replaced with either the maximum value or zero, usually 255 and 0.

How is the watermark recovered? By averaging pixels. Let $w'_{a,b}$ be the average intensity of all pixels, $p_{i,j}$ such that $i \bmod m = a$ and $j \bmod n = b$. In the 4×4 example, $w'_{0,1}$ is the average of pixels like $p_{0,1}, p_{4,1}, p_{8,1}, p_{0,5}, p_{4,5}, p_{8,9}$, and so on.

The success of this step assumes that the patterns of the image do not fall into the same $m \times n$ rhythm as the watermark. That is, the average value of all of the pixels will be the same. A light picture may have a high average value while a dark picture may have a low average value. Ideally, these numbers balance out. If this average value is S, then the goal is to find the best watermark that matches $w' - S$.

This is simple to do if the image has not been cropped or changed. $w' - S$ should be close to, if not the same as, the inserted watermark. The only inaccuracy occurs when the watermark value is added to a pixel and the pixel value overflows.

Recovering the watermark is still simple to do if the image is cropped in the right way. If the new boundaries are an integer multiple of m and n pixels away from the original boundaries, then the values of w' and w will still line up exactly.

This magical event is not likely to occur, and any of the mn possible orientations could occur. One simple solution is to compare the values recovered from the image to a database of known watermarks. This takes kmn steps where k is the number of known watermarks. This may not be a problem if the system uses only a small number of watermarks, but it could become unwieldy if k grows large.

Another solution is to create a canonical order for the watermark matrix. Let p and q be the canonical offsets. The goal is to find one pair of values for p and q so that we always find the same order for the watermark, no matter what the scheme. This is a bit cumbersome, and there are other solutions.

1. For this example, let $z_{i,j} = 5^{4i+j}$. Five is the number of possible values of the watermark.

2. Let $F(w, p, q) = \sum z_{i,j}(2 + w_{(i+p) \bmod 4, (j+q) \bmod 4})$.

3. Try all possible values of $F(w, p, q)$ and choose the maximum (or minimum). This is the canonical order of w.

If mn is a reasonable value, then it might make more sense to store mn versions of each watermark in a database. If it is large, then a canonical order might make more sense.

It should become clear at this point that all possible 5^{16} watermarks can't be used. Some of them have identical canonical values. Every watermark has 15 other shifty cousins. Others turn out to be identical because of patterns inside the watermark.

16.3.1 Effects of Distortion

Much of the success of this watermark depends upon the way that the averaging balances out any potential changes. If the noise or distortion in the image is uniformly distributed, then the changes should balance out. The averages will cancel out the changes.

Not all distortions are equal. Several of the Stirmark changes introduce or delete rows or columns of pixels from the middle of the image. This can throw off the averaging completely and destroy this kind of watermark. While it may be possible to recover it by sampling sections of the image, the process is neither simple nor guaranteed.

16.4

Summary

Watermarking is not an easy challenge for steganography. Many of the researchers exploring the area have high ideals and want their watermarks to remain intact even after a fairly daunting array of distortions and changes.

   This chapter offers two basic algorithms that resist some basic distortions. The discussion avoids much of the complexity involved in determining when a watermark may or may not be present. Finding the watermark is easy if the image is not changed. Finding it afterward becomes an exercise in informed guessing. Just when is one vector of numbers close enough to another? Which is the best match for a watermark? These are questions of engineering and design not answered in this chapter. Finding the best solution requires building a system and testing it with a collection of sample images and sound files. Much of the real challenge is tweaking the coefficients.

- *The Disguise.* Watermarks are steganographic solutions designed to withstand more general attacks from a savvy set of users and potential pirates. The ideal watermark will embed information in such a way that the only way to destroy it is to introduce so much noise and distortion that the original image is unusable and perhaps unrecognizable.

- *How Secure Is It?* None of the watermarks come close to this ideal, but some are quite useful. Systems like Digimarc's are in wide use thanks to the company's partnership with Adobe. While they can be circumvented, they can withstand many casual distortions. Much of the success depends upon the individual algorithm and the sample files.

- *How to Use It.* Find an image, introduce some changes, and then hope to track down the person violating your copyright. In practice, the legal and logistical headaches may be greater than the problems of making the watermark work. If you get really frustrated, just start suing people as some companies have done.

chapter seventeen

Steganalysis

Code Words

Authors of recommendation letters often add a secret layer of meaning hidden beneath the surface of a letter that is ostensibly positive.

- All of his colleagues are astounded by his scrupulous attention to detail *and* the zeal with which he shares this information.

- Let us just say that his strength is his weakness.

- Bold words and sweeping statements are his friend.

- We continue to be amazed by his ability to whip off articles, journal papers, and conference talks with such a minimal time in the lab.

- This candidate is a master of the art of not saying what he means. He slips quickly between two-faced disinformation and carefully worded calumny.

17.1
Finding Hidden Messages

Many of the techniques in this book are far from perfect. A wise attacker can identify files with hidden information by looking carefully for some slight artifacts created by the process of hiding information. In some cases, the tests are simple enough to be automated with a high degree of reliability. This field is often called *steganalysis*, a term that mimics the word *cryptanalysis*, the study of breaking codes.

The field of steganalysis is usually more concerned with simply identifying the existence of a message instead of actually extracting it. This is only natural because the field of steganography aims to conceal the existence of a message, not scramble it. Many of the basic tests in steganalysis will just identify the possible existence of a message. Recovering the hidden data is usually beyond the capabilities of the tests because many algorithms use simple cryptographically secure random number generators to scramble the message as it is inserted. In some cases, the hidden bits are spread throughout the file. Some of these algorithms can't tell you where they are, but they can tell that the hidden bits are probably there.

Identifying the existence of a hidden message can often be enough for an attacker. The messages are often fragile, and an attacker can destroy the message without actually reading it. Some data can be wiped out by storing another message in its place. Others can be nullified by flipping a random number of the least significant bits. Many small, simple distortions can wipe out the information, which after all is stored in the form of small, simple distortions. While the attacker may not read the message, the recipient won't either.

All of these attacks depend upon identifying some characteristic part of an audio or image file that is altered by the hidden data—that is, finding where the steganography failed to imitate or camouflage enough. In many cases, the hidden data is more random than the data it replaces, and this extra "perfection" often stands out. The least significant bits of many images, for instance, are not random. In some cases, the camera sensor is not perfect, and in others the lack of randomness is introduced by some file compression. Replacing the least signficant bits with a more random (i.e., higher entropy) hidden message removes this artifact.

There are limitations. Many of these techniques must be tuned to attack the output from particular software programs. They can be highly effective in the hands of a skilled operator searching for hidden information created by known algorithms, but they can begin to fail when the methods encounter the results from even slightly different algorithms. There is no guarantee that the steganalysis algorithms can be automatically extended to each version of the software. There is no magic antisteganography bullet.

But there are also no guarantees that any steganographic algorithm can withstand clever steganalysis. None of the algorithms in this book offer any mathematical guarantees that they are free from statistical or computational artifacts. Many of the automatic steganographic programs introduce errors if they are used without care. Many are very simple to detect if used without caution.

17.2

Typical Approaches

Much of the early work on this topic was done by Sushil Jajodia, Neil Johnson, Andreas Pfitzmann, Niels Provos, and Andreas Westfeld [WP99, JJ98a, JJ98b], but new work is emerging frequently.

The basic approaches can be divided into these categories:

- *Visual or Aural Attacks.* Some attacks strip away the significant parts of the image in a way that facilitates a human trying to search for visual anomalies. One common test displays the least significant bits of an image. Completely random noise often reveals the existence of a hidden message because imperfect cameras, scanners, and other digitizers leave echoes of the large structure in the least significant bits.

  The brain is also capable of picking up very subtle differences in sound. Many audio watermark creators are thwarted by very sensitive ears able to pick up differences. Preprocessing the file to enhance parts of the signal makes their job easier.

- *Structural Attacks.* The format of the data file often changes as hidden information is included. Often these changes can be boiled down to an easily detectable pattern in the structure of the data. In some cases, steganographic programs use slightly different versions of the file format, and this gives them away. In others, they pad files or add extra information in another way.

- *Statistical Attacks.* The patterns of pixels and their least significant bits can often reveal the existence of a hidden message in the statistical profile. The new data doesn't have the same statistical profile as the standard data is expected to have.

Of course, there is no reason to limit the approaches. Every steganographic solution uses some pattern to encode information. Complex computational schemes can be created for every algorithm to match the structure. If the algorithm hides the information in the relative levels of pairs of pixels, then an attack might compute the statistical profile of pairs. If an algorithm hid data in the order of certain elements, then one attack may check the statistical profile of the orders.

There is no magic theoretical model for either steganalysis or anti-steganalysis. This is largely because theoretical models are always limited in their power. The mimic functions described in Chapters 7 and 8 are theoretically hard to break. The classical work from Kurt Gödel, Alan Turing, and others firmly establishes that computer programs can't analyze other computer programs effectively.

Such theoretical guarantees are comforting, but they are rarely as strong as they sound. To paraphrase Abraham Lincoln, "You can fool all of the computer programs some of the time, and some of the computer programs all of the time, but you can't fool all of the computer programs all of the time." Even if no program can be created to crack mimic functions all of the time, there's no reason why something might not detect imperfections that happen most of the time. For instance, the software for hiding information in the voiceover of baseball games is going to become repetitive after some time. Some form of statistical analysis may reveal something. It won't work all of the time, but it will work some of the time.

The best the steganographer can do is constantly change the parameters and the locations used to hide information. The best the steganalyst can do is constantly probe for subtle patterns left by mistake.

17.3

Visual Attacks

The simplest form of steganalysis is to examine the picture or sound file with human eyes or ears. Our senses are often capable of complex, intuitive analysis that can, in many ways, outstrip the power of a computer. If the steganographic algorithm is any good, the changes should not be apparent at first. Hiding the information from human eyes is the first challenge. Some basic algorithms will make mistakes and make large color changes in the process of hiding the information, but most should produce a functionally identical image or sound file.

A bit of computer enhancement, however, can quickly make a hidden message apparent to our eyes. If the most important parts of the image are stripped away, the eye can often spot encoded information without any trouble. Figures 17.1 and 17.2 show the least significant bits of an image before and after information is hidden with the EzStego program.

The figures illustrate how the least significant bits in an image are often far from random. Notice how the saturated areas of the image can still be seen in the least significant bits. When the image is either all white or all black, the least significant bit is far from random. It's usually pegged at either a 0 or a 1. Even the nonsaturated

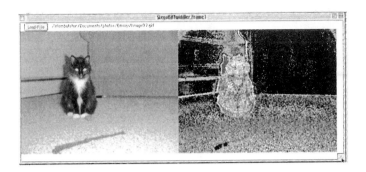

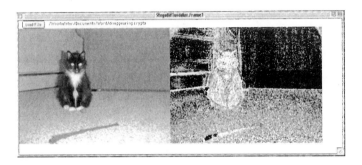

Figure 17.1   The top window shows a picture and its least significant bits before approximately 6000 bytes were hidden in the image with EzStego. The image had a capacity of 15,000 bytes. The bottom window shows the image and the least significant bits afterward.

sections are far from random. The positions of the objects in an image and the lights that illuminate them guarantee that there will often be gradual changes in colors. These gradients are also far from random. And then there's just pure imperfection. Digital cameras do not always have a full 24 bits of sensitivity. The software may pump out 24-bit images, but only after padding the results and adding extra detail. The least significant bits are not always assigned randomly when the sensors do not have sufficient resolution.

In some cases, file-compression algorithms can leave large areas with the same least significant bits. The JPEG algorithm, for instance, stores each image as the weighted sum of some cosine functions. If the 64 pixels in the 8×8 block are sufficiently similar, the algorithm will simply store the average value. The GIF algorithm will also replace similar colors with the same value in the interest of saving space. Both of these effects conspire to prevent the least significant bits from being truly random.

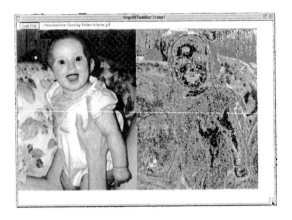

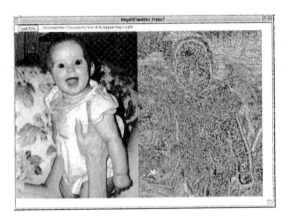

Figure 17.2   The top window shows a picture and its least significant bits before approximately 17,000 bytes were hidden in the image with EzStego. The image had a capacity of 20,000 bytes. The bottom window shows the image and the least significant bits afterward.

After information is hidden in the least significant bits, though, all of these regions become much more random. The eye is often the fastest tool for identifying these changes. It's very easy to see the effects in Figures 17.1 and 17.2.

There is no reason why more complicated visual presentations can't be created. Information does not need to be hidden in the least significant bits, in part because it is often very fragile there [SY98]. More complicated presentations might combine several bit planes and allow the attacker to try to identify where the extra information may be hidden.

17.3.1 Aural Attacks

Skilled audio technicians and musicians can often hear changes ignored by the average pair of ears. Many creators of watermarks for music systems find it simple to inject extra echoes in places that are never heard by most people. Trained ears, however, can detect them immediately.

Average ears can pick up information if the data is normalized. Most techniques depend upon the way that the human brain picks up the most significant frequency while ignoring softer versions of similar frequencies.

17.4

Structural Attacks

In many cases, steganographic algorithms leave behind a characteristic structure to the data. This is often as distinctive as a person's handwriting or an artist's brushstroke. If you know what to look for, you can often spot the effects of some algorithms very quickly.

Many of the basic steganographic solutions that hide information in the least significant bits of images are hampered by the data formats used to represent images. Hiding information in the least significant bit is simple when each pixel is represented by 24 bits with 8 bits allocated for the amount of red, green, and blue. Scanners and cameras often leave enough randomness in the 3 least significant bits assigned to each pixel to make it feasible to store the data.

Unfortunately, most images don't allocate 24 bits for each image. File formats such as GIF or PNG allocate 8 bits or fewer by building a *palette* of selected colors. An i-bit palette means 2^i possible colors. These can significantly reduce the size of the images, especially when they're combined with run-length encoding to compress long stretches of identical pixels.

In some cases, the structure used by the software hiding the data is different from the standard. Many GIF files are written with entries for 256 colors, even if only a small number are needed. The software SysCop only writes out the colors in the image. The extra efficiency may shrink the file, but it can distinguish the output.

There are many glitches and minor incompatibilities in many of the current packages. Version 4.1 of Hide and Seek, for instance, requires all images to be 320×480 arrays of pixels. StegoDos uses 320×200 pixel images. None of these limitations are difficult to fix, but they show how dangerous quick and dirty steganography software can be [JJ98a].

Hiding information in the compressed GIF or PNG format by tweaking the least significant bit can fail dramatically because the palette entries are often not close enough to each other. Entry 01001001 may be a deep blue, while entry 01001000 may be a hot pink. Twiddling the last bit will distort the image.

Many of the steganographic schemes in Chapter 9 try to avoid this problem by constructing a special palette. This process can leave a damning mark.

A simple technique is to choose a smaller palette and then add duplicate colors that can be used to hide information. S-Tools, for instance, first creates an optimal 32-color palette for the image. Then it creates 7 near-duplicate colors that differ by one pixel in either the red, green, or blue component. If one of the 32 chosen colors has the RGB profile of $(64, 250, 120)$, then 7 additional colors will be added with the RGB values of $(64, 250, 121)$, $(64, 251, 120)$, $(64, 251, 121)$, $(65, 250, 120)$, $(65, 250, 121)$, $(65, 251, 120)$, and $(65, 251, 121)$. Less dramatic versions of this approach are also common. MandelSteg, for instance, reduces the size of the palette to 128 different colors and then creates only one near-duplicate of each color.

This approach can hide up to 3 extra bits of information at every pixel—a significant payload—but one that comes with a cost. Palettes like these are also easy to detect. When clusters of colors appear in the palette, they are often indicators of bit-twiddling schemes such as this. Natural palette creation algorithms try to choose colors as widely dispersed as possible in order to minimize the error of reducing the number of colors.

Section 13.6 describes how to hide information in the *order* of the colors, a technique used in GifShuffle.

In other cases, the algorithms try to order the elements of the palette to place similar colors next to each other. Flipping the least significant bit should not distort the image too much because a similar color should be nearby. EzStego, a program written by Romana Machado, uses this technique with some success.

The attacker may be able to intercept the bits if the sorting method is publicly known or easy to figure out. If the data is protected by an additional layer of encryption, then the message will be indistinguishable from random noise.

An attacker may still detect the presence of a message by examining the statistical profile of the bits. An encrypted hidden message should come with an equal probability of 0s and 1s. If the numbers of 0s and 1s are equal, then the odds point toward a hidden message.

There are two ways to thwart these attacks. The first is to use some keyed version of the sorting routine in order to prevent an eavesdropper from assembling the sorted palette. The palette-sorting algorithm is not deterministic because it tries to arrange points in a three-dimensional space so that the distance between adjacent points is minimized. This is a discrete version of the Traveling Salesman Problem, a known difficult problem. EzStego uses one reasonable approximation that makes guesses. Instead of using a random source to make decisions, a cryptographically secure keyed random number generator can take the place and create a keyed sorting algorithm.

The second is to use the statistical mimic functions described in Chapter 6 to create a statistically equivalent version of least significant bits. The patterns from the least significant bits of the original image can be extracted and then used to encode the data. This approach may fool some statistical tests, but not all of them. It may also fail some of the visual tests described in Section 17.3.

17.5

Statistical Attacks

Much of the study of mathematical statistics is devoted to determining whether some phenomenon occurs at random. Scientists use these tools to determine whether their theory does a good job of explaining the phenomenon. Many of these statistical tools can also be used to identify images and music with a hidden message because the hidden message is often more random than the information it replaces. Encrypted information is usually close to random unless it has been reprocessed to add statistical irregularities.

The simplest statistical test for detecting randomness is the χ^2 (*chi-squared*) test, which sums the square of the discrepancies. Let $\{e_0, e_1, \ldots\}$ be the number of times that a sequence of events occurs. In this case, it may be the number of times that a least significant bit is 1 or 0. Let $E(e_i)$ be the expected number of times the event should occur if the sample was truly random. The amount of randomness in the sample is measured with this equation:

$$\chi^2 = \sum \frac{(e_i - E(e_i))^2}{E(e_i)}.$$

High scores indicate an unrandom condition—one that was probably part of an original picture or sound file created by an imperfect set of sensors. Low scores indicate a high degree of randomness—something that is often connected with encrypted hidden information.

Table 17.1 Turning two bits into events.

Event	Bit	Neighbor Bit
e_0	0	0
e_1	0	1
e_2	1	0
e_3	1	1

The χ^2 test can be applied to any part of the file. The least significant bits can be analyzed by looking at two events, e_0 when the least significant bit is 0 and e_1 when the bit is 1. A low score means the bits occur with close to equal probability, while a higher one means that one bit outnumbers the other. In this case, $E(e_0) = E(e_1) = .5$.

A better solution is to create four events that look at the pattern of neighboring least significant bits (see Table 17.1). Natural images often leave neighboring bits set to the same value. Files with hidden information have neighbors that are often different.

Files with a high amount of hidden information will usually have low scores in this χ^2 test. More natural, undoctored images often have higher scores, as Figures 17.1 and 17.2 indicate.

Neil Johnson, Sushil Jajodia, J. Fridrich, Rui Du, and Meng Long report that measuring the number of close colors is a good statistical test for detecting images with data hidden in the least significant bits. A pair of close colors differs by no more than one unit in each of the red, green, and blue components. Naturally constructed files have fewer close pairs than ones with extra inserted data. This is especially true if the image was stored at one time by a lossy-compression mechanism like JPEG. Testing for the number of close pairs is an excellent indicator [JJ98a, JJ98b, FDL, Mae98].

Section 13.6 describes how to hide information in the sorted order of pixels.

These tests will often do a good job of identifying basic least-significant-bit steganography. More complicated mechanisms for hiding data, however, would avoid this simple test and require one tuned to the algorithm at hand. Imagine the sender was hiding information by choosing pairs of pixels and occasionally swapping them to encode either a 0 or a 1. The overall distribution of colors and their least significant bits would not be changed in the process. Swapping doesn't change the statistical profile of the least significant bits.

An enhanced version of the test can identify a hidden collection of bits in some cases if the attacker can identify the pairs. The order of pairs in an image with hidden information should occur with equal frequency, while those in a natural image should probably come with some imperfection.

More sophisticated tests can be tuned to different applications. The program JSteg hides information by changing the least significant bit of the integer coefficients used in the JPEG algorithm. In normal pictures, smaller coefficients are more common than larger ones. The value of 1 is more than twice as common as the value 2, a value that is in turn about twice as common as 3 [Wes01]. When the least significant bits of these values are tweaked to hide information, the occurrences equalize. The numbers of 1s and 2s become equal, the occurrences of 3s and 4s become equal, and so on. If two coefficients differ by only the least significant bits, then their occurrences become equal as information is hidden.

The χ^2 test can help identify JPEG photos where the coefficients occur with too much similarity.

17.5.1   Sophisticated Statistics

Another solution is to examine the statistics produced by applying a set of functions to the image. Hany Farid noted that many of the wavelet functions used to model images often produced distinctive statistical profiles [RC95, Sha93, BS99]. He applied one set, the *quadrature mirror filters* (QMF), at multiple scales and found that the basic statistical profile of the coefficients generated by these wavelet decompositions could predict the presence or absence of a message in some cases. That is, the mean, variance, skewness, and kurtosis were different enough to be distinctive.

Messages from basic programs like JSteg and EzStego could be detected with accuracy rates approaching 98 percent, while those from more careful programs like Outguess could be found as often as 77 percent of the time. Of course, the success depended heavily on the size of the message encoded in the images. The high success rate came when the hidden message was about 5 percent of the carrier image's size. If the image size dropped, the success rate dropped to next to nothing (2 percent).

Some of the success is no doubt due to the fact that a program like Outguess only tries to balance the first-order statistics. Multiscale decompositions with more complicated statistics are still affected by even these balanced tweaks. A more sophisticated version of Outguess designed to keep the QMF statistics in balance could probably defeat it. Of course, keeping the message small is one of the simplest solutions.

17.6

Summary

For every steganographic algorithm, there may be a form of steganalysis that detects it. Many of the early algorithms were relatively easy to detect because they left statistical anomalies. The newest algorithms are much more secure, but only time will tell whether they are able to withstand sophisticated analysis.

A good open question is whether there can be any solid description of which tweaks change which class of statistics. It would be nice to report that simply swapping the least significant bits will change a particular set of stats and leave another particular set unchanged. This work, however, needs a deeper understanding of how digital cameras, scanners, and microphones convert our world into numbers.

Mark Ettinger uses game theory to model the cat and mouse game between hider and attacker [Ett98].

In the meantime, the easiest way to slip by steganographic attacks is to minimize the size of the message. The smaller the message, the fewer the changes in the file and the slighter the distortion in the statistics. In this realm, as in many others, the guiding rule is "Don't get greedy."

- *The Disguise.* Data mimicry often fails to completely hide the existence of a message because the efforts to blend the data often leave other marks. The efforts at steganalysis often detect these patterns and reveal the existence of the message.

- *How Secure Is It?* Many of the early software packages for hiding information in the noise of an image are easy to detect. Images have more structure than we can easily describe mathematically. In many cases, the cameras or scanners don't generate files with true noise in the least significant bits, and this means that any efforts to hide information there will be defeated.

- *How to Use It.* The best steganalysis is aimed at individual algorithms and the particular statistical anomalies they leave behind. The best solution is to learn which software is being used and analyze it for characteristic marks. More general solutions are usually far from accurate. The best general solution is to check the randomness of the least significant bits. Too much randomness may be a sign of steganography—or a sign of a very good camera.

Afterword

While writing this book, I've been haunted by the possibility that there may be something inherently evil or wrong in these algorithms. If criminals are able to hide information so effectively, justice becomes more elusive. There is less the police can do before a crime is committed, and there is less evidence after the fact. All of the ideas in this book, no matter how philosophical or embellished with allegory or cute jokes, carry this implicit threat.

This threat is a bit more obvious after the destruction of the World Trade Center on September 11, 2001. Some news reports offered the supposition that the attackers may have coordinated their efforts by hiding information in images. While there is no evidence that this occurred as I rewrite this chapter, there's no doubt that it could have happened.

The U.S. Federal Bureau of Investigation or at least its senior officers are clearly of the opinion that they need ready access to all communications. If someone is saying it, writing it, mailing it, or faxing it, the FBI would like to be able to listen in so they can solve crimes. This is a sensible attitude. More information can only help make sure that justice is fair and honest. People are convicted on the basis of their own words—not the testimony of stool pigeons who often point the finger in order to receive a lighter sentence.

The arguments against giving the FBI and the police such power are more abstract and anecdotal. Certainly, the power can be tamed if everyone follows proper procedures. If warrants are filed and chains of evidence are kept intact, the abuse of power is minimized. But even if the police are 100 times more honest than the average citizen, there will still be rogue cops on the force with access to the communications of everyone in the country. This is a very powerful tool, and corruption brought by power is one of the world's oldest themes.

Both of these scenarios are embodied in one case that came along in the year before I began writing the first edition of this book. The story began when a New Orleans woman looked out the window and saw a police officer beating her son's friend. She called the internal affairs department to report the officer. By lunchtime, the officer in question knew the name of the person making the accusation, her address, and even what she was wearing. He allegedly ordered a hit and by the end of the day, she was dead.

How do we know this happened? How do we know it wasn't a random case of street violence? Federal authorities were in New Orleans following the officer and bugging his phone. He was a suspect in a ring of corrupt cops who helped the drug trade remain secure. They audiotaped the order for the hit.

There is little doubt that secure communications could have made this case unsolvable. If no one heard the execution order except the killer, there would be no case and no justice.

There is also little doubt that a secure internal affairs office could have prevented the murder. The leak probably came from a colleague, but the corrupt cops could have monitored the phones of the internal affairs division. That scenario is quite conceivable. At the very least, the murder might have been delayed until a case was made against the officer. The right to confront our accusers in court means that it would have been impossible to keep the caller's identity secret forever.

Which way is the right way? Total openness stops many crimes, but it encourages others forms of fraud and deceit. Total secrecy protects many people, but it gives the criminals a cover.

One solution is to encrypt the session key with a special public key. Only the government has access to the private key.

In the past, the FBI and other groups within the law enforcement community suggested a system known as "key escrow" as a viable compromise. The escrow systems broadcast a copy of the session key in an encrypted packet that can only be read by designated people. Although Department of Justice officials have described extensive controls on the keys and access to them, I remain unconvinced that there will not be abuse. If the tool is going to be useful to the police on the streets, they'll need fast access to keys. The audit log will only reveal a problem if someone complains that his or her phone was tapped illegally. But how do you know your phone was tapped? Only if you discover the tapes in someone's hands.

There really is no way for technology to provide any ultimate solution to this problem. At some point, law enforcement authorities must be given the authority to listen in to solve a crime. The more this ability is concentrated in a small number of hands, the more powerful it becomes and the more alluring the corruption associated with breaking the rules. Even the most dangerous secret owned by the United States, the technology for building nuclear weapons, was compromised by an insider. Is there any doubt that small-time criminals won't be able to pull off small-time corruption across the country?

The depth and complexity of this corruption can lead to ironic situations. Robert Hanssen, an FBI agent who worked on counterespionage, turned out to be spying for the Russians at the same time. In September 2001, the head of the Cuban desk at the Defense Intelligence Agency was arrested and charged with being a spy for, of all places, Cuba. If the goal is to protect U.S. information from Russian or Cuban ears, we must realize that putting eavesdropping technology in the hands of the FBI or the DIA may also be putting this technology at the disposal of foreign powers.

If giving into widespread eavesdropping is not a cure, then allowing unlimited steganography and cryptography is not one either. The technology described in this book offers a number of ways for information to elude police dragnets. Encrypted files may look like secrets and secrets can look damning. Although the Fifth Amendment to the U.S. Constitution gives each person the right to refuse to incriminate him- or herself, there is little doubt that invoking that right can look suspicious.

The mimic functions, anonymous remailers, and photographic steganography allow people to create files and hide them from sight. If no one can find them, no one can demand the encryption key. This may offer a powerful tool for the criminal element.

There are some consolations. Random violence on the street really can't be stopped by phone taps. Muggers, rapists, robbers, and many other criminals don't rely upon communications to do their job. These are arguably some of the most important problems for everyone and something that requires more diligent police work. None of the tools described in this book should affect the balance of power on the street.

Nor will banning cryptography or steganography stop terrorism. The hijackers used knives and guile, not a bunch of cutting epigrams floating around in the netherworld of stegospace. The pen is not always mightier than the box cutter.

In reality, very few crimes can be readily solved through wiretaps because very little crime depends upon communications and the exchange of information. Bribery of officials, for instance, is only committed when two people sit down in private and make an agreement.

> But in the end it doesn't matter what they see or think they see. The terminals are equipped with holographic scanners, which decode the binary secret of every item, infallibly. This is the language of the waves and radiation, or how the dead speak to the living. And this is where we wait together, regardless of age, our carts stocked with brightly colored goods.
>
> —Don DeLillo,
> *White Noise*

If the money can't be traced (as it so often can't be), then the only way to prove the crime happened is to record the conversation or get someone to testify. Obviously, the recorded conversation is much more convincing evidence. State and local police in some states are not allowed to use wiretaps at all. Some police officers suggest that this isn't an accident. The politicians in those states recognized that the only real targets for wiretaps were the politicians. They were the primary ones who broke laws in conversation. Almost all other law-breaking involved some physical act that might leave other evidence.

The power for creating secret deals that this technology offers is numbing. The only consolation is that these deals have been made in the past and only a fool would believe that they won't be made in the future. All of the wiretap laws didn't stop them before cryptography became cheap. Meeting people face to face to conduct illegal business also has other benefits. You can judge people better in person. Also, the places where such deals may be made, such as bars, offer drinks and often food. You can't get that in cyberspace.

The fact that crooks have found ways to elude wiretaps in the past can be easily extended to parallel a popular argument made by the National Rifle Association. If cryptography is outlawed, only outlaws will have cryptography. People who murder, smuggle, or steal will probably not feel much hesitation to violate a law that simply governs how they send bits back and forth. Honest people who obey any law regulating cryptography will find themselves easy marks for those who want to steal their secrets.

I mulled over all of these ideas while I was writing this book. I had almost begun to feel that the dispute is not really about technology. If criminals can always avoid the law, this wasn't really going to change with more technology. The police have always been forced to adapt to new technology, and they would have to do the same here.

In the end, I began concentrating on how to balance the power relationships. If power can be dispersed successfully, then abuse can be limited. If individuals can control their affairs, then they are less likely to be dominated by others. If they're forced to work in the open, then they're more likely to be controlled.

The dishonest will never yield to the law that tells them not to use any form of steganography. The cliché of gangsters announcing the arrival of a shipment of 10,000 bananas will be with us forever. The question is whether the honest should have access to the tools to protect their privacy. Cryptography and steganography give individuals this power, and, for better or for worse, that's the best place for this power to be.

Java Mimic Code

Here is the source code for a Java version of the context-free grammar-based mimic functions described in Chapter 7. The code is Copyright © 1997 by Peter Wayner, but you're welcome to use it as long as you obey all U.S. export laws and identify all changes as your own. At this point it is functional, but it could use a better random number generator, a mechanism for detecting run-on grammars, and a more efficient parser. You may find a number of other ways to improve it.

BitInput Interface

```java
public interface BitInput {
  public boolean nextBit();
  public void startBitSource(String s);
  public void startBitSource();
  public boolean atEnd();
    /// Returns true if everything has been outputted.
}
```

CTMimicCentral Class

```java
import java.applet.*;
import java.io.*;
import java.net.*;
import java.awt.*;
public class CTMimicCentral extends Applet {
  TableSetter ts;
  OutSpitter os;
  MimicParser mp;

  Label mainAnnounce;
  TextField inputLine,outputLine;
```

```
TextArea outputMimic, inputMimic;
  // The main part of the input
Button inMimic,outMimic;
  // For getting to go.
boolean startedUp=false;

public void init(){
  this.setBackground(Color.white);
  ts=new TableSetter(getCodeBase());
  os=new OutSpitter();

  add(inputLine=new TextField("PUT MESSAGE HERE"));
  add(outputLine=new TextField(""));
  add(outputMimic=new TextArea(""));
  //add(inputMimic=new TextArea(""));

  add(inMimic=new Button ("Push for Mimicry"));
  add(outMimic=new Button("Remove Mimicry"));

  add(mainAnnounce=new Label("Loading Table. Please wait."));

  ts.setAnnounceHere(mainAnnounce);
  ts.run();

  startedUp=true;

}

public void layout(){
    int textWidth=400;
  if (startedUp){
    mainAnnounce.reshape(0,0,textWidth,20);
    if (inputLine!=null)
      {inputLine.reshape(5,20,textWidth,20);}
    if (inMimic!=null)
      {inMimic.reshape(5,45,200,18);}
    if (outputMimic!=null)
      {outputMimic.reshape(5,70,textWidth,150);}
    if (inputMimic!=null)
      {inputMimic.reshape(5,220,textWidth, 150);}
    if (outMimic!=null)
      {outMimic.reshape(5,240,200,18);}
    if (outputLine!=null)
      {outputLine.reshape(5,270,textWidth,20);}
  }
}

public void start(){

}

public boolean action(Event e, Object arg){
  boolean answer=false;
  if (ts.tableLoaded) {
    if (e.target == inMimic){
      os.setTableSource(ts);
```

```
      os.setTableSource(ts);
      os.setOutputTextArea(outputMimic);
      os.DoSomeMimicry(inputLine.getText());
      answer=true;

    } else if (e.target == outMimic){
      mp=new MimicParser(ts,outputMimic.getText());
      mp.setOutputLocation(outputLine);
      mp.DoItAllLoop();
      answer=true;
    }
  }
  return answer;
}

}
```

Globals Class

```
import java.awt.*;
import java.applet.Applet;

class Globals {
  public static final char StoppingCharacter = '/';
  // In the definition of section where the grammar is defined,
  // this character is used to separate the different
  // productions that could occur. When it occurs twice,
  // it signifies the end of the production...
  public static final char VariableSignifier = '*';
    // If the first character of a word equals this, then the program
    // shall treat the word as a variable which
    // will undergo more transformations. Note the program
    // ASSUMES that a variable is one word.
  public static final char EqualityCharacter = '=';
    // There is a character that signifies the equality
    // between a variable and set of productions.
  public static final char EndOfFileSignifier =  (char)(0);
    // This is passed back from NextWord when
    // it finds it is at the end of the file...
  public static final String NullWord = " ";
    // This is what comes back from NextWord
    // if it can't find something...
  public static final char Space = ' ';
    // This is something different, but the same.
    // It is the same thing, but used in a different fashion.

  public static final boolean AddCarriageReturns=true;
    // If we want to do some word wrapping, this is inserted.
  public static final int RightMargin=50;
    // The margin for wrapping.
  }
```

WordNode Class

```
class WordNode {
  String w1;
```

```java
    // The string being stored here.
  WordNode next;
    // What comes next in the list. null is nothing.

  public WordNode(){
    w1="";
    next=null;
  }

  public void setW1(String s){
    w1=s;
  }

  public WordNode (String s){
    w1=s;
    next=null;
  }

  public WordNode (String s, WordNode n){
    w1=s;
    next=n;
  }

  public void setNext(WordNode n){
    next=n;
  }

  public WordNode getNext(){
    return next;
  }
}
```

BitNode Class

```java
class BitNode {
  int bitNumber=-1;
    // This is the number of a central register of bits.
  boolean polarity=true;
  double probability;
    // The total probability of all subordinate nodes.
  BitNode up;
    // What comes up.
  BitNode left,right;
    // For building a tree.
  ProductionNode theProductionNode;
      /*Well, technically, I could get away
        with storing this pointer in either left or
        right because left and right will equal nil if
        and only if TheProductionNode <> nil, but
        I don't feel like packing this too tightly
        right now. I'm being lavish with memory.*/

  public BitNode(){
    up=null;
    left=null;
    right=null;
```

```
      bitNumber=0;
      polarity=true;
      probability=1.0;
    }
    public void setProbability(double d){
      probability=d;
    }
}
```

ProductionNode Class

```
    class ProductionNode {
    double probability;
      // The Probability that this particular
      // production will be chosen.
    BitNode itsBit;
      // Follow this up to the root to find the bits
      // associated with this production.
    WordNode theWords;
      // This is the list of words that come from
      // the Production. Variables are at the end.
    ProductionNode next;
      // This is the next in the list.

    public ProductionNode(){
      probability=1.0;
      itsBit=null;
      theWords=null;
      next=null;
    }
    public void setProbability(double d){
      probability=d;
    }
    public void setNext(ProductionNode n){
      next =n;
    }
    public ProductionNode getNext(){
      return next;
    }
    public void setTheWords(WordNode w){
      theWords=w;
    }
}
```

VariableNode Class

```
    class VariableNode {
     String w1;
       // This is the identity of the variable.
     ProductionNode productions;
```

```
  // This is the list of productions associated
  // with the variable.
BitNode itsBitRoot;
  // This is the top of the bit tree. When
  // random characters are being generated,
  // it follows this down to the bottom.
VariableNode next;

public VariableNode(){
  wl="";
  productions=null;
  itsBitRoot=null;
  next=null;
}

public void setProductions(ProductionNode p){
  productions=p;
}

public ProductionNode getProductions(){
  return productions;
}

public void setWl(String w){
  wl=w;
}

public void setNext(VariableNode n){
  next=n;
}

public VariableNode getNext(){
  return next;
}
}
```

MimicProdNode Class

```
class MimicProdNode{
 WordNode ww;
 MimicProdNode next;

public  MimicProdNode() {
  ww=null;
  next=null;
}

public void setNext(MimicProdNode n){
  next =n;
}

public MimicProdNode getNext(){
  return next;
}
```

```
  public void setWW(WordNode a){
    ww=a;
  }

  public WordNode getWW(){
    return ww;
  }
}
```

MimicParseFrame Class

```
class MimicParseFrame {
 VariableNode theVariable;
 WordNode theWordsToMatch;
   // Once a production is matched,
   // this baby is loaded with words to check.

  public MimicParseFrame(){
    theVariable=null;
    theWordsToMatch=null;
  }
}
```

NextWordResponse Class

```
class NextWordResponse {
  String w;
  char stopChar;
  boolean doubleStop;

  public NextWordResponse(String s, char stop, boolean ds){
    w=s;
    stopChar=stop;
    doubleStop=ds;
      // set to be true when we hit a double slash.
  }
}
```

CTTableSetter Class

```
import java.applet.*;
import java.io.*;
import java.net.*;

public class CTTableSetter {
  WordEater we;
  NextWordResponse n;

  public TableSetter(){
    we= new WordEater();
    we.initializeScanHashTable();
  }
}
```

MyIntegerWrapper Class

```
import java.io.*;
import java.net.*;
```

```java
import java.awt.*;
class MyIntegerWrapper {
  int x;
    // Used to pass by reference.

  public MyIntegerWrapper(int zz){
    x=zz;
  }

  public void setX(int y){
    x=y;
  }
  public int getX(){
    return x;
  }
}
```

MimicParser Class

```java
public class MimicParser {

  public final static int spacer=1;
  public final static int normal=2;
  public final static int stopper=3;

  public final static char equalityCharacter='=';
  public final static char stoppingCharacter='/';

  public final static int MaxLookAhead=200;
  public final static int StandardLookAhead=20;
      /* MaxLookAhead is the absolute maximum permitted
      by the sizes of the array. StandardLookAhead is
      the usual amount to search. Note that the running
      time is potentially exponential in the
      LookAhead. Don't be greedy. Sorry I didn't write
      a better algorithm. */

    public RandomBits rb=new RandomBits();
      // For synchronizing things. ...
    public boolean debug=false;
    public int debugStackDepth=0;
      // For controlling the printout.

    public int offsetTraffic=0;
      // Used for passing information.
  public TableSetter ts;
    // Where the information is kept.

  public TextField outputLocation=null;
    // Where the data goes.

  public String[] LookAheadTable;
      /* The next MaxLookAhead words are kept in this
      circular array. When the end of file is found, the
      table contains nullWord. */
```

```java
public int LookAheadOffset=0;
   /* Keeps track of where the first word will be. */

public boolean FoundAmbiguity=false;
      /* When the machine starts to do some parsing and
      discovers that there are two different paths for
      each production, this baby is set to true. */

public int SoftMaxLookAhead;
      /* This allows the parser to set its lookahead on
      the fly if it wants to increase it. */

public boolean ReachedEndOfFile=false;
   /* Set true when everything is exhausted... */

StringBuffer outputStrings;
   /// Where the data is going.

int tempOutputBits=0;
int tempOutputBitsPosition=0;

public void openOutputFile(){
   outputStrings= new StringBuffer("");
}

String toBeParsed;
   // What will be parsed.
int toBeParsedPosition=0;
   // The current characters.

public int[] scanTable=new int[256];
   // This is a scan table used for parsing.

public void setOutputLocation(TextField f){
   outputLocation=f;
}


public void initializeScanHashTable()\{
   /* The Scanning Hash Table has 256 entries. They
   identify a character as either a letter, stop
   character,} a space or a comment. */
   int i;
   for (i=14; i<=255; i++){
     scanTable[i]=normal;
   }
   for (i=0; i<=13; i++){
     scanTable[i]=spacer;
   }
     scanTable[(byte)(equalityCharacter)] = stopper;
     scanTable[(byte)(stoppingCharacter)]  = stopper;
     scanTable[(byte)(' ')] = spacer;
}
```

```java
  public void debugFirstPrint(String s){
    for (int i=0; i<debugStackDepth;i++){
      System.out.print("-");
    }
    System.out.print(s);
  }

  public void debugPrintln(String s) {
    for (int i=0; i<debugStackDepth;i++){
      System.out.print("-");
    }
    System.out.println(s);
  }

  public String parserNextWord(){
    // Pull off the next word.
    String answer ="";
    while ((toBeParsedPosition < toBeParsed.length())
        && (scanTable[toBeParsed.charAt(toBeParsedPosition)] != normal)) {
      toBeParsedPosition++;
    }
    while ((toBeParsedPosition < toBeParsed.length())
        && (scanTable[toBeParsed.charAt(toBeParsedPosition)] == normal)) {
      answer=answer+toBeParsed.charAt(toBeParsedPosition++);
    }
    if (toBeParsedPosition >= toBeParsed.length()){
      ReachedEndOfFile = true;
    }
    return answer+" ";
  }


/* Sets up the lookahead buffer
to keep all of the words in place. */

  public void InitLookAhead(){
    int i;
    char Stopper; /* to be ignored. */
    LookAheadTable = new String[MaxLookAhead+1];

    LookAheadOffset = 0;
    for (i = 0; i<= MaxLookAhead - 1; i ++){
        LookAheadTable[i]= parserNextWord();
      }
  }

  public MimicParser(TableSetter tt, String doMe){
      ts=tt;
      toBeParsed=doMe;
      toBeParsedPosition=0;
      initializeScanHashTable();
      InitLookAhead();
    }
```

```java
public String  TimeDelayNextWord(){
  String result;

  result=LookAheadTable[LookAheadOffset];
  LookAheadTable[LookAheadOffset]=parserNextWord();

  LookAheadOffset = (LookAheadOffset + 1) % MaxLookAhead;
  return result;
}


  public char convertNumToChar(int c){
    // Just converts things back.

    switch(c){
      case 23:
      case 31:
      case 26:
      case 0: return ' ';
      // 29=11101=10111=23
      // 31=11111=11111=31
      // 11=01011-11010=26
      // 00000=00000
      case 16: return 'A';
      // 00001=10000=16
      case 8: return 'B';
      // 00010=01000=8
      case 24: return 'C';
      // 00011=11000=24
      case 4: return 'D';
      // 00100=00100=4
      case 20: return 'E';
      // 00101=10100=20
      case 12: return 'F';
      // 00110=01100=12
      case 28: return 'G';
      // 00111=11100=28
      case 2: return 'H';
      // 01000=00010=2
      case 18: return 'I';
      // 01001=10010=18
      case 10: return 'J';
      // 01010=01010=10
      case 15: return 'K';
      // 01011=11010=26
      // K is now 30=11110=01111=15
      case 6: return 'L';
      // 01100=00110=6
      case 22: return 'M';
      // 01101=10110=22
      case 14: return 'N';
      // 01110=01110=14
      case 30: return 'O';
```

```java
    // 01111=11110=30
    case 1: return 'P';
    // 10000=00001=1
    case 17: return 'Q';
    // 10001=10001=17
    case 9: return 'R';
    // 10010=01001=9
    case 25: return 'S';
    // 10011=11001=25
    case 5: return 'T';
    // 10100=00101=5
    case 21: return 'U';
    // 10101=10101=21
    case 13: return 'V';
    // 10110=01101=13
    case 29: return 'W';
    // 10111=11101=29
    case 3: return 'X';
    // 11000=00011=3
    case 19: return 'Y';
    // 11001=10011=19
    case 11: return 'Z';
    // 11010=01011=11
    case 27: return '-';
    // 11011=11011=27
    default: return '*';
  }
}


public void storeOutputBit(boolean b){
  if (b) {
    tempOutputBits=(tempOutputBits << 1) +1;
  } else
    tempOutputBits = (tempOutputBits <<1);
  tempOutputBitsPosition++;
  if (tempOutputBitsPosition>=5){
    tempOutputBitsPosition = 0;
    outputStrings.append(convertNumToChar(tempOutputBits));
    tempOutputBits = 0;
  }
}

public boolean RandomBit(int a){
  return true;
  // No random synchronization at this time.
}


public void ProductionToBits(ProductionNode p){
  BitNode BitPointer;
    /* This will lead the way. */
  long TempBit;
    /* This will hold the bits. */
```

```java
    int BitCounter=0;
      /* This is position of the next bit to be stored. */
    boolean[] store=new boolean[30];
      // This should be enough.
    rb.updateRandomBits();
      /* Get a new group of random
         bits for the random generator. */
    TempBit=0;
    BitCounter=0;
    BitPointer=p.itsBit;
      /* We're not concerned about the first node because
         it is just an interface. */
    //debugFirstPrint("Bits:");
    while (BitPointer.up != null) {
        if (BitPointer.polarity) {
            store[BitCounter++]=(rb.randomBit(BitPointer.up.bitNumber) && true);
            // System.out.print("T");
          } else {
            store[BitCounter++]=(rb.randomBit(BitPointer.up.bitNumber) ^ true);
            // System.out.print("F");
          }
        BitPointer= BitPointer.up;
    }
    for (int i=BitCounter-1;i>=0;i--){
      storeOutputBit(store[i]);}
      // These are backward. We can reverse them here.
//   System.out.print(" ");
}


    /* Imagine this case. You are now trying to decide
    whether the next token, say "Ernest", came for the
    production of a variable "*Dudes" or "*Duds". It
    could be from either. This tries to lookahead to
    see if there is any clue that says, Hey, it can't
    be "*Dudes" because the production of the token
    "Ernest" is always followed by the token "Rex" to
    indicate his stature. */

public ProductionNode TokenInVariable(MyIntegerWrapper MoreOffsetWrapper,
VariableNode v){
  ProductionNode ProductionNumber;
    /* Well not as much a number as a pun. */
  boolean OneFound;
    /* This is just set to look for
    ambiguities...Problems, you know.... */
    int   RealOffset;
    /* This holds the temporary Offset that is passed
    to the CheckWordList function. */
    MyIntegerWrapper tempOffset=new MyIntegerWrapper(0);
  ProductionNode result = null;


  ProductionNumber = v.productions;
  OneFound = false;
  RealOffset = MoreOffsetWrapper.getX();
```

```java
   while ((ProductionNumber != null) && !OneFound) {
       tempOffset.setX(RealOffset);
       debugStackDepth += 2;
       if (CheckWordList(tempOffset, ProductionNumber.theWords)) {
     if (debug) {
       WordNode temp = ProductionNumber.theWords;

         debugPrintln("TokenInVariable found production of "+v.w1+":" + tempOffset+":");
         while (temp != null) {
             System.out.print(temp.w1);
             temp = temp.next;
           }
         System.out.println(" ");
       }

         OneFound = true;
         MoreOffsetWrapper.setX(tempOffset.getX()-1);
         result = ProductionNumber;
         }
             debugStackDepth -= 2;
       ProductionNumber = ProductionNumber.next;
     }
 return result;
 }

       /* This compares the words in the word list with
       the words in the lookahead buffer.  If they all
       match, then BINGO! */

 public  boolean CheckWordList(MyIntegerWrapper offset, WordNode www) {
   WordNode checkMe = www;
   int newOffset = offset.x;
   MyIntegerWrapper passItOn=new MyIntegerWrapper(0);
   // debugFirstPrint("Offset:"+passItOn.x+" Comparing word:"+checkMe.w1);

   while ((newOffset < SoftMaxLookAhead )&& (checkMe != null)) {
       if (checkMe.w1.charAt(0) == Globals.VariableSignifier) {
         passItOn.setX(newOffset);
                 debugStackDepth += 2;
         if (TokenInVariable(passItOn, ts.FindVariable(checkMe.w1)) == null) {
            offset.setX(passItOn.getX());
            return false;
          }
                 debugStackDepth -= 2;
                     offset.setX(passItOn.getX());

         newOffset= passItOn.getX()+1;
         checkMe = checkMe.next;
       } else if (LookAheadTable[(newOffset + LookAheadOffset)
           % MaxLookAhead].compareTo(checkMe.w1) != 0) {
     //    System.out.println(""+checkMe.w1+"::FAILED");
      offset.setX( newOffset);
       return false;
       } else {
```

```
    //   System.out.print(""+checkMe.w1);
        newOffset ++;
        checkMe = checkMe.next;
      }
  }


  offset.setX(newOffset);
  // debugPrintln("Found at offset:"+newOffset);
return true;
}

        /* The Serious Version Checks for Parsing
        Ambiguities.... This is only done on the first
        call. You could get rid of this and just let the
        program choose the first production it finds. This
        will be faster, but it might lead to errors. I've
        chosen to include this because it is
        computationally difficult (at least for now) to
        ensure that CFLs are non-ambiguous. */

  public ProductionNode SeriousTokenInVariable(int MoreOffset, VariableNode v){
    ProductionNode ProductionNumber; /* Well, not as much a number as a pun. */
    boolean OneFound;
        /* This is just set to look for ambiguities. Problems, you know.... */
    int    RealOffset, bestOffset;
    MyIntegerWrapper tempOffset=new MyIntegerWrapper(0);
        /* This holds the temporary Offset that is passed to the CheckWordList
            function. */
    ProductionNode result = null;

    ProductionNumber = v.productions;
    OneFound = false;
    RealOffset = MoreOffset;
        bestOffset = MoreOffset+1;
        tempOffset.setX(RealOffset);

    while (ProductionNumber != null) {
      tempOffset.setX(RealOffset);
        if (OneFound) {
        if (CheckWordList(tempOffset, ProductionNumber.theWords)) {
          if (tempOffset.getX() == bestOffset) {
          System.out.println("Parsing Ambiguity Here!!! Try growing the lookahead. ");
          FoundAmbiguity = true;
          return null;
        } else if (tempOffset.getX() > bestOffset) {
          bestOffset = tempOffset.x;
          result = ProductionNumber;
        }
            /* else ignore shorter match */
          }
        } else if (CheckWordList(tempOffset, ProductionNumber.theWords)) {
          OneFound = true;
          bestOffset = tempOffset.x;
```

```
        result = ProductionNumber;
      }
      ProductionNumber = ProductionNumber.next;
    }
    if (debug) {
    WordNode temp = result.theWords;
      //System.out.print("TokenInVariable found production of "+v.w1+":" +
tempOffset+":");
      while (temp != null) {
          System.out.print(temp.w1);
        temp = temp.next;
      }
    // System.out.println(" ");
    }
return result;
}


/* This routine takes the frame and figures out that pointer would match... */
 public void DoFrame(MimicParseFrame f){
  ProductionNode Prod;  /* This is the location of the pointer... */
  MimicParseFrame NewFrame; /* If a new frame is needed... */
  int CurrentDepth; /* Used to halt the spread of the search. */
  MyIntegerWrapper curDepth=new MyIntegerWrapper(0);

  FoundAmbiguity = false;
  SoftMaxLookAhead = StandardLookAhead;
  CurrentDepth = 0;
  // debugPrintln("Looking up variable:"+f.theVariable.w1);
  debugStackDepth+=3;
  curDepth.setX(CurrentDepth);
  Prod = TokenInVariable(curDepth, f.theVariable);

        /* I realize that it is a bit of an overkill to
        use a big hammer like SeriousTokenInVariable, but
        it is late at night and I don't want to bother
        writing an elegant method that uses breadth first
        instead of depth-first. */

    debugStackDepth-=3;
  if (FoundAmbiguity) {
    FoundAmbiguity = false;
     SoftMaxLookAhead = MaxLookAhead;
     /* This just doubles the lookahead for the fun of it... */
     CurrentDepth = 0;
       curDepth.setX(CurrentDepth);
     Prod = TokenInVariable(curDepth, f.theVariable);

  }
  if (Prod == null) {
    System.out.println("Can't seem to find a production for:"+f.theVariable.w1);
     curDepth.setX(CurrentDepth);
     Prod = TokenInVariable(curDepth, f.theVariable);
   //longjmp(LABEL\_199, true);
  } else if (!FoundAmbiguity) {
```

```
      /* We've found something.... */
    ProductionToBits(Prod);
    /* Store the bits... */
     NewFrame= new MimicParseFrame();
   f.theWordsToMatch = Prod.theWords;
   while (f.theWordsToMatch != null) {
     if (f.theWordsToMatch.wl.charAt(0) == Globals.VariableSignifier) {
       NewFrame.theVariable = ts.FindVariable(f.theWordsToMatch.wl);
           debugStackDepth+=3;
         DoFrame(NewFrame);
         debugStackDepth-=3;

     } else {
       String theOther = TimeDelayNextWord();

         if (f.theWordsToMatch.wl.compareTo(theOther) != 0) {
       System.out.println("Problem in parsing the file. The Word "+f.theWordsToMatch
.wl+" doesn't belong here.");
       System.out.println("Supposed to match:"+theOther);
       //          longjmp(LABEL\_199, true);
         }
       }
       f.theWordsToMatch = f.theWordsToMatch.next;
     }
  }
}

public String stripSpaces(String  s){
  int i=s.length()-1;
  while (s.charAt(i)==' ') {
    i--;
  }
  return s.substring(0,i+1);
}

public void DoItAllLoop(){
  MimicParseFrame BaseFrame;
    /* This is the first frame allocated. */
  int i=0;
  rb.syncRandomBits();
  openOutputFile();
 BaseFrame = new MimicParseFrame();
  BaseFrame.theVariable = ts.GetStartVariable();
  do {
    DoFrame(BaseFrame);
    i++; // This is a safety net to pull us out of the loop.
    } while ((i<10) && !
       (ReachedEndOfFile &&
         LookAheadTable[LookAheadOffset].compareTo(Globals.NullWord) == 0));
    if (outputLocation!=null){
      outputLocation.setText(stripSpaces(outputStrings.toString()));
    }
  //  System.out.println("Finished.");
```

```java
 // rb.outputDebugArray();
}

}
```

OutSpitter Class

```java
import java.io.*;
import java.net.*;
import CTMimicGlobals;
import java.awt.*;
public class OutSpitter extends Thread {
  BitInput bitSource;
    // This gets the bits.
  TableSetter tableSource;
    // What we use to get everything in shape.
  StringBuffer outputForMimicry;
    // Where the data goes.

  TextArea outputTextArea=null;

  RandomBits rb;
    // Where the random bits come from
  MimicProdNode TheOutputStack;
    /* This is the stack of variables that are unproduced... */
   int CarriagePosition=0;
      /* This is the location of the last character printed
         out on the page. For justification. */

  int StackCount=0;

  public OutSpitter(){
    super();
    rb=new RandomBits();
  }

  public void setTableSource(TableSetter t){
    tableSource = t;
  }

  public void setOutputTextArea(TextArea t){
    outputTextArea = t;
  }


public void OpenForOutput(){
  outputForMimicry= new StringBuffer("");
}

public boolean RandomBit(int i){
  return true;
  // This is just a placeholder for a synchronized random number generator.
}
```

```java
        /* This baby takes a variable and follows its way
        down to the production using the bit tree. */

  public ProductionNode VariableToProduction(VariableNode v){
    BitNode Bitto; /* This is the position that the bit tree should follow. */

    rb.updateRandomBits(); /* Cycle the random number generator. */
    Bitto = v.itsBitRoot;
    while (Bitto.theProductionNode == null) {
        if (bitSource.nextBit()) {
          if (rb.randomBit(Bitto.bitNumber))
            Bitto = Bitto.right;
          else
             Bitto = Bitto.left;
        } else {
          if (rb.randomBit(Bitto.bitNumber))
            Bitto = Bitto.left;
          else
            Bitto = Bitto.right;
        }
      }
    //  System.out.print(" ");
    return Bitto.theProductionNode; /* TheAnswer. */
}

/* This will do the correct thing with the word
node w. If it is a terminal, it will write it out.
Otherwise it will start a new frame... */

public  void DoWord(WordNode w){
  MimicProdNode StackFrame; /* For creating new ones... */

if (w.w1.charAt(0) == Globals.VariableSignifier) {
  StackFrame = new MimicProdNode();
  StackFrame.setNext(TheOutputStack);
  TheOutputStack = StackFrame;

StackFrame.setWW(VariableToProduction(tableSource.FindVariable(w.w1)).theWords);
  if (StackCount++ <500) {
    //System.out.println("Going down:"+w.w1);
    DoStack(StackFrame);
  //  System.out.println("Coming up:"+w.w1);
  } else {
  //  System.out.println("Ignoring:"+w.w1);
  }
  } else {
  /* Write it out. */
  outputForMimicry.append(w.w1);
  // System.out.print();
  /* Assuming there is a space at the end of each word. */
  if (Globals.AddCarriageReturns) {
    CarriagePosition += (w.w1.length());
    if (CarriagePosition > Globals.RightMargin) {
      // Not Sure How to do this...  fprintf(OpenMimicryFile, "\\n");
```

```
//  System.out.println("");
      CarriagePosition = 0;
      }
    }
  }
}


public void DoStack(MimicProdNode s){
WordNode wurds;
 /* This just goes through the list of words on the stack until they are gone. */
wurds = s.getWW();
while (wurds != null) {
  //System.out.println("About to DoStack on word:"+wurds.wl);
  DoWord(wurds);
  wurds = wurds.getNext();
  }
 TheOutputStack = TheOutputStack.getNext();
}

public void DoSomeMimicry(String s){
  // This starts it up.
  rb.syncRandomBits(); // We're not going to do that right now.
  OpenForOutput();
  bitSource= new StringBufferBitInput();
  bitSource.startBitSource(s);
  //System.out.println("Initialized bit source. Read to start generating.----");

  while (!bitSource.atEnd()) {
    TheOutputStack = new MimicProdNode();

TheOutputStack.setWW(VariableToProduction(tableSource.GetStartVariable()).theWords);
      DoStack(TheOutputStack);
    }
  outputTextArea.setText(outputForMimicry.toString());
  //System.out.println();
  //rb.outputDebugArray();
  //  System.out.println();

}}
```

RandomBits Class

```
public class RandomBits {
      /*  This uses an outdated random number generator
      created by Stephen Wolfram. The original one was
      considered to be cryptographically secure, but
      others have found a way to break it. I wish I
      could use a better one, but I don't have time to
      research it. */

  int initialKey, randomBits;
    // For holding the information.
```

```java
public boolean[] debugArray=new boolean[10000];
public int debugArrayPos=0;

public RandomBits(){
  initialKey=0xbaad111f;
  randomBits=initialKey;
}

public void syncRandomBits(){
  randomBits=initialKey;
  debugArrayPos=0;
}

public void updateRandomBits(){
  randomBits = (randomBits << 1) ^ ( randomBits | (randomBits >> 1));
}

public boolean randomBit(int i){
  return true;
  /*  i = i % 32;

  if ((1 & (randomBits >> i)) == 1 ){
    debugArray[debugArrayPos++]=true;
    return true;
  } else {
    debugArray[debugArrayPos++]=false;
    return false;
  }
  */
}

public void outputDebugArray(){
  for (int i=0;i<debugArrayPos;i++){
    if (debugArray[i]){
      System.out.print('T');
    } else {
      System.out.print('f');
    }
  }
  System.out.println(' ');
}
}
```

StringBufferBitInput Class

```java
public class StringBufferBitInput implements BitInput {

  StringBuffer text;
    // This is what comes next.
  int nextBitsSource;
    // This is what is going out next.
  int nextBitsPosition;
    // This points to the bit to leave.

  boolean atTheEndOfBuffer=false;
```

```java
    // Set to be true.
  int textPosition=0;
    // Where it is found.

  public boolean atEnd(){
    return atTheEndOfBuffer;
  }

  public void setText(StringBuffer s){
    text = s;
  }

  public void loadNextBits(char c){
    // This just inserts the right set of bits into place.
    // This version uses an abbreviated set of values between 0 and 31 to use only
5 bits.
    // This is a short way of compressing things.

    nextBitsPosition=0;
    if (c==' ') {
      double r=Math.random();
      if (r<.25){
        nextBitsSource=0;
      } else if (r<.5) {
        nextBitsSource=29;
      } else if (r<.75) {
        nextBitsSource=11;
      } else {
        nextBitsSource=31;
      }} else {
      switch(c){
        case ' ': nextBitsSource=0; break;
        case 'A': case 'a': nextBitsSource=1; break;
        case 'B': case 'b': nextBitsSource=2; break;
        case 'C': case 'c': nextBitsSource=3; break;
        case 'D': case 'd': nextBitsSource=4; break;
        case 'E': case 'e': nextBitsSource=5; break;
        case 'F': case 'f': nextBitsSource=6; break;
        case 'G': case 'g': nextBitsSource=7; break;
        case 'H': case 'h': nextBitsSource=8; break;
        case 'I': case 'i': nextBitsSource=9; break;
        case 'J': case 'j': nextBitsSource=10; break;
        case 'K': case 'k': nextBitsSource=30; break;
        case 'L': case 'l': nextBitsSource=12; break;
        case 'M': case 'm': nextBitsSource=13; break;
        case 'N': case 'n': nextBitsSource=14; break;
        case 'O': case 'o': nextBitsSource=15; break;
        case 'P': case 'p': nextBitsSource=16; break;
        case 'Q': case 'q': nextBitsSource=17; break;
        case 'R': case 'r': nextBitsSource=18; break;
        case 'S': case 's': nextBitsSource=19; break;
        case 'T': case 't': nextBitsSource=20; break;
        case 'U': case 'u': nextBitsSource=21; break;
        case 'V': case 'v': nextBitsSource=22; break;
        case 'W': case 'w': nextBitsSource=23; break;
```

```java
          case 'X': case 'x': nextBitsSource=24; break;
          case 'Y': case 'y': nextBitsSource=25; break;
          case 'Z': case 'z': nextBitsSource=26; break;
          case '-':nextBitsSource=27;
          default: nextBitsSource=28;
      }
    }
  }


  public boolean nextBit(){
    boolean answer;
    if ((nextBitsSource & 1)!=0){
      answer=true;
    } else {
      answer = false;
    }
    nextBitsPosition++;
    if (nextBitsPosition>=5) {
      textPosition++;

      if (textPosition>=text.length()){
        atTheEndOfBuffer = true;
        loadNextBits(' ');
      } else {
        loadNextBits(text.charAt(textPosition));
      }
    } else {
      nextBitsSource = nextBitsSource>>1;

    }
  /*  if (answer) {
      System.out.print("T");
    } else {
      System.out.print("F");
    } */
    return answer;
  }

  public void startBitSource(){
    textPosition=0;
    text = new StringBuffer("hi mom.");
    loadNextBits(text.charAt(textPosition));
  }
  public void startBitSource(String s){
    textPosition=0;
    text = new StringBuffer(s);
    loadNextBits(text.charAt(textPosition));
  }
}
```

TableSetter Class

```java
import java.io.*;
import java.net.*;
import java.awt.*;
```

```java
public class TableSetter extends Thread{
  boolean tableLoaded=false;
  WordEater we;
  NextWordResponse n;
  VariableNode CurrentVariable;
    // What is currently being parsed.
  VariableNode VariableListRoot=null;
      /// The list of all variables.
  boolean WasThereNoError=true;

  URL base;
    // This must be passed down because
    // only applets can discover their URL base.

  Label announceHere=null;

  public void setAnnounceHere(Label s){
    announceHere=s;
  }

      /* This returns the variable that starts out every
      production. This is just set to be the first one
      alphabetically in the list. It would be possible to
      put some sort of random selection here too if you
      wanted to add an additional signifier that said "I'm
      a good candidate to start a production." */

VariableNode GetStartVariable()  {
  return VariableListRoot;
}

  public boolean loadTable(){
    //This function tries to load the information
    // from the currently opened file into table.
    // Returns true if it succeeds. False if it signals an error.
      boolean looping;

      VariableListRoot = null;
      looping = true;
      while (looping) {
        try {
          sleep(40);
        } catch (InterruptedException e) {
        }
        if (HandleFirst()) {
          looping = HandleProduction();
        } else {
          looping = false;
        }
      }
      BuildBitTable();
      // PrintVariableList(VariableListRoot);
```

```java
      return  WasThereNoError;
    }

public void run(){
  //System.out.println("Starting the run thing.");
  if (announceHere!=null){
    announceHere.setText("Loading Grammar Table. Please Wait.");
  }
    try {
        sleep(40);
      } catch (InterruptedException e) {
      }
  we.initializeScanHashTable();
  we.openGrammarURL("BASE.CFL",base);
      //System.out.println("Opened the grammar thing.");

  loadTable();

  if (announceHere!=null){
    announceHere.setText("Table Loaded. Ready to go.");
  }
  tableLoaded=true;
}

public TableSetter(URL u){
  base=u;
  we= new WordEater();

}

public void AddVariable (VariableNode v ){
  //This adds it to the root.}
    VariableNode previous, node;
  //For scanning along the list.}
    int Relativity;

    node = VariableListRoot;
    previous = null; // Must init it.
    if (VariableListRoot == null) {
    VariableListRoot = v;
    v.setNext(null);
    } else if (node.w1.compareTo(v.w1)>0) {
    VariableListRoot = v;
      v.next = node;
    } else {
    while (node != null ) {
      Relativity = node.w1.compareTo(v.w1);
          if (Relativity<0) {
            previous = node;
            node = node.next;
          } else  if  (Relativity == 0) {
            System.out.println("'"+  v.w1 +"'  has been previously defined.");
        } else {
            previous.setNext(v);
```

```
                    v.setNext(node);
                  node = null;
                v=null;
            }
            }
            if (v != null) {
            previous.setNext(v);
            v.setNext(null);
            }
        }
    }

    /* Looks up the list and finds the variable
    corresponding to it. Note that everything is
    extremely slow to just keep this in a list! */

VariableNode FindVariable(String name){
 VariableNode temp;
   /* Sort of a stunt double for FindVariable. */
 int relativity;
   /* Just for storing the relative differences between strings. */

 temp = VariableListRoot; /* Start at the very beginning. */
 while (temp != null) {
        relativity = name.compareTo(temp.wl);
     if (relativity > 0) {
       temp = temp.next;
     } else {
       if (relativity == 0)
          return temp;
       else
         return null;
       }
     }
   return null;
 }

 public boolean HandleFirst(){
  // The first word in a line must be a variable.
  // This will be used to set up the variable list.

    VariableNode v;
    // This is what is going to get built.}
    NextWordResponse wa,wb;

  boolean answer=true;

   wa = we.nextWord();
   if (wa.stopChar == Globals.EndOfFileSignifier) {
     if (! wa.w.equals(Globals.NullWord)) {
      System.out.println("Unexpected end of the file.");
 }
```

```java
        return false;
      }
      if ((wa.w.equals(Globals.NullWord)) ||
         (wa.w.charAt(0) != Globals.VariableSignifier)) {
       System.out.println("Here's the first char:"+wa.w.charAt(0)+
                          "::"+ Globals.VariableSignifier+"::");
       System.out.println("Expected a variable name at the beginning of the line:");
      } else {
         v=new VariableNode();
         v.setW1(wa.w);
      // Now add it to the list in the right place.}
         AddVariable(v);
         CurrentVariable = v;
      }
      if (wa.stopChar != Globals.EqualityCharacter) {
         do {
             wa = we.nextWord();
         } while ((wa.stopChar == Globals.Space) && (wa.w.equals(Globals.NullWord)));
          if (! wa.w.equals(Globals.NullWord)) {
            System.out.println("The Variable should only be one word. "+ wa.w+" is too
much. Error in line:");
         }
      }
       return true;
      }

    public void  SkipToEnd(){
    // This procedure just keeps hitting NextWord until
    // it hits the double StoppingCharacter, which when
    // I wrote this line was defined to be '//'.
    NextWordResponse wa;
    char previous;
    boolean dontStopNow=true;

    // WasThereNoError := false;

     wa = we.nextWord();
     do {
       previous = wa.stopChar;
       wa = we.nextWord();
       if (wa.stopChar==Globals.EndOfFileSignifier) {
          dontStopNow=false;
       } if ((wa.w.equals(Globals.NullWord))
             && (previous == Globals.StoppingCharacter)
             && (wa.stopChar== Globals.StoppingCharacter)) {
        dontStopNow=false;
       }
     } while (dontStopNow);
    }

/*public double wordToValue(String s){
 double answer = Double.valueOf("0"+s).doubleValue();
 return answer;
}
*/
```

```java
public double wordToValue(String s){
    double answer = 0.0;
    boolean fraction=false;
    int count = 0;
    for (int i=0;i<s.length();i++){
        switch (s.charAt(i)){
            case '0':
                answer=10*answer+0;break;
            case '1':
                answer=10*answer+1;break;
            case '2':
                answer=10*answer+2;break;
            case '3':
                answer=10*answer+3;break;
            case '4':
                answer=10*answer+4;break;
            case '5':
                answer=10*answer+5;break;
            case '6':
                answer=10*answer+6;break;
            case '7':
                answer=10*answer+7;break;
            case '8':
                answer=10*answer+8;break;
            case '9':
                answer=10*answer+9;break;
            case '.':
                fraction = true;break;
        }
        if (fraction) count++;
    }
    for (int i=0;i<count;i++){
        answer=answer/10;
    }
    return answer;
}

public boolean HandleProduction(){
// Keeps Adding Production until it
// encounters a double Stopping Character.

    WordNode    LastAddedWord=null;
    // This is just a place keeper which points
    // to the last word added so the next can
    // be updated when another one is added.
    ProductionNode TheProduction=null;
    //This is where the info goes.
    NextWordResponse wa;
    //For local reasons.

    boolean startedVariables=false;
    //Variables can only come at the end of productions.
    boolean IsError;
    //If there is a problem this get's set to be true.
    boolean answer=true;
```

```java
    do {
      do {
        wa = we.nextWord();
        if (wa.stopChar == Globals.EndOfFileSignifier) {
          if (LastAddedWord != null) {
            System.out.println("Just parsed something left incomplete by the end of
the file:");
            // PrintWordList(LastAddedWord);
            System.out.println("Unexpected end of the file.");
            answer = false;
          }
          return answer;
        }
        if (! wa.w.equals(Globals.NullWord)) {
          if (LastAddedWord == null ) {
          // Start a new production.
            if (wa.w.charAt(0) == Globals.VariableSignifier){
              System.out.println("'The first word of a production, '"+ wa.w+"' cannot
be a variable. Ignoring Production.");
              SkipToEnd();
              wa.stopChar = Globals.StoppingCharacter;
              wa.w = Globals.NullWord;
          } else {
            // System.out.print(":"+wa.w);
            TheProduction = new ProductionNode();
              TheProduction.setNext(CurrentVariable.getProductions());
              CurrentVariable.setProductions(TheProduction);
              // Put it at the beginning of the list...
            LastAddedWord = new WordNode(wa.w);
            TheProduction.setTheWords(LastAddedWord);
            startedVariables = false;
          }
        } else {
            LastAddedWord.setNext(new WordNode(wa.w));
              LastAddedWord = LastAddedWord.getNext();
              if (wa.w.charAt(0) == Globals.VariableSignifier) {
                if (! startedVariables) {
                startedVariables = true;
              }
            } else if (startedVariables) {
            System.out.println("The format of a production is terminal, terminal ...
terminal, variable... varable. A terminal comes before the variable in line:");
            CurrentVariable.productions = null;
            //Clean out this baby to signal a problem.}
            }
          }
        }
        } while (wa.stopChar!= Globals.StoppingCharacter);

      if (LastAddedWord != null) {
      LastAddedWord.next = null;
      LastAddedWord = null;
    }
```

```java
          if (! wa.doubleStop) {
    // At this point a production has been stored away. Now get its probability.}
        wa  = we.nextWord();
          if (wa.stopChar == Globals.EndOfFileSignifier) {
            System.out.println("Unexpected end of the file when looking for a
probability.");
               answer = false;
               return answer;
          }
            //System.out.print(":N:"+wa.w);
            TheProduction.setProbability(wordToValue(wa.w));

    }      else if (wa.stopChar != Globals.StoppingCharacter) {
            wa = we.nextWord();
            System.out.println("The word "'+ wa.w+'" does not belong in the
probability field. ");
    //    write('The error occurs in production:');
     //   PrintWordList(LastAddedWord)
    }
  }
  while ( ! wa.doubleStop);
  return answer;
}

   public BitNode InsertIntoBitList (BitNode node, BitNode ListStart){
    //This is just a temporary procedure
    // that maintains a list of BitNodes Sorted by Probability.
    BitNode Previous, Scanner;
    //For scanning along the list.
   BitNode answer=ListStart;
    if (ListStart ==null) {
      answer = node;
      node.up = null;
    } else if (node.probability <= ListStart.probability) {
      node.up = ListStart;
      answer = node;
    }  else {
      Scanner = ListStart;
      Previous = ListStart;
      while (Scanner != null) {
        if (node.probability > Scanner.probability){
           Previous = Scanner;
           Scanner = Scanner.up;
        } else {
            Previous.up = node;
           node.up = Scanner;
           Scanner = null;
           node = null;// To signal that it was added...
      }
    }
    if (node != null) {
        Previous.up = node;
```

```
            node.up = null;
        }
    }
    return answer;
}

public void BuildBitTable(){
// It is important that there be a tree that
// describes how the bits are assigned to each production.}

    BitNode IntermediateBitList;
    //  This contains the list of bit nodes that
    //  don't have a root. When there is only
    //  one left, then this is crowned king and
    //  assigned to the variable's ItsBitRoot.
    BitNode TempBit;
    // Used in the building.}
    ProductionNode productionList;
    // This is the list of productions that
    // the bit list will be built out of.
    int NextBitNumber;
    // This is used for assigning a unique
    // number to each node.
    VariableNode v;
    // This is so the list can do this
    // for every variable.

    v  = VariableListRoot;
    while (v != null) {
        productionList = v.productions;
        //This is the list.}
        IntermediateBitList = null;
        NextBitNumber = 0;
        while (productionList != null)  {
            TempBit = new BitNode();
            TempBit.setProbability(productionList.probability);
            TempBit.left = null;
            TempBit.right = null;
            TempBit.polarity = true;
            TempBit.bitNumber = -1;
            TempBit.theProductionNode = productionList;

            productionList.itsBit = TempBit;
            IntermediateBitList=InsertIntoBitList(TempBit, IntermediateBitList);
            productionList = productionList.next;
        }
    // Now one bit for each production list;
    // let's start making pairs.
    while (IntermediateBitList.up != null)  {
        //  While there is more than one node in the list.
        TempBit = new BitNode();
        TempBit.setProbability(IntermediateBitList.probability
                            + IntermediateBitList.up.probability);
        TempBit.left = IntermediateBitList;
```

```
        TempBit.right = IntermediateBitList.up;
        TempBit.bitNumber = NextBitNumber++;
        TempBit.polarity = true;
        TempBit.theProductionNode = null;

        IntermediateBitList = IntermediateBitList.up.up;
          // Get Rid of the top two.
        TempBit.left.polarity=false;
          // Flip one. One son should be true and the other false.
        TempBit.left.up = TempBit;
        TempBit.right.up = TempBit;
        IntermediateBitList=InsertIntoBitList(TempBit, IntermediateBitList);
    }
        // There should only be one left at this point.
      v.itsBitRoot = IntermediateBitList;
      IntermediateBitList.up = null;
      v = v.next;
  }
}
}
```

WordEater Class

```java
import java.net.*;
import java.io.*;
public class WordEater {

  URL u;
  URLConnection uc;
  StringBuffer grammarBuffer;
  int grammarBufferPos=0;
  boolean readComplete=false;
  int numCharacters=-1;
    // For reading in the data.

  public final static int spacer=1;
  public final static int normal=2;
  public final static int stopper=3;

  public final static char equalityCharacter='=';
  public final static char stoppingCharacter='/';
  public final static char doubleStopCharacter=(char)(1);
    // This is sent out when a double slash is encountered.

  public int[] scanTable=new int[256];
    // This is a scan table used for parsing.

    public void initializeScanHashTable(){
    // The Scanning Hash Table has 256 entries.
    // They identify a character as either a letter, stop character,
    // a space or a comment.
    int i;
    for (i=14; i<=255; i++){
```

```
      scanTable[i]=normal;
  }
  for (i=0; i<=13; i++){
    scanTable[i]=spacer;
  }

    scanTable[(byte)(equalityCharacter)] = stopper;
     scanTable[(byte)(stoppingCharacter)] = stopper;
     scanTable[(byte)(' ')] = spacer;
}

public  void openGrammarURL(String a, URL u){
  // Takes a URL for a Grammar URL and reads it in line by line.
  // We just
  String line;

  if (a!="") {
        try{
           grammarBuffer = new StringBuffer();
           grammarBufferPos = 0;
           int pos=0;
           int len;
           u= new URL(u,a);
           uc=u.openConnection();
           DataInputStream theHTML = new DataInputStream(uc.getInputStream());
           while ((line= theHTML.readLine()) != null) {
               grammarBuffer.append(line);
             }
           grammarBuffer.append(' ');
        } catch (MalformedURLException e) {
           System.err.println(a+ " is a bad URL.");
           System.err.println(e);
        } catch (IOException e){
           System.err.println("IO Error reading in the data.");
        }
      }
  // System.out.println("Hey, I found it.");
  }
public NextWordResponse nextWord () {
  String answer;
    // What goes back. Null if eof.
  answer = "";
  boolean ds=false;

  while ((grammarBufferPos<grammarBuffer.length())
     && (scanTable[grammarBuffer.charAt(grammarBufferPos)]==spacer)){
    grammarBufferPos++;
  }

  while ((grammarBufferPos<grammarBuffer.length())
     && (scanTable[grammarBuffer.charAt(grammarBufferPos)]==normal)){
    answer=answer+grammarBuffer.charAt(grammarBufferPos++);
  }
  answer=answer+" ";
```

```java
//System.out.println("Found:"+answer+":");


    if (grammarBufferPos>=grammarBuffer.length()){
      return new NextWordResponse(answer,Globals.EndOfFileSignifier,false);
    } else if (scanTable[grammarBuffer.charAt(grammarBufferPos)]==spacer) {
      grammarBufferPos++;
      return new NextWordResponse(answer,' ',false);
    } else {
      if ((scanTable[grammarBuffer.charAt(grammarBufferPos)]==stopper) &&
      (scanTable[grammarBuffer.charAt(grammarBufferPos-1)]==stopper)) {
        ds=true;
      }
      grammarBufferPos++;
      return new NextWordResponse(answer,grammarBuffer.charAt(grammarBufferPos-1),ds);
    }

  }

}
```

Baseball CFG

This appendix contains a sample context-free grammar designed to simulate the voiceover from a baseball game. The grammar is printed in the format required by the program in Appendix A.

Each variable begins with an asterisk. Each production has two components that are broken up by forward slashes. The first part is the mixture of variables and terminals that will replace the variable in question during the production. The second is the weight given to one production in the random selection process. The final production for each variable is ended with a double forward slash.

```
*period = ./1//
*questionmark = ?/1//
*WeatherComment = Hmm . Do you think it will rain ? /.1/
     What are the chances of rain today ? /.1/
     Nice weather as long as it doesn't rain . /.1/
     Well, if rain breaks out it
      will certainly change things . /.1/
     You can really tell the mettle
      of a manager when rain is threatened . /.1//
*BlogsOutfielder = Orville Baskethands /.1/
                Robert Liddlekopf /.1/
                Harrison "Harry" Hanihan /.1//
*BlogsInfielder = Gerry Johnson /.1/
                Lefty Clemson /.1/
                Robby Rawhide /.1/
                Alberto Juan Turbosino /.1//
*BlogsManager = Billy Martin /.1/
                Hanson Haversham /.1//
*BlogsCatcher = Bloaty Von Ripple /.1//
*BlogsPitcher = Mark Markinson /.1/
                Andy Anteriority /.1//
*BlogsPlayer= Orville Baskethands /.1/
             Robert Liddlekopf /.1/
```

```
                    Harrison "Harry" Hanihan /.1/
                    Gerry Johnson /.1/
                    Lefty Clemson /.1/
                    Robby Rawhide /.1/
                    Alberto Juan Turbosino /.1/
                    Bloaty Von Ripple /.1/
                    Mark Markinson /.1/
                    Andy Anteriority /.1//
*WhapperOutfielder = Prince Albert von Carmichael /.1/
                    Parry Posteriority /.1/
                    Herbert Herbertson /.1//
*WhapperInfielder = Johnny Johanesberger /.1/
                    Frank Gavi /.1/
                    Harry Dolcetto /.1/
                    Sal Sauvignon /.1//
*WhapperManager = Bob Von Bittle /.1/
                    Hank Von Bittle /.1//
*WhapperCatcher = Mark Cloud /.1//
*WhapperPitcher = Jerry Johnstone /.1/
                    Albert Ancien-Regime /.1//
*WhapperPlayer = Prince Albert von Carmichael /.1/
                    Parry Posteriority /.1/
                    Herbert Herbertson /.1/
                    Johnny Johanesberger /.1/
                    Frank Gavi /.1/
                    Harry Dolcetto /.1/
                    Sal Sauvignon /.1/
                    Jerry Johnstone /.1/
                    Albert Ancien-Regime /.1/
                    Mark Cloud /.1//
*Announcer= Bob /.1/
            Ted /.1/
            Mike /.1/
            Rich /.1//
*DumbComment = Some kind of Ballplayer, huh ? /.1/
        These guys came to play ball ./.1/
        What a game so far today ./.1/
        How about those players ./.1/
        Got to love baseball ./.1/
        Hey, they're playing the organ ./.1//
*WhapperOutfieldOut = He pops one up into deep left field . /.1/
            He lifts it back toward the wall where it is caught
            by *BlogsOutfielder *period/.1/
            He knocks it into the glove of
             *BlogsOutfielder *period /.1/
            He gets a real piece of it and
             drives it toward the wall
             where it is almost ... Oh My God! ... saved by
             *BlogsOutfielder *period /.1/
            He pops it up to *BlogsOutfielder *period /.2//
*WeirdOutfield = who is too deep to get it. Base hit! /.1/
        who bobbles the catch! /.05/
        who trips on his Nikes! Time for a new sponsor. /.05/
        who loses it in the sun. It drops in the warning track. /.1/
```

```
      whose mind seems lost thinking of investments. He starts
      moving too late! Hit. /.1//
*OutfieldResult = for a double! /.1/ for a stand-up double. /.1/
      for a stand-up double ... wait he's going to stretch
      it for a triple and ... he's safe. /.1/
      to grab another hit . /.1/
      to bump his average up . His salary is up for renegotiation
      this year . /.1//
*WhapperOutfieldHit = knocks it toward *BlogsOutfielder
          *WeirdOutfield /.1/
          line-drives toward the outfield where *BlogsOutfielder
          *WeirdOutfield /.1/
          puts it into the back corner of right field. /.1/
          lifts it over the head of *BlogsOutfielder
          *OutfieldResult /.1/
          drives it into the stands for a home run! /.1/
          lifts it toward heaven ! Home Run !/.1/
          sends it to the man upstairs . Home run !/.1/
          clears the stadium wall . Whoa ! home run !/.1/
          and it's ... La Bomba ! Home Run !/.1//
*BlogsOutfieldHit = knocks it toward *WhapperOutfielder
          *WeirdOutfield /.1/
          line-drives toward the outfield where *WhapperOutfielder
          *WeirdOutfield /.1/
          puts it into the back corner of right field. /.1/
          lifts it over the head of *WhapperOutfielder
          *OutfieldResult /.1/
          drives it into the stands for a home run! /.1/
          lifts it toward heaven ! /.1/
          sends it to the man upstairs . /.1/
          clears the stadium wall . Whoa ! /.1/
          and it's ... La Bomba ! /.1//
*BlogsOutfieldOut = He pops one up into deep left field . /.1/
          He lifts it back toward the wall where it is caught
          by *WhapperOutfielder *period/.1/
          He knocks it into the glove of
           *WhapperOutfielder *period /.1/
          He gets a real piece of it and
           drives it toward the wall
          where it is almost ... Oh My God! ... saved by
          *WhapperOutfielder *period /.1/
          He pops it up to *WhapperOutfielder *period /.2//
*BuntResponseHit = bobbles it ./.1/
      trips on it . /.1/
      scoops it up and realizing that he's too late
      signs it and throws it to a kid in the stands . / .01 /
      gets to, but the throw is ... late! /.1/
      grabs it, but the throw is too low ! /.1//
*BuntResponseOut = grabs it and makes the out . /.1/
      scoops it up and tosses him out . /.1/
      passes it on to first . /.1/
      nabs it ./.1/
      picks it up, laughs and tosses him out . /.1/
      grabs it and tosses it to first . /.1//
```

```
*InfieldLocation = first base /.1/
                   second base/.1/
                   the pitcher's mound/.1/
              short stop/.1/
              third base/.1/
              third base foul line/.1/
              first base foul line/.1//
*BadThrow = in the dirt ./.1/
            digging a ditch ./.1/
            too wide ./.1/
            into the umpire's head ! Whoa ! /.01/
            way too wide to make the tag ./.1/
          too high ./.1/
          too high to make the tag ./.1/
          in his chest ./.1//
*BaseReached = for a single ./.1/
              for a double ./.1/
              for a triple ./.1/
              for an easy single ...
                Wait he's going to try for more and the
                throw is *BadThrow /.1/
                for a stand-up double. But is that young
                Charlie Hustle going to wait ?
                No . He's going for the triple and
                the throw is *BadThrow /.1/
                for a close single and the the toss is
                *BadThrow /.1/
                for a dangerous double and the
                throw is *BadThrow /.1//
*HitResult = into short right field *BaseReached /.1/
        into short left field *BaseReached / .1/
        and the ball bounces past the shortstop *BaseReached/.1/
        and the ball takes a weird bounce at *InfieldLocation
        *BaseReached /.1/
        and the ball flies down the foul line .
         It stays fair *BaseReached /.1/
        in the short left field where it
        bounces into the stands . Ground rule
        double for the young man ./.1//
*WhapperInfieldHit = He tries to bunt, and *BlogsInfielder
          *BuntResponseHit /.1/
          He knocks it down the line between
          the legs of *BlogsInfielder *period /.1/
          He waps it into the shortstop's glove,
          but he can't control it . Safe at first . /.1/
          He lifts it over the head of *BlogsInfielder
           *HitResult /.1/
          The batter gets a piece of it *HitResult /.1/
          It's contact time  *HitResult /.1/
          Nice hit *HitResult /.1/
          Whoa ! That swing was on the money  *HitResult /.1/
          Nice job *HitResult /.1/
          Great hit *HitResult /.1/
          Super looper for a hit ./.1/
```

```
              He knocks a line-drive into the head of
                 *BlogsInfielder /.05//
*WhapperInfieldOut = He grounds out to *BlogsInfielder *period/.1/
              He pops it up to *BlogsInfielder *period/.1/
              He tries to bunt, and *BlogsInfielder
                 *BuntResponseOut /.1/
              He knocks a line-drive into the glove of
                 *BlogsInfielder /.1/
              He knocks an easy bouncer to *BlogsInfielder
                 *period /.1/
              He bounces one off the ground into the
                 first-baseman's glove ./ .1//
*BlogsInfieldHit = He tries to bunt, and *WhapperInfielder
              *BuntResponseHit /.1/
              He knocks it down the line between the legs of
                 *WhapperInfielder *period /.1/
              He lifts it over the head of *WhapperInfielder
                 *HitResult /.1/
              The batter gets a piece of it *HitResult /.1/
              Nice job *HitResult /.1/
              Great hit *HitResult /.1/
              It's contact time  *HitResult /.1/
              Nice hit *HitResult /.1/
              He waps it into the shortstop's glove,
              but he can't control it . Safe at first . /.1/
              Whoa ! That swing was on the money  *HitResult /.1/
              Super looper for a hit ./.1/
              He knocks a line-drive into the head of
                 *WhapperInfielder /.05//
*BlogsInfieldOut =
              He grounds out to *WhapperInfielder *period/.1/
              He  knocks a line-drive into the glove of
                 *WhapperInfielder /.1/
              He tries to bunt, and
                 *WhapperInfielder *BuntResponseOut /.1/
              He knocks an easy bouncer to
                 *WhapperInfielder *period /.1/
              He  pops it up to *WhapperInfielder *period/.1/
              He  bounces one off the ground into the
                 first-baseman's glove ./ .1//
*EndOfInning =
        Well, that's the end of their chances in
        this inning, *Announcer *period *Commercial/.1/
        No more at bats left in this inning. *Commercial /.1/
        The inning's over . Some kind of ballplayer, huh,
         *Announcer *period *Commercial /.1/
        Yowza! End of the inning . Hard to imagine
         life without baseball? Right, *Announcer
         *questionmark *Commercial /.1/
        That inning proves why baseball is
        the nation's game . *Commercial /.1//
*Return = Back to the game, *Announcer *period /.1/
        We now return to the game between the Blogs and
         the Whappers . /.1/
```

```
       Now back to the game . /.1/
       Just wanted to say thanks to our sponsors for
       those great messages . /.1//
*Commercial = This is WZZZ-TV bringing you the ballgame!
         *BeerCom *BeerCom
         *CarCom *Return/.1/
       We're here at WZZZ-TV bringing you the ballgame!
       *CarCom *CarCom
       *BeerCom *Return /.1/
       This is the WZZZ baseball network!
       *BeerCom *CarCom *CarCom
       *BeerCom *BeerCom *Return /.1/
       Now a message from our sponsors. *BeerCom *BeerCom
       *BeerCom *Return /.1/
       Now a very special message from our sponsors.
       *CarCom *BeerCom
       *CarCom *Return /.1//
*BeerOne = Imported Name . / .1/
           Imported Label ./.1/
           Imported Aura . /.1/
           Imported Concept ./.1/
           Imported Danger Warning in German . /.1//
*BeerTwo = American Taste . /.1/
           American Flavor . /.1/
           Clean American Taste ./.1/
           No Overly-flavorful Assault on your Tongue . /.1//
*BeerThree = fermentation is natural ? /.1/
        yeast is one of Mother Nature's Creatures ? /.1/
        yeast is a beast of Nature ? /.1/
        beer is natural ? /.1//
*BeerFour = Support Mother Nature and drink. /.1/
        Go green and support the environment . /.1/
        Support Natural Things and drink another ! /.1/
        Live a natural life and drink some more ! /.1//
*BeerCom = St. Belch . *BeerOne *BeerTwo /.1/
      Longing for adventure ? Open a bottle of St. Belch ! /.1/
      Did you know that *BeerThree *BeerFour /.1/
      Hey! *BeerFour /.1/
      Man comes up to Bob on the street and says,
      "Want a St. Belch ?" and his friend says, "Sure, I'm a man
      and I love to drink ." It turns out the Man was the head of
      a Fortune 500 company looking for a new Chairman of the
      Board of Directors . He hires Bob for
      $350,000 a year . /.1/
      St. Belch Beer: Especially tailored for men who watch
      ballgames . /.1//
*Car = Chevy Cordon-Bleu / .1 /
         Chevy Coq-au-Van /.1/
         Ford Platzer /.1/
         Ford Wienerschnitzel / .1/
         Chevy Choucroute /.1/
         Ford Weisswurst /.1/
         Chevy Crouton /.1//
```

```
*CarFoodAdj = Scrumptious ! /.1/
                Delicious ! /.1/
                Mouth-watering !/.1/
                Tasty! /.1/ Rich ! /.1/
                Sinfully Sweet ! /.1/
                Organically Grown/.1//
*CarRegAdj = Fast ! / .1/
                Bold ! / .1/ Ambitious ! /.1/
                Nocturnal ! /.1/ Adiabatic ! /.1/
                Anti-establishmentary !/.1/ Plenary ! /.1/
                Easy ! /.1/ Capitalistic ! /.1//
*CarLink = That's the new /.1/
            What a car, the /.1/
            How about that /.1/
            That's it. The new /.1//
*CarCom = Wow! *CarFoodAdj *CarRegAdj *CarFoodAdj *CarRegAdj
    *CarLink *Car *period /.1/
    What do these words mean? *CarRegAdj *CarFoodAdj *CarRegAdj
    *CarLink *Car *period /.1/
    Yowza! *CarFoodAdj *CarRegAdj *CarFoodAdj *CarLink
    *Car *period /.1/
    The way to a man's heart is through his stomach. Ergo we want
    you to think of our car as *CarFoodAdj *period *CarLink *Car
    *period /.1//
*PlateAction = comes to the plate ./.1/
        swings the bat to get ready and enters
          the batter's box ./.1/
        adjusts the cup and enters the batter's box ./.1/
        swings the baseball bat to stretch and enters
          the batter's box ./.1//
*NewBlogsBatter = Now, *BlogsPlayer *PlateAction /.1/
        Here we go. *BlogsPlayer *PlateAction /.1/
        The pitcher spits. *BlogsPlayer *PlateAction /.1/
        The crowd is nervous. *BlogsPlayer *PlateAction /.1//
*NewWhapperBatter = Now, *WhapperPlayer *PlateAction /.1/
        Here we go. *WhapperPlayer *PlateAction /.1/
        The pitcher spits. *WhapperPlayer *PlateAction /.1/
        The crowd is nervous. *WhapperPlayer *PlateAction /.1//
*Strike = Swings and misses ! /.1/ Fans the air ! /.1/
    No contact in Mudsville ! /.1/
    Whooooosh! Strike ! /.1/ Steeeriiiiike ! /.1/
    No wood on that one . /.1/
    He just watched it go by ./.1/ No contact on that one . /.1/
    Nothing on that one ./.1/
    He swings for the stands, but no contact . /.1//
*BallCall = Ball ./.1/ The umpire calls a ball ./.1/
    Definitely a ball ./.1/
    No strike this time . /.1//
*Ball = High and outside . *BallCall /.1/
        Whoa, he's brushing him back . *BallCall/.1/
        Short and away . *BallCall/.1/
        OOOh, that's almost in the dirt . *BallCall/.1/
        No good. *BallCall /.1/
        High and too inside. *BallCall/.1//
```

```
*ThePitchType = a curveball ./.1/
     a flaming fastball ./.1/
     a screaming fast ball ./.1/
     a change-up ./.1/
     a knuckler ./.1/
     what looks like a spitball ./.1/
     a spitter ./.1/
     a split-fingered fastball ./.1/ a rising fast ball ./.1/
     a fast one that looked like it was rising ./.1/
     a screamer ./.1/
     a torcher ./.1/ a blaster ./.1/a knuckleball ./.1/
     a breaking curve ./.1/
     a slow change-up ./.1/ a toaster ./.1/
     a rattling corkscrew ./.1/
     a curvaceous beauty ./.1/
     a wobbling knuckler ./.1/
     a bouncing knuckleball ./.1/
     a smoking gun ./.1/ a blazing comet ./.1/
     a rattler ./.1/
     a heckraising fastball ./.1/
     a rocket booster ./.1/ a fastball with wings ./.1//
*ThePitch = Checks first base . Nothing. Winds up and pitches
     *ThePitchType /.1/
     Here's the pitch . It's *ThePitchType /.1/
     Here comes the pitch . It's *ThePitchType/.1/
     He's winding up . What *ThePitchType /.1/
     And the next pitch is *ThePitchType /.1/
     The next pitch is *ThePitchType /.1/
     A full windup and it's *ThePitchType /.1/
     He's uncorking *ThePitchType /.1/
     It's *ThePitchType /.1//
*StrikeOut = He's out of there . / .1/
     Strike out . He's swinging at the umpire .
     The umpire reconsiders until
     the security guards arrive . /.1/
     Strike out ! /.1/
     Yes. Another wiffer ./.1/
     Strike out . There goes his batting average . /.1/
     Strike three . Some sports writer figured that
     each strike cost the ball
     player about $1,530 at today's average rate . /.1/
     The last strike . Only three chances in this game . /.1//
*BlogsHit = Here we go. *ThePitch *Ball *ThePitch *BlogsInfieldHit /.1/
     Okay. *ThePitch *Ball *Strike *Strike *BlogsInfieldHit /.1/
     The crowd is roaring . *ThePitch *Ball *ThePitch
      *Ball *BlogsOutfieldHit/.1/
     Here we go . *Ball *ThePitch *Ball
      *ThePitch *BlogsOutfieldHit /.1/
     Here's the pitch . *Strike *ThePitch *Strike *ThePitch
      *BlogsOutfieldHit /.1//
*BlogsOut = Yeah. *ThePitch *Strike *ThePitch *Strike *ThePitch
     *Strike *StrikeOut /.1/
     The pitcher is winding up to throw. *Strike
      *ThePitch *Ball *ThePitch
```

```
      *BlogsInfieldOut /.1/
      Here's the fastball . *BlogsInfieldOut /.1/
      He's trying the curveball . *BlogsOutfieldOut /.1/
      Love that baseball game. *ThePitch *Ball
       *ThePitch *Ball *ThePitch
      *Strike *ThePitch *Strike *ThePitch *Strike *StrikeOut /.1/
      Another fastball . *Strike *ThePitch
       *BlogsOutfieldOut /.1//
*WhapperHit = Here we go. *ThePitch *Ball *ThePitch
      *WhapperInfieldHit /.1/
      Okay. *ThePitch *Ball *Strike *Strike *WhapperInfieldHit /.1/
      The crowd is roaring . *ThePitch *Ball *ThePitch
      *Ball *WhapperOutfieldHit/.1/
      Here we go . *Ball *ThePitch *Ball
       *ThePitch *WhapperOutfieldHit /.1/
      Here's the pitch . *Strike *ThePitch
       *Strike *ThePitch
       *WhapperOutfieldHit /.1//
*WhapperOut = Yeah. *ThePitch *Strike *ThePitch *Strike
      *ThePitch *Strike *StrikeOut /.1/
      The pitcher is winding up to throw. *Strike *ThePitch *Ball
      *ThePitch
      *WhapperInfieldOut /.1/
      Here's the fastball . *WhapperInfieldOut /.1/
      He's trying the curveball . *WhapperOutfieldOut /.1/
      Love that baseball game. *ThePitch *Ball
       *ThePitch *Ball *ThePitch
       *Strike *ThePitch *Strike *ThePitch
       *Strike *StrikeOut /.1/
      Another fastball . *Strike *ThePitch
       *WhapperOutfieldOut /.1//
*OneWhapperLeft = Only one more out needed . *NewWhapperBatter
     *WhapperHit
     *OneWhapperLeft /.1/
     The Blogs only need to get one more out . *NewWhapperBatter
     *WhapperHit *OneWhapperLeft /.1/
     The Blogs are trying for the last out .  *NewWhapperBatter
     *WhapperHit *OneWhapperLeft /.1/
     The crowd is looking for the last out !   *NewWhapperBatter
     *WhapperHit *OneWhapperLeft /.1/
     Before the last out, let's get a message in from our
     sponsors. *Commercial    *NewWhapperBatter
     *WhapperHit *OneWhapperLeft /.05/
     Only one out left.   *NewWhapperBatter
     *WhapperHit *OneWhapperLeft /.1/
     Yup, the Blogs only need to get one more out.
      *NewWhapperBatter
     *WhapperHit *OneWhapperLeft /.1/
     Hey, two down, one to go. *NewWhapperBatter
     *WhapperOut *EndOfInning /.1/
     Only one chance left for the Whappers . *NewWhapperBatter
     *WhapperOut *EndOfInning /.1/
     Two big outs for the Blogs. *NewWhapperBatter
     *WhapperOut *EndOfInning /.1/
```

```
          What a game ! *NewWhapperBatter
          *WhapperOut *EndOfInning /.1/
          These are the times that make baseball special .
            *NewWhapperBatter
          *WhapperOut *EndOfInning /.1/
          One more thin out stands between the Whappers and the end of
          this inning's chances . *NewWhapperBatter
          *WhapperOut *EndOfInning /.1/
          Yowza. *NewWhapperBatter
          *WhapperOut *EndOfInning /.1/
          He's hefting some wood . *NewWhapperBatter
          *WhapperOut *EndOfInning /.1//
*TwoWhappersLeft = Hey, one down, two to go.   *NewWhapperBatter
          *WhapperHit *TwoWhappersLeft /.1/
          The Whappers have only one out .          *NewWhapperBatter
          *WhapperHit *TwoWhappersLeft /.1/
          One down, two to go.  *NewWhapperBatter
          *WhapperHit *TwoWhappersLeft /.1/
          Only one out into the inning.  *NewWhapperBatter
          *WhapperHit *TwoWhappersLeft /.1/
          One out against the Whappers.  *NewWhapperBatter
          *WhapperHit *TwoWhappersLeft /.1/
          The Blogs need two more outs. *NewWhapperBatter
          *WhapperOut *OneWhapperLeft /.1/
          Two more outs to go. *NewWhapperBatter
          *WhapperOut *OneWhapperLeft /.1/
          The Whappers have two outs to spare. *NewWhapperBatter
          *WhapperOut *OneWhapperLeft /.1/
          Plenty of room. Only one out. *NewWhapperBatter
          *WhapperOut *OneWhapperLeft /.1/
          How about those ballplayers.
           One out so far. *NewWhapperBatter
          *WhapperOut *OneWhapperLeft /.1/
          Some day for a ballgame, huh? *WeatherComment *NewWhapperBatter
          *WhapperOut *OneWhapperLeft /.1/
          Wow. Only one out. *NewWhapperBatter
          *WhapperOut *OneWhapperLeft /.1/
          Somekind of ballgame, huh, *Announcer
           *questionmark *NewWhapperBatter
          *WhapperOut *OneWhapperLeft /.1/
          Yup, got to love this stadium. *NewWhapperBatter
           *WhapperOut *OneWhapperLeft /.1//
 *ThreeWhappersLeft = No damage yet, *Announcer *period
            *NewWhapperBatter
          *WhapperHit *ThreeWhappersLeft /.1/
          No outs . *NewWhapperBatter
          *WhapperHit *ThreeWhappersLeft /.1/
          No outs yet for the Whappers . *NewWhapperBatter
          *WhapperHit *ThreeWhappersLeft /.1/
          No trouble yet . *NewWhapperBatter
          *WhapperHit *ThreeWhappersLeft /.1/
          Check out the Whappers' mascot a Weasel.
           He's biting a 7-year old !
           Some kind of mascot, huh, *Announcer *questionmark
```

```
        *NewWhapperBatter
    *WhapperOut *TwoWhappersLeft /.01/
    Nobody out yet . *NewWhapperBatter
    *WhapperOut *TwoWhappersLeft /.1/
    Whappers are up with no outs . *NewWhapperBatter
    *WhapperOut *TwoWhappersLeft /.1/
    Nothing's happened yet to the Whappers . *NewWhapperBatter
    *WhapperOut *TwoWhappersLeft /.1/
    No outs yet . *NewWhapperBatter
    *WhapperOut *TwoWhappersLeft /.1/
    What a day . *NewWhapperBatter
    *WhapperOut *TwoWhappersLeft /.1/
    I could go for a home run,
     *Announcer *period *NewWhapperBatter
    *WhapperOut *TwoWhappersLeft /.1/
    Baseball and Apple Pie . *NewWhapperBatter
    *WhapperOut *TwoWhappersLeft /.1/
    Yup. *DumbComment *NewWhapperBatter
    *WhapperOut *TwoWhappersLeft /.2//
*OneBlogsLeft = Only one more out needed . *NewBlogsBatter *BlogsHit
    *OneBlogsLeft /.1/
    The Whappers only need to get one more out . *NewBlogsBatter
    *BlogsHit *OneBlogsLeft /.1/
    The Whappers are trying for the last out .  *NewBlogsBatter
    *BlogsHit *OneBlogsLeft /.1/
    The crowd is looking for the last out !   *NewBlogsBatter
    *BlogsHit *OneBlogsLeft /.1/
    Before the last out, let's get a message in from our
    sponsors. *Commercial    *NewBlogsBatter
    *BlogsHit *OneBlogsLeft /.05/
    Only one out left.   *NewBlogsBatter
    *BlogsHit *OneBlogsLeft /.1/
    Yup, the Whappers only need to get
     one more out.   *NewBlogsBatter
    *BlogsHit *OneBlogsLeft /.1/
    Hey, two down, one to go. *NewBlogsBatter
    *BlogsOut *EndOfInning /.1/
    Only one chance left for the Blogs . *NewBlogsBatter
    *BlogsOut *EndOfInning /.1/
    Two big outs for the Whappers. *NewBlogsBatter
    *BlogsOut *EndOfInning /.1/
    What a game ! *NewBlogsBatter
    *BlogsOut *EndOfInning /.1/
    These are the times that make baseball
     special . *NewBlogsBatter
    *BlogsOut *EndOfInning /.1/
    One more thin out stands between the Blogs and the end of
    this inning's chances . *NewBlogsBatter
    *BlogsOut *EndOfInning /.1/
    Yowza. *NewBlogsBatter
    *BlogsOut *EndOfInning /.1/
    He's hefting some wood . *NewBlogsBatter
    *BlogsOut *EndOfInning /.1//
```

```
*TwoBlogsLeft = Hey, one down, two to go.     *NewBlogsBatter
        *BlogsHit *TwoBlogsLeft /.1/
        The Blogs have only one out .        *NewBlogsBatter
        *BlogsHit *TwoBlogsLeft /.1/
        One down, two to go.  *NewBlogsBatter
        *BlogsHit *TwoBlogsLeft /.1/
        Only one out into the inning.  *NewBlogsBatter
        *BlogsHit *TwoBlogsLeft /.1/
        One out against the Blogs.  *NewBlogsBatter
        *BlogsHit *TwoBlogsLeft /.1/
        The Whappers need two more outs. *NewBlogsBatter
        *BlogsOut *OneBlogsLeft /.1/
        Two more outs to go. *NewBlogsBatter
        *BlogsOut *OneBlogsLeft /.1/
        The Blogs have two outs to spare. *NewBlogsBatter
        *BlogsOut *OneBlogsLeft /.1/
        Plenty of room. Only one out. *NewBlogsBatter
        *BlogsOut *OneBlogsLeft /.1/
        How about those ballplayers. One out so
         far. *NewBlogsBatter
        *BlogsOut *OneBlogsLeft /.1/
        Some day for a ballgame, huh?
         *WeatherComment *NewBlogsBatter
        *BlogsOut *OneBlogsLeft /.1/
        Wow. Only one out. *NewBlogsBatter
        *BlogsOut *OneBlogsLeft /.1/
        Some kind of ballgame, huh, *Announcer
         *questionmark *NewBlogsBatter
        *BlogsOut *OneBlogsLeft /.1/
        Yup, got to love this stadium. *NewBlogsBatter
        *BlogsOut *OneBlogsLeft /.1//
*ThreeBlogsLeft = No damage yet, *Announcer *period *NewBlogsBatter
        *BlogsHit *ThreeBlogsLeft /.1/
        No outs . *NewBlogsBatter
        *BlogsHit *ThreeBlogsLeft /.1/
        No outs yet for the Blogs . *NewBlogsBatter
        *BlogsHit *ThreeBlogsLeft /.1/
        No trouble yet . *NewBlogsBatter
        *BlogsHit *ThreeBlogsLeft /.1/
        Check out the Blogs' Weasel. He's biting a 7-year old !
        Some kind of mascot, huh, *Announcer *questionmark
        *NewBlogsBatter
        *BlogsOut *TwoBlogsLeft /.01/
        Nobody out yet . *NewBlogsBatter
        *BlogsOut *TwoBlogsLeft /.1/
        Blogs are up with no outs . *NewBlogsBatter
        *BlogsOut *TwoBlogsLeft /.1/
        Nothing's happened yet to the Blogs .
         *NewBlogsBatter
        *BlogsOut *TwoBlogsLeft /.1/
        No outs yet . *NewBlogsBatter
        *BlogsOut *TwoBlogsLeft /.1/
        What a day . *NewBlogsBatter
        *BlogsOut *TwoBlogsLeft /.1/
```

```
            I could go for a home run,
             *Announcer *period *NewBlogsBatter
            *BlogsOut *TwoBlogsLeft /.1/
            Baseball and Apple Pie . *NewBlogsBatter
            *BlogsOut *TwoBlogsLeft /.1/
            Yup.   *DumbComment *NewBlogsBatter
            *BlogsOut *TwoBlogsLeft /.2//
*BlogsHalf = Time for the Blogs to see what they can do .
            *ThreeBlogsLeft /.1/
            It's the Blogs' turn at bat . *ThreeBlogsLeft /.1/
            Bottom half of the inning .
            The Blogs must prove their stuff .
            *ThreeBlogsLeft /.1/
            Let's get on with the inning . *ThreeBlogsLeft /.1/
            Well, another half of the inning, *Announcer *period
            *DumbComment
            *ThreeBlogsLeft /.1/
            Let's get moving  with this half of the inning, but first,
            another message from our sponsors . *Commercial
            *ThreeBlogsLeft /.1//
*WhapperHalf = Top of the inning. *ThreeWhappersLeft /.1/
        Another new inning . Ain't life great, *Announcer *questionmark
        *ThreeWhappersLeft /.1/
        Start of another inning . *ThreeWhappersLeft /.1/
        Yes, it's time for the Whappers to lead off the inning .
        *ThreeWhappersLeft /.1/
        Time for another inning . The Whappers will be leading off .
        *ThreeWhappersLeft /.1//
*NineInnings = Let's get going ! *WhapperHalf *BlogsHalf
            *WhapperHalf *BlogsHalf
            *WhapperHalf *BlogsHalf
            *WhapperHalf *BlogsHalf
            *WhapperHalf *BlogsHalf
            *WhapperHalf *BlogsHalf
            *WhapperHalf *BlogsHalf
            *WhapperHalf *BlogsHalf
            *WhapperHalf *BlogsHalf /.1/
            The Umpire throws out the ball . *WhapperHalf *BlogsHalf
            *WhapperHalf *BlogsHalf
            *WhapperHalf *BlogsHalf
            *WhapperHalf *BlogsHalf
            *WhapperHalf *BlogsHalf
            *WhapperHalf *BlogsHalf
            *WhapperHalf *BlogsHalf
            *WhapperHalf *BlogsHalf
            *WhapperHalf *BlogsHalf /.1/
            Play ball ! *WhapperHalf *BlogsHalf
            *WhapperHalf *BlogsHalf
            *WhapperHalf *BlogsHalf
            *WhapperHalf *BlogsHalf
            *WhapperHalf *BlogsHalf
            *WhapperHalf *BlogsHalf
            *WhapperHalf *BlogsHalf
            *WhapperHalf *BlogsHalf
```

```
            *WhapperHalf *BlogsHalf /.1/
            It's a fine day for a game . *WhapperHalf *BlogsHalf
            *WhapperHalf *BlogsHalf
            *WhapperHalf *BlogsHalf
            *WhapperHalf *BlogsHalf
            *WhapperHalf *BlogsHalf
            *WhapperHalf *BlogsHalf
            *WhapperHalf *BlogsHalf
            *WhapperHalf *BlogsHalf
            *WhapperHalf *BlogsHalf /.1//
*OneInning = Let's get going !
              *WhapperHalf *BlogsHalf/.1/
              The umpire throws out the ball .
              *WhapperHalf *BlogsHalf/.1/
              Play ball ! *WhapperHalf *BlogsHalf/.1/
            It's a fine day for a game . *WhapperHalf
              *BlogsHalf/.1//
*AAStart = Well Bob, welcome to yet another game between the
    Whappers and the Blogs here in scenic downtown
    Blovonia . I think it is fair to say that there is
    plenty of BlogFever brewing in the stands as the
    hometown comes out to root for its favorites .
     *OneInning /.1/
    It's time for another game between the Whappers and
    the Blogs in scenic downtown Blovonia . I've just got
    to say that the Blog fans have come to support their
    team and rant and rave . *OneInning /.1//
```

Reversible Grammar Generator

Here is the LISP source code for the reversible grammar generator described in Chapter 8. It was written for XLISP, a version of LISP that can be found in many archives throughout the Internet. The structure is very basic, however, and so it should be useful.

```
;;; Reversible Grammar Machine
;;; Copyright 1996 Peter Wayner
;;; All rights reserved.
;;; Permission is granted to copy the file as long as no charge
;;; is made. Permission is also granted to make changes as long as
;;; the author of the changes is indicated in the comments.
;;;
;;;
;;; This code is designed to implement a reversible computer. If
;;; it can be reversed, then the data used to create it can be extracted.
;;;
;;;
;;; constant-list contains constant values that are left unchanged.
;;; var-list contains variables that are changed by the person.
;;; procedure-list includes all of the procedures that are executed.

(setq constant-list
        '(
                (c1 ("Bob " "Ray " "Loraine " "Carol " "Gilda "))
                (c2 ("Lucy " "Ricky " "Ethel " "Fred "))
                (c3 ("Fred " "Barney " "Wilma " "Betty "))

                (v1 ("considered insubordination "
                    "redirected commercial inertia "
                    "smiled knowingly "
                    "reundeconstructed comedic intent "
                    "ladled laugh slop "
                    "insinuated a nervous satire "))
```

```
                (cs 1) (ci 1) (ce 5)

        ))

(setq var-list
        '(
                (va 3) (vb 4) (vc 45) (vd 1) (ve 41) (vf 11)
        ))

(setq procedure-list
        '(
                (main ((add va vb)
                        (whi vf cs ci (gt vf ce) t1)
                        (chz (c1)) (chz (c1 c2)) (add vb vc)
                        (chz (v1)) (chz (c2 c3)) (mul vc va)
                        (chz (v1))))

                (t1          ((add va vb)
                        ;;(add vb vc) (mul vd va) (mul vc vd)
                        (if (gt va vb) b1 b2) (add vc vd) (add vd ve)))

                (b1   ((mul vd ve) (mul vb ve)))
                (b2   ((add vd vc) (add vc ve)))
        )
)

(defun Record-Error (error-string)
;;; If something goes wrong, this indicates the error.
        (print error-string))

(defun eval-tag (tag)
;;; Finds the right match for the tag.
        (setq temp nil)
        (setq temp (assoc tag constant-list))
        (cond ((not temp)
                        (setq temp (assoc tag var-list))))
        (cond ((not temp)
                        (Record-Error (concatenate 'string
                                                "Missing Tag:"
                                                (symbol-name tag)))))
        temp)
(defun test-change (tag new-value)
        (setq temp (assoc tag var-list))
        (cond (temp
                        (setf (cdr temp) new-value))))


(defun do-addition (tag1 tag2)
;; Add tag2+tag1 and store in tag1
        (setq temp (eval-tag tag2))
        (setq temp2 (assoc tag1 var-list))
        (cond ((not temp2)
                        (Record-Error (concatenate 'string
                                                "Missing Variable Tag:"
                                                (symbol-name tag1)))))
```

```
                           ((and temp (numberp (cadr temp))
                                      (numberp (cadr temp2)))
                               (setf (cdr temp2)
                                     (list (+ (cadr temp) (cadr temp2)))))
                          (t
              (Record-Error (concatenate 'string
                                         "Problems with adding:"
                                         (symbol-name tag1)
                                         (symbol-name tag2))))))


(defun do-subtraction (tag1 tag2)
;; Subtract tag1-tag2 and store in tag1
       (setq temp2 (eval-tag tag2))
       (setq temp1 (assoc tag1 var-list))
       (cond ((not temp1)
                     (Record-Error (concatenate 'string
                                                "Missing Variable Tag:"
                                                (symbol-name tag1))))
                ((and temp2 (numberp (cadr temp1))
                             (numberp (cadr temp2)))
                       (setf (cdr temp1)
                             (list (- (cadr temp1) (cadr temp2)))))
                (t
                  (Record-Error (concatenate 'string
                                             "Problems with subtracting:"
                                             (symbol-name tag1)
                                             (symbol-name tag2))))))


(defun do-multiplication (tag1 tag2)
;; Add tag2+tag1 and store in tag1
       (setq temp (eval-tag tag2))
       (setq temp2 (assoc tag1 var-list))
       (cond ((not temp2)
                     (Record-Error (concatenate 'string
                                                "Missing Variable Tag:"
                                                (symbol-name tag1))))
                ((and temp (numberp (cadr temp))
                             (numberp (cadr temp2)))
                 (cond ((or (= 0 (cadr temp2)) (= 0 (cadr temp)))
                               (Record-Error (concatenate 'string
                                             "Multiply by zero error: "
                                             (symbol-name tag1) " by "
                                             (symbol-name tag2))))
                          (t
                           (setf (cdr temp2)
                           (list (* (cadr temp) (cadr temp2)))))))
                (t
                  (Record-Error (concatenate 'string
                                             "Problems with multiplying: "
                                             (symbol-name tag1) " by "
                                             (symbol-name tag2))))))


(defun do-division (tag1 tag2)
;; Add tag2+tag1 and store in tag1
```

```
        (setq temp (eval-tag tag2))
        (setq temp2 (assoc tag1 var-list))
        (cond ((not temp2)
                    (Record-Error (concatenate 'string
                                        "Missing Variable Tag: "
                                        (symbol-name tag1))))
               ((and temp (numberp (cadr temp))
                        (numberp (cadr temp2)))
                  (cond ((or (= 0 (cadr temp2)) (= 0 (cadr temp)))
                            (Record-Error (concatenate 'string
                                        "Divide by zero error: "
                                        (symbol-name tag1) " by "
                                        (symbol-name tag2))))
                         (t
                          (setf (cdr temp2)
                          (list (/ (cadr temp2) (cadr temp)))))))
               (t
                 (Record-Error (concatenate 'string
                                    "Problems with Dividing: "
                                    (symbol-name tag1) " by "
                                    (symbol-name tag2)))))))
(defun Do-Swap (var1 var2)
;;; Swap the values stored here.
        (setq temp (cdr (assoc var1 var-list)))
        (setf (cdr (assoc var1 var-list)) (cdr (assoc var2 var-list)))
        (setf (cdr (assoc var2 var-list)) temp))


;;;;;;;;;;;;;;;;;;;;;;;;;;;;;;;;;;;;;;;;
;;;; Eval Operations
;;;; Used to step through lists of ops.
(defvar Forbidden-List nil)
;;; This is the list of variables that can't be touched.
;;; This feature is used when progressing down paths chosen
;;; by an if statement. If the variable used to choose the
;;; path is changed along the path, then bad things can happen
;;; and the world can't be reversed correctly.
(defun check-if-test (if-test)
;;; Evaluate test.
 (setq ans nil)
   (setq side1 (cadr (eval-tag (cadr if-test))))
   (setq side2 (cadr (eval-tag (caddr if-test))))
   (cond ((eq (car if-test) 'lt) ;; less-than
         (setq ans (< side1 side2)))
        ((eq (car if-test) 'gt) ;; greater-than
         (setq ans (> side1 side2)))
            ((eq (car if-test) 'eq) ;; equal-than
         (setq ans (= side1 side2)))
        ((eq (car if-test) 'le) ;; less-or-equal
         (setq ans (<= side1 side2)))
        ((eq (car if-test) 'ge) ;; greater-or-equal
         (setq ans (>= side1 side2)))
        (t
         (Report-Error (concatenate 'string
                    "Error evaluating If-then:"
```

```
                              (symbol-name (car if-test))))))
          ans)
(defun Do-If (if-test if-clause else-clause)
;;; Evaluate an if-then branch.
;;;
;;; This current version can CREATE bugs when
;;; the program takes one path and then CHANGES
;;; the value of one of the variables used to
;;; choose the path. Reversing this is filled
;;; with ambiguities and is prohibited.
;;;
        (setq ans (check-if-test if-test))
      (setq Forbidden-List (append
                            (list (cadr if-test) (caddr if-test))
                            Forbidden-List))
     (cond (ans
            (Do-Op-List if-clause))
           (t
            (Do-Op-List else-clause)))
     (setq Forbidden-List (cdr (cdr Forbidden-List)))
     )
(defun Do-Reverse-If (if-test if-clause else-clause)
;;; Evaluate an if-then branch.
;;; This goes backward. I could remove some of this
;;; extra code by embedding a strategic reverse, but I
;;; think it might be better to build the separate code
;;; now.
   (setq ans (check-if-test if-test))
   (cond (debug
          (print (list "In Rev If. Taking path:" ans))))
   (cond (ans
          (Do-Reverse-Op-List if-clause))
         (t
          (Do-Reverse-Op-List else-clause))))
(defun Do-While (var init-const inc-const if-test branch)
;;; A while operation looks like this: '(whi var init-const inc-const
;;; test branch). var is the variable that is used to keep track of the
;;; progress of the loop. The first pass through the loop, var is set
;;; to init-const. Then if-test is checked. When it becomes true, then
;;; the loop breaks out. Otherwise the branch is executed. Then
;;; inc-const is ADDed to var and we go back to if-test.
;;;
;;; There is something irreversible going on here!!! The prior contents
;;; of var are destroyed. This is only bad if you use the variable
;;; before it gets to the loop. The solution is to use a new variable
;;; for each loop. This is, alas, a requirement. Something must keep
;;; track of the number of passes through the loop.
        (setf (cdr (assoc var var-list))
              (append (cdr (assoc init-const constant-list)) nil))
        (setq ans (check-if-test if-test))
        (do () (ans)
           (Do-Op-List branch)
                (Do-Addition var inc-const)
                (setq ans (check-if-test if-test)))
)
```

```lisp
(defun Do-Reverse-While (var init-const inc-const if-test branch)
;;; The while loop run in reverse!
        (do () ((= (cadr (assoc var var-list))
                   (cadr (assoc init-const constant-list))))
           (Do-Reverse-Op-List branch)
               (Do-Subtraction var inc-const)
         )
)


(defun Do-Operation (op)
;;; An operation looks like this: '(op var1 var2)
;;; Do the right thing.
        (cond (debug
                        (print (list "Doing Op:" op))))

        (cond ((member (cadr op) Forbidden-List)
              (Record-Error (concatenate 'string
                        "Attempt to influence op on Forbidden List:"
                        (symbol-name (cadr op)))))

              ((eq (car op) 'add)
               (Do-Addition (cadr op) (caddr op)))
              ((eq (car op) 'sub)
               (Do-Subtraction (cadr op) (caddr op)))
              ((eq (car op) 'mul)
               (Do-Multiplication (cadr op) (caddr op)))
              ((eq (car op) 'div)
               (Do-Division (cadr op) (caddr op)))
              ((eq (car op) 'swp)
               (Do-Swap (cadr op) (caddr op)))
              ((eq (car op) 'if)
               (Do-If (cadr op) (caddr op) (cadddr op)))
              ((eq (car op) 'chz)
               (Do-Choice (cadr op)))
              ((eq (car op) 'whi)
               (Do-While (cadr op) (caddr op) (cadddr op)
                        (nth 4 op) (nth 5 op)))
                 (t
                        (Record-Error (concatenate 'string
                                "Undefined Operation: "
                                (symbol-name (car op)))))))
        ))
(defun Do-Reverse-Operation (op)
;;; An operation looks like this: '(op var1 var2)
;;; Do the right thing.
        (cond (debug
                        (print (list "Doing Reverse Op:" op))))
        (cond ((eq (car op) 'add)
              (Do-Subtraction (cadr op) (caddr op)))
              ((eq (car op) 'sub)
               (Do-Addition (cadr op) (caddr op)))
              ((eq (car op) 'mul)
```

```
                (Do-Division (cadr op) (caddr op)))
              ((eq (car op) 'div)
               (Do-Multiplication (cadr op) (caddr op)))
              ((eq (car op) 'swp)
               (Do-Swap (cadr op) (caddr op)))
              ((eq (car op) 'if)
               (Do-Reverse-If (cadr op) (caddr op) (cadddr op)))
                  ((eq (car op) 'chz)
               (Do-Reverse-Choice (cadr op)))
              ((eq (car op) 'whi)
               (Do-Reverse-While (cadr op)
                                 (caddr op) (cadddr op)
                                 (nth 4 op) (nth 5 op)))

              (t
                        (Record-Error (concatenate 'string
                                      "Undefined Operation: "
                                      (symbol-name (car op)))))
          ))

(defun Do-Op-List (ls)
;;; Look up the tag in the procedure list.
    (do ((l (cadr (assoc ls procedure-list)) (cdr l)))
        ((null l))
      (Do-Operation (car l))))
(defun Do-Reverse-Op-List (ls)
;;; Look up the tag in the procedure list.
    (do ((l (reverse (cadr (assoc ls procedure-list))) (cdr l)))
        ((null l))
      (Do-Reverse-Operation (car l))))
;;;;;;;;;;;;;;;;;;;;;;;;;;;;;;;;;;;;;;;;;
;;;; File Operations
;;;; Used for going backward.
(defvar Backwards-Text nil)
;;; This file is where the text will be removed.
(defvar Backwards-Buffer "")
;;; This holds the reversed version of the string.
(defun File-To-String (name)
;;; Reads in a file. Might be faster if AREF is used
;;; to index the string.
        (setq temp "")
        (setq Backwards-Text
          (open name))
        (setq a (read-char backwards-text))
        (do ()
             ((null (peek-char 'nil backwards-text)))
           (setq temp (concatenate 'string temp (string a)))
           (setq a (read-char backwards-text)))
        (setq temp (concatenate 'string temp (string a)))
        (close backwards-text)
        temp)

(defun File-To-BitString (name)
;;; Reads in a file and converts it into a bit string.
```

```
;;; Might be faster if AREF is used
;;; to index the string.
;;;
;;; This is a really inefficient way to do things. It
;;; is silly to load an entire file into memory. But,
;;; I'm getting lazy in these days of cheap memory.
;;; If this isn't changed to buffer things, then I
;;; didn't have time to be efficient.
        (setq temp "")
        (setq temp-file
          (open name))
        (setq a (read-byte temp-file))
        (do ()
                ((null (peek-char 'nil temp-file)))
            (setq temp (concatenate 'string temp (Num-To-Bits a 256)))
            (setq a (read-byte temp-file)))
        (close temp-file)
        (setq BitSourcePointer 0)
        (setq MaxBitSourcePointer (length temp))
        temp)

(defun BitString-To-File (str name)
;;; Take a bit string and convert it into bytes.
        (setq out-file (open name :direction :io ))
        (setq tot-bytes (ceiling (/ (length str) 8)))
        (setq ptr 0)
        (do ((i 0 (+ 1 i))) ((= tot-bytes i))
                (setq cur-byte 0)
                (setq cur-value 128)
                (do ((j 0 (+ 1 j))) ((= j 8))
                        (cond ((eq (aref str ptr) #)
                                (setq cur-byte (+ cur-byte cur-value))))
                        (setq cur-value (/ cur-value 2))
                        (setq ptr (+ 1 ptr)))
                (write-byte cur-byte out-file))
        (close out-file))


(defun write-string (st stream)
  (do ((i 0 (+ 1 i))) ((= i (length st)))
    (write-char (aref st i) stream)))


;;;;;;;;;;;;;;;;;;;;;;;;;;;;;;;;;;
;;;; Choose Operation and its reverse.
(defun Flatten-Choice-List (ls)
;;; ls is presented as a list of variables and constants.
;;; Some of these variables and constants might be lists
;;; of variables and constants.
;;; This current version is NOT recursive. It can
;;; handle ONE level of indirection.
        (setq answer nil)
        (do ((l ls (cdr l))) ((null l))
          (cond ((stringp (car l))
                  (setq answer (cons (car l) answer)))
```

```
                  ((atom (car l))
                   (setq answer (append
                                      (cadr (eval-tag (car l)))
                                      answer)))
                  (t
                   (Report-Error (concatenate 'string
                                    "Something wrong with: "
                                    (symbol-name (car l))))))))
          answer)
(defun Stringify (i)
;;; Make sure that i is a string.
          (cond ((listp i)
                 (Flatten-Choice-List i))
                ((stringp i) i)
                ((integerp i)
                 (format nil "~d" i))
                ((floatp i)
                 (format nil "~g" i))
                ((rationalp i)
                 (format nil "~d" i))))

(defun Find-Reverse-Choice (ls)
;;; Scans down ls and looks for the first complete match with
;;; the Backwards-Buffer.
          (setq answer nil)
          (setq counter 0)
          (do ((l (car ls) (cdr l)))
                  ((null l))
            (setq ttt (reverse (car l)))
            (cond ((string= ttt Backwards-Buffer :end2 (length ttt))
                     ;;; We have a match!!!
                     (setq answer counter)
                     (setq l nil)
                     )
                  (t (setq counter (+ 1 counter)))))
          answer)

(defun Num-To-Bits (value top)
;;; There are top choices between 0 and top-1.
;;; Find the bits to this value.
          (setq bot 0)
          (setq top (- top 1))
          (setq answer "")
          (do ()
                  ((= top bot))
          ;; (print (list bot top))
            (cond ((> value (+ (/  (- top bot) 2) bot))
                     (setq bot (ceiling (+ (/ (+ 1 (- top bot)) 2) bot)))
                     (setq answer (concatenate 'string answer "1")))
                  (t
                   (setq top (floor (+ (/  (- top bot) 2) bot)))
                   (setq answer (concatenate 'string answer "0")))))
          answer)
```

```
(defun test-num (j)
  (setq answer nil)
  (do ((i 0 (+ 1 i))) ((= i j))
    (setq temp (num-to-bits i j))
    (cond ((not (= i (Bits-To-Num temp j)))
          (print (list i (Bits-To-Num temp j) j))))))
(defun Bits-To-Num (bits top )
;;; Reverse Num-To-Bits.
;;; This consumes bits from the BitFile.
;;; Choose them at random if the file is finished.
    (setq bot 0)
    (setq top (- top 1))
        (do ((i BitSourcePointer (+ 1 i))) ((= top bot))
            (setq BitSourcePointer (+ 1 BitSourcePointer))
            (cond (debug
                    (print (list "taking bit: " (aref bits i) i))))
                (cond ((> BitSourcePointer MaxBitSourcePointer)
                        (cond ((= 0 (rand 1))
                        (setq top (floor (+ (/  (- top bot) 2) bot))))
                        (t
                        (setq bot
                        (ceiling (+ (/ (+ 1 (- top bot)) 2) bot))))))

                ((eq (aref bits i) #)
                (setq top (floor (+ (/  (- top bot) 2) bot))))
                (t
                (setq bot (ceiling (+ (/ (+ 1 (- top bot)) 2) bot))))))
      bot)
(defun Old-Bits-To-Num (bits top )
;;; Reverse Num-To-Bits.
    (setq bot 0)
    (setq top (- top 1))
        (do ((i 0 (+ 1 i))) ((= top bot))
                (cond ((eq (aref bits i) #)
                (setq top (floor (+ (/  (- top bot) 2) bot))))
                (t
                (setq bot (ceiling (+ (/ (+ 1 (- top bot)) 2) bot))))))
      bot)
(defun Do-Choice (ls)
;;; This is presented by the Do-Op function.
;;; Make a choice and spit it out the right stream.
  (setq temp (Flatten-Choice-List ls))
  (setq t1 (Bits-To-Num BitSource (length temp)))
  (cond (debug
          (print (list "In Do Choice with choice:" t1))))
    (write-string
      (nth t1
           temp)
      output-stream))
(defun Do-Reverse-Choice (ls)
;;; Reverse the effects of do-choice.
  (setq answer nil)
  (setq temp (Flatten-Choice-List ls))
  (setq len (length temp))
```

```
   (setq counter 0)
   (do ((l temp (cdr l))) ((null l))
      (cond (debug
             (print (list "Checking :" counter (reverse (car l))))))
      (cond ((string= TextSource (reverse (car l))
                     :start1 TextSourcePointer
                     :end1 (+ TextSourcePointer (length (car l))))
             (setq answer
                   (Num-To-Bits counter len))
             (setq TextSourcePointer
                   (+ TextSourcePointer (length (car l))))
             (setq l nil)))
      (setq counter (+ 1 counter)))
   (cond (debug
          (print (list "Found bits: " (reverse answer)))))
   (setq output-bits (concatenate 'string output-bits (reverse answer)))
   answer)
;;;;;;;;;;;;;;;;;;;;;;;;;;;;;;;;
;;;; Main Code Section
;;;;
;;;;    This is the mastermind.
;;;;    It must open up the correct files and start processing.
;;;;
(defun Encode (In-Data-Name Out-Text-Name &optional (Grammar-File nil))
;;; Encode information so it ends up in a funky grammar file.
      (cond (Grammar-File
             (load Grammar-File))) ;;; If Grammar-File is declared,
                                   ;;; then load more information.
      (setq BitSource (File-To-BitString In-Data-Name))
      (setq output-stream (open Out-Text-Name
                                :direction :output
                                :if-does-not-exist :create))
   (setq Forbidden-List nil)
      (Do-Op-List 'main)
      (close output-stream))
(defun Decode (In-Data-Name Out-Text-Name &optional (Grammar-File nil))
;;; Decode information so it comes out in the correct format.
      (cond (Grammar-File
             (load Grammar-File))) ;;; If Grammar-File is declared,
                                   ;;; then load more information.
      (setq TextSource (reverse (File-To-String In-Data-Name)))
      (setq output-bits "")
      (setq TextSourcePointer 0)
      (Do-Reverse-Op-List 'main)
      (BitString-To-File output-bits Out-Text-Name)
)
```

Software

Many useful programs can be found in Internet archives. Some of the better ones include the following:

- *http://www.stegoarchive.com*
- *http://crypto.radiusnet.net/archive*
- *http://www.cl.cam.ac.uk/~fapp2/steganography*
- *http://www.geocities.com/Paris/9955/priv.html*
- *http://www.student.seas.gwu.edu/~sowers/digwat.html*
- *http://www.isse.gmu.edu/~njohnson/Steganography*
- *http://www.watermarkingworld.org*
- *http://www.funet.fi/pub/crypt/steganography*
- *http://glu.freeservers.com/stegano.htm*

Specific software packages available on the Internet are listed here.

http://www.stego.com   Romana Machado distributes the Java version of her Stego and EzStego software from here. This cross-platform tool hides information in the least significant bit of an image *after* the colors in the image are sorted. This usually works quite well, but there can be some inconsistencies. See Sections 9.2 and 17.4. The software is distributed with the GNU Public License.

http://wwwrn.inf.tu-dresden.de/~westfeld/f5.html   Offers the F5 software used for hiding information in JPEG images and includes a number of enhancements designed to avoid steganalytic techniques discovered by the creator, Andreas Westfeld [Wes01, WP99].

http://www.mcdonald.org.uk/StegFS   The source for the Steganographic File System described in Section 4.4. This software works well with Linux file systems and can probably be extended to any other file systems with some work. It is released under the GNU GPL.

http://www.smalleranimals.com/stash.htm   The StashIt software hides data in the least significant bits of images with five different techniques. There is no charge for the software.

http://www.darkside.com.au/snow   The Snow software developed by Matthew Kwan will insert extra spaces at the end of each line. Three bits are encoded in each line by adding between 0 and 7 spaces that are ignored by most display programs including Web browsers.

ftp://ftp.csua.berkeley.edu/pub/cypherpunks/steganography/ mandelSteg1.0.tor.Z   The MandelSteg software hides information in the least significant bit of an image of the Mandelbrot set. The set can be synthesized for any set of coordinates in the plane with 7 bits of accuracy. The last bit is the message.

http://www.stella-steganography.de   The Stella (Steganography Exploration Lab) software is both a tool for hiding information in bitmaps and a lab for exploring how hidden the information may be. The software includes a number of different tools for taking apart the images to see the effects.

http://www.darkside.com.au/gifshuffle   The GifShuffle program written by Matthew Kwan hides information in the ordering of the palette of an image. If there are $n!$ different ways to arrange n objects, then $\log_2(n!)$ bits can be hidden in the choice of which sorting to choose. GifShuffle hides 209 bytes in the way that it selects 256 colors.

http://glu.freeservers.com/sgpo.htm   David Glaude and Didier Barzin created this program (SteganoGifPaletteOrder) that hides information in the permutation of the colors in the GIF palette in the same manner as GifShuffle.

http://www.steganos.com   Steganos sells a suite of security products that includes The Safe, a "hard drive that disappears at the click of a button."

http://www.tiac.net/users/korejwa/jsteg.htm   Offers the JSteg software enhanced with a Windows shell.

http://linux01.gwdg.de/~alatham/stego.html   The JPHide and JPSeek programs written by Allan Latham hide information in the JPEG coefficients using classical algorithms. The software keeps track of the change in the statistical profile of the coefficients to help you avoid steganalysis. (See Chapter 17.)

http://www.compris.com/subitext   Compris sells TextHide, a software program that hides information by changing the structure of sentences. That is, sentences are changed to hide information. The text should, in theory, say the same thing after the extra information is inserted.

http://www.ctgi.net/nicetext   Mark Chapman created NiceText as his Master's thesis project during his time at the University of Wisconsin studying with George Davida. The software assembles a dictionary and classifies words to make it possible to approximate styles while also hiding information in text [CD97].

http://www.datamark-tech.com   DataMark Technologies sells four programs using steganography. One offers watermarking, one embeds raw information, one adds a digital signature to an image, and one builds a "safe."

http://www.stealthencrypt.com   Stealth Encrypt bundles a steganography wizard with its security suite.

http://www.heinz-repp.onlinehome.de/Hide4PGP.htm   Hide4PGP stores data in the least significant bits of either BMP or WAV files. It's a small, free program.

http://www.blindside.co.uk   Blindside hides information in bitmapped images after using a proprietary encryption algorithm for extra protection.

http://steghide.sourceforge.net   The Steghide software is a GPL-protected package started by Stefan Hetzl for hiding information in the least significant bits of images (BMPs) or sound files (WAV or AU).

http://www.brasil.terravista.pt/Jenipabu/2571/e_hip.htm   Hide In Picture stores information in the least significant bits of image files.

http://www.intar.com/ITP/itpinfo.htm   In The Picture hides information in 4-bit, 8-bit, and 24-bit images. The software can also store multiple files protected with different passwords.

http://sourceforge.net/projects/mixmaster   Mixmaster is an excellent set of tools for running and using anonymous remailers.

ftp://idea.sec.dsi.unimi.it/pub/security/crypt/code/s-tools4.zip Andrew Brown wrote S-Tools, one of the first programs for hiding information in image and sound files.

http://www.neobytesolutions.com/invsecr/index.htm   Invisible Secrets is a shareware program for storing information in the usual places. It is a well-designed and highly polished program. A version supported by banner ads is also available.

http://www.neobytesolutions.com/invsecr/index.htm   S-Mail hides information in x86 executable files (.exe or .dll). The programs still work after the information is inserted.

http://www.camouflagesoftware.co.uk   Camouflage is a basic tool for compressing, encrypting, and then appending the information to the end of a file. The information isn't inserted steganographically into the actual data, it's just stuck at the end. This is often good enough and it is guaranteed not to leave any distortion to the cover file.

http://wbstego.wbailer.com   wbStego is a polished, professional tool for hiding information in sound, image, and text formats. The latest version can also store them in Adobe PDF files in order to help establish ownership.

http://www.scramdisk.clara.net   If you want to hide information in a scrambled directory on your hard drive, Scramdisk provides the mechanism.

http://www.cl.cam.ac.uk/~fapp2/steganography/mp3stego   Fabien A. P. Petitcolas created MP3Stego for hiding information in the very popular MP3 files. The mechanism tweaks the parity of some of the quantized coefficients chosen using a random number generator [AP98].

http://www.outguess.org   Niels Provos built the Outguess system to hide information in JPEG files without distorting the statistical profile. He also distributes the StegDetect program, which will detect distortions in other steganographic systems.

http://www.psionic.com/papers/covert   Psionic Software created this package for hiding information in the redundant or optional bits of the TCP/IP headers (the IP packet identification field, the TCP initial sequence number field, and the TCP acknowledged sequence number field).

ftp://ftp.funet.fi/pub/crypt/steganography/PGM.stealth.c.gz
PGMStealth hides data in the least significant bits of PGM files on UNIX boxes.

ftp://ftp.funet.fi/pub/crypt/steganography/piilo061195.tar.gz
Piilo hides data in the least significant bits of PGM files on UNIX boxes.

http://www.cl.cam.ac.uk/~fapp2/watermarking/stirmark   The Stirmark software helps test watermark or image steganographic methods by scrambling the images in subtle ways. The software treats the image like a rubber sheet by stretching some parts, blurring other parts, destroying some parts, and even duplicating small parts. The meddling is controlled with parameters so watermark creators can make claims like, "This software resists Stirmark at settings up to 1.5."

Further Readings

This book is quite incomplete because it only offers the reader an introduction to many of the topics. Other topics are simply left out because of time and space constraints. This section is intended to offer some suggestions for further reading and exploration.

A good place to begin is with history. David Kahn's *Codebreakers* is an excellent survey of the history of cryptology [Kah67]. There are numerous descriptions of steganographic solutions like secret inks and microdots. More recent histories are published in *Cryptologia*.

There are also a number of other good books on the subject. Stefan Katzenbeisser and Fabien Petitcolas edited a collection of essays from the leading researchers entitled *Information Hiding Techniques for Steganography and Digital Watermarking* [SKE00]. Neil F. Johnson, Zoran Duric, and Sushil Jajodia's recent addition, *Information Hiding: Steganography and Watermarking*, is the first part of a series [JDJ01]. Ross Anderson's general survey, *Security Engineering*, also includes some information on steganography and watermarking [And01].

Some of the best material can be found, in its original form, in the Proceedings of the Information Hiding Workshop. There have been four conferences, and more are scheduled.

Other more specific information can be found in these areas.

Error-Correcting Codes. Chapter 3 in this book cannot do justice to the wide field. There are many different types of codes with different applications. Some of the better introductions are [LJ83] and [Ara88]. There are many others.

Compression Algorithms. Compression continues to be a hot topic, and many of the latest books are no longer current. The best solution is to combine books like [Bar88, BS88] with papers from the proceedings from academic conferences like [Kom95]. I also wrote an introductory book on compression recently [Way99].

Subliminal Channels.   This idea is not covered in the book, but it may be of interest to many readers. Much of the work in the area was done by Gus Simmons, who discovered that many digital signature algorithms had a secret channel that could be exploited to send an extra message [Sim84, Sim85, Sim86, Sim93, Sim94]. This is pretty easy to understand in the abstract. Many of the algorithms like the El Gamal signature scheme [ElG85] or the Digital Signature Algorithm [NCSC93] create a new digital signature at random. Many different valid signatures exist, and the algorithm simply picks one at random. It is still virtually impossible for someone without the secret key to generate one, but the algorithms were intended to offer authentication without secrecy.

Imagine that you want to send a 1-bit message to someone. The only encryption software you can use is a DSA signature, which is not designed to hide secrets. You could simply send along a happy message and keep recomputing the digital signature of this message until the last bit is the bit of your message. Eventually, you should find one because the algorithm chooses among signatures at random.

This abstract technique only shows how to send one bit. There are many extra bits available for use, and the papers describe how to do the mathematics and exploit this channel.

The algorithms form an important example for political discussions about cryptography. The U.S. government would like to allow people to use authentication, but they would like to restrict the use of secrecy-preserving encryption. Algorithms such as the DSA appear to be perfect compromises. The existence of subliminal channels, however, shows how the current algorithms are not a perfect compromise.[1]

Covert Channels.   This is, in many ways, just an older term for the same techniques used in this book. The classic example comes from operating system design: imagine that you run a computer system that has an operating system that is supposed to be secure. That means the OS can keep information from traveling between two users. Obviously, you can implement such an OS by shut-

---

[1]They may be a perfectly adequate practical compromise because implementing the software to use this additional channel is time consuming.

ting down services like file copying or electronic mail. It is not clear, however, that you can completely eliminate every way of communicating.

The simplest example for sending a message is to tie up some shared resource like a printer. If you want to send a 1 to a friend, then you print a file at 12:05 and tie up the printer. If you want to send a 0, then you print the file at 12:30. The other person checks the availability of the printer. This may not be a fast method, but it could work. The speed of the channel depends upon the shared system resources and the accuracy of detection. Obviously, one way to defend against covert channels is to create timing errors, but then that just creates other problems.

Some beginning sources are [NCSC93, PN93, MM92].

Digital Cash. There are many different ways to exchange money over digital wires, but some of the most interesting systems offer complete anonymity. People are able to spend their money without fear of records being kept. This is a fairly neat trick because digital cash must be counterfeit-resistant. Paper cash achieves this goal when it is printed with a sophisticated press. Digital copies, on the other hand, are easy to make. If people can copy files of numbers meant to represent cash, then anonymity would seem to allow people the freedom to counterfeit without being caught.

The cleverest schemes involve a complicated spending system that forces the spender to reveal part of his or her identity. If the spender tries to use a bill twice, enough of the identity should be revealed to expose the criminal.

Anonymous Voting. People often want to cast their votes anonymously because this can prevent coercion. Paper ballots are generally successful if no one checks the ballot before the voter enters the box. Providing the same accountability and security is no simple feat.

K. Sako and J. Kilian [SK95], for instance, modified the Mixmaster protocol described in Chapter 10 to provide a simple way for people to cast their vote. Each person can check the tally and compare their vote to the recorded vote to guarantee that the election was fair. Other systems include [BY86, Boy90, FOO93, CC96].

Finally, newer and better papers can be found through electronic paper archives such as the CiteSeer system run by NEC (*http://citeseer.nj.nec.com*). This is an invaluable source of knowledge.

Bibliography

[Age95]   National Security Agency. N.S.A. press release: Venona documents released. Technical report, National Security Agency, July 1995.

[AHU83]   A. V. Aho, J. E. Hopcroft, and J. D. Ullman. *Data Structures and Algorithms*. Addison-Wesley, Reading, MA, 1983.

[AK91]   Dana Angluin and Michael Kharitonov. When won't membership queries help? In *Proceedings of the Twenty-Third Annual ACM Symposium on Theory of Computing*, pages 444–454. ACM Press, 1991.

[And01]   Ross J. Anderson. *Security Engineering: A Guide to Building Dependable Distributed Systems*. John Wiley and Sons, New York, 2001.

[ANS98]   Ross Anderson, Roger Needham, and Adi Shamir. The steganographic file system. In *IWIH: International Workshop on Information Hiding*, 1998.

[AP98]   Ross Anderson and Fabien Petitcolas. The limits of steganography. *IEEE Journal on Selected Areas in Communications*, pages 474–481, May 1998.

[Ara88]   Benjamin Arazi. *A Commonsense Approach to the Theory of Error Correcting Codes*. MIT Press, Cambridge, MA, 1988.

[ARC+01]   Mikhail Atallah, Victor Raskin, Michael Crogan, Cristian Hempelmann, Florian Kerschbaum, Dina Mohamed, and Sanket Naik. Natural language watermarking: Design, analysis and a proof-of-concept. In *Fourth Information Hiding Workshop*, 2001.

[Are00]   S. Areepongsa, N. Kaewkamnerd, Y. F. Syed, and K. R. Rao. Exploring steganography for low bit rate wavelet based coder in image retrieval system. In *Proceedings of TENCOM '00 3*, Kuala Lumpur, Malaysia, September 2000.

[Aur95]   Tuomas Aura. Invisible communication. Technical report, Helsinki University of Technology, November 1995.

[Bar88]   Michael F. Barnsley. Fractal modelling of real world images. In Heinz-Otto Peitgen and Dietmar Saupe, editors, *The Science of Fractal Images*, Chapter 5, pages 219–239. Springer-Verlag, 1988.

[Bar93]   Michael F. Barnsley. *Fractals Everywhere*. 2nd edition. Academic Press, Cambridge, MA, 1993.

[BB00]   Mihir Bellare and Alexandra Boldyreva. The security of chaffing and winnowing. In *Lecture Notes in Computer Science, ASIACRYPT*, 1976: 517–530. Springer-Verlag, 2000.

[BBWBG98]   S. Blackburn, S. Blake-Wilson, M. Burmester, and S. Galbraith. Shared generation of shared RSA keys. CORR98-19, Department of Combinatorics and Optimization, University of Waterloo, Canada, 1998.

[BF97]   D. Boneh and M. Franklin. Efficient generation of shared RSA keys. *Lecture Notes in Computer Science, CRYPTO '97*, 1294: 425–439, 1997.

[BFHMV84]   I. F. Blake, R. Fuji-Hara, R. C. Mullin, and S. A. Vanstone. Computing logarithms in finite fields of characteristic two. *SIAM Journal on Algebraic Discrete Methods*, 5, 1984.

[BGML96]   Walter Bender, D. Gruhl, N. Morimoto, and A. Lu. Techniques for data hiding. *IBM Systems Journal*, 35(3): 313. 1996.

[BH92]   M. Barnsley and L. Hurd. *Fractal Image Compression*. AK Peters, Ltd., Wellesley, MA, 1992.

[BJNW57]   F. P. Brooks, A. L. Hopkins Jr., Peter G. Neumann, and W. V. Wright. An experiment in musical composition. *IRE Transactions on Electronic Computers*. EC-6(3), September 1957.

[BL85]   Charles Bennett and Rolf Landauer. The fundamental physical limits of computation. *Scientific American*, pages 48–56, July 1985.

[BLMO94]   J. Brassil, S. Low, N. Maxemchuk, and L. O'Gorman. Electronic marking and identification techniques to discourage document copying. In *Proceedings of IEEE Infocom 94*, pages 1278–1287, 1994.

[BLMO95]   Jack Brassil, Steve Low, Nicholas Maxemchuk, and Larry O'Gorman. Hiding information in document images. In *Proceedings of the 1995 Conference on Information Sciences and Systems*, March 1995.

[Blu82]   M. Blum. Coin flipping by telephone: A protocol for solving impossible problems. *Proceedings of the 24th IEEE Computer Conference (CompCon)*, 1982.

[BMS01]   Adam Back, Ulf Moeller, and Anton Stiglic. Traffic analysis attacks and trade-offs in anonymity providing systems. In *Fourth Information Hiding Workshop*, pages 257–269, 2001.

[BO96]   Jack Brassil and Larry O'Gorman. Watermarking document images with bounding box expansion. In *Information Hiding, Lecture Notes of Computer Science (1174)*. Springer-Verlag, New York, Heidelberg, 1996.

[Boy90]   C. Boyd. A new multiple key cipher and an improved voting scheme. In *Advances in Cryptology—EUROCRYPT '89 Proceedings*. Springer-Verlag, 1990.

[Bra93]   S. A. Brands. An efficient off-line electronic cash system based on the representation problem. Technical Report CSR9323, Computer Science Department, Centrum voor Wiskunde en Informatica, Amsterdam, March 1993.

[Bra95a]   Stefan A. Brands. *Rethinking Public Key Infrastructure and Digital Certificates—Building in Privacy*. Ph.D. thesis, Amsterdam, 1995.

[Bra95b]   Stefan A. Brands. Secret-key certificates. Technical Report CS-R9510, Centrum voor Wiskunde en Informatica, Amsterdam, 1995.

[Bri82]   E. F. Brickell. A fast modular multiplication algorithm with applications to two key cryptography. In *Advances in Cryptology: Proceedings of Crypto 82*. Plenum Press, 1982.

[BS88]   Michael F. Barnsley and Alan D. Sloan. A better way to compress images. *Byte Magazine*, pages 215–223, January 1988.

[BS95]   D. Boneh and J. Shaw. Collusion-secure fingerprinting for digital data. In *15th Annual International Cryptology Conference*, number 963, pages 452–465, Santa Barbara, CA, 1995.

[BS99]   R. W. Buccigrossi and E. P. Simoncelli. Image compression via joint statistical characterization in the wavelet domain. *IEEE Transactions on Image Processing*, 8(12): 1688–1701. 1999.

[BY86]   J. C. Benaloh and M. Yung. Distributing the power of government to enhance the privacy of voters. *Proceedings of the 5th ACM Symposium on the Principles in Distributed Computing*, 1986.

[CC96]   Lorrie Cranor and R. Cytron. Design and implementation of a practical security-conscious electronic polling system. Technical Report WUCS-96-02, Washington University Department of Computer Science, St. Louis, 1996.

[CD97]   Mark Chapman and George Davida. Hiding the hidden: A software system for concealing ciphertext as innocuous text. In *International Conference on Information and Computer Security (ICICS '97)*, Beijing, P.R. China, November 1997.

[Cha81]   D. Chaum. Untraceable electronic mail, return addresses, and digital pseudonyms. *Communications of the ACM*, 24(2), February 1981.

[Cha95a]   David Charlap. The BMP file format, Part i. *Dr. Dobbs Journal*, March 1995.

[Cha95b]   David Charlap. The BMP file format, Part ii. *Dr. Dobbs Journal*, April 1995.

[CKLS96]   Ingemar Cox, Joe Kilian, Tom Leighton, and Talal Shamoon. A secure, robust watermark for multimedia. In *Information Hiding, Lecture Notes of Computer Science (1174)*. Springer-Verlag, New York, Heidelberg, 1996.

[Cla83]   F. Clarke. *Optimization and Nonsmooth Analysis*. John Wiley, New York, 1983.

[Cla99]   Ian Clarke. A distributed decentralised information storage and retrieval system. Department of Combinatorics and Optimization, University of Waterloo, 1999.

[CM58]   Noam Chomsky and G. A. Miller. Finite state languages. *Information and Control*, 1: 91–112. 1958.

[CM97]   Ingemar J. Cox and Matt L. Miller. A review of watermarking and the importance of perceptual modeling. In *Proceedings of Electronic Imaging '97*, February 1997.

[CM98]   J. Camenisch and M. Michels. A group signature scheme with improved efficiency. In *ASIACRYPT: Advances in Cryptology—ASIACRYPT: International Conference on the Theory and Application of Cryptology*. LNCS, Springer-Verlag, 1998.

[CMB01]   Ingemar J. Cox, Matthew L. Miller, and Jeffrey A. Bloom. *Digital Watermarking*. Morgan Kaufmann, San Fransisco, CA, 2001.

[CSWH00]   I. Clarke, O. Sandberg, B. Wiley, and T. Hong. Freenet: A distributed anonymous information storage and retrieval system. In *Proceedings of the ICSI Workshop on Design Issues in Anonymity and Unobservability*, Berkeley, CA, 2000.

[CW93]   K. W. Campbell and M. J. Wiener. DES is not a group. In *Advances in Cryptology—CRYPTO '92 Proceedings*. Springer-Verlag, 1993.

[DF00]   D. M. Roger Dingledine and Michael J. Freedman. The Free Haven project: Distributed anonymous storage service. In *Proceedings of the Workshop on Design Issues in Anonymity and Unobservability*, July 2000.

[DR00]   Joan Daemen and Vincent Rijmen. The block cipher Rijndael, pages 288–296. Springer-Verlag, 2000.

[DR01]   Joan Daemen and Vincent Rijmen. Rijndael, the advanced encryption standard. *Dr. Dobb's Journal*, 26(3): 137–139, March 2001.

[DIF76a]   W. Diffie and M. E. Hellman. Multiuser cryptographic techniques. In *Proceedings of AFIPS National Computer Conference*, 1976.

[DIF76b]   W. Diffie and M. E. Hellman. New directions in cryptography. *IEEE Transactions on Information Theory*, IT-22(6), November 1976.

[ElG85]   T. El Gamal. A public-key cryptosystem and a signature scheme based on discrete logarithms. In *Advances in Cryptology: Proceedings of CRYPTO 84*. Springer-Verlag, 1985.

[ESG00a]   Joachim J. Eggers, Jonathan K. Su, and Bernd Girod. Asymmetric watermarking schemes. In *Sicherheit in Mediendaten*, Berlin, September 2000.

[ESG00b]   Joachim J. Eggers, Jonathan K. Su, and Bernd Girod. Public-key watermarking by eigenvectors of linear transforms. In *EUSIPCO 2000*, Tampere, Finland, September 2000.

[Ett98]   J. Mark Ettinger. Steganalysis and game equilibria. In *Information Hiding Workshop, Lecture Notes of Computer Science (1525)*. Springer-Verlag, New York, Heidelberg, 1998.

[FBS96]   J. Fridrich, Arnold Baldoza, and Richard Simard. Robust digital watermarking based on key-dependent basis functions. In *Information Hiding Workshop, Lecture Notes of Computer Science (1525)*. Springer-Verlag, New York, Heidelberg, 1996.

[FDL]   J. Fridrich, Rui Du, and Meng Long. Steganalysis of LSB encoding in color images. In *Proceedings of the IEEE International Conference on Multimedia and Expo,* August 2000.

[FG99]   J. Fridrich and M. Goljan. Protection of digital images using self embedding. In *Proceedings of NJIT Symposium on Content Security and Data Hiding in Digital Media,* Newark, NJ, May 1999.

[FMY98]   Yair Frankel, Philip D. MacKenzie, and Moti Yung. Robust efficient distributed RSA-key generation. In *Symposium on Principles of Distributed Computing,* page 320, 1998.

[FOO93]   A. Fujioka, T. Okamoto, and K. Ohta. A practical secret voting scheme for large scale elections. In *Advances in Cryptology—AUSCRYPT '92 Proceedings*. Springer-Verlag, 1993.

[Fou98]   Electronic Frontier Foundation. *Cracking DES: Secrets of Encryption Research, Wiretap Politics and Chip Design*. O'Reilly, 1998.

[Fre82]   Ed Fredkin. Conservative logic. *International Journal of Theoretical Physics*, 21, 1982.

[Fri99]   J. Fridrich. A new steganographic method for palette-based images. In *Proceedings of the IS&T PICS Conference,* Savannah, GA, April 1999.

[FT82]   Edward Fredkin and Tommaso Toffoli. Conservative logic. *International Journal of Theoretical Physics*, 21: 219–253. 1982.

[GB98]   Daniel Gruhl and Walter Bender. Information hiding to foil the casual counterfeiter. In *Information Hiding Workshop, Lecture Notes of Computer Science (1525)*. Springer-Verlag, New York, Heidelberg, 1998.

[GJ79]   Michael R. Garey and David S. Johnson. *Computers and Intractability: A Guide to the Theory of NP-Completeness*. W. H. Freeman and Company, New York, 1979.

[GJKR]   R. Gennaro, T. Rabin, S. Jarecki, and H. Krawczyk. Robust and efficient sharing of RSA functions. *Journal of Cryptology: The Journal of the International Association for Cryptologic Research*, 13(2): 273–300. 2000.

[Gro]   Wendy Grossman. alt.scientology.war. *Wired*, 3(2): 172, December 1995.

[Gun88]   C. G. Gunther. A universal algorithm for homophonic coding. In *Advances in Cryptology—Eurocrypt '88 Lecture Notes in Computer Science* (330), pages 405–414. Springer-Verlag, New York, 1988.

[Hec82]   Paul Heckbert. Color image quantization for frame buffer display. In *Proceedings of SIGGRAPH 82*, 1982.

[HG]   Frank Hartung and Bernd Girod. Fast public-key watermarking of compressed video. In *Proceedings of International Conference on Image Processing (ICIP '97) 1*, Santa Barbara, CA, 1997.

[Hil91]   David Hillman. The structure of reversible one-dimensional cellular automata. *Physica D*, 54: 277–292, 1991.

[HSG99]   Frank Hartung, Jonathan K. Su, and Bernd Girod. Spread spectrum watermarking: Malicious attacks and counterattacks. In *Security and Watermarking of Multimedia Contents, Proceedings for SPIE (The International Society for Optical Engineering) (3657)*, pages 147–158, January 1999.

[HU79]   John Hopcroft and Jeffrey Ullman. *Introduction to Automata Theory, Languages and Computation*. Addison-Wesley, Reading, MA, 1979.

[JDJ01]   Neil F. Johnson, Zoran Duric, and Sushil Jajodia. *Information Hiding: Steganography and Watermarking—Attacks and Countermeasures (Advances in Information Security, Volume 1)*. Kluwer Academic Publishers, 2001.

[JJ98a]   Neil F. Johnson and Sushil Jajodia. Steganalysis of images created using current steganography software. In *Information Hiding, Second International Workshop*, pages 273–289, 1998.

[JJ98b]   Neil F. Johnson and Sushil Jajodia. *Steganalysis: The investigation of hidden information*. 1998.

[JKM90]   H. N. Jendal, Y. J. B. Kuhn, and J. L. Massey. An information-theoretic treatment of homophonic substitution. In *Advances in*

Cryptology—Eurocrypt '89, Lecture Notes of Computer Science. Springer-Verlag, New York, 1990.

[KA98]   Markus G. Kuhn and Ross J. Anderson. Soft tempest: Hidden data transmission using electromagnetic emanations. In *Information Hiding Workshop, Lecture Notes of Computer Science (1525).* Springer-Verlag, New York, Heidelberg, 1998.

[Kah67]   David Kahn. *The Codebreakers.* Macmillan, New York, 1967.

[KBC+00]   John Kubiatowicz, David Bindel, Yan Chen, Patrick Eaton, Dennis Geels, Ramakrishna Gummadi, Sean Rhea, Hakim Weatherspoon, Westly Weimer, Christopher Wells, and Ben Zhao. Oceanstore: An architecture for global-scale persistent storage. In *Proceedings of ACM ASPLOS.* ACM, 2000.

[Kea89]   Michael Kearns. *The Computational Complexity of Machine Learning.* Ph.D. thesis, Harvard University Center for Research in Computing Technology, May 1989.

[KH98]   Deepa Kundur and Dimitrios Hatzinakos. Digital watermarking using multiresolution wavelet decomposition. In *International Conference on Acoustic, Speech and Signal Processing (ICASP),* volume 5, pages 2969–2972. 1998.

[KH99]   Deepa Kundur and D. Hatzinakos. Digital watermarking for telltale tamper-proofing and authentication. *Proceedings of the IEEE Special Issue on Identification and Protection of Multimedia Information,* 87(7): 1167–1180, July 1999.

[Knu81]   D. Knuth. *The Art of Computer Programming: Volume 2, Seminumerical Algorithms.* 2nd edition. Addison-Wesley, Reading, MA, 1981.

[KO84]   Hugh Kenner and Joseph O'Rourke. A travesty generator for micros. *BYTE,* page 129, November 1984.

[Kob87]   Neal Koblitz. *A Course in Number Theory and Cryptography.* Springer-Verlag, New York, 1987.

[Kom95]   John Kominek. Convergence of fractal encoded images. In J. A. Storer and M. Cohn, editors, *Data Compression Conference 1995,* pages 242–251, Snowbird, UT, March 1995.

[KQP01]   Farinaz Koushanfar, Gang Qu, and Miodrag Potkonjak. Intellectual property metering. In *Fourth Information Hiding Workshop,* 2001.

[KV89]   Michael Kearns and Leslie Valient. Cryptographic limitations on learning boolean formulae and finite automata. In *Proceedings of the Twenty-First Annual ACM Symposium on Theory of Computing*, pages 433–444, Seattle, May 1989.

[Leh82]   D. J. Lehmann. On primality tests. *SIAM Journal on Computing*, 11(2), May 1982.

[Lia95]   Wilson MacGyver Liaw. Reading GIF files. *Dr. Dobbs Journal*, February 1995.

[Lic]   Vinicius Licks and R. Jordan. On digital image watermarking robust to geometric transformations. In *Proceedings of IEEE International Conference on Image Processing 2000*, Vancouver, Canada, 2000.

[LJ83]   Shu Lin and Daniel J. Costello Jr. *Error Control Coding: Fundaments and Applications*. Prentice Hall, Englewood Cliffs, NJ, 1983.

[LMBO95]   Steve Low, Nicholas Maxemchuk, Jack Brassil, and Larry O'Gorman. Document marking and identification using both line and word shifting. In *Proceedings of the 1995 Conference on Infocom '95*, April 1995.

[LMSP98]   John Lach, William H. Mangione-Smith, and Miodrag Potkonjak. Fingerprinting digital circuits on programmable hardware. In *Information Hiding Workshop, Lecture Notes of Computer Science (1525)*. Springer-Verlag, New York, Heidelberg, 1998.

[Mae98]   Maurise Maes. Twin peaks: The histogram attack to fixed depth image watermarks. In *Information Hiding Workshop, Lecture Notes of Computer Science (1525)*. Springer-Verlag, New York, Heidelberg, 1998.

[Mar84]   N. Margolus. Physics-like models of computation. *Physica D*, 10: 81–95, 1984.

[MBR99]   L. Marvel, C. Boncelet, and J. Retter. Spread spectrum image steganography. *IEEE Transactions on Image Processing*, 8(8): 1075–1083. 1999.

[McH01]   John McHugh. Cover image. In *Fourth Information Hiding Workshop*. 2001.

[Mer93]   Ralph Merkle. Reversible electronic logic using switches. *Nanotechnology*, 4: 21–40. 1993.

[MM92]   I. S. Moskowitz and A. R. Miller. The channel capacity of a certain noisy timing channel. *IEEE Transactions on Information Theory*, IT-38(4): 1339–1343. 1992.

[Mon85]   P. L. Montgomery. Modular multiplication without trial division. *Mathematics of Computation*, 44: 170. 1985.

[MWC00]   Aviel D. Rubin, Marc Waldman, and Lorrie Faith Cranor. Publius: A robust, tamper-evident, censorship-resistant, web publishing system. In *Proceedings of the 9th USENIX Security Symposium*, pages 59–72, August 2000.

[NCSC93]   A guide to understanding covert channel analysis of trusted systems. Technical Report TG-030, NCSC, November 1993.

[Neu64]   P. G. Neumann. Error-limiting coding using information-lossless sequential machines. *IEEE Transactions on Information Theory*, IT-10: 108–115, April 1964.

[NY89]   M. Naor and M. Yung. Universal one-way hash functions and their cryptographic applications. In *Proceedings of the 21st Annual ACM Symposium on Theory of Computing*, pages 33–43. ACM, 1989.

[NY90]   M. Naor and M. Yung. Public-key cryptosystems provably secure against chosen ciphertext attacks. In *Proceedings of the 22nd Annual ACM Symposium on Theory of Computing*, pages 427–437. ACM, 1990.

[PBBC97]   A. Piva, M. Barni, F. Bartolini, and V. Cappellini. DCT-based watermark recovering without resorting to the uncorrupted original image. In *IEEE Signal Processing Society 1997 International Conference on Image Processing (ICIP '97)*, Santa Barbara, CA, October 1997.

[PN93]   N. Proctor and P. Neumann. Architectural implications of covert channels. In *Proceedings of the 15th National Computer Security Conference*, 1993.

[PP90]   B. Pfitzmann and A. Pfitzmann. How to break the direct RSA-implementation of mixes. In *Advances in Cryptology—Eurocrypt '89*, number 434. Springer-Verlag, 1990.

[Pro]   Niels Provos. Defending against statistical steganalysis. In *Proceedings of the 10th USENIX Security Symposium*, pages 323–335. 2001.

[Pro01]   Niels Provos. Probabilistic methods for improving information hiding. Technical Report 01-1, University of Michigan, January 2001.

[QC82]   J.-J. Quisquater and C. Couvreur. Fast decipherment algorithm for RSA public-key cryptosystem. *Electronic Letters*, 18. 1982.

[Qu01]   Gang Qu. Keyless public watermarking for intellectual property authentication. In *Fourth Information Hiding Workshop*. 2001.

[Rab89]   Michael Rabin. Efficient dispersal of information for security, load balancing and fault tolerance. *Journal of the ACM*, 38: 335–348. 1989.

[RC95]   R. Rinaldo and G. Calvagno. Image coding by block prediction of multiresolution subimages. *IEEE Transactions on Image Processing*, 4: 909–920. 1995.

[RDB96]   J. Ruanaidh, W. Dowling, and F. Boland. Phase watermarking of digital images. In *Proceedings of ICIP '96*, 3: 239–242, Lausanne, Switzerland, September 1996.

[Riv]   Ron Rivest. Chaffing and winnowing: Confidentiality without encryption. *Crypto Bytes* (RSA Laboratories), 4(1): 12–17, Summer 1998.

[Rob62]   L. G. Roberts. Picture coding using pseudo-random noise. *IRE Transactions on Information Theory*, IT-8, February 1962.

[RR98]   Michael K. Reiter and Aviel D. Rubin. Crowds: Anonymity for Web transactions. *ACM Transactions on Information and System Security*, 1(1): 66–92. 1998.

[RSG98]   M. G. Reed, P. F. Syverson, and D. M. Goldschlag. Anonymous connections and onion routing. *IEEE Journal on Selected Areas in Communications*, 16(4): 482–494, May 1998.

[Sch94]   Bruce Schneier. *Applied Cryptography*. John Wiley and Sons, New York, 1994.

[SGR97]   P. F. Syverson, D. M. Goldschlag, and M. G. Reed. Anonymous connections and onion routing. In *Proceedings/1997 IEEE Symposium on Security and Privacy, May 4–7, 1997, Oakland, California*, pages 44–54. IEEE Computer Society Press, Silver Springs, MD, 1997.

[Sha79]   A. Shamir. How to share a secret. *Communications of the ACM*, 24(11), November 1979.

[Sha93]   J. Shapiro. Embedded image coding using zerotrees of wavelet coefficients. *IEEE Transactions on Signal Processing*, 41(12): 3445–3462. 1993.

[Sha01]   Toby Sharp. An implementation of key-based digital signal steganography. In *Fourth Information Hiding Workshop*, 2001.

[Shi99]   Natori Shin. One-time hash steganography. In *3rd Information Hiding Workshop, Lecture Notes of Computer Science (1768)*. Springer-Verlag, New York, Heidelberg, 1999.

[Sim84]   G. J. Simmons. The prisoner's problem and the subliminal channel. In *Advances in Cryptology: Proceedings of CRYPTO '83*. Plenum Press, 1984.

[Sim85]   G. J. Simmons. The subliminal channel and digital signatures. In *Advances in Cryptology: Proceedings of EUROCRYPT 84*. Springer-Verlag, 1985.

[Sim86]   G. J. Simmons. A secure subliminal channel. In *Advances in Cryptology—CRYPTO '85 Proceedings*. Springer-Verlag, 1986.

[Sim92]   G. J. Simmons, ed. *Contemporary Cryptology: The Science of Information Integrity*. IEEE Press, Piscataway, NJ, 1992.

[Sim93]   G. J. Simmons. The subliminal channels of the U.S. Digital Signature Algorithm (DSA). In *Proceedings of the Third Symposium on State and Progress of Research in Cryptography*, Fondazone Ugo Bordoni, Rome, 1993.

[Sim94]   G. J. Simmons. Subliminal communication is easy using the DSA. In *Advances in Cryptology—EUROCRYPT '93 Proceedings*. Springer-Verlag, 1994.

[SK95]   K. Sako and J. Kilian. Receipt-free mix-type voting schemes. In *Advances in Cryptology—Eurocrypt '95*, pages 393–403. Springer-Verlag, 1995.

[SKE00]   Fabien Petitcolas and Stefan Katzenbeisser (Editors). *Information Hiding Techniques for Steganography and Digital Watermarking*. Artech House. 2000.

[SRG00]   Paul F. Syverson, Michael G. Reed, and David M. Goldschlag. Onion routing access configurations. In *DISCEX 2000: Proceedings of the DARPA Information Survivability Conference and Exposition*, Volume I, pages 34–40, Hilton Head, SC, January 2000. IEEE CS Press.

[Sto88]   James Storer. *Data Compression*. Computer Science Press, Rockville, MD, 1988.

[STRL00]   Paul F. Syverson, Gene Tsudik, Michael G. Reed, and Carl E. Landwehr. Towards an analysis of onion routing security. In *Workshop on Design Issues in Anonymity and Unobservability*, Berkeley, CA, July 2000.

[SY98]   Sabrina Sowers and Abdou Youssef. Testing digital watermark resistance to destruction. In *Information Hiding Workshop, Lecture Notes of Computer Science (1525)*. Springer-Verlag, New York, Heidelberg, 1998.

[Tah92]   H. Taha. Operations Research: An Introduction. Macmillan, New York, 1992.

[TM87]   Tommaso Toffoli and Norman Margolus. *Cellular Automata Machines*. MIT Press, London, 1987.

[Tof77a]   T. Toffoli. *Cellular Automata Mechanics*. Ph.D. thesis, University of Michigan, 1977.

[Tof77b]   Tommaso Toffoli. Computation and construction universality of reversible cellular automata. *Journal of Computer and System Sciences*, 15: 213–231. 1977.

[Tur36a]   Alan Turing. On computable numbers with an application to the entscheidungsproblem. *Proceedings of the London Math Society*, 2(42): 230–265. 1936.

[Tur36b]   Alan Turing. On computable numbers with an application to the entscheidungsproblem. *Proceedings of the London Math Society*, 2(43): 544–546. 1936.

[Val84]   Leslie G. Valient. A theory of the learnable. *Communications of the ACM*, 27: 1134–1142. 1984.

[Wal95]   S. Walton. Image authentication for a slippery new age. *Dr. Dobbs Journal*, 20(4): 18–26, April 1995.

[Way85]   Peter Wayner. Building a travesty tree. *BYTE*, page 183, September 1985.

[Way92]   Peter C. Wayner. Content-addressable search engines and DES-like systems. In *Advances in Cryptology: CRYPTO '92 Lecture Notes of Computer Science (740)*, pages 575–586. Springer-Verlag, New York, 1992.

[Way95]   Peter Wayner. Strong theoretical steganography. *Cryptologia*, 19(3): 285–299, July 1995.

[Way99]　　　Peter Wayner. *Data Compression for Real Programmers*. AP Professional, Chesnut Hill, MA, 1999.

[Wei76]　　　Joseph Weizenbaum. *Computer Power and Human Reason: From Judgment to Calculation*. W. H. Freeman, San Francisco, 1976.

[Wes01]　　　Andreas Westfeld. High capacity despite better steganalysis: F5, a steganographic algorithm. In *Fourth Information Hiding Workshop*, pages 301–315. 2001.

[WH94]　　　Peter Wayner and Dan Huttenlocher. Image analysis to obtain typeface information. *U.S. Patent*, 5253307, 1994.

[Won98]　　　P. Wong. A public key watermark for image verification and authentication. In *Proceedings of ICIP '98 1*, pages 425–429, Chicago, IL, October 1998.

[WP99]　　　Andreas Westfeld and Andreas Pfitzmann. Attacks on steganographic systems. In *Information Hiding, Third International Workshop, IH '99* (1768), pages 61–76. Springer-Verlag, Dresden, Germany, 1999.

[WRC00]　　　Marc Waldman, Aviel D. Rubin, and Lorrie Faith Cranor. Publins: A robust, tamper-evident, censorship-resistant, Web publishing system. In *Proceedings of 9th Security Symposium*, pages 59–72, August 2000.

[WS99]　　　Wright and Spalding. Experimental performance of shared RSA modulus generation (short). In *SODA: ACM-SIAM Symposium on Discrete Algorithms (A Conference on Theoretical and Experimental Analysis of Discrete Algorithms)*, 1999.

[XBA97]　　　X.-G. Xia, C. Boncelet, and G. Arce. A multiresolution watermark for digital images. In *IEEE Signal Processing Society 1997 International Conference on Image Processing (ICIP '97)*, Santa Barbara, CA, October 1997.

Index

About the Author

Peter Wayner is a writer living in Baltimore and is the author of *Digital Cash* and *Agents at Large* (both Academic Press). His writings appear in numerous academic journals as well as the pages of more popular forums such as *MacWorld* and *The New York Times*. He has taught various computer science courses at Cornell University and Georgetown University.